MW01127202

To the memory of Michael Gilbert and Lester Young

Contents

Preface and Acknowledgments

This book grew out of lectures I gave at the Collège de France in 2008–09, 2009–10, and 2010–11. In the first year, I considered collective decision making quite generally, from both a normative and an explanatory point of view. In the present work, the focus is on normative analysis. The topics of the second and third sets of lectures were the Federal Convention in Philadelphia (1787) and the first French Constituent Assembly (1789–91). In this book I draw extensively on the debates in these two assemblies.

A few years earlier, I had become aware of Bentham's writings on the design of political assemblies. Although I did not immediately recognize their full significance, I have come to believe that Bentham's negative approach to institutional design – *providing securities against misrule* – is more robust and realistic than the numerous positive approaches proposed in the literature. Shorn of their eccentric and occasionally ridiculous aspects, his analyses of assemblies and legislation have provided the lodestar for my work. I thank the director of the Bentham Project at University College London, Philip Schofield, for helpful guidance and, more generally, the editors of Bentham's *Collective Works* for their superb scholarship. Although most work on Bentham has been devoted to his writings on the law, a few kindred spirits, notably Philippe Urfalino and Adrian Vermeule, have shared my enthusiasm for his work on political decision making. I suspect there is much yet to be mined in Bentham's writings.

In drawing out the implications of Bentham's ideas, I have benefited much from an encyclopedic treatise by Eugène Pierre, *Traité de droit politique électoral et parlementaire* (1893), which offers fine-grained procedural descriptions of a kind Bentham would have appreciated but that are rarely found in works of political science. The writings of, among others, James Bryce, André Castaldo, Adhémar Esmein, Roger Hoar, Paul Langford, François-Olivier Martin, Peter Novick, and J. R. Pole have also been invaluable in this respect. My hero Montaigne, and his hero Plutarch, have also provided regular inspiration. Although as lawyers and historians these writers are obviously concerned with particulars, they are also, by virtue of their ability to locate the revealing detail and the compelling counterexample, immensely helpful to the would-be generalist. Some readers will no doubt find that my borrowings give the book the appearance of an overloaded Christmas tree. I hope others will share my delight in discovering the "differences in similarity, similarity in difference" – in political institutions over nearly thirty centuries. Also, I believe the tree has a trunk.

The work may be read as a companion volume to *Explaining Social Behavior* (2007). In that work I argued, in a skeptical vein, against the excessive explanatory ambitions of much of recent social science. In the present volume, I argue against the excessive ambitions of normative political theory. This criticism relies in part on the earlier one, since some political theories rely on unrealistic claims about our ability to determine the optimal means to realize a given end. One could not implement utilitarianism, for instance, without causal theories telling us the costs and benefits of reform. In my earlier work, I argued that such theories are often lacking. The present criticism goes beyond this argument, however, by arguing that in many cases the end itself is ill-defined. In the case of utilitarianism, we do not know how to compare and add the welfare of different individuals.

Jakob Elster and Bernard Manin offered useful comments on the discussion of arguing in Chapter 1. Michael Balinski kindly and critically read the sections of Chapter 1 devoted to his work with Rida Laraki that, I believe, has the potential for revolutionizing the theory and practice of voting. Allan Gibbard commented on a very early draft of Chapter 1. In this chapter I devote some space to social-choice theory, an area where non-specialists such as myself fear to tread. Richard Posner commented usefully on Chapter 2. There is little new in what I say, but I hope there is also little that is outright wrong. In thinking about cross-voting and Numa, I was guided by Alain Boyer. I have benefited greatly from discussions of drafts of Chapters 2 and 3 at Harvard Law School and of drafts of Chapters 3 and 4 at the University of Chicago Law School. I presented an early draft of Chapter 5, which vegetated on my hard drive for a decade before it found its proper place, to seminars at Columbia Law School and Stanford Law School. In a focused workshop in Paris, Vermeule, Aanund Hylland, and John Ferejohn offered detailed comments on an early draft of the whole manuscript. Over and above Hylland's contributions on that occasion, his effort to keep me honest has been invaluable, continuing a collaboration dating back to 1973. I am also thankful for the comments of two anonymous readers for Cambridge University Press.

My research assistants at the Collège de France, Hélène Landemore, Stéphanie Novak, and Arnaud Le Pillouer, provided a constantly stimulating environment. Lectures at that institution do not allow for exchanges with the audience. My students at Columbia University have, however, offered useful comments, objections, and suggestions in the classes I have taught there in recent years on constitution-making, on the Federal Convention, and on collective decision making. Exchanges with Felix Gerlsbeck and Jeffrey Lenowitz have been especially valuable.

Unless otherwise noted, translations from French are my own. I do not signal my occasional corrections in published translations.

The dedication of the book to the memory of Michael Gilbert (1912–2006) and of Lester Young (1909–59) may require an explanation. Although I never met either man, I have read and reread Gilbert's novels since about 1955 and listened to Young's music on a more or less daily basis from the same time onward. They have not only provided a thread of continuity in my life but have also offered a window into worlds I have come to appreciate.

Michael Gilbert wrote crime novels. In my view, he was the best crime writer ever. Many of his novels are minor masterpieces – minor because of the genre to which they belong, masterpieces because of the skills he brought to his craft. He combined lightness of touch with deftness of plotting, together with the ability to use dialogue and indirect speech to create interesting and credible, two-and-a-half dimensional characters. His main profession as a solicitor enabled him to anchor many of his stories in the complexities of the British legal system. The observations in Chapter 4 on the 1964 Trade Union (Amalgamations) Act were taken from his novel *Flash Point*. His insight in the law also benefited him when compiling the often hilarious *Oxford Book of Legal Anecdotes*, cited several times in this book.

These facts might not be worth mentioning but for an amazing coincidence. My father, Torolf Elster (1911–2006), also wrote crime novels, among the many things he did. He was a great admirer of Gilbert and introduced me to his books at an early age. Each new novel was eagerly awaited and immediately purchased. Like Gilbert, he continued to write crime novels well into his eighties. They both escaped from the Germans during the war. Gilbert got away from a prisoner of war camp in Italy in 1943. My father jumped from the balcony at the back of his apartment when the Gestapo knocked on the front door one morning in 1942. More important, my father and Gilbert, at least as I reconstruct him from his books, had many character features in common: fundamental decency, compassion, utter lack of dogmatism and pretentiousness, as well as a puckish sense of humor.

Lester Young was a jazz musician, playing the tenor saxophone and occasionally the clarinet. On one recording, *Two to Tango*, one can even hear him sing. In my view, he was the best jazz musician ever. Artistically, his achievements tower over those of Gilbert: there is nothing minor about his masterpieces. Many critics prefer his prewar recordings, which convey utter, relaxed self-confidence and unsurpassed creativity in improvising. When we have access to alternate takes of his recordings, they are almost invariably as good as the released takes, and entirely different. Although his recordings with the Count Basie orchestra are mostly up-tempo, his duos with Billie Holiday show an exquisite romantic sensibility (miles away from sentimentalism).

By all accounts, Young had a sweet, conflict-avoiding personality. He was fully absorbed by his music. Perhaps as a result of these traits, he had a bad war. He ignored his army summons and was put in detention barracks, a traumatic experience that may have contributed to the sometimes darker and more hesitant style of his later recordings. The contrast with the prewar work can be exaggerated, however. While finishing the present book, I was constantly listening to his wonderfully light and inventive live performances in Washington, DC, from 1956. Other postwar soliloquies and meditations express emotions rarely found in the earlier recordings. As in Billie Holiday's parallel development over the same 25 years, the loss of technical fluency somehow seems unimportant. When I was young I preferred their exuberant early work, but with age I have become more attuned to the gains from age and experience.

Introduction

Securities Against Misrule was the title of a work by Bentham from 1822–23, one of several writings on a proposed constitution for Tripoli. The main idea was already stated in *Political Tactics* (1789):

The tactics of political assemblies form the science . . . which teaches how to guide them to the end of their institution, by means of the order to be observed in their proceedings.

   In this branch of government, as in many others, the end is so to speak of a *negative character*. The object is to avoid the inconveniences, to prevent the difficulties, which must result from a large assembly of men being called to deliberate in common. *The art of the legislator is limited to the prevention of everything which might prevent the development of their liberty and their intelligence.*[1]

The aim of the present book is to develop, generalize, and, to some degree, modify the claim made in the sentence I have italicized.

   Before deciding on the title, I thought of calling the book *Bentham against Condorcet*. In Chapter 1 I argue, in fact, that the social-choice tradition stemming from Condorcet has little relevance for the normative theory of collective decision making. In Chapter 3 I make a similar claim with regard to the Condorcet Jury Theorem. By contrast, Bentham's relentless realism and his insight into the operations and the failings of actual institutions provide, or so I shall argue throughout the book, a superior guide to institutional reform. To get a feeling for the drift of my argument, readers are encouraged to consult the list – which is far from exhaustive – of Benthamite schemes that I offer in the Conclusion (p. 272).

   In Bentham's view, the object of institutional design is security against misrule, or the prevention of mischief – the removal of obstacles that will thwart the realization of the greatest good for the greatest number. In a sense, I go further than he did, since I do not stipulate any particular goal to which the removal of these obstacles is conducive. I shall argue that once collective decisions have been

---

[1] Bentham (1999), p. 15. For Bentham, the subject matter of "tactics" was not strategic behavior (which I discuss in Chapter 1), but the design of political institutions that promote the "greatest happiness of the greatest number."

shielded as much as possible from distortion*s*, we have to let the chips fall where they may. In this respect I follow the memorable Conclusion to John Hart Ely's *Democracy and Distrust*, which I cite and discuss in the Conclusion. The distortions stem from *self-interest* ("sinister interest" in Bentham's phrase) and from *irrationality*: passion, prejudice, and bias.

Ely and, above all, Bentham are the direct sources of inspiration for this book. Other partial ancestors or precursors can also be cited. Given that action depends on opportunities as well as on motives, institutional designers can try to prevent undesirable actions either by acting on the motives of the agents (the incentive approach) or by limiting their opportunities to do harm (the Benthamite approach). The American framers used both strategies. In Chapter 5 I provide an example of how Madison relied on incentives in designing the mechanism for electing the President. According to an authoritative interpretation of *The Federalist*, he also proposed to act on opportunities:

Madison's idea that a republican government will deprive corrupt representatives of the opportunity to carry out schemes of oppression is evident in *Number 63*, when he says that even if indirectly elected senators were to be impelled by corrupt motives, the system of government provided for in the Constitution would *deny them the opportunity to act corruptly*. It is hard to exaggerate the extent to which Madison and his fellow authors employed the concepts of motive and opportunity.[2]

In a very different way, the Benthamite approach may also be seen as a generalization of Habermas's idea of "the uncoerced force of the better argument." It is a generalization of his idea, because it takes account of other distorting factors than coercion. Coercion – the threat of violence – may induce either prudential, interest-based fear or visceral, emotion-based fear (see Chapter 4). My conjecture – based on the lack of any sustained discussion by Habermas of the role of emotions in public life – is that he refers to prudential fear. In that case, his theory needs to be supplemented by an account of emotion. Also, bribes can be as powerful as threats. Plutarch tells us that Solon "with good reason [thought] that being seduced into wrong was as bad as being forced ... , since both may equally suspend the exercise of reason" (*Solon* XXI.4). Institutional designers should insulate the decision makers from both, as well as from the other distortions I mentioned.

The idea of "preventing the prevention of intelligence" has a strong verbal resemblance to the claim of the British idealists that the main task of the state is to "hinder hindrances" or "remove obstacles" to the free development of the individual. Yet these writers did not focus, as I shall, on removing obstacles to *collective* decision making. They did, for instance, endorse restrictions on the sale and purchase of alcohol so that individuals "may become more free to exercise the faculties and improve the talents which God has given them."[3]

---

[2] White (1987), pp. 145–46; my italics.
[3] Green (1986), p. 212. I am grateful to Claus Offe for directing my attention to Green's work.

From the Benthamite perspective, the relevant task would be to limit the sale of alcohol to jurors, deputies, and voters. Let me give some examples.

A handbook for jurors in Minnesota tells them, "While serving as a juror, do not drink alcoholic beverages during trials breaks." In *Tanner v. United States*, the Supreme Court found that copious consumption of alcohol by jurors during a trial did not constitute grounds for overturning the verdict: "However severe their effect and improper their use, drugs or alcohol voluntarily ingested by a juror seems no more an 'outside influence' than a virus, poorly prepared food, or a lack of sleep." (I return to this amazing piece of bad reasoning in Chapter 1.) From the Benthamite perspective, the Minnesota ex ante ban solves the problem. When the French *constituants* abolished feudalism on the night of August 4, 1789, some of them may have been, in the words applied to a later self-denying ordinance, "drunk with disinterestedness."[4] In addition, it is likely that a good portion were drunk in the literal sense of the term. One historian claimed that a few days later, "to avoid nocturnal and intemperate deliberations, and the reproaches that good Frenchmen who are not deputies could make to good patriots for deliberating upon coming from the dinner table, it was decided that in future votes on important matters the assembly should be fasting (*à jeun*)."[5] Many countries and American states, finally, ban the sale of liquor on election day, partly no doubt because of the historical practice of candidates plying voters with liquor[6] and partly, I assume, because voters are believed to be more open to reason when not "under the influence."

The natural standard for assessing the institutions I discuss in this book – jury trials, political assemblies, and electoral systems – might seem to be whether they tend to *produce good outcomes*. In Chapter 1 I discuss some of the problems raised by that approach. One difficulty is that of defining what counts as good outcomes.[7] Political and legal philosophers have proposed a number of answers, and it is not clear how we can choose among them. Assuming that we opt for one of them, we then have to assess institutions in light of their tendency to promote the chosen conception of goodness. To do so, we need a causal theory (a purely non-consequentialist theory will never be sufficient in institutional design). Social scientists have produced a number of such theories, and it is not clear how we can choose among them. Over the last few years the *Financial Times* has probably published dozens of different theories of what caused the current financial crisis, together with equally many remedy proposals. The number of theories and proposals is matched only by the certainty with which each of them

---

[4] Lebègue (1910), p. 261, referring to the decision by the Assembly on May 16, 1791, to render its members ineligible to the first ordinary legislature (see Chapter 4).

[5] Kessel (1969), p. 193.

[6] Pierre (1893) pp. 266–68.

[7] This is not a problem if the good outcome is defined as finding a factual truth, as in jury verdicts. The Condorcet Jury Theorem is often, in fact, held up as an example of how institutional design can promote good outcomes. I believe the relevance of the theorem to actual decisions is minimal. Also, as I explain in Chapter 3, Bentham spotted a possibly fatal weakness in Condorcet's argument.

is propounded. The large number of competing theories should, however, undermine our confidence that *any* of them is right.[8]

I believe that this *double indeterminacy* – of plausible-sounding but unprovable normative views, and of plausible-sounding but unprovable causal theories – has led to a deep disillusionment in public debates. References to the common good or the general interest are routinely dismissed as cant. There is, in fact, hardly any policy proposal – however partial in its origins – that cannot be justified on impartial grounds. Blue-collar and white-collar workers tend to invoke different norms of equity, the former arguing that work should be rewarded according to the burdens imposed on the workers and the latter that wages should reflect skills and benefit to society.[9] A study of the appeal to principles of equity in allocating the burdens of climate change abatement found that "the economic costs implied by the respective equity rules explain the perceived support by EU, Russia, and the USA."[10] These examples could be multiplied indefinitely.

Tocqueville's observation still rings true:

A politician first tries to identify his own interests and finds out what similar interests might be joined with his. He then casts about to discover whether there might not by chance exist some doctrine or principle around which this new association might be organized, so that it may present itself to the world and gain ready acceptance.[11]

He might also have accepted the following variation on his theme:

A politician first tries to identify his own interests and finds out what similar interests might be joined with his. He then casts about to discover whether there might not by chance exist some causal theory or statistical model according to which the promotion of these interests coincides with the general interest, so that it may present itself to the world and gain ready acceptance.

Thus Chicago-style economists find that for each murderer who is executed, up to 18 murders are not committed, and also that the right to carry concealed handguns saves lives. To buttress these claims, they engage in fragile statistical analyses that amount to little more than data-mining or curve-fitting.[12] Although in

[8] "Where we have several competing theories, which give different predictions, all these theories should be regarded with suspicion, and we should be prepared for a risk that is higher than what is predicted by any of the theories" (Føllesdal 1979, pp. 405–6).

[9] Hyman and Brough (1975), p. 49.

[10] Lange et al. (2010), p. 367.

[11] Tocqueville (2004a), p. 202. Anticipating and influencing a more famous statement by Pascal, Montaigne (1991), p. 635, asked, "What kind of truth can be limited by a range of mountains, becoming a lie for the world on the other side?" Tocqueville might have observed that this relativism creates an incentive to *cross* the mountain. Under the entry "Morals," Bierce (2002), p. 166, cites the following passage from the mythical *Gooke's Meditations*: "It is sayd there be a raunge of mountaynes in the Easte, on one syde of the which certayn conducts are immorall, yet on the other syde they are holden in good esteeme; whereby the mountaineer is much conveenyenced, for it is given to him to goe downe eyther way and act as it shall suite his moode, withouten offence."

[12] For a general criticism of many uses of statistical models (admitting my lack of firsthand expertise), see Elster (2009d). Concerning the death penalty and handguns see, respectively, Donohue and Wolfers (2005) and Ayres and Donohue (2003).

their case it is not a matter of self-interest but of ideology, the general point is the same. To justify a policy to which one is attached on self-interested or ideological grounds, one can shop around for a causal or statistical model just as one can shop around for a principle. Once it has been found, one can reverse the sequence and present the policy as the conclusion. This process can occur anywhere on the continuum between deception and self-deception (or wishful thinking), usually no doubt closer to the latter.

Being aware of these temptations and suspecting oneself of being subject to their influence, what should one do? Mme de Staël wrote that in "this world, there is no greater trial for morality than political employment, for the arguments one can invoke on this subject, to reconcile one's conscience with one's interest, are without number. Yet the principle from which one ought not to deviate is to support the weak; one rarely goes wrong in orienting oneself by this compass."[13] The Norwegian writer Helge Krog told his readers that when in doubt, they should adopt the policy that would harm themselves the most. Along the same lines, Proust refers to "the soldier who chooses the post not where he can be of most use but where he is most exposed."[14] While these reactions may seem morally admirable, they can lead one astray. Pascal wrote, "The most equitable man in the world is not permitted to be judge in his own cause: I know some who, in order not to be entrapped by this amour-propre, have been *as unjust as possible by a counter-bias*; the sure way to lose a perfectly just cause was to get it commended to them by their near kinsfolk."[15] Also, and more relevant for my purposes, the injunction "Distrust thyself" has no clear institutional implications. Although the idea of distrust points in the right direction, it needs to be spelled out in a different way.

My proposal is to consider procedural accounts of good institutional design. I shall discuss three versions of this idea, and opt for the last and least ambitious.

First, we might ask whether institutions can be designed to *select good decision makers*. "Anyone who could discover the means by which men could be justly judged and reasonably chosen would, at a stroke, establish a perfect form of commonwealth."[16] In later chapters, I discuss some proposals to this effect. Toward the end of Chapter 2 I discuss procedures intended to select competent jurors. Chapter 5 as a whole is devoted to a device – cross-voting – that has been adopted at various times and places to generate impartial representatives from an electorate of partial voters. Although the idea is intuitively attractive, it has rarely worked well. Trivially, members of expert bodies such as central bank committees are selected on grounds of competence. In this book, however, I am not concerned, except occasionally, with expert decision making, but with *democratic decisions*.

---

[13] De Staël (2000), p. 208.
[14] Proust (1988b), p. 228.
[15] *Pensée* 78, ed. Sellier; my italics. See also the comments in Chapter 1 on the tendency of the French revolutionaries to think or to claim that the only disinterested attitudes were *counterinterested* ones.
[16] Montaigne (1991), p. 1057. He believes, of course, that it can't be done.

Second, we may ask whether institutions can be designed to *eliminate bad decision makers*, such as the biased, the prejudiced, and the incompetent. Trivially, this is what happens when children are not allowed to vote. In criminal jury selection, the aim is not to eliminate jurors who would be unsuitable in *any* trial, but only those with biases and prejudices that might be triggered by particular aspects of a given case or a given defendant. Allegedly, female jurors are hard on female defendants, middle-class jurors soft on middle-class defendants, and overweight jurors either hard or soft on overweight defendants. One famous American defense attorney, Clarence Darrow, preferred older jurors: they "are generally more charitable and kindly disposed than young men."[17] Another, Samuel Leibovitz, preferred them young: "They're not set in their ways. They are tolerant."[18] As these examples suggest, there are no hard facts in this area. If jury selection were an exact science, the challenges by prosecutors and defense attorneys would tend to cancel each other in their effects, the only effect being wasteful costs and delays. If, as I believe, it is not, it does not even have the virtue of neutrality.

Third, we may ask whether decision making by ordinary citizens can be improved by *structuring their relation to the environment*. This process involves three main procedures: preventing the decision makers from learning certain things (*ignorance*), preventing others from learning certain things about them (*secrecy*), and enabling others to learn certain things about them (*publicity*). These are central notions throughout the book. As we shall see, secrecy and publicity are relative to an audience and to a point in time. A vote by a juror, for instance, may be known to other jurors but not to the public at large. It may be unknown to other voters at the time of voting but be made known to them afterward.

In addition, *rotation* can serve the function of insulating decision makers from corrupting influences, a technique used, among other places, in the Roman Empire, the Chinese empire, and in the French ancien régime.[19] In a compelling metaphor, John Lilburne told the private soldiers in the New Model Army, "Suffer not one sort of men too long to remaine adjutators [delegates], least they be corrupted by bribes of offices, or places of preferment, for *standing water though never so pure at first, in time putrifies*."[20] Rotation may need to be supplemented by a mechanism – election or randomization – that makes it difficult to *predict* who will replace the departing decision maker. In fact, "rapid rotation of assignments can lead to 'judge shopping' by litigants through the mechanism of delaying a case until judicial assignments have been rotated."[21] Yet, as I shall argue,

---

[17] Cited in Gilbert (1986), p. 101.
[18] Cited in ibid., p. 199.
[19] For these cases, see, respectively, Olivier-Martin (2010), pp. 64, 106; Skinner (1975), p. 341; and Olivier-Martin (2010), pp. 267, 626. In China, rotation was supplemented by the "law of avoidance" that kept officials from serving in their native provinces.
[20] Woolrych (1986), p. 192; my italics.
[21] Hurst (1990–91), p. 14.

because rotation can also undermine epistemic competence it can be difficult to tell when it is appropriate.

In the cases I shall consider, the requirement of ignorance applies mainly to jurors. As we shall see in Chapter 2, members of a jury are not supposed to know certain facts about the case, the defendant, or the law. (Sometimes they are also, more paradoxically, requested to act as if they did not know some facts they do know.) Although the jury seems to be the most important institution in which a group of individuals is asked to make decisions behind an artificial "veil of ignorance," other examples can be cited. Holding the assets of politicians in blind trust offers one illustration. The use of need-blind committees for college admission and of gender-blind committees for musical auditions relies on the same principle. Double-blind line-ups in criminal investigations and double-blind medical studies, while important, do not involve collective decisions.[22]

The main reason for inducing ignorance in the jury is the belief that knowledge would trigger passions, biases, or prejudices that are likely to have a negative impact on the decision. A standard example is knowledge of a defendant's previous criminal record. A secondary reason is that the admission of certain kinds of evidence might have undesirable incentive effects on cases other than the one that is being decided. A standard example is the ban on eating from the fruit of the poisoned tree.

The use of secrecy aims at eliminating undesirable incentives – bribes, threats, social ostracism – for deciding one way rather than another. To be effective, secrecy typically has to be mandatory rather than optional, since a demand for secrecy often allows others to infer how the person requesting it will vote. Also, if a person has received a bribe to vote in a certain way, she can hardly then opt for secrecy.

In juries, deliberations are shrouded in secrecy, always during the trial and often afterward. Except when unanimity is required, the identity of those who voted for and against conviction is usually also kept secret. The jury itself may practice secret voting. In some countries, this procedure is mandatory; in others it is up to the jurors to decide whether they shall decide by public or secret voting. Little seems to be known about optional jury practices, except that it is apparently common to begin the deliberations by a secret straw ballot.

In elections, even when secrecy is mandatory, it is rarely perfect, or believed to be perfect. The micro-technolology of the secret ballot can be decisive.[23] In

---

[22] A veil of ignorance can also be a useful device for preventing data-mining and curve-fitting: "you put half the data in cold storage, and look at it only after deciding which models to fit" (Freedman 2005, p. 64). For some reason, this salutary but costly procedure (also called out-of-sample testing), which is "commonplace in the physical and health sciences," is "rare in the social sciences" (ibid.). Not only may social scientists be subject to ordinary self-deception when they mine the data, but even to second-order self-deception ("I never deceive myself") when they believe they have no use for a tool that would keep them honest.

[23] For Imperial Germany, Leemann and Mares (2011) demonstrate the importance of the color, shape, and transparency of ballots as well as the design of urns. Pierre (1893) offers numerous examples from France.

Colombia, electoral fraud is made possible by the use of mobile phones to take a picture of the ballot and send it to the briber. "In Chiapas, Mexico, during the 2000 elections ... voters worried that the ruling party had a satellite watching the ballot box or that ballots could be linked to them by finger prints."[24] In 2010, the Icelandic Supreme Court invalidated the elections to the Constitutional Council on the grounds that the secrecy of the vote had been jeopardized in five different ways.[25] Yet compared to previous centuries, the secret ballot has undoubtedly reduced the power of the state, political parties, local communities, or powerful individuals to shape voting behavior. One might also extend the logic of the secret ballot to campaign contributions, by imposing donor anonymity.[26] In some American states this idea has been used, with mixed success, in the election of judges.[27]

It may be worthwhile emphasizing the difference between *secrecy* and *privacy*. Carl Schmitt confuses these two notions when he argues against the secret ballot in elections by contemplating a possible extension of the practice:

It is fully conceivable that one day through ingenious discoveries, every single person, without leaving his apartment, could continuously express his opinions on political questions through an apparatus and that all these opinions would automatically be registered by a central office, where one would only need to read them off. That would ... provide a proof that the state and the public were fully privatized. It would not be public opinion, for even the shared opinion of millions of private people produces no public opinion. ... In this way, no common will arises, no *volonté générale*; only the sum of all individual wills, a *volonté de tous*, does.[28]

Today, of course, that apparatus exists in the form of the Internet.

The vote in the privacy of one's apartment could not always, however, be kept secret. A vote buyer could send his agent to the home of the voter to verify that she votes for him; and ten agents might reach enough voters to tip the balance in a local election. *The very publicity of the voting process makes the secret vote possible.* Together with the requisite technology, voting officials recruited from different political parties, monitoring the voters and each other, are the guarantors of the secret ballot. Schmitt compounds his mistake when he asserts that

<hr/>

[24] Desposato (2007), p. 76. Modern technology also creates problems for maintaining *ignorance*; see "Judge Considers Pledge for Jurors on Internet Use," *New York Times*, September 18, 2011, p. A 23.

[25] Axelsson (2011). The Court did not assert that the secrecy had actually been violated but, using the tenuous possibilistic reasoning discussed in Chapter 1, claimed that it *could* have been. In all likelihood, the Court's decision was politically motivated (Gylfason 2012).

[26] As suggested by Ayres (2000), who also discusses some formidable technical obstacles to the implementation of the idea. In this context, donor anonymity means that neither the candidate nor the public at large would know the identity of the donors. Alternatively, as argued by the Supreme Court in the otherwise disastrous *Citizens United* decision in 2010, one could require full public disclosure so that voters could decide for themselves "whether elected officials are 'in the pocket' of so-called moneyed interests." The current situation is inferior to both options.

[27] Banner (1988).

[28] Schmitt (2008), p. 274. Schmitt's implicit view that Rousseau was an opponent of secret voting does not seem to have a firm basis in the texts (see note 64 in Chapter 1).

"the current electoral and voting secrecy is *not a genuine secret* at all. According to their discretion, the voters can decide whether to disclose and make this secret public; its preservation is only a right, not a duty of the state citizen."[29] From the point of view of democratic theory, however, the crucial question is whether the citizen can *credibly communicate* her vote to a prospective vote buyer, since if she cannot he will not pay for it. She can do so in the privacy of her home, not in the public space of the polling booth.[30]

In contemporary assemblies, secrecy is exceptional. Citizens can listen to the debates in public galleries, and votes are public and usually recorded. In most assemblies, discussions are reported verbatim, allowing only for correction of grammatical mistakes and elimination of redundancies. In the American Congress, representatives can alter their speeches before they go into the Congressional Record, but in recent years revised remarks have been printed in a different typeface. Historically, assemblies have not always granted publicity of their debates.[31] They have often denied the public access to their proceedings and also used secret voting to allow their members to shield themselves from the public, from the executive, or from the political parties to which they belong. As I argue in Chapter 4, secrecy may in fact be a desirable feature of constituent assemblies. In ordinary legislatures, though, publicity is usually essential to prevent self-dealing.[32]

Let me illustrate the pressure on assemblies to deliberate and vote in public.

In 1401, Sir Arnold Savage complained that certain members of the House of Commons reported their deliberations to the King.[33] In 1532, Henry VIII forced a division in the House of Commons, that is, a physical separation of the members, that enabled him to identify who voted his way and who voted against him. "Several who had earlier been in opposition joined the 'yeas' for fear of the king's indignation, and a majority was obtained."[34] In 1633, Charles I experienced

---

[29] Ibid.

[30] Buchstein (2000), p. 22.

[31] See Vermeule (2004) for overview and discussion of American practice. Pierre (1893), pp. 824–25, 834–37, has a full discussion of the practices in the French Senate and National Assembly. The principle of publicity was often undermined by the transformation of the assembly into a "secret committee" at the request of a small number of deputies (ranging from 5 to 20). Before 1870, the names of the requesters were not inserted into the record. Similarly, before the abolition of the right to demand a *secret vote*, the insertion of the names of the requesters into the record was refused as being contrary to the principle of the secret ballot (ibid., p. 1010). Demands for secrecy were to be kept secret. Conversely, when deputies or senators demanded a *public vote* (written or viva voce from the tribune), their names had to be entered into the record so that "it would not be possible to impose a long and fastidious process on the assembly in secondary matters without incurring accountability" (ibid., p. 1027). Demands for publicity had to be made publicly.

[32] *Ignorance* can achieve the same aim, if politicians are required to put their assets in a blind trust. In the United States, there are no strict requirements to this effect, but some members of Congress choose to adopt this practice. The Congressional Blind Trust Act introduced in 2011 would, if adopted, make it mandatory.

[33] Adams and Stephens (1914), p. 172.

[34] Lehmberg (1970), p. 138.

difficulties getting his most cherished measures through the Scottish Parliament, despite the fact that he was present in the assembly and "ostentatiously took down the names of those who spoke against them."[35] In 1641, "[The] trial of Strafford ... produced the first exercise in parliamentary history of the coercive use of publicity of members' votes in the chamber. The names of fifty-nine M.P.s who had voted against Strafford's attainder were posted up on the Royal Exchange under the title, 'The names of those men, who to save a Traytor, would betray their Country.' It is hardly surprising that attendance in Parliament began to fall."[36]

In two constituent assemblies, demands for public voting came from representatives branding the threat of popular action. In 1789, radical members of the Assemblée Constituante insisted on roll-call voting on controversial issues to scare their opponents into voting against their conviction. Although no framers were killed or physically injured, many feared for their lives and for those of their families. To explain why some members voted against bicameralism, a liberal deputy for the nobility wrote to his constituency, "Some deputies from the third estate have told me, I do not want my wife and children to have their throats cut."[37] When radicals in the 1848 Frankfurt constituent assembly used the same tactic, "the work of parliament was ... threatened by the hunt of the crowd for unpopular members of the assembly."[38] One member of the Center Right was beaten up and two killed.

In modern political systems, parties are usually able to enforce discipline on deputies, since voting in Parliament is almost invariably public. Until 1988, the Italian Parliament was a rare exception to this rule. In that year, "party leaders promoted the abolition of secret vote as it prevented them from monitoring organized intra-party factions that used secret voting as a tool to undermine incumbent governments."[39]

To my knowledge, when the publicity of *debates* has been induced by pressure, it has always been by popular demand. The principal naturally wants to know not only how its agents are voting but also what they are saying. Reporting of debates and access of the public to assemblies were nevertheless contentious issues in British and American history for centuries.[40] Deputies claimed they were fighting a two-front war against the executive and the people and needed to be protected from both. Progress was interrupted by reversals until by the early 19th century publicity imposed itself irreversibly.

In modern societies, publicity and the related norm of transparency impose themselves in an increasing number of domains.[41] Historically, the secrecy of

---

[35] Woolrych (2002), p. 90.
[36] Pole (2008), p. 101; see also Woolrych (2002), p. 177.
[37] Lally-Tolendal (1790), p. 141.
[38] Eyck (1968), p. 312.
[39] Gianetti (2010).
[40] Pole (2008), chs. 4 and 5.
[41] There does not seem to be a well-established distinction between publicity and transparency as features of decision-making processes. In an administrative context, when the reasons for a decision are made known to the individual whom it concerns but not to anyone else, intuition

jury deliberations has been matched by the publicity of the trial itself. A more recent development is the demand that the jury give *reasons* for its verdict (see Chapter 2). After the accidental revelation in 1993 that the Open Market Committee of the Federal Reserve Board had been taping the debates, as a help in preparing the minutes, and that the tapes had been preserved, Congress pressured the board into publishing the transcripts with a five-year delay.[42] The decision by the European Council of Ministers in that same year to publish the votes of individual member states was probably also due to a diffuse pressure for transparency. Yet since, for a number of reasons, the published votes do not reflect the true positions of the member states, publicity actually has had the effect of making the process more opaque.[43]

Normatively grounded devices for creating or maintaining ignorance, secrecy, and publicity are the main organizing topics of this book. Yet from the normative point of view, five more questions need to be raised. I discuss them at greater length in the Conclusion.

First, whereas the guiding idea in the book is to design institutions so as to reduce the exposure of decision makers to distorting factors, one might also consider other goals.[44] Specifically, one might assess institutions by their *cost*, their *legitimacy*, and their *impact on the character of the participants*. Of these, I believe that only the costs of decision making – direct costs, opportunity costs, and delays – are relevant.[45] To take an excessively simple example, even if we believed that the Condorcet Jury Theorem is fully valid, in the sense that the likelihood of a collective decision being correct converges toward 100 percent as the number of participants increases indefinitely, the cost of gathering millions of people to decide in a small-tort case would obviously be prohibitive. In that

---

may suggest that there is transparency without publicity. In judicial and legislative contexts, it seems harder to drive a wedge between the two ideas. In some cases, one can perhaps define transparency as what is *not hidden* (but may be costly to find) and publicity as what is *revealed* (with low or zero costs).

[42] Stasavage and Meade (2008), p. 697. The delayed revelation in 2011 that Ben Bernanke and other members of the Federal Reserve Board had minimized the subprime risk in 2006, one year before it erupted, provided a telling illustration, if one was needed, of the fragility of financial models.

[43] Novak (2011), ch. 3.

[44] Tideman (2006), p. 35, proposes to evaluate collective decisions by the following criteria: outcome efficiency, procedural efficiency (costs of decision making), symbolic equality, material equality, productivity-based inequality (merit-based rewards), restoration (undoing past injustice), and preservation (creating a stable environment for decisions). The list seems somewhat ad hoc.

[45] In my opinion, the criterion of (perceived) legitimacy is too arbitrary to serve as a normative yardstick. Many institutions acquire the appearance of legitimacy simply by virtue of having been in place for a long time (Zajac 1995). In the Conclusion I cite an example from jury reform. Tocqueville (2004a), p. 316, and Stephens (1883), vol. 1, pp. 572–73, cite the impact on the character of jurors as a "collateral benefit" of the jury system. I have argued elsewhere (Elster 1983, Chapter 2), that it is incoherent to assume that one could propose this effect as a justification *to the jurors*, since the impact on their character depends on their belief that the goal is something external to themselves. "All public offices, like all professional skills, aim at something beyond themselves: *nulla ars in se versetur*" (Montaigne 1991, p. 1022).

sense, the question of *good collective decisions* (Chapter 1, IV) diverges from that of *good collective decision-making procedures* (Chapter 1, V).

Second, my case for negative institutional design ignores the crucial positive desideratum of *epistemic competence*. At the individual level, such competence can be enhanced not only by removing distorting factors but also by providing opportunities to learn. At the collective level, it can be enhanced by ensuring that the decision-making body has sufficient *diversity*. It has been said that the aim of college admission should be to create not a group of well-rounded individuals, but a well-rounded group of individuals.[46] Similarly, a diverse collection of ordinary individuals may outperform the best single person. The idea goes back to Aristotle (*Politics* 1281b–1282a) and has recently been subject to formal analysis.[47] The best rationale for the idea that the jury should form a microcosm of society at large is not that it should be representative or that all citizens have the right to serve as jurors, but that the jury should be *diverse*.[48] Similarly, I argue in Chapter 4 that diversity is of great value in constituent assemblies, while perhaps less necessary in ordinary legislatures. Diversity allows for deliberation among individuals with different experiences that can supplement each other.[49] I reserve a general discussion of the value of diversity for the Conclusion.

Third, my case for negative design also needs to be supplemented along a different dimension. I have asserted that once we have done our best to minimize passion, interest, bias, and prejudice, using the tools of ignorance, secrecy, publicity, randomization, and rotation, we should let the chips fall where they may. The problem is that our best may not be very good. In the Conclusion, therefore, I consider when and how we might want to create institutional mechanisms for *overriding* bad collective decisions.

Fourth, here as elsewhere it is a fallacy to assume that all good things go together. An institutional device that reduces the impact of passion on decision makers may enhance that of self-interest (Chapter 4). A system of rotating officials that promotes impartiality by preventing them from being captured by local interests can also undermine epistemic competence by limiting their opportunities to learn. Sieyes advocated a very rapid turnover in the Presidency of the Constituante to prevent capture by the executive,[50] whereas Bentham argued that the President of an assembly had to be permanent so that he could acquire the necessary experience.[51] The idea of designing institutions to minimize the impact of interest, passion, prejudice, and bias while at the same time promoting

---

[46] J. C. Kemeny, cited in Dawes (1964).

[47] Page (2007). The contributions to Landemore and Elster (2012) develop (and sometimes question) the idea of the "wisdom of crowds" from different perspectives.

[48] Abramson (2000), ch. 3.

[49] Diversity may also be valuable in expert bodies. The French constitutional court has had some members without legal training, such as the sociologist Dominique Schnapper. Blinder (2007) argues for diversity on Central Bank committees.

[50] Sieyes (1789), p. 82.

[51] Bentham (1999), pp. 66–67.

epistemic competence may, in fact, be conceptually incoherent, or coherent only by accident. We cannot assume that several distinct functions of a given variable will reach their maximum (or minimum) for the same value of the variable. In some cases we may be confident that a reform addressed to reducing the impact of one of the distorting factors will not enhance that of the others, but this happy situation cannot be taken for granted.

To answer this objection by citing the need to find an "optimal compromise" between, say, expertise and impartiality is to presuppose that we can determine the trade-off between these two values. One might affirm, for instance, that the benefits from learning created by extending the tenure of rotating officials from one year to two years exceed the costs arising from the risk of capture. Similarly, one might affirm that the benefits of a two-terms-only rule for deputies exceed the costs. It follows from my general argument, however, that such claims will in general be unsustainable. They assume that we have a normative theory of what constitutes a good outcome and a causal theory of how to bring it about by institutional means. The present work as a whole is directed against this assumption.

This being said, it would be absurd to be dogmatic on this issue. In some cases where a proposed reform would entail costs as well as benefits, one can confidently claim that the net effect will be positive. Examples include the abolition of life tenure for judges (an American practice created when life expectancies were less than half of what they are today) or of annual elections to Parliament (also a practice that may have made sense in the 18th century but not in the 21st). By contrast, the merits of triennial versus quadrennial elections or of six-year versus eight-year tenure for judges on constitutional courts seem entirely indeterminate.

Finally, there is a question of agency or political will: why would political actors implement Benthamite reforms if they stand to lose from them? Assuming that it would be desirable if elected officials put their financial assets in a blind trust, so that their votes on issues that might affect their interest would be made behind a veil of ignorance, why would they adopt this regime? Why would French deputies abolish the *cumul des mandats* in France? Why would government delegate control over monetary policy to an independent central bank? These issues can be resolved at a constitutional stage, but only if framers do not expect to be in power at the post-constitutional stage.

The strength and generality of the argument in the book is to some extent limited by the opacity or contemporary irrelevance of the main empirical cases. My discussion of legislatures and constituent assemblies reflects my immersion in the late 18th century. Compared to contemporary politics, it was a different world. Today, an elected political assembly is dominated by political parties, and its work is largely done in committees. Free plenary exchanges among representatives willing to change their mind upon conviction is largely a thing of the past.[52]

---

[52] Writing in 1927, Carl Schmitt (2008), p. 341, singled out the French Chamber of Deputies as a "noteworthy exception" to the general fact that parliaments were "no longer the site of reciprocal rational persuasion."

(Because of the relative lack of party discipline in the major American parties, the U.S. Congress forms an important exception.) Some of the issues that I discuss may, therefore, seem marginal or of historical relevance only. I hope nevertheless that the underlying psychological mechanisms have a more general interest.

The jury offers a contemporary example, in miniature, of the plenary debates of the past. Unfortunately, we know so little about what goes on inside the jury room that it is hard to make robust assertions about the impact of institutional design on the quality of the deliberations. Moreover, there is little one can affirm confidently about the impact of design on the quality of outcomes (verdicts, sentences, and awards) since we cannot measure the dependent variable. As we have to study the jury by triangulating evidence from many sources, our conclusions are mostly tentative.

I am not using the case studies to "prove" anything. Rather, I alternate between two argumentative strategies. One is to assume the correctness of my basic proposal (the negative Benthamite approach supplemented by epistemic and override mechanisms) and draw implications for institutional design. The other strategy is to show the appeal of that proposal by pointing to the failure of more ambitious approaches and by showing what can go wrong if one fails to reduce the impact of distorting factors on the decision makers. I offer an "essay in persuasion," not a demonstration.

I

The Normative Study of Collective Decision Making

I. INTRODUCTION: INDIVIDUAL CHOICE

Individual and collective decision making can be studied either from a positive (descriptive or explanatory) point of view or in a normative perspective. Here I first briefly consider individual decisions.[1] A standard classification is the following:

Decision analysis

Positive	Normative
Behavioral economics	Rational-choice theory (expected-utility theory)
Behavioral ethics	Ethical theories

Let me briefly consider the four categories.

Rational-choice theory tells an agent how to choose the means that will best realize her ends, given her beliefs. It also offers normative advice on belief formation and information gathering. Given her information, the beliefs ought to be shaped by truth-tracking procedures, that is, by the procedures that in the long run and on the average are most conducive to true beliefs. Finally, given her beliefs and her preferences, the agent should gather information up to the point (which in practice may be impossible to determine) at which the expected marginal value of information equals the expected marginal cost.

Ethical theories tell the agent how to act morally. There are many such theories, the main varieties being consequentialist and non-consequentialist proposals. Each variety, if taken to extremes, can have absurd implications. At the same time, there is no agreement on how each should be tempered to yield reasonable prescriptions. A consequentialist ethical theory will also tell the agent to act rationally. If her aim is to alleviate poverty in developing countries, she ought to make sure that her donations benefit poor individuals rather than lining the pockets of bureaucrats or dictators.

---

[1] Baron (2008) is a useful overview.

Over the last four decades, behavioral economics has documented numerous cases in which actors trying to behave rationally are influenced by "rationally irrelevant" factors, such as whether a glass is described as half empty or as half full. Similarly, the partially overlapping field of "behavioral ethics" has identified a number of ways in which individuals seeking to act morally are influenced by "morally irrelevant" factors, such as the difference between omission and commission.

Going beyond this typology, I shall propose *a normative behavioral approach*. I shall first explain what this means for individual decisions; in later sections and chapters the idea will be extended to collective decisions.

To motivate the proposal, let me note that the standard normative theories are, in many situations, hopelessly demanding.[2] They presuppose that agents have stable and fine-grained preference rankings and subjective probabilities on which they can rely to calculate and compare the expected utility of their various options. In many situations, however, preferences and beliefs are neither stable nor fine-grained. Moreover, even if they were, the agents would not be able to carry out, *in real time*, calculations that may occupy many pages in a mathematical appendix to an article in the rational-choice framework. This is not a matter of the *irrationality of the agents*, but of the *indeterminacy of the theory*.

Yet even when rational-choice theory is indeterminate, we may be able to offer some normative advice. Behavioral economics and behavioral ethics tell us that desires and beliefs can be shaped by irrelevant features of the agent's internal state and external situation. Hence she has *nothing to lose and possibly something to gain* from preventing the emergence of these states and situations or from blocking their effects. It is not a question of debiasing, which is a procedure of dubious effectiveness,[3] but of either preventing biases from arising in the first place or of making oneself unable to act on them. For individual decisions, the story of Ulysses and the sirens is a paradigm of this strategy.[4] Other devices include "Counting to 10," never shopping on an empty stomach if you want to lose weight, and not reassessing your portfolio stock too frequently. A large part of the present book is devoted to *bias prevention in collective decision making*.

Implicit in the preceding remarks is a distinction between substantively good decisions and good decision-making procedures. In what we may call the standard approach, the purpose of good procedures is seen as that of promoting *independently defined* good outcomes. At the individual level, the use of "fast and frugal heuristics" is often defended on these grounds.[5] In this case, we are dealing with *truth tracking*. More controversially, it has been claimed that the

---

[2] Elster (2009d).
[3] Fischhoff (1982).
[4] Elster (1984, 2000).
[5] Gigerenzer and Goldstein (1996); Goldstein and Gigerenzer (2002).

"affect heuristic" can *track morality*.[6] At the collective level, Bentham thought that majority voting would track what he somewhat misleadingly called the greatest happiness for the greatest number.

These are strong claims. For my purposes, I do not need to address the efficacy of heuristics of individual choice. In Chapter 3 I briefly observe that even if we ignore the paradox of cycling majorities, Bentham's claim cannot be defended. The approach I shall propose is substantially weaker, and negative rather than positive. As I said, I shall be concerned with removing – or blocking the effect of – known obstacles to good decision making. I shall not claim that we can establish an empirical correlation between features of the decision-making process and the quality of the outcome, since we usually have no independent measure of the latter. There is no way to measure, for instance, rates of false acquittals and false convictions by juries in different settings.[7] If we could, there would be no need for juries.

In Rawlsian terms, we can exclude an understanding of good collective decisions in terms of *perfect procedural justice*.[8] We might then turn to what Rawls calls *imperfect procedural justice*, which he illustrates by the example of the criminal trial (trial by jury). If the only task for juries were to decide between conviction and acquittal, they would indeed match his characterization of imperfect procedural justice: "while there is an independent criterion for the correct outcome, there is no feasible procedure that is sure to lead to it." Yet the existence of an independent *criterion* is irrelevant in the absence of an independent *procedure for determining* how often it is satisfied. Moreover, some juries have the task of sentencing in criminal cases and of awarding damages in civil cases. In these cases, there is not even an independent criterion for the correct outcome, no fact of the matter.

It might then seem more appropriate to characterize good collective decision making in terms of *pure procedural justice*, in which "there is a correct or fair procedure such that the outcome is likewise correct or fair, whatever it is, provided that the procedure has been properly followed." This is how Rawls argues for his theory of justice. If we try to apply the idea to actual decisions, however, it is still too demanding. Even if (*per impossibile*) all systematic biases, prejudices, and the like were removed, jury deliberations could still contain random idiosyncratic components that might cause one jury to award higher damages than what might be awarded by another equally unbiased jury in an

---

[6] Sinnott-Armstrong, Young, and Cushman (2010).

[7] Although DNA testing has made it possible to produce estimates of the frequency of wrongful convictions (Risinger 2007; Garrett 2011), nobody to my knowledge has tried to use this frequency as a dependent variable with alternative jury procedures (or jury-versus-judge) as independent variables. In his discussion of reforms of the criminal justice system that might reduce the frequency of miscarriages of justice, Garrett (2011, ch. 9) does not mention jury reform. In any case, as DNA testing is becoming standard practice at the initial trial, and not just a tool in exonerating the innocent convicted in the pre-DNA era, this retrospective assessment will be less feasible in the future.

[8] Rawls (1971), §14. The two quotations in the text are taken from this paragraph.

identical case.[9] The generally accepted principle that jurors should be chosen by lot might in one case produce an all-male and in another an all-female jury. Although the awards might differ, neither plaintiff would have grounds for complaints.

Also, no procedure for selecting members of juries, committees, or assemblies can screen out domineering individuals or spoilers (*mauvais coucheurs*, as an untranslatable French expression has it). An English proverb says that "There is a black sheep in every flock." A French proverb tells us that "It takes only one bad sheep to spoil a flock." Together, they imply that every flock will be spoiled. The proverbs exaggerate, as usual, but they still provide a useful warning. The two disastrous decisions of the 1848 French constituent assembly to allow Louis Bonaparte to be elected as deputy and to have the President chosen in direct elections were arguably due to the eloquence of a few deputies, notably Lamartine (see Chapter 4). To prevent candidates from standing on the ground that they are too eloquent is hardly imaginable. Sometimes, the best we can do is to pursue *impure procedural justice*. In the Conclusion, I ask what if anything one can do when the best is not good enough.

In the remainder of this chapter I begin by offering a survey of collective decisions (Section II) and an analysis of "the elementary forms of collective decision making" (Section III). From descriptive I then turn to normative issues. I first discuss the idea of good collective decisions (Section IV) and then the idea of good procedures for making collective decisions (Section V). In Section VI I consider how these procedures can be affected by various forms of strategic behavior. Whereas Sections IV through VI mainly have the form of a critical exposition of existing theories (together with an argument for the recently proposed alternative of "majority judgment"), in Section VII I turn to my own "Benthamite" view that in various forms will be developed in the rest of the book.

II. COLLECTIVE DECISIONS

Collective decisions are the result of collective decision making. Hence beginning with the decisions rather than with the processes might seem to be putting the cart before the horse. I believe it may nevertheless be useful to begin with a sample of cases on which I can draw in the next section. Although my main concern in later chapters is with juries, assemblies, and electorates, it will prove helpful to have a richer array of examples as background material. In the survey that follows, I shall also include some cases of *failures* to arrive at a collective decision. In such cases the parties may disband, go to war, or go to court.

Before I proceed to the examples, I should make it clear that I shall adopt an expansive notion of what counts as a decision. One might prefer a restricted notion and limit oneself to decisions that have a direct *causal impact* on their

---

[9] For the distinction between random and systematic imperfections in jury trials, see Kassin and Wrightsman (1988), p. 110.

intended objects. "I tell this one, 'Go,' and he goes; and that one, 'Come,' and he comes." I shall refer to these as *effective decisions*. I choose, however, to construe the concept of a decision more broadly to include *decisions to propose*, that is, decisions to propose to make an effective decision. Thus a proposer and an effective decider would act as joint decision makers. Following Harrington, "I divide, you choose" is the canonical case.[10] The Athenian practice of *antidosis* relied on a related, more complex mechanism.[11]

I shall often use the Federal Convention as a paradigm of collective decision making although, strictly speaking, it decided nothing. Responding to the objection that the Convention was going beyond its mandate, James Wilson said that "He conceived himself authorized to conclude nothing, but to be at liberty to propose any thing."[12] The effective decision was left to the state conventions of ratification. The Council of the Five Hundred had a crucial role in the Athenian democracy, yet its only function was to prepare cases for the assembly to decide. Although the Spartan *gerousia* did not make decisions, it had the exclusive right to make proposals to the decision-making body of the *apella*. (The Athenian Council did not have this monopoly.) Some recent instances of deliberative democracy involve only the right to debate and to propose, not the right to decide.[13]

I shall also extend the idea of a collective decision to the case of *collective belief formation*. Strictly speaking, a jury doesn't decide anything when it pronounces a verdict. It is just reporting the beliefs of the jurors, or a majority among them. The announcement of this belief may *trigger* a decision, as when the judge, upon the pronouncement of a verdict of not guilty, orders the immediate release of the accused, but it does not *constitute* a decision. (In fact, as we shall see, judges can sometimes override jury decisions.) Because of the close link between the belief formation and the decision in such cases, I shall count the former *as* a decision. Although one can imagine processes of collective belief formation that are not harnessed to decisions, as when a group of historians might try to reach agreement about some past event, these are unlikely to occur when the decision has no practical relevance. One might establish a "jury" of historians to reach a collective conclusion about the alleged Armenian genocide, but hardly about genocides in Antiquity.

Let me first consider some small-scale decisions, beginning with the allocation of household work and child care between husband and wife jointly with the determination of the total work to be performed. Family work involves tasks

---

[10] Harrington (1977), p. 417, also wanted to reserve the right to *debate* to the proposing assembly, leaving the deciding assembly no other task than to vote the proposals up or down. Although he cites Sparta as an example, it seems that the *apella* did have the right to debate the proposals, but not to modify them (Levy 2003, pp. 210–16). That was also true of the conventions that ratified the American Constitution.

[11] MacDowell (1978), pp. 162–64. In inheritance cases, when there were two heirs only, the Athenians also used the practice "I divide, you choose" (ibid., p. 93).

[12] Farrand (1966), vol. 1, 253.

[13] For some experiments in deliberative democracy, see Lang (2007) on British Columbia, Fishkin et al. (2010) on China, and Fishkin et al. (2008) on Greece.

that the spouses (1) are more or less good at, (2) find more or less irksome, and (3) assess as more or less important. Thus one spouse may find it easy and not too unpleasant to clean the house, but care little about the house being clean. The other may differ on one or several of these dimensions. Sometimes, they may find it in their interest to misrepresent these differences, notably with regard to intrapersonal or interpersonal differences in preference intensity along dimensions (2) and (3). If they cannot reach an agreement, they may split up.

For another two-person example, suppose that Peter and Paul are playing tennis in five sets for a prize, and that rain interrupts the game at the beginning of the fourth set, when Paul has a lead of two sets to one. For some reason, it is not possible to continue the game on a later occasion. How should the prize be divided? Paul might say that he should get it, since he is ahead. Others may propose to give 2/3 of the prize to Paul and 1/3 to Peter. As for Peter, he might argue for equal division, backing his claim by asserting that he had been deliberately saving his forces for the last two sets. If they can't agree on a proposal to present to the organizers, neither gets anything.

Consider also the decision by passengers in a train compartment to keep the window open or closed. Some passengers may claim that a closed window is the default position,[14] just as silence is the default position when one person wants to play the trumpet and his neighbor wants to sleep. Others might claim that an open window is the default, or that there is no default. If they can't agree, some of them may decide to leave for another compartment where their preferred practice is observed, or get off the train.

In the first of these cases, the two spouses typically make many decisions over time, reflecting new problems and changing circumstances. Moreover, their decisions at one time create premises for later decisions. By contrast, the second and the third cases involve one-off decisions. The same distinction applies to committee decision making. The governing boards of central banks and constitutional courts are called upon to make many decisions over a period of many years. Earlier decisions constrain or form precedents for later ones. By contrast, trial juries only meet once and, today at least, only to decide a single case. (Grand juries differ in both respects.)

At a more aggregate level, legislative assemblies and (some) constituent assemblies also differ in this respect. In 1787, the Federal Convention was called only to reform the constitution, and that is all it did (stretching its mandate, however). By contrast, the concurrently operating Continental Congress met periodically until it was replaced by the body established by the new constitution. To be sure, the task of a constituent assembly is vastly more complex than that of a jury. Altogether, the Federal Convention took 569 roll-call votes over roughly three months. Yet these votes built up to one single decision, the adoption of the constitution to be proposed for ratification, whereas ordinary legislatures take separate and binding decisions on many unconnected issues.

---

14 In Paris buses, there are signs saying "In case of disagreement, priority is given to those who want the window to be closed."

The French Estates-General provide an example of *episodic* decision-making bodies,[15] which are intermediate between one-off bodies and bodies that meet on a regular basis, at scheduled times and places and with fixed procedures. On each occasion, the procedures were up for grabs. "The modes of convocation, election and holding of the Estates-General had never been clearly determined."[16] The successive kings had a strong interest in cultivating this procedural indeterminacy. "The king was careful not to enact rules of order that might be used as argument for regular meetings of the Estates.... The royal prudence avoided any enactment of general statutes."[17] Furthermore, as long as there were no standing rules, the King retained the option of soliciting subsidies from the provincial Estates when he expected strong resistance from the Estates-General.[18] Guy Coquille, a deputy to the Estates of 1560, 1576, and 1588 as well as a theoretician of the absolute monarchy, stated the matter very clearly: "The government of this Kingdom is a true monarchy, which has no relation to democracy or aristocracy, as some have claimed because of the existence of the Estates and of the *parlements* [quasi-legislative judicial bodies]. This opinion is far from the truth; for if the Estates were a form of democracy, there would be regular times and places for their meetings, which is not the case."[19] There would also, of course, have to be regular procedural rules. Several Estates collapsed because of disagreements over the second-order decision about how to vote.[20]

Any deciding body does indeed need some procedural rules adopted by second-order decisions – decisions about how to decide. It might, for instance, have the options of using premise-based or conclusion-based aggregation (see Section V), to decide by simple majority voting, weighted majority voting, supermajority, or unanimity, and so on.

In some cases, the group that is to make the first-order decisions also makes the second-order decision. In that case, I shall say that the group is *autonomous*. In some cases, a jury can sovereignly decide whether to reach its decision by secret ballot or by public voting. A union may decide to use postal ballot when its members vote on a negotiated wage increase. The European Central Bank is partly governed by its autonomously adopted rules of procedure. Legislatures are to a large extent, although far from completely, masters of their own rules of order. A famous and puzzling example is the 60 percent majority rule in the American Senate.[21] Constituent assemblies are usually held to be completely free to decide on their own procedural rules. When Louis XVI tried to tell the

---

[15] For the contrast between periodic and episodic institutions, see Vermeule (2010).
[16] Marion (1923), p. 217.
[17] Tanchoux (2004), pp. 24, 25.
[18] Konopczynski (1930), p. 70.
[19] Coquille (1789), pp. 294–95.
[20] See the journals of Jean Masselin (1835), pp. 99–101, 221; Jean Bodin (1788), p. 228; and Florimond Rapine (1651), p. 362, for, respectively, the Estates of 1484, 1576, and 1614; also Mousnier (2005), p. 791.
[21] See Eule (1987) for history and discussion.

Estates-General of 1789 how to organize their vote – they could vote by head, but only if each of the three estates agreed to it – they ignored him.

The question raises the specter of an infinite regress, however, since it invites us to ask about the third-order decision by which the assembly adopts the second-order decision rule, and so on. As an example, consider the opening session of the First Continental Congress in Philadelphia on September 5, 1774. The appointment of the twelve state delegations was a pretty haphazard process.[22] It seems that each state sent as many delegates as it could easily afford. Not only were the delegations of unequal size, but the numbers were not in any way proportional to the population or wealth of the respective states. Once the delegates were in place, they had to decide on how they were to decide in the future. The second-order options were

1. Each state will cast one vote
2. Each delegate will cast a vote
3. Each state will cast a number of votes that is proportional to its population, wealth, or some combination of the two.

There were strong objections to each proposal. The first was seen as *unfair*, given the ratio of 10:1 of the populations of the most and the least populated states. The second was seen as *arbitrary*, given that the size of the delegations was largely a matter of chance. The third was seen as *impractical*, both because it would be difficult to reach agreement on the appropriate basis for apportionment (ought slaves to be included?) and because there were no reliable statistics.

On September 6, the Congress adopted the first procedure:

Resolved, That in determining questions in this Congress, *each Colony or Province shall have one Vote*. The Congress not being possess'd of, or at present able to procure proper materials for ascertaining the importance of each Colony.

As this was objected to as unequal, an entry was made on the journals to prevent it being drawn into a precedent.

Virtually all commentators content themselves with affirming that Congress "decided" to adopt the principle of one state, one vote, without specifying how the decision was made.[23] A partial exception is Richard Barry (a biographer of the delegate John Rutledge), who may be read as stating that the decision was taken by a close vote among the delegates.[24] He claims, moreover, that

---

[22] Jillson and Wilson (1994), ch. 2.

[23] "In the end each colony *was given* one vote" (Jensen 1959, p. 59); "it *was agreed* that each colony should have one vote" Burnett (1964, p. 38); "the delegates then *resolved* 'that ... each colony or province should have one vote' " (Jillson and Wilson 1994, pp. 52–53). The authors of the phrases I have italicized do not indicate the voting rule.

[24] Barry (1942), pp. 161–62. The text is ambiguous, but I believe my interpretation is at least plausible. He states, without citing his sources, that "the decision to vote by colonies was carried by the narrow margin of two votes." This statement probably refers to voting by voice, since a margin of two state votes among the eleven states assembled, for example, 6 to 4 with one delegation divided, would hardly be a "narrow" one.

whereas a majority among the *delegates* were against breaking with Great Britain, a majority of the *states* favored a rupture, adding that while this fact was not common knowledge among the delegates, it was known to Sam Adams from Massachusetts. Hence to ensure the rupture, Adams cleverly engineered the second-order decision of voting by states by having the third-order decision made by a vote by delegates. Although I cannot vouch for the historical accuracy of this account, it brings out the important conceptual point that the self-government of collective bodies may have an inevitable component of arbitrariness.

The attempt to prevent the decision from serving as a precedent turned out to be completely ineffective. When the framers met in Philadelphia thirteen years later, the principle "one vote, one state" had been transmuted from a temporary expedient into an immutable right. This tendency for solutions that were intended to be temporary and reversible to harden into unalterable rules by virtue of their focal-point quality is quite common.

In 2002, the Convention for drafting the European Constitution also faced a bootstrapping problem.[25] As the upstream authority (the Laeken Declaration) did not contain any instructions about how the Convention was to vote, it had to make up its own rules. Abstractly speaking, one might have given each of the 14 states one vote, used the weighted voting scheme established by the Treaty of Nice, or adopted some other weighted scheme. The last option was unfeasible, since each state would have favored the scheme more likely to favor the decision (including its future voting weight) favoring it. The second option may also have been unviable, as the Nice voting scheme was widely perceived as giving too much weight to Spain and Poland. The first option was apparently ruled out of court because of the possibility that the draft might be adopted by a majority of the states representing a minority of their population. Instead, the President of the Convention, Giscard d'Estaing, imposed the rule of decision by non-opposition (see below), *using that very rule* in imposing it.

In many cases, procedural decisions that govern or constrain substantive decisions in one body are taken by a different body. In that case, the body is *heteronomous*. Some examples follow. In 16th-century England, the boards of corporations were required by law to decide by majority rule, except when the private interests of board members were involved, in which case unanimity was required.[26] In Norway, the law says that jury forepersons must be chosen by secret ballot. In 1984, the Thatcher Parliament enacted laws restricting the immunities of workers against court actions following a strike to unions that had secured majority support for the strike in a secret ballot. Previously, unions, operating autonomously under an open-vote second-order system, had favored

---

[25] For the observations in this paragraph, see Miller (2002), Magnette (2004), Magnette and Nicolaïdis (2004), and Zhao (2008). The contradiction regarding the Laeken Declaration between note 15 and note 19 in Magnette and Nicolaïdis (2004) should be resolved in favor of the former.

[26] Konopczynski (1930), pp. 59–60; Gialdroni (2009).

the open vote for first-order decisions. The European Central Bank is partly governed by externally imposed statutes. Legislatures, too, are usually heteronomous in some respects. Quorum rules, the majority needed for legislation, mandatory delays, publicity of the proceedings, and similar principles are often laid down in the Constitution.[27] Until the recent constraints imposed by the European Convention of Human Rights, the British Parliament was completely autonomous, a feature greatly praised by Bentham.

The question of *deciding how to decide* is related to, but distinct from, the question of *deciding who shall decide*.[28] Like the former, the latter has the potential for an infinite regress, a problem that can be avoided if the assembly is *self-created*. That solution may, however, create a new problem, if there are several groups of would-be constitution makers. In the quasi-constitutional debates at Putney, Cromwell raised precisely this issue: "How doe we know if whilest wee are disputing these thinges another companie of men shall gather together, and they shall putt out a paper as plausible perhaps as this?"[29]

Important and successful instances of self-creation include the First Continental Congress and the German assembly of notables who elected the *Vor-Parlament* that in turn established the rules for electing delegates to the 1848 constituent assembly in Frankfurt. In the American states, there have been several attempts at bootstrapping or unauthorized constitutional conventions. In Michigan in 1835, the attempt succeeded: "Congress accepted [the process] as satisfactory and by its acceptance ratified the action of the irregular convention."[30] A famous unsuccessful attempt was an effort by the citizens of Rhode Island in 1841 to "overthrow the tyrannical rule of the landholding classes" by holding an unauthorized convention that adopted a democratic constitution.[31] In 1855 and in 1857, while Kansas was still a territory, two competing self-appointed conventions – the first anti-slavery, the second pro-slavery – submitted constitutions to Congress, seeking the rights and title of a state. Congress accepted neither.[32] In the irregular context of the Civil War, successful self-appointed conventions were also held in Arkansas in 1864[33] and in Tennessee in 1865.[34] By definition, such bodies have no upstream legitimacy: they will be judged only by the downstream effects of their decisions.

Decisions about the deciders may *cascade* and *cycle*. A cascade occurs, for instance, if the members of a constituent assembly decide that the voters shall

---

[27] Pierre (1893), p. 431.
[28] For simplicity, I ignore the issue of deciding *what* to decide. The U.S. Supreme Court, for instance, spends a great deal of time deciding (by a submajority of four) whether to grant certiorari (Perry 1991). Committees in Congress decide what to forward to floor debate. A submajority of Congress can, however, force a bill out of committee. On submajorities in general, see Vermeule (2005).
[29] Firth (1891), p. 237.
[30] Hoar (1917), p. 20.
[31] Ibid., p. 21.
[32] Borgeaud (1895), pp. 175–77.
[33] Cowan (1959).
[34] Harris (1997), pp. 219–21.

elect representatives to decide on their behalf. An elected parliament may delegate decisions to the administration. A cycle occurs, for instance, if deputies, once chosen by the voters, decide to let the voters decide in a referendum.

The ideas of autonomy and of self-creation must be distinguished from that of *self-government*. To explain the latter idea, let me distinguish between the agents of a collective decision (the *deciders*) and the *targets* of the decision. The latter are the individual or individuals on whom the decision has *an intended or expected effect*. The *primary targets* are those whose behavior the deciders intend to affect, whereas *collateral targets* are those whom the deciders expect to be affected by the decision.[35] These targets often form a much smaller group than the set of individuals *actually affected* by the decision.

In Boolean terms, the relation between deciders and targets can take five different forms: (1) the agents and the targets coincide; (2) the deciders are a proper subgroup of the targets; (3) the targets are a proper subgroup of the deciders; (4) the deciders and the target overlap, but neither group is included in the other; and (5) the deciders and the targets are disjoint groups. I define *self-government* as case (1), *the coincidence of deciders and targets*. The adoption of laws by referendum provides an example if the laws apply, at least potentially, to all voters and only to voters. When an assembly adopts rules of order, it is also self-governing. (When it adopts income tax legislation it is not, since the agents then are a proper subgroup of the targets.) When a jury decides to vote by secret ballot, it is self-governing. (When it produces a verdict it is not, since in that case the agents and the target are disjoint.) Although in these examples self-government involves second-order decisions, it can also be a matter of first-order decisions, as when an assembly or workers' cooperative votes a salary increase for its members.

Suppose that the extension of the franchise is a subject of referendum. If only those already enfranchised are allowed to vote, deciders and targets are disjoint. I conjecture that this is the normal pattern. In at least two cases, however, more fully described in Chapter 5, the prospectively enfranchised have also been allowed to vote, making the targets a proper subgroup of the deciders. The 1830 Virginia constitution was "ratified in an election open to all who were prospectively enfranchised by it."[36] The same procedure gave the opposite result in 1953, when revisions in the Danish constitution were submitted to referendum.

Elections may be seen as a form of self-government if active and passive suffrage coincide. The voters choose some among themselves to rule them. Although this way of stating the matter might suggest that the targets are a proper subgroup of the deciders, this is not how I intend my terminology to be understood. By targets I have in mind a *preexisting* groups of individuals, such as those between 21 and 25 years of age, whose opportunities or obligations the

---

[35] In the United States, the Unfunded Mandates Reform Act of 1995 requires deciders to take account of collateral targets (Vermeule 2007, pp. 228–31). In Chapter 3 I return to the rationale for this requirement.

[36] Pole (1966), p. 332.

agents seek to regulate. Elected officials, by contrast, do not preexist the decision by the deciders: they are created by that decision. The decision targets everybody, at least potentially.

Age qualifications (or other qualifications) for active and passive suffrage do not always coincide, however. The most common divergence no doubt occurs when the targets (the eligible) form a proper subgroup of the deciders (the electors). Bentham argued, as we shall see in Chapter 3, that there is no good rationale for this restriction on eligibility. Instead, he claimed, the deciders ought to form a proper subgroup of the targets. In some historical cases, restrictions on grounds of income, age, or gender have in fact been less restrictive for representatives than for voters. In the 1776 constitution of Virginia, voters had to be freeholders with at least 50 acres of land or satisfy other property conditions, whereas representatives only had to be freeholders. Eugène Pierre lists the following examples from the late 19th century:[37] Great Britain had economic qualifications for active suffrage, but not for passive; in the Danish elections to the lower chamber, voters had to be at least 30 years of age, but anyone above 25 could be elected; in Spain, voters had to be at least 25 years old, but one only had to be of age (21 years) to be eligible. More recently, in Holland and Spain women became eligible before they could vote.[38]

The three-tiered voting system adopted in the French constitution of 1791 is somewhat anomalous. Here an electorate with low tax-paying qualifications chose electors with high property qualifications to elect deputies with low tax-paying qualifications. De jure, this may be seen as a form of self-government. De facto, the targets formed a proper subgroup of the deciders. The goal of the three-tiered system was to ensure that only wealthy individuals would be chosen as deputies. Once the direct method for achieving this aim – requiring high property or tax-paying qualifications for the deputies – had been discarded as incompatible with the Declaration of Rights, the property-owning majority in the Assembly opted for the three-tiered system as an indirect method that was sure to give the same result, since wealthy electors could be counted on to choose wealthy deputies.[39]

Among the five Boolean relations, the most frequent seem to be the first, the second, and the fifth. Although I have given several examples of the third, it seems to be comparatively rare. I have not found any important cases of the fourth. A marginal case could be a workers' cooperative with some outside owners that voted to reduce the wages of a proper subgroup of its members.[40]

Pursuing this example, many cooperatives are, of course, *self-governing*. Frequently, they are also *autonomous* (although subject to general workplace and company legislation). Finally, they are often *self-created*. The governing board of a central bank is at the opposite ends on each of these three dimensions.

---

[37] Pierre (1893), pp. 126–28, 163–64.
[38] See entries on "Netherlands" and "Spain" in Hannan, Auchterlonie, and Holden, eds. (2000).
[39] Guennifey (1993), pp. 51–62; Elster (2006a).
[40] Aanund Hylland points out to me that the election of the German President offers another example.

The members are appointed from outside, they are (to variable degrees) subject to externally imposed rules, and their decisions flow mainly from the intention of benefiting the economy as a whole. Other institutions may occupy the positions of high-high-low, high-low-high, high-low-low, low-high-high, low-high-low, and low-low-high on the three dimensions. There may be systematic relations among these positions, but I have not been able to determine any.

III. COLLECTIVE DECISION-MAKING PROCESSES

Assuming methodological individualism, it makes intuitive sense to think of collective decision making as the outcome of *organized horizontal interaction among individuals.*[41] True, in some collective decisions the deciding units appear to be aggregates. In the Continental Congress, in the Federal Convention, and in the French Estates-General, votes were taken by states or by estates (or by collective subunits of the estates, which could be either provinces or *bailliages*). However, the vote to be cast by an aggregate would ultimately be determined by individual voting within the aggregate.

I shall now try to spell out the intuition italicized above.

By interaction *in the strong sense* I shall mean influences mediated by communication with others and observation of others. I exclude the use of physical force, but include verbal threats to use force. Although most processes of collective decision making are interactive in one of these senses, some are not. Members of the Athenian juries were discouraged from communicating with each other and prevented by the secret ballot from observing how other jurors voted (Chapter 2). As we shall also see in Chapter 2, the law governing contemporary Brazilian juries forbids interaction among the jurors. Although political assemblies typically involve some form of interaction, there are exceptions. When municipal councils in the Third French Republic elected members of the college that elected senators, debates were forbidden and votes were secret. "The fact that a vote had been preceded by a debate would have made a case for invalidation."[42]

These processes were nevertheless interactive if we understand interaction in a *weaker sense*, in which interaction includes not only the causal impact of other agents on the *acts* of a given agent, but also the impact of other agents on the *impact of the acts* of a given agent on the outcome. Thus if we consider elections to be only a matter of *choosing one of two candidates*, the impact of my vote depends on the votes of others. For my vote to be pivotal, the other votes have to be equally divided between the candidates. By contrast, if we see elections as also *conferring a mandate* on the winner or as *conferring legitimacy* on the loser, the

---

[41] In a rare explicit definition, Tideman (2006, p. 6) writes, a "Collective decision . . . is a process that identifies a pattern of future coordinated actions as the intended actions of the members of a collectivity, and creates corresponding intentions in enough members of the collectivity that in the ordinary course of events the pattern is realized." It makes no sense to quarrel over definitions, but this one does not seem very useful. Nothing in Tideman's excellent book turns on it.

[42] Pierre (1893), p. 149.

stronger the effect the larger the number of votes in their favor, the impact of my vote does not depend, on a first approximation, on how others vote. If the formal powers of elected officials or the length of their tenure depended (continuously) on the size of the majority by which they were elected, the collective decision-making process would to some extent be additive and not even weakly interactive.[43] As we shall see later, lottery voting has the same property.

The requirement of *horizontal* interaction is intended to exclude imposed, dictatorial decisions. It should not be taken to imply that all members are on a par, in the sense of having equal powers to shape the outcome. Collective decision making is compatible with the presence of a primus inter pares. In even-numbered groups, the oldest member or the most senior one may have the right to break ties. In many committees, the chairperson may have a greater influence than the others. In descending order of influence of the chairperson, she may appoint the other members (as in many cabinets), be appointed separately by an external instance (as in the French constitutional court), or be chosen by and from the members (as in the Italian constitutional court or in some university departments). The chairperson will usually exercise greater influence by virtue of her agenda-setting power and her greater knowledge of the preferences of other members. An exception, sometimes observed in university departments, may arise when the members of the body deliberately choose a weak chairperson.

In practice, the distinction between dictatorial and collective decision making is easily blurred. A committee may be dominated by a single individual. "Alan Greenspan chaired the [Open Market Committee of the Federal Reserve Board] for 18 years and was never on the losing side of a vote. Nor did he ever eke out a close victory."[44] To an unknowable extent Greenspan may of course have been constrained by the knowledge that he might be outvoted ("the law of anticipated reactions").[45] Conversely, even a supposedly absolute monarch may be unable to impose his will. Although Louis XIV managed to do so, his predecessors were often constrained by unruly nobles and by the Estates-General, and his successors by recalcitrant courts or *parlements*, which were de facto co-legislators by virtue of their credible threat to delay or shut down essential legal functions.[46] Judges have sometimes tried to influence or harass jurors. As these brief comments suggest, the simple dichotomy between vertical and horizontal decision procedures risks being simplistic. In Chapter 4 I shall examine two particularly poignant instances in which this dichotomy breaks down: the making of the Japanese constitution of 1947 and of the German constitution of 1949.

Collective decision making is also consistent, although sometimes tenuously, with individual influence *weighed* by income, tax payment, property, education,

---

[43] The proposal by Durant and Weintraub (2011) that the first and second placed candidates should take alternating years in office if no candidate achieves a supermajority of 60 percent does not satisfy the continuity condition.

[44] Blinder (2007), p. 111.

[45] Ibid., p. 115.

[46] See Olivier-Martin (2010), pp. 582–607, for a succinct description of the *parlements*.

age, number of children, or marital status. All of these criteria have been proposed at various times, and some have been implemented. Property is by far the most important criterion. In cooperative buildings, votes at the annual meeting are routinely weighed by square feet. In Britain around 1900, a man could vote in all the electoral districts where he possessed property. In 1911, it was estimated that 7 percent of the electorate were "plural voters."[47] A similar arrangement obtained in Virginia in the 18th century. There it was supplemented by "a remarkable fractional vote to joint owners. Provided that their joint freehold was big enough to qualify, and that they could agree with each other, they might unite to cast a single vote for their freehold."[48]

From the conceptual point of view, it is important to distinguish between (say) property as a criterion for *excluding* certain members of the community from the decision-making process, thereby relegating them to the status of targets of decisions, and property as a criterion for *weighing* the votes of the deciders. The case of the Virginia fractional vote shows that the distinction is not clear-cut, since small owners could not cast a vote unless they agreed. Bracketing that question, I shall count any non-dictatorial decision procedure as a collective one, even when the influence of the deciders on the outcome is highly unequal and many members of the community are non-deciders.

Nor does horizontal interaction imply that all deciders participate in all decisions. A collective may divide itself into *sub-collectives*, or committees. In assemblies, there are three kinds of committees.[49] First, they may be made up of deputies who already possess specialized knowledge, members of the finance committee having experience from private business or public finance, members of the committee on health and social security having a background in public health or social services administration, and similarly for other committees. Second, they may be made up of members who are not chosen for their preexisting expertise but who develop specialized knowledge by serving on the committee over an extended period of time. Third, they may be made up of members who are chosen without preexisting knowledge and who turn over frequently, with no opportunity to become specialized.

Condorcet's jury theorem would seem to suggest that committees are less efficient truth trackers than the larger bodies from which they are recruited. Accepting for the sake of argument the validity of his reasoning (see Chapter 3 for some doubts), what might justify their existence? If the assembly itself deliberates in public, committees have the advantage of being able to deliberate calmly without undue pressure or influence from an audience.[50] This argument

---

[47] Blewett (1965), p. 46. This percentage represented between 500,000 and 600,000 voters.

[48] Pole (1966), pp. 140–41.

[49] The first corresponds to the case envisaged by List and Pettit (2011), p. 95; the second and the third to the case they discuss in ibid., p. 96.

[50] Committees may, however, be open to other members of the assembly. Pierre (1893), pp. 773–76, details the varying French practices from 1789 onward. When access of non-members was abolished, it was because "the publicity disturbed, without any benefits, discussions that ought to be calm and thoughtful" (ibid., p. 785). At the Continental Congress, "Grand Committees appointed to deal

applies to all three types of committees. Also, the epistemic gains from special-
ization might more than offset the loss from their small size. This argument
would obviously apply to the first and second types of committee only.[51]
Specialized committees are likely to be more competent than the not specialized ones,[52] while sharing the advantage of being insulated from popular
pressure. They might, therefore, seem to dominate the third model. Yet since
specialized bodies risk being captured by *special interests*, committees with
rotating membership might also have their advantages. As we shall see in
Chapter 4, the French revolutionaries initially preferred the third model over
the specialized ones.

In earlier writings, I have distinguished decision-making processes by two
dichotomies. First, I opposed the aggregation of preferences through *voting* to
the transformation of preferences through *arguing*.[53] Later, I contrasted *arguing*
with *bargaining*.[54] It would seem, however, to make more sense to consolidate
the two dichotomies into a trichotomy: arguing, bargaining, and voting.[55] We
find an unusually explicit presentation of these three modes of deciding in a
comment on the edicts of pacification issued at the end of each of the eight
French wars of religion:

> Wherever religious pacification confirmed and consolidated confessional dispersal and
> the appearance of biconfessional territories, towns and institutions, these immediately
> raised a problem that was destined to attain decisive importance over the years: *which
> mode of decision to adopt* in religious matters? Should one at any price and despite the
> inevitable delays pursue a unanimous decision [*arguing*]? Or let each camp take separate
> votes before negotiating a compromise that satisfies them [*voting + bargaining*]? Or
> exploit the seductive possibilities – clarity, rapidity, efficiency – of majority voting
> [*voting*]?[56]

For reasons I explain at greater length in Section IV, the category of voting may,
however, be too narrow. Voting and elections rely on the aggregation of ordinal
preferences, which are information-poor inputs to the social decision. Michel
Balinski and Rida Laraki argue that one can improve the decision by asking
participants to provide an information-richer input in the form of *judgments*.[57]
This practice is, for instance, often used in wine tasting. When wine tasters make

---

with the most critical business before the Congress were open to all members of the Congress"
(Jillson and Wilson 1994, p. 55). The intention was to guarantee "every member the right to monitor
the committee's work" (ibid.). Modern assemblies, by contrast, monitor only the *outputs* of their
committees.

[51] List and Pettit (2011), pp. 95–97, state conditions under which the epistemic gains from "decom-
position" dominate the information-pooling benefits of large groups.

[52] Standing committees can also be inefficient, however, if their membership is not reasonably stable.
At the Continental Congress, the "substantial turnover on standing committees undermined the
development of expertise" (Jillson and Wilson 1994, p. 105).

[53] Elster (1986).

[54] Elster (1999–2000).

[55] Elster (2007a), ch. 25.

[56] Christin (1997), p. 135; my italics.

[57] Balinski and Laraki (2010).

a collective decision about the relative merits of wines, for instance, they often use absolute qualitative criteria rather than rank orderings. In the first step of the process, "each [wine] receives a rating which is the median rating based on the ratings resulting from the calculations of each of the jurors."[58] This rating is the *majority grade*. In the second step, the *majority judgment* selects the option with the highest majority grade. I shall use *aggregation* as a term of art for the broader category that includes both traditional voting and majority judgment. When discussing aggregation, I shall systematically consider these two procedures separately. Although the theory of majority judgment is novel and (in the legal and political domains that are my main focus here) untested in practice, I believe it has considerable intrinsic virtues, notably that of eliminating many of the pathologies of preference aggregation discussed later.

The procedures of argument, aggregation, and bargaining constitute, I believe, the *elementary forms* of interactive collective decision making. All procedures known to me can be analyzed, as I do later, as combinations of these. Yet even if the three categories form an exhaustive classification, they are not always unambiguously exclusive of one another. It can be difficult to tell whether a given speech act counts as an argument, as an input to an aggregation procedure, or as a threat. Three examples will illustrate the problem. (1) When an oral vote is accompanied by a comment, the meaning of the vote may not be clear. In the transcripts of the debates in the advisory committees to the Federal Drug Administration, a vote that is stated as *"yes, but"* or *"no, unless"* is sometimes counted, improperly, as, respectively, a positive or a negative vote.[59] (2) What appears to be a factual statement, made as part of an argument, may in reality be closer to a threat. On July 8, 1789, when the troops were converging toward the National Assembly, Mirabeau spoke directly to the King in language that seemingly only *predicted* his own behavior while in reality amounting to a threat: "The danger, Sire, is threatening the efforts that are our main duty, and which can only succeed fully and durably if the people perceive them as entirely free. Passionate movements are subject to contagion; we are only men; our distrust of ourselves, the fear of appearing to be weak, may carry us beyond the goal; we will become obsessed by violent and excessive proposals." (3) When a minority accepts defeat in voting, it may do so under the shadow of threat. "Parliamentary government is simply a mild and disguised form of compulsion. We agree to try strength by counting heads instead of breaking heads, but the principle is exactly the same."[60]

Pure argument is observed, or at least supposed to be the rule, in juries that require unanimity. Although jurors also vote, the purpose of the vote is to

---

[58] OIV (1994) cited after Balinski and Laraki (2010), p. 154.

[59] Urfalino and Costa (2010). See also Bentham (1999), pp. 93–101, and Konopczyński (1930), pp. 19–20, for the importance of a clear separation between the debate and the vote.

[60] James Fitzjames Stephen as cited in Vermeule (2009), who explores many aspects of this connection.

verify that they agree, not to force a decision.[61] Multimember courts and central bank committees that decide by consensus rather than by voting also fall into this category. Even here, some members may resort to tacit bargaining by virtue of their greater ability to hold out, that is, their lesser impatience to get out of the committee and back to their ordinary life. Because time is always important when a decision has to be made – if it didn't matter *when* a decision is made, it wouldn't matter *whether* it is made – and because the participants in the process typically have different degrees of impatience, this case may in fact be typical.

Pure bargaining is illustrated by sequential "divide-a-dollar" games in which the parties make successive offers and counteroffers. The outcome is determined by the bargaining mechanism and the bargaining power of the parties, that is, by the resources that enable them to make credible threats and promises. In rational-choice models of pure bargaining, no actual bargaining occurs. The bargainer who has the right to make the first offer proposes a division of the dollar, and the second accepts it. This artificial result is due not only to the assumption of rationality but also to the assumption that the utility functions and time preferences of the bargainers are common knowledge. By contrast, actual bargaining, in which these features are often shrouded in (Knightian) uncertainty, may go on for a long time and even fail to yield an agreement.

Bargaining can also take place among more than two agents. It seems fair to say that we do not understand multilateral bargaining very well, mostly because it is hard to predict which coalitions will form. In domestic politics, the best-known claim, that the minimum winning coalition will form, has poor theoretical and empirical support. In international politics, the interaction of economic, political, and psychological forces produces a cloud of uncertainty that is hard to pierce analytically, as the recent European debt crises illustrate. I shall limit myself, therefore, to the two-person case.

Pure aggregation is illustrated by the wine-tasting system mentioned earlier, by ice-skating and ski-jump competitions, and many similar procedures. Although judges in these sports sometimes engage in vote trading[62] (a form of bargaining), they are not supposed to. In sport competitions, they are neither supposed to nor able to argue about the merits of the contenders. In political choice, pure voting was Rousseau's conception of collective decision making. The citizens were to form their preferences in isolation from one another so as not to be contaminated by eloquence and demagogy.[63] Because they would also cast their vote without communicating with one another, vote trading would be

---

[61] "The requirement of unanimity ... contributes to an understanding among the jurors that their function is to persuade, not to outvote one another" (Abramson 2000, pp. 195–96).

[62] Zitzewitz (2006).

[63] At least Rousseau thought that under certain circumstances this isolation was a sufficient condition for the formation of the general will. It is not clear (to me) whether he also thought it was a necessary condition.

excluded.[64] The same was true of Harrington's popular assembly and, according to him, of the Spartan model. Earlier, I cited the Athenian and Brazilian juries as examples, along with the French municipal elections. This mode may also be illustrated by certain low-stake decisions, such as the election of members to a scientific academy the main function of which is to elect new members.[65]

Social-choice theory (discussed later) usually assumes that the only function of aggregation is to pick a winner. That assumption is, however, unrealistic and misleading. "Extending the concept of [voters'] utilities to all the outputs of an election ... helps to explain many obscure phenomena.... Examples abound. Take first-past-the post. Abstention: perhaps a voter does not wish a winner to win by too much. Participation: perhaps the contrary (e.g., Chirac versus Le Pen, which brought out a record number of voters). Votes given small party candidates: voters know they cannot win and may wish they do not win, and yet they vote for them."[66] A voter might also desire the election of a consensual candidate rather than the one she would personally prefer.

Mixed arguing and aggregation without bargaining may be illustrated by tenure decisions in American university departments. These decisions are supposed to be governed only by deliberating about the merits of the candidate followed by an open vote. In good departments there is a norm against logrolling. In the best departments this norm is actually adhered to: that is why they are the best. (Needless to say, perhaps, these claims are based on my personal impressions only.) In some French academic institutions, logrolling is more rigorously prevented by the rule that professors are elected by secret ballot, so that members cannot make credible promises to reciprocate (or observe whether others reciprocate). The downside of this system is that the quality of argument is reduced by the fact that the electors do not have to put their vote where their mouth is.

Many other committees only use, or are supposed only to use, arguing and voting. Examples include the Federal Drug Administration (FDA) committees on drug safety, the U.S. Supreme Court, the German Constitutional Court, the Open Market Committee of the Federal Reserve Board, and the Governing Council of the European Central Bank. Given the opacity of all these institutions but the first, it is usually impossible to tell whether some issue-based bargaining also takes place – for instance, in the form of vote trading. Later I cite a rare documented example of vote trading on the U.S. Supreme Court. I would be surprised if the practice were not quite common on other multi-member bodies operating as ongoing institutions with high degree of continuity of membership.

The Federal Reserve Board and the Governing Council of the European Central Bank have the interesting feature that some members (chosen by

---

[64] It is also unclear whether Rousseau thought that the citizens should vote without *observing* the votes of others, that is, whether they should use the secret ballot. Bertram (2004), p. 107, assumes that Rousseau intended the vote to be secret to prevent the formation of coalitions.

[65] Elections to the American Academy of Arts and Sciences also have an element of arguing, since highly negative assessments of candidates are discarded if the elector does not offer her or his *reasons*.

[66] Balinski and Laraki (2010), p. 374.

rotation) are allowed to participate in the discussion, but not to vote. In some other cases, non-voting membership is determined by *age* (in the Norwegian Academy of Sciences members above the age of 70 cannot vote in the election of new members) or by *status* (apprentices and students sometimes do not have voting rights on bodies where they serve as representatives). On the FDA committees that evaluate drugs, the representative of the drug industry does not vote. Generally speaking, little seems to be known about the rationales for, and the effects of, the presence of non-voting members in a decision-making body.

Mixed arguing and bargaining, without aggregation, is illustrated by collective wage bargaining. When a union and a management are deciding how to divide the income of the firm, it might appear as if only bargaining is taking place. On closer inspection, however, there is always a substantial amount of arguing about factual matters, such as the financial well-being of the firm and the productivity of the labor force. The allocation of household work and child care can also happen in this mixed mode. The spouses might argue from a number of distinct principles: we should devote equal time to the tasks, we should suffer equal disutility from the tasks, or we should minimize joint (total) disutility from the tasks. Since the very plurality of plausible-sounding arguments provides an opportunity for each spouse to adopt the one that serves his or her self-interest, the threat of a divorce may be needed to reach agreement.

Mixed bargaining and aggregation (by majority voting) was institutionalized in the British Wages Councils and Boards in the 1950s. The *possibility* of a vote shaped wage bargaining even though in most cases no vote took place.[67] The crucial factor was the presence at the bargaining table of an uneven number of independent members, along with equal numbers of members representing employers and workers. The first group served both as a mediator between the two others in the course of the bargaining process and, by virtue of their uneven number, as a guarantee that the wage would be settled by a decisive vote if no negotiated agreement was reached. In 1945, out of 51 decisions 37 were reached by agreement, 5 by a voting majority of employer representatives and independent members, and 9 by a voting majority of worker representatives and independent members.[68]

Assembly decision making usually involves *all three procedures.* Again, this fact follows from the need to reach a decision sooner rather than later. *Voting* will tend to arise when an issue has to be decided urgently, so that the participants do not have the time to deliberate until they reach unanimity. More prosaically, they may not be motivated to search for unanimity. As I mentioned,

[67] Bayliss (1957).
[68] Theories of majoritarian bargaining (e.g., Baron and Ferejohn 1989) also describe cases of mixed bargaining and voting. Most models in this tradition seem to have little purchase on actual behavior, perhaps because of their "cognitively demanding" character (Diermeier and Gailmard 2006, p. 330). This is, of course, an objection that can be raised to a large class of formal theories (Elster 2009d).

bargaining will tend to arise when some of the participants are more impatient to finish than others. Bargaining also arises through logrolling, due to unequal intensity of preferences over the issues to be traded off against each other, and through a number of other mechanisms. Members may, for instance, use the threat of filibustering, of endless amendment proposals, or of time-consuming voting procedures to obtain concessions. When a quorum is essential, they may use the threat of staying away from the assembly.

Arguing and aggregation (voting) can also occur in *virtual* form. Philippe Urfalino observes that many small groups *decide by non-opposition*.[69] The decision to do X is made when one member (usually a chairperson) asserts, after some discussion, that "Unless someone objects I take it that *the sense of the meeting* is that we do X," and nobody objects.[70] As we saw earlier, Giscard d'Estaing used this rule both for the meta-decision and the first-order decisions at the European Convention. Cabinet decision making, too, often takes this form.[71] Although a prime minister may take a straw poll to get a feel for the sense of the meeting, it does not amount to a formal vote. On a central bank committee, the Governor "may listen to the debate and then announce the group's decision, expecting everyone else to fall in line."[72]

In the European Council of Ministers, the President can impose a decision in this way, even when there is actually a minority block of states that, according to the voting rules of the Council, could prevent it.[73] Because bilateral talks with member delegates allow the President to be much better informed about their voting intentions than the members are about each other, she may not encounter any opposition if she asserts, contrary to fact, that the required qualified majority for a proposal has been reached. No minority delegation objects because each thinks, wrongly, that there is no blocking minority (a case of pluralistic ignorance). Whereas a prime minister can dominate a cabinet by virtue of his greater authority, the President dominates the Council by virtue of her greater information. Decision by non-opposition clearly presupposes the *possibility* of opposition, minimally in the form of saying "I object, for the following reasons" and sometimes in the form of demanding a formal vote. In other words, decision by non-opposition occurs *in the shadow of arguing and voting*.

As noted, the European Convention used the same procedure for its meta-decision and for its substantive decisions. In general, however, there is no reason to think that the mix of mechanisms used for the second-order decision will be transferred to the first-order level. An association might require, at its founding meeting, that its bylaws be adopted by unanimity. One of the bylaws might be

---

[69] Urfalino (2007). The practice of deciding "nemine contradicente" has a long history. As noted by Konopczynski (1930), p. 58 n. 3, it is perfectly compatible with a majority of the voters being against the decision (see discussion later in the chapter).

[70] See also Novak (2011), ch. 5, for many examples.

[71] Jones (1985).

[72] Blinder (2007), p. 114.

[73] Novak (2011).

that future decisions should be made by majority voting. The decision that municipal elections to the French senatorial college should take place without prior debate was presumably made by a vote in the national assembly following a debate, or at least without a ban on debate.

IV. GOOD COLLECTIVE DECISIONS

In this section and in the two following ones, I shall discuss good decisions and good decision-making procedures within the framework of existing theories of preference aggregation, judgment aggregation, and belief aggregation. Although I try to some extent to assess the theories as more or less adequate, this is somewhat marginal to my main concern, which is to argue that, *whichever theory we adopt*, its aim will be better realized within the Benthamite framework.

In the analysis of good collective decisions, *goodness for the targets* is in an obvious sense the most relevant idea. I shall argue, however, that in the general case we have to limit ourselves to *goodness for the deciders*. Sometimes, to be sure, this is not true. Even in the case of disjoint deciders and targets, the deciders might want to achieve overall goodness rather than goodness for one group only. When adult voters adopt child-related legislation, it is not a given that the aim be defined either in terms of goodness for adults only (as was often the case in the past) or in terms of goodness for children only (as is often the case today). Although one can understand why, in child custody disputes, the law in many countries says that custody should follow the best interest of the child (but see Section VII for some objections), arguments for giving custody to one or the other parent might also have some weight.

Let me illustrate the tension between deciders and targets by the debates over extension of the suffrage at the Federal Convention. John Dickinson saw "the restriction [of the right to vote to freeholders] as a necessary defence agst. the dangerous influence of those multitudes without property & without principle with which our Country like all others, will in time abound."[74] His was an overt defense of the interest of the deciders. Others took an indirect route to the same conclusion, arguing that only the rich would benefit from giving the poor the right to vote. Gouverneur Morris, for instance, argued that "Give the votes to people who have no property, and they will sell them to the rich who will be able to buy them. We should not confine our attention to the present moment. The time is not distant when this Country will abound with mechanics & manufacturers who will receive their bread from their employers. Will such men be the secure & faithful Guardians of liberty? Will they be the impregnable barrier agst. aristocracy?"[75] In the same breath Morris also pointed to the pressure that the wealthy could exercise on the votes of their dependents. No carrot would be necessary to make them vote the right way; the stick would do it.[76] In either

---

[74] Farrand (1966), vol. 2, p. 202.
[75] Ibid. Madison (Farrand 1966, vol. 2, pp. 203–4) combined both arguments.
[76] Ibid., p. 203.

version, the argument was that extension of the suffrage to the propertyless would de facto amount to greater representation of *property*. It was, therefore, in the interest of the poor themselves that they be deprived of the vote.

The last argument is an old one. In the Roman Republic, some voting restrictions may have been motivated by "the desire to limit the influence of patrons over their former slaves."[77] In the Putney debates, Colonel Rich cited this precedent to argue against unrestricted democracy: in Rome, he said, "the peoples voices were bought and sold, and that by the poore, and thence it came that the richest man ... made himself a perpetuall dictator."[78] However, the Romans also used the secret ballot to limit the influence of the rich. If the American framers had been seriously concerned with vote buying or with the pressure the wealthy could exercise on their clients, they, too, could have proposed a secret ballot. Since the debates at the Convention are full of references to the institutional arrangements of Classical Antiquity,[79] ignorance of the secret ballot was not the reason why nobody proposed it. I agree, therefore, with Alexander Keyssar when he writes that the American founders "were performing an impressive feast of ideological alchemy: providing an ostensibly egalitarian defense of an overtly anti-egalitarian policy"[80] or, in my terminology, defending the interests of the deciders by ostensibly appealing to the interests of the targets.

Abstractly speaking, it would seem both desirable and possible to define goodness of collective decisions in terms of the targets. The most prominent candidate – the principle of adopting the policy that maximizes the sum-total of happiness or welfare in society – makes no reference to the preferences, judgments, or beliefs of the deciders. The proposal presupposes, however, that we can make reasonably accurate interpersonal comparisons of utility. The conceptual and practical obstacles to such comparisons are known to be formidable.[81] To be sure, in practice we sometimes do use this utilitarian approach in a rough and ready manner. On the reasonable assumptions (1) that individuals are pretty much similar in their capacity for transforming money into subjective welfare and (2) that the marginal utility of money is decreasing, we feel justified in transferring some income from the rich to the poor. We can also temper these consequentialist considerations with distributive concerns. The recognition that some individuals are less efficient than others in transforming money into welfare,

---

[77] Lintott (1999), p. 204.

[78] Firth (1891), p. 239.

[79] Richards (1994).

[80] Keyssar (2000), p. 11. Sydnor (1952), p. 123, asserts that the main aim of the exclusion of tenants from the suffrage in the 1776 Virginia constitution (or rather the maintenance of the suffrage restrictions in the 1762 colonial charter) was to "restrict the political power of the very rich" by disenfranchising their dependents. He also, and inconsistently, claims (ibid., p. 164) that the reduction of the freehold size required for suffrage was "an attempt to multiply the votes of men of property" who held land in several counties. Whereas Wood (1991), p. 178, cites the first passage, Pole (1966), p. 144, refers to the second.

[81] Elster and Roemer, eds. (1991).

notably if they have a disability of some kind, can provide an additional justification for transfers.

In many cases, however, the utilitarian approach provides no guidance for action. If some members of the municipal council want to build a swimming pool, others a school library, and still others to fund an orchestra, interpersonal comparisons of the utility the citizens would derive from the various options are likely to be unfeasible. Moreover, even if such comparisons could be carried out with precision across currently living individuals, the approach fails completely with respect to future generations. We do not know how many individuals there will be in the future. Although that number could in theory be determined by a collective decision by the present generation, the idea is chimerical. In any case, our knowledge about how our actions will affect the welfare of future generations is shrouded in deep uncertainty. Even the much weaker criterion of *Pareto-optimality for the targets*, inducing a partial rather than a complete ranking of the options, is vulnerable to this objection.

For these reasons, I shall only consider how collective decisions may be good *for the deciders*. This sense of goodness is obviously highly relative. As an analogy, take the fact that rational-choice theory tells agents how best to realize their desires, *whatever these might be*. If Hitler had listened to such advice, he might have won the war. Instead, his emotions caused him to act irrationally: his hubris triggered by the victory against all odds over France led to his disastrous conduct of the war in the East, his anger at the British bombing of Hamburg caused him to direct air attacks against London instead of targeting airfields, his contempt for the Slavs made him blind to the benefits of cooperating with the Western Ukrainians, and his hatred of Jews made him divert scarce resources to the Holocaust. In all these cases, a less emotional response would have better served his ends, *such as they were*. Similarly, the normative question asked by social-choice theory, for instance, is how to aggregate individual preferences, *whatever these might be*. If all deciders prefer exterminating all Jews to eliminating some Jews or none, the Holocaust will be the socially preferred outcome. Like rational-choice theory, social-choice theory and its cognates are in an important sense normatively neutral. The "general will," however defined and operationalized, has no privileged normative status.

Social-choice theory is the dominant framework for assessing the goodness of (noncognitive) collective decisions. I shall first state some basic features of the theory and then discuss the powerful alternative approach of "majority judgment" recently proposed by Michel Balinski and Rida Laraki. On both approaches, it is assumed that the collective has to *choose* one from a set of alternatives – policies, candidates, or other objects of evaluation – or *rank* the options from better to worse. I begin by considering social-choice theory.

In the language of that theory, the goodness of a collective decision is an *intra-profile* matter. A profile is a constellation of individual preference rankings over a set of options. For a given profile, the normative question is to determine the option society should choose or, more generally, the social preference ranking that it should use as the basis of its decision. For instance, if all members of society prefer x to y, society should choose x over y. Since unanimity is rare, one must also determine what counts as a good collective decision in its absence. One might lay down, for instance, that when a majority prefers x to y, society should choose x over y.

By contrast, the goodness of a collective decision-making *procedure* is an *inter-profile* matter, defined with reference to a *set* of profiles, perhaps the set of all possible profiles, rather than a given profile. As an example, consider the requirement of non-dictatorship. The existence of an intra-profile dictator, whose preferences coincide perfectly with the social ranking, can be consistent with genuine collective decision making. Such a person might just be a chameleon. By contrast, the existence of an inter-profile dictator such that the social preferences always coincide with hers, even when she is in a minority of one, is inconsistent with the very idea of collective decision making. I discuss other inter-profile requirements in Section V and in Section VI.

Condorcet noted that as a way of realizing intra-profile goodness of decisions, majority voting can be indeterminate. With three voters and three alternatives, a majority of two may prefer the first alternative over the second, another majority prefer the second over the third, and yet another majority prefer the third over the first. I shall offer several examples of such cycles. (Moreover, attempts to overcome this problem by requiring a supermajority will not work, since cycles can appear for any supermajority short of 100 percent.) While some scholars claim that majority cycles are rare and others that they are pervasive,[82] nobody denies that they logically can and at least occasionally do occur. From this fact, some have drawn the conclusion that the idea of the "general will," as conceived by Rousseau, is meaningless.

Some aspects of Rousseau's theory may in fact seem to be meaningless, such as the idea that a person who finds himself voting against the majority ipso facto is shown to be mistaken, as if majority voting is supposed to *reveal* rather than to *determine* the general will. Given the ambiguity of Rousseau's writing, it is hard to determine whether he held this view. Some of the French revolutionaries certainly claimed to understand (and endorsed) him in this sense.[83] Be this as it may, the idea that the existence of majority cycles invalidates the idea of the general will is clearly wrong. The cycles show that majority voting is a poor instrument for determining the general will, not that the idea itself is incoherent.[84] In fact, the method of majority judgment offers a coherent version of the idea.

Votes are a poor instrument because they contain so little information. A voter can convey either the minimal information that one option is top-ranked, by voting for one candidate or policy rather than another, or the somewhat fuller but still impoverished information embodied in an ordinal ranking of the

---

[82] For these two views, see Mackie (2003) and Riker (1982).

[83] Martineau, AP 10, p. 423; Camus, AP 30, pp. 134–35; see also Castaldo (1989), pp. 272–73, for other examples. The ancient practice of punishing minority members of a jury (Konopczynski 1930, pp. 14–17) may perhaps be seen as a forerunner of this idea.

[84] Grofman and Feld (1988), p. 574.

alternatives. I shall return later to the virtues and flaws of the Borda count, which tries to make use of this ordinal information. First, however, I want to discuss the information-richer procedure of asking voters to *judge* the alternatives.[85]

We first assume that the judges have a shared language in which they can express their qualitative evaluations of the options or candidates. Balinski and Laraki argue, on the basis of extensive empirical investigations of grading in wine tasting, ice skating, and other domains, that "inputs [to an aggregation mechanism] given in the six-word language of grades *Excellent*, *Very Good*, *Good*, *Acceptable*, *Poor*, and *To Reject* convey much more precise common meanings within a culture, than the input of rank-order, the name of one candidate, or the names of several candidates."[86] Crucially, for my purposes here, politics also seems to have a common language. In a survey where 1,752 persons were asked to grade twelve French politicians for the office of President of the Republic, "more than one of every three participants gave their highest grade to two or more candidates. Only half of the voters used the grade of *Excellent*.... *This proves that voters do not have in mind rank-orderings of the candidates.*"[87]

Once the voters or judges have assigned grades to the candidates, we define the *majority grade* as the median of all the grades. We then rank the candidates according to their majority grades, the winner being the candidate with the highest majority grade. (I skip complications due to ties and to an even number of judges.) This procedure cannot give rise to cycles. Moreover, it eliminates the problem caused by extreme or "cranky voters," whose votes would receive excessive weight if the procedure used the mean rather than the median.[88] Finally, if candidates are placed on a left-right spectrum, majority judgment has neither a bias against centrist candidates nor a bias in favor of centrist candidates. Other systems tend to have one of these biases. Majority judgment also has other desirable properties that I discuss in the next section.

The following example offers a striking illustration of the superiority of the grading method over voting:

Suppose three grades – *Good*, *Pass*, and *Bad* – and an electorate that evaluated two candidates A and B as follows:

	Good	Pass	Bad
A:	40%	35%	25%
B:	35%	30%	35%

[85] The following is a non-technical and approximate summary of much more complex and nuanced arguments, which interested readers should consult in the original (Balinski and Laraki 2010, 2012).

[86] Balinski and Laraki (2010), p. 389.

[87] Ibid., p. 13; italics in original.

[88] As they show (ibid., pp. 100–102), Galton explicitly argued for the use of the median rather than the mean in his famous weight-judging competition, to avoid an undue influence of outliers or "cranks"; see also Levy and Peart (2002). Many writers nevertheless affirm that Galton proposed to use the mean (e.g., Surowiecki 2005, p. xiii; Philippe Maier 2010, p. 325; List and Pettit 2011, p. 86).

A's percentages of *Good* and *Pass* are both above B's, her percentage of *Bad* below B's, so there is no doubt that in the electorate's evaluation A leads B. But what does a majority vote say? That all depends. If the electorate's preference profile is

	30%	10%	10%	25%	25%
A:	Good	Good	Pass	Pass	Bad
B:	Pass	Bad	Good	Bad	Good

(consistent with the distributions of grades) then A wins with 65 percent of the votes (assuming a voter gives her vote to the candidate with the higher grade). On the other hand, if the electorate's profile is

	5%	35%	35%	25%
A:	Good	Good	Pass	Bad
B:	Pass	Bad	Good	Pass

(also consistent with the distributions of grades) then B wins with 60 percent of the votes. Thus more precise information about voters' evaluations of candidates shows that majority voting and the traditional model may fail even when comparing only two candidates.[89]

When voters have to choose among policy options – for example, where to build a road or which weapon system to adopt – rather than among candidates, they may not have a common language in which they can express their judgment. Instead, they may have to use ordinal rankings. Balinski and Laraki argue that in such cases, some of the advantages of majority judgment can be retained if one uses the Borda Count (defined in the next section) and chooses the option with the highest *median* rather than, as in the usual procedure, the highest mean. This procedure is both "crankiness-proof" and, as we shall see in Section VI, at least partly manipulation-proof.

Although I believe that Balinski and Laraki have shown that majority judgment is superior to traditional voting procedures, I shall continue to discuss both systems. Since the traditional procedures are likely to remain in place for some time, it is important to assess their normative properties.

V. GOOD COLLECTIVE DECISION-MAKING PROCEDURES

In this section I focus on the goodness of procedures rather than on the goodness of outcomes, to assess arguing, aggregation (of votes and judgments), and bargaining as mechanisms for making collective decisions.[90] Arguing can occur among two

---

[89] Balinski and Laraki (2012), p. 18.
[90] Tideman (2006), p. 69, defines good collective decisions by three criteria : "(1) The decision is made by a procedure that is accepted by the members of the collectivity. (2) The outcome does not

or more individuals, aggregation among three or more individuals, and bargaining (for reasons explained earlier) only between two individuals.

Before I proceed, I shall raise a question that readers may already have asked themselves. Would not the question of determining the best procedure for collective decision making be pointless if some forms of decision making by a *single* individual could be shown to be superior to all forms of collective decision making? Might not judges perform better than juries, an individual central banker better than a central bank committee, or a single founder better than a constituent assembly? R. V. Jones claimed that no committee of intelligence analysts in World War II could have outperformed him when he collected all information and collated it in his own mind.[91] Although I shall touch on this question from time to time, I do not propose a general analysis. Let me observe, though, that the mechanism for selecting this single individual would itself involve a collective decision.

In this section I assume throughout that participants are *sincere*: there is no difference between what they believe or prefer and what they say, or between what they believe or prefer and how they vote. In the next section I consider the effects of *strategic* non-sincere behavior, with respect both to verbal behavior and to the nonverbal behaviors of voting and judging. In the final section I also consider the effects of *hypocritical* non-sincere *behavior*, verbal and nonverbal. The reasons for and effects of these two kinds of misrepresentation, while sometimes overlapping, can diverge quite widely.

Arguing Toward Unanimity

My aim in this subsection is to elucidate the properties of arguments that *work in practice*, that is, arguments that succeed in persuading others. The analysis depends therefore to some extent on empirical material. The empirical study of argumentative processes is, however, fraught with a basic methodological dilemma. If debates are recorded for posterity or are conducted before a public, one can never be certain whether the participants are partly or wholly speaking to one of these two audiences rather than to each other. If they are not recorded or are conducted behind closed doors, they may not leave any material for empirical analysis. Later accounts by the participants may be unreliable or self-serving. The most satisfactory material would be provided if a participant in a debate behind closed doors took notes of what was being said, either

---

conflict with reasonable claims of persons who are not members of the collectivity. (3) Any member of the collectivity who disagrees with the outcome can leave on reasonable terms." This definition has more bite than his definition of collective decisions cited earlier. The exit option is valuable and could easily be incorporated into my analysis. It tacitly presupposes that collective decisions are *binding*, so that members of the collectivity are not free to ignore decisions they disagree with (Przeworski 2010, p. 36, cites two cases in which members did feel free to do so). The question of exit becomes especially crucial when a community votes on which religion to follow, as happened in Switzerland during the Reformation (Christin, 2009).

[91] Jones (1978), pp. 494–97.

unbeknownst to the others or with a shared understanding that the notes would remain unpublished until the participants would be unaffected by their publication.

There are few cases that satisfy this criterion. In Chapter 2 I discuss the unsuccessful attempt by Harry Kalven and Hans Zeisel to have jury deliberations tape-recorded without the jurors being aware of it. A small window into deliberation unconstrained by expectations of posterity or by the presence of a public exists in the transcripts of the meetings of the Open Market Committee of the Federal Reserve Board from 1989 to 1992. When the existence of these transcripts became known, Congress pressured the Federal Reserve into adopting the policy that future transcripts would be published with a five-year delay. The knowledge that their debates would be published may have had a chilling effect on the participants.[92]

On some occasions, assemblies debating behind closed doors have benefited from the presence of a diligent note taker.[93] Jean Masselin's notes from the Estates-General of 1484 contain many illuminating vertical exchanges between the royal household and the estates as well as horizontal ones among the deputies. The debates among British officers and soldiers at Putney in October 1647 were taken down in shorthand by a secretary, William Clarke, who subsequently wrote them out in longhand. When his notes were discovered in 1890, they turned out to include remarkable (although often tantalizingly opaque) exchanges among Cromwell, General Ireton, Colonel Rainborowe, and others on both substantive and procedural constitutional matters. Even more important are Madison's notes from the Federal Convention. The exchanges he reports are unique in their spontaneity and directness, and his report itself is unique in its accuracy when held up against other accounts. Like Masselin, and unlike Clarke, Madison was also a very active participant in the debates he recorded.

The classical works on argumentation, from Aristotle's *Rhetoric* to *The New Rhetoric* by Perelman and Olbrects-Tyteca, mostly address the question of adversarial argument *before an audience*. The debaters do not try to persuade each other, but a third party who is either supposed to be silent or limited to expressions of approval and disapproval. By contrast, I shall mainly focus on arguments aimed at persuading an opponent or someone who has not yet made

[92] Meade and Stasavage (2008). I am not convinced, though, that the proxy they use to control for Greenspan's increasing dominance is sufficient to eliminate the alternative hypothesis that *he* chilled the debates.

[93] On other occasions, participants have agreed not to take notes, as in the 1865 Hampton Roads conference between Lincoln and southern envoys (Foner 2010, p. 315) and in some meetings of the Nuremberg Tribunal. At the last, Francis Biddle took notes anyway, for the sake of posterity (*St. Petersburg Times*, October 3, 1969). According to Bogdanor (2003), p. 9, "it was considered contrary to etiquette to take notes at a [British] Cabinet meeting." The reason Richard Crossman (unlike Barbara Castle) based his revelations from Cabinet meetings on diaries dictated once a week rather than on notes was hardly respect for etiquette but the fact that he did not know shorthand (Theakston 2003, p. 23).

up her mind. For instance, speeches for the prosecution and defense in a jury trial are less relevant than the deliberations among the jurors themselves (if only we could have access to them!). In some cases, to be sure, the dividing line is blurred. In the French Constituante, with 1,200 deputies, "250 deputies spoke more than three times and 80 among them pronounced several substantial speeches."[94] The majority of potential orators were only an audience to which the elite speakers addressed themselves. At the Federal Convention, with 55 delegates, 27 spoke 10 times or more, whereas 10 never said a word.[95] The latter assembly offers a rich material for the analysis of *argument*, whereas the former illustrates many of the devises of *rhetoric*.

Arguing *to* unanimity is a relatively rare path to collective decisions. Jury deliberations and expert committees sometimes instantiate this idea, but in practice it is almost always impossible to tell whether the unanimity is genuine or due to inner conformism or peer pressure. In fact, one sometimes encounters the assertion that unanimous agreement, like 99 percent majorities in sham elections, is intrinsically suspect.[96] Often, the *urgency* of decision may prevent the full deployment of arguments that might have brought about unanimity. In the Putney debates, Cromwell referred to possible moves by the King or Parliament when he warned that "I have butt one word to prevent you in, and that is for imminent danger. It may be possibly *soe imminent that it may not admit of an houres debate.*"[97]

It seems clear, nevertheless, that argument is capable of moving the participants *toward* unanimity by narrowing down the set of defensible solutions, at the very least by eliminating Pareto-dominated options, even though at the end a vote may be needed to choose among the remaining ones. At the same time, in the process of arguing the participants might generate *new* alternatives to be considered. This dual process of *eliminating and inventing options* is a central feature of argumentation.

At the most abstract level, argument consists in offering *reasons* for a proposition rather than simply stating it. If participants come with a mandate from their constituents to insist on certain demands with instructions to leave if they are not satisfied, there is no room for argument. As Cromwell said in the Putney debates, "If any come to us tomorrow onely to instruct us and teach us, how farre that will consist with the liberties of a free debate . . . I referre to every sober spirrited man to thinke of and determine. I thinke itt is such a *preengagement* that there is noe need of talke of the thinge."[98] In the 18th century, many

---

[94] Aulard (1882), p. 50.

[95] Vile (2005), vol. 2, pp. 740–41.

[96] Perelman and Olbrechts-Tyteca (1969), p. 473.

[97] Firth (1891), p. 292; my italics. Colonel Rainborowe said that "I think a very little delay will undoe us; and therefore I should onely desire . . . the lesse wee speake itt may bee the better" (ibid., p. 273).

[98] Firth (1891), p. 270; my italics. At the Federal Convention, delegates from Delaware came with a "preengagement" not to accept "an abolition of the fifth article of the confederation, by which it is declared that each state shall have one vote" (Farrand 1966, vol. 1, p. 6). In the French

politicians and political thinkers voiced the same objection to imperative mandates (see Chapter 5).

Reasons have to be *impartial*, in the sense that they must appeal to general principles and not merely to the naked self-interest of the speaker. In a debate in the municipal council, a speaker cannot expect to persuade others by saying, "We should build the road so that it passes by my house, because that's most convenient for me." She may, however, hope to persuade them by saying "We should build the road so that it passes by my house, because that is the cheapest option" or even "We should build the road so that it passes by my house, given that I can only get around in a wheelchair." Similarly, if in a debate over whether to keep a window open or closed one passenger can credibly claim to have asthma, the *urgency* of her need for a closed window trumps the mere *preferences* of the others.[99]

In general, arguments for any decision rely on normative as well as factual premises: the *fundamental preferences* of the speaker[100] and (when relevant) her factual and causal *beliefs*. Jointly, these premises yield a *policy preference*. If other participants fail to share the speaker's fundamental preferences or beliefs, she can try to persuade them by offering reasons. (She does not need to do so if differences in fundamental preferences and in factual or causal beliefs cancel each other.)[101] The normative analysis of argumentation is relatively simple as far as factual and causal arguments go but becomes more complex when we turn to the fundamental preferences of the agents.

I begin with factual and causal arguments. These aim at truth but in practice cannot offer more than possibility, probability, and plausibility. Interpersonal agreement on these properties of statements, however, is often difficult to achieve, as some examples will suggest.

In some contexts, the mere possibility that a given policy might lead to a very bad outcome may count against it. It is not clear, however, how to distinguish possibilities that are "real" in the sense of having implications for action and those that are mere figments of the imagination, such as the existence of a Cartesian demon that systematically misleads us. Some believe, for instance, that the possibility that laboratory experiments might cause the production of a strangelet that would make the earth collapse into a hyperdense sphere a hundred meters across is "real."[102] To my knowledge no action has been taken on this particular possibility. By contrast, the Extra-Terrestrial Exposure

Estates-General, deputies often tried to bind themselves by asking their constituencies for imperative mandates.

[99] Scanlon (1975); Yaari and Bar-Hillel (1984).
[100] I use "preference" as shorthand for any causally efficacious motivation, be it self-regarding or other-regarding. For a full analysis of the concept of preference, see Hausman (2011).
[101] Suppose that representatives in one group are in favor of a bill and believe it will be upheld by the Supreme Court. Those in another group are against the bill, yet want to please their constituents, who favor it. If members of the second group believe the Court will invalidate the bill, they may join forces with the first and vote for it (Diller 2008, p. 303).
[102] Posner (2005). Randall (2011) argues that this fear is misguided. For a similar worry about the H-bomb, see Ohanian (2008), p. 168.

Act of 1969 mandated quarantining astronauts returning from the first missions to the moon, to prepare for the possibility that they were harboring unknown lunar organisms that might endanger life on earth. No one tried to quantify the risk.

The question that concerns me here is not so much how an individual should make up her mind in such cases as what arguments she could offer to persuade others. The debates on the precautionary principle in general and on global warming in particular have demonstrated how difficult it is to reach interpersonal agreement when navigating in unknown waters. According to the Arrow-Hurwicz theorem for deciding under uncertainty, both acting on best-case scenarios (maximax) and on worst-case scenarios (maximin) can be rationally defended. In fact, any weighted sum of the best and worst outcomes could be the maximand.[103]

Political debates also offer many examples of possibility arguments. Edmund Burke's speeches in Parliament were often marred by his "strategy of arguing from remote and seemingly improbable consequences. . . . No wonder that Lord North, wearied with Burke's perpetual alarmism, compared him to the boy who cried 'Wolf!' too often."[104] In the French constituent assembly of 1848, one deputy criticized a proposal to have the people elect one of five candidates for the Presidency proposed by the national assembly, on the grounds that the procedure would allow the assembly to impose its choice by proposing four impossible candidates.[105] One can also cite examples of possibility arguments from the Federal Convention and the subsequent ratification debates. At the Convention, Gouverneur Morris proposed to leave Congress entirely free to impose eligibility constraints on representatives, to which the deputy Williamson retorted that "This could surely never be admitted. Should majority of the Legislature be composed of any particular description of men, of lawyers for example, which is no improbable supposition, the future elections might be secured to their own body."[106] Nobody bothered to refute this fanciful suggestion. In the ratification debates, many opponents (notably George Mason) made equally flimsy and speculative objections to the proposed constitution.[107] In the Virginia debates, Henry Lee correctly observed that "the opposition continually objected to possibilities with no consideration of probabilities."[108] Madison, too, objected to the supposition that "the general legislature will do every thing

---

[103] Arrow and Hurwicz (1971). Since the theorem assumes that all possible outcomes are *known* – an assumption that is hard to justify in the presence of uncertainty regarding their probability of occurrence – the direct relevance of the theorem is tenuous. Yet it captures the general idea that when people differ along an optimism-pessimism scale, they may not be open to rational persuasion.

[104] Lock (1998), pp. 266–67; also pp. 308, 357.

[105] Coutant (2009), p. 239. A similar argument had been deployed in the making of the French constitution of 1795 (Troper 2006, pp. 50, 86).

[106] Farrand (1966), vol. 2, p. 250.

[107] See, for instance, the exchanges between Mason and Madison in Elliot (1836), vol. 3, pp. 415–16, 431–32.

[108] Pauline Maier (2010), p. 283.

mischievous they possibly can."[109] At the same time, in the Pennsylvania ratification debates James Wilson defended the document by claiming that "we were obliged to guard even against possibilities, as well as probabilities."[110] At no time did anyone address the underlying epistemological issues, which remain unresolved or ill-understood to this day.

Establishing quantifiable probabilities can in some cases be a more feasible aim. I am not referring to frequency-based probabilities, which are mostly debated by experts and less likely to be affected by legal and political debates, but to subjective probabilities. (For the sake of argument I am bracketing my deep doubts about the reliability of these assessments.) In an exchange of information, each participant may provide new data that will enable the others to update their estimates in accordance with Bayes's rule. Yet their updated estimates may remain very different from each other if their initial priors diverge greatly. It follows from Bayes's rule that it is impossible to persuade a *fanatic*, defined as someone who attaches a 100 percent probability to a certain state of affairs. The impermeability of many conspiracy theorists to argument may be due in part to this fact. It will also be impossible to persuade a *skeptic*, defined as someone who refuses to assign any prior probabilities and, in particular, refuses the idea that equiprobability of outcomes is a good way of modeling ignorance.[111]

The jury provides a good vehicle to explain what I mean by plausibility. For many jurors in criminal cases, the conviction of the guilt of the accused depends on a plausible *story*.[112] Yet plausibility may diverge from probability. A plausible story must take the form of a *downhill narrative*, in which the transition from one step to the next seems unstrained and uncontrived. Suppose the storyteller – the prosecutor or the defense attorney – has the choice between getting from A to B in a narrative in two steps or in six steps. For specificity, suppose that the two steps require events that will occur with likelihood 0.9 and 0.2, respectively, whereas each of the six events will occur with likelihood 0.75. Assuming the events in each sequence to be independent of each other, the two-step sequence is more likely to occur (0.18 versus 0.178), yet only the six-step sequence will be seen as having the desirable downhill property. "[The] plausibility of a scenario depends much more on the plausibility of its weakest links than on the number of links."[113]

Moreover, the assignment of probability to each chain in the link may be indeterminate. One juror will say, plausibly, "If he had really committed the murder, he would not have left the weapon," and another, also plausibly, "He left the weapon precisely because he expected people to say he would not have left it had he been guilty." Either juror might be unable to persuade the other that

[109] Elliot (1836), vol. 3, p. 536.
[110] Ibid., vol. 2, pp. 440–41.
[111] For a similar assimilation of the fanatic and the skeptic (defined, however, in different terms), see Perelman and Olbrechts-Tyteca (1969), p. 62.
[112] Hastie, Penrod, and Pennington (1983).
[113] Kahneman and Tversky (1982), p. 207.

her story is more probable. At one trial "the judge noted during sentencing that 'both defendants walked into the courtroom with a swagger' as evidence that neither exhibited any signs of remorse. Their attorney tried to respond, 'I think that is clearly indicative of innocence, that you don't feel remorse for something you didn't do.'"[114] Either story is plausible. Similarly in a speech by Antiphon (III.8–10), "the prosecutor of a young man who has accidentally killed a young man while practising javelin-throwing argues that the young man may have been guilty of an impiety and so, being 'stained,' was manoeuvred by the gods into a predicament which would result in his condemnation for accidental homicide, while the defendant argued that if it was the divine will that the boy should die, it would be impious to condemn the young man who was the instrument of death."[115] For the Greeks, either story was presumably plausible.

The preceding comments were not intended to convey wholesale skepticism about the value of argument with regard to factual and causal issues. It should go without saying that in many cases such arguments matter. The Federal Convention at one point voted for the President to be named by electors chosen by popular votes in the states and meeting in the national capital. When the delegate Houston then "urged the extreme inconvenience & the considerable expense of drawing together men from all the States for the single purpose of electing the Chief Magistrate,"[116] the Convention reverted to its earlier decision to have the President elected by Congress. This debate provides a clear example of how a new *factual observation* can shape a policy decision. The importance of Keynesian ideas provides a clear case of how *causal theories* may shape policy. As I noted in the Introduction, such genuine cases of the ex ante "causal power of causal theories" should be sharply distinguished from the ex post use of theories to rationalize policies adopted on other grounds.

At a later stage in the Federal Convention, debates over the election of the President also provide an example of how *creativity* – in this case adding a new option – can allow for the reconciliation of different views. The Committee on Postponed Matters managed to meet Houston's objection as well as the objections to congressional election by proposing that the President be chosen by electors meeting in their respective state capitals. For another example of on-the-spot inventiveness in this context, we can cite the proposal that each elector vote for two presidential candidates, one of whom could not be from his state (see Chapter 5). Like many other decisions at the Convention, this one rests on a sophisticated incentive argument (a causal mechanism), but one that came up in the give-and-take of discussion rather than being part of a preexisting tool box of any of the founders. Because of the importance of creativity quite generally, defining argument as an exchange of preexisting ideas and information would provide a very impoverished notion of the contribution of argument to good decisions. Whereas voting systems "require some prior statement of what the

[114] Garrett (2011), p. 162.
[115] Dover (1994), p. 150.
[116] Farrand (1966), vol. 2, p. 95.

alternatives are,"[117] that is not true for arguing. For the same reason, the idea of *formalizing* the process of arguing toward a conclusion is doomed to fail.

I do not think we have a good understanding of how to promote creativity in legal and political debates. Having a deadline can help to focus the mind but can also impede free-wheeling exchanges. Participants unencumbered by specialized knowledge may be more able to come up with unorthodox proposals, but they might also ignore obvious objections and spend their time reinventing the wheel. In the general Benthamite spirit of the present work, we may ask whether it could be more feasible to *remove obstacles to creativity*. One might, for instance, impose secrecy of the debates to ensure that nobody risks being penalized later for coming up with seemingly wild ideas in a brainstorming session.[118] If we depart from the negative Benthamite approach, we may also conjecture that *diversity* can be conducive to creativity.

I shall now consider a harder question: can one change *fundamental preferences* by means of argument?[119] Can one, for instance, turn egoists into moral agents by offering them *reasons* to be moral? As an example, can a juror who is concerned only with coming to a speedy decision and not with making the right decision be persuaded to change his mind? What arguments can defenders of the right to abortion offer to its opponents and vice versa? What arguments are available to those who want to lower the voting age to 16 years? I shall use these and other examples to explore some of the normative argumentative strategies available to the participants in collective decision making. The main thrust of the analysis will be to bring out the *conditional character* of much normative reasoning. Often, moral argument is ad hominem in the sense in which Locke used that expression: "to press a man with consequences drawn from his own principles or concessions,"[120] to which we may add consequences drawn from his past behavior. In a sense, of course, any argument – reaching a conclusion from the reasons that support it – is conditional. What I want to emphasize, however, is the relative difficulty of persuading others by arguing from first principles and from first principles only.

Consider first the case of the selfish juror. One might try to persuade him to take his task more seriously by asking, "If *you* were on trial, wouldn't you want the jury to be conscientious?" This is the Golden Rule argument from reciprocity: do unto others as you would wish them to do unto you. Unlike the "everyday-Kantian" argument from universalizability – "What would happen to the defendant if all your co-jurors were equally lax?" – the argument from

[117] Fearon (1998), p. 49.
[118] The alleged chilling effect of the publication (with a five-year delay) of the minutes of the Open Market Committee of the Federal Reserve Board may provide an example (Meade and Stasavage 2008). See also Philippe Maier (2010), p. 335. It seems that criticism *during* the brainstorming sessions enhances creativity (Nemeth et al. 2004).
[119] I bracket a question I shall discuss at some length later, the possibility of making such persons change the outward profession of their fundamental preferences. Here I consider only inward changes brought about by the "uncoerced force of the better argument."
[120] Locke (1979), p. 686.

reciprocity might work precisely because it appeals to the selfishness of the juror rather than to concern for the accused.[121] It would not, however, appeal to a juror who was both selfish and *rational*. It relies, in fact, on a form of magical thinking, similar to what animates the Narrator's friend in *A la recherche du temps perdu*, who refrains from "taking an active interest in [the Narrator's] girls" out of "an almost superstitious belief that on his own fidelity might depend that of his mistress."[122] *Arguments* cannot rely on magic, although *persuasion* can.

Perelman and Olbrechts-Tyteca also consider what they call "arguments of reciprocity." They do not, however, appeal to the selfishness of the agent to which the argument is addressed. Rather, they appeal to the moral symmetry of cases where two agents are involved on opposite sides of a transaction:

Among the examples which Aristotle considers to be drawn from "reciprocal relations" we find that of the tax-farmer Diomedon speaking on the subject of taxes: "If it is no disgrace for you to sell them, it is no disgrace for us to buy them." Quintillian supplies an example of the same sort of propositions "which confirm one another": "What it is honorable to learn it is also honorable to teach." By a reasoning of the same nature, La Bruyère condemns the Christians who attend plays, since the actors are condemned for performing in these plays.[123]

Clermont-Tonnerre's speech in the French Constituante on December 23, 1789, offers a very influential instance of this kind of reasoning. It is in part a development of La Bruyère's observation, but also goes far beyond it to attack discrimination against executioners and Jews:

The professions that the adversaries of my opinion claim to mark as infamous come down to two: the executioners and the actors who occupy our various theaters. . . . What the law orders is inherently good; the law orders the death of a guilty person, the executioner only obeys the law. It is against all justice for the law to inflict upon him a legal punishment; it is against reason to tell him, do this and if you do it, you will be considered infamous. . . .

We should either forbid plays altogether or remove the dishonor associated with acting. Nothing infamous should endure in the eyes of the law, and nothing that the law permits is infamous. . . .

There is no middle way possible: either you admit a national religion, subject all your laws to it, arm it with temporal power, exclude from your society the men who profess another creed and then, erase the article in the declaration of rights [that ensures freedom of religion]; or you permit everyone to have his own religious opinion, and do not exclude from public office those who make use of this permission. (my italics)

These arguments are strictly conditional: you must accept behavior A if you accept behavior B. Nothing forces you to accept B, but, as Clermont-Tonnerre says, the "middle way" of accepting B and rejecting A is not available to you.

---

[121] For the relation between the Golden Rule and the categorical imperative, see Parfit (2011), pp. 327 ff. My concern here, however, is only with the psychological efficacy of the arguments, not with their intrinsic moral standing.

[122] Proust (1988a), p. 165. As is clear from the context, this inference does not rely on a causal link, but on a magical "action at a distance" (Elster 2010b).

[123] Perelman and Olbrechts-Tyteca (1969), p. 221.

In another argumentative strategy the speaker affirms that the interlocutor must accept behavior A if he accepts behavior B, *and* that he must accept behavior B. An argument in favor of abortion will illustrate this strategy. In one of the best philosophical analyses of public policy decisions, Judith Jarvis Thompson imagines the following case:

You wake up in the morning and find yourself back to back in bed with an unconscious violinist. A famous unconscious violinist. He has been found to have a fatal kidney ailment, and the Society of Music Lovers has canvassed all the available medical records and found that you alone have the right blood type to help. They have therefore kidnapped you, and last night the violinist's circulatory system was plugged into yours, so that your kidneys can be used to extract poisons from his blood as well as your own. The director of the hospital now tells you, "Look, we're sorry the Society of Music Lovers did this to you – we would never have permitted it if we had known. But still, they did it, and the violinist is now plugged into you. To unplug you would be to kill him. But never mind, it's only for nine months. By then he will have recovered from his ailment, and can safely be unplugged from you. Is it morally incumbent on you to accede to this situation?[124]

As will be obvious, the answer is No; and as is also obvious, the negative answer supports a positive answer to the question whether a woman who gets pregnant as the result of a rape has a right to abortion. The argument relies on (1) a partial analogy between two cases, (2) a strong moral intuition about one of them, and (3) a claim that the aspects in which the cases are not analogous are morally irrelevant. Since those who oppose the right to abortion even in a pregnancy resulting from rape will probably share the moral intuition about the violinist, they will have to change their opinion unless they can point to some morally relevant differences between the two cases.

Thompson's analogical argument for the right to abortion is limited to pregnancy following rapes. Cass Sunstein uses a different analogical argument to justify abortion in all cases. He takes Thompson's article as his point of departure, but goes beyond it in a crucial respect:

We might explore ... another argument on behalf of [the right to abortion], one that sounds in principles of equal protection. This argument sees a prohibition on abortion as invalid because it involves a cooptation of women's bodies for the protection of fetuses. It claims that abortion restrictions *selectively* turn women's reproductive capacities into something for the use and control of others. *No parallel disability is imposed on men.*[125]

The question is what counts as a "parallel disability." Sunstein cites the fact that (presumably male) "parents are not compelled to devote their bodies to the protection of children, even if, for example, a risk-free transplantation is

---

[124] Thompson (1971), pp. 48–49. Although Thompson also addresses the issue of abortion in cases other than rape, I limit myself to her discussion of that issue.
[125] Sunstein (1992), pp. 31–32; my italics. "Equal protection" here refers to equality of men and women, not of the woman and her fetus.

necessary to prevent the death of their child."[126] The argument seems to be the following. (1) If the law accepts behavior B (men do not have to donate their organs in risk-free operations to save their children), it should accept behavior A (women do not have to carry their unborn children to birth). (2) The law does accept behavior B. Hence (3) the law should accept behavior A. The relevance of the second premise might be questioned, at least from a moral point of view. The acceptance of B does not correspond to a firm *moral* intuition, the way Thompson's refusal of the violinist's right to protection does. Yet since Sunstein's argument concerns the law and the constitution, not morality, this issue is perhaps secondary. The first premise is more obviously questionable. Sunstein is aware that the parallel is imperfect, but argues as follows:

> To be sure, nothing is quite like pregnancy. It is plausible that there are relevant differences between a prohibition on abortion and other forms of legally compelled use of bodies for the protection of others. But the fact that the burden of bodily cooptation is imposed in this setting alone *at least suggests* that the interest in protection of human life is found adequate only as a result of impermissible sex stereotypes. The fact that an abortion is treated as a killing, whereas other refusals to allow one's body to be used are treated as mere refusals to protect, *suggests* precisely the same thing.[127]

Unlike Thompson's sharp analogy, Sunstein's parallel relies on the more diffuse idea of a "suggestion." As a result, it is difficult to evaluate his argument. Analogies with blunt edges are rarely persuasive.

The law is replete with such analogies: "Just as no event and no form completely resembles another, neither does any completely differ.... All things are connected by some similarity; yet *every example limps* and any correspondence which we draw from experience is always feeble and imperfect; we can nevertheless find some corner or other by which to link our comparisons. And that is how laws serve us: they can be adapted to each one of our concerns by means of some twisted, forced or oblique interpretation."[128] In a classical example, Demosthenes "justifies the killing of an adulterer on the grounds that an adulterer identifies himself with the enemies against whom we wage war in order to save our wives and children from the sexual outrage consequent on captivity."[129] For a contemporary example, consider again the decision in *Tanner v. United States* cited in the Introduction. In this case, seven jury members regularly consumed alcohol during the noon recess. Whereas the Court focused on the superficial analogy between the state of alcoholic intoxication and a virus-induced state, arising from the fact that both are due to "internal" rather than "external" influences, it ignored the morally relevant difference that only the former is due to a voluntary choice.

---

[126] Ibid., p. 34. As a matter of fact, since transplantations are never risk-free, a law compelling parents to donate their organs when they would be pointless. Also, women are not forced to donate their organs either.

[127] Ibid., pp. 34–35; my italics.

[128] Montaigne (1991), p. 1213; my italics.

[129] *Against Aristocrates* 56, as summarized by Dover (1994), p. 218.

Arguments for and against lowering the voting age to sixteen years can illustrate another use of (good or bad) arguments from symmetry. We find minimum age legislation in many arenas: admission to employment, serving in the army, obtaining a driver's license, buying cigarettes or alcohol, marrying without parental consent, being subject to criminal prosecution – and of course voting. In a given country, the minimum ages may differ across arenas. In the United States, the 18-year-old can vote but, in many states, not buy liquor. In Brazil, the 16-year-old can vote, but is not subject to criminal prosecution. In France, you have to be 18 years old to vote, but offenders between 16 and 18 are subject to criminal prosecution. This combination also exists in some American states. In American states the minimum age for obtaining a driver's license is lower than the minimum age for voting, but in Brazil it is the other way around (16 vs. 18 in both countries). Some might use the right to drive a car at 16 as an argument for the right to vote at the same age. Others might use the ban on buying liquor before 18 as an argument against lowering the voting age to 16. The validity of these arguments depends on the presence or absence of morally relevant differences.[130]

In politics, bad arguments based on halting comparisons abound. In the Putney debates, General Ireton argued from analogy that manhood suffrage would lead to universal communism:

Now I wish wee may all consider of what right you will challenge, that all the people should have right to Elections. Is itt by the right of nature? If you will hold forth that as your ground, then I thinke you must deny all property too, and this is my reason. For thus: by that same right of nature, whatever itt bee that you pretend, by which you can say, "one man hath an equall right with another to the chusing of him that shall governe him" – by the same right of nature, hee hath an equal right in any goods hee sees: meate, drinke, cloathes, to take and use them for his sustenance. Hee hath a freedome to the land, [to take] the ground, to exercise itt, till itt; he hath the [same] freedome to any thinge that any one doth account himself to have any propriety in.[131]

In Chapter 5 I cite an equally dubious argument from analogy to justify the right of church members in 17th-century Connecticut to a monopoly on being elected as magistrates. In Chapter 2, I cite an argument from the 1835 jury reform in France based on an imperfect analogy between jurors and voters. As I also observe in Chapter 2, scholars, too, have relied on that analogy, when claiming that juries should use majority voting and that jurors should be anonymous.

[130] In my view, both arguments would be invalid: whereas voting requires *intellectual competence*, driving and buying liquor require *self-control*. These two qualities do not mature at the same age.
[131] Firth (1891), p. 307. The *Agreement of the People*, the text Ireton reacted to, did not include a proposal for manhood suffrage. The issue came up because Ireton himself asserted (ibid.), p. 299, that the army's claim for apportionment proportional to population implied a claim for manhood suffrage. Woolrych (1987), p. 220, seems to accept this implication. These two aspects of democracy are, however, quite independent of one another. Interestingly, Ireton did not make the *causal* argument that became central in the next century, that if the propertyless got the right to vote they would choose representatives hostile to property.

Analogical arguments often rely on a claim that conditions for being able to do X are sufficient conditions for being able to do Y. In the United States, "proposals for lowering the age limit [for voting] had appeared during or after every major war, on the grounds that men who were old enough to fight for their country were old enough to participate in political decisions."[132] A different kind of argument states that *doing* X ipso facto confers the right to do Y. Historically, the most poignant example concerns the right to vote of soldiers who have risked their lives for their country (and not merely done military service in peacetime). In the Putney debates, General Ireton had defended the proposition that the right to vote should be conditional on the possession of an estate bringing an income of 40 shilling a year. Some argued against his view from first principles, claiming that the right to vote was a "birthright." Others used a conditional argument, which seems to have been the more effective. Colonel Rainborowe responded that "I doe [think] and am still of the same opinion; that every man born in England cannot, ought nott, neither by the law of God nor the law of nature, to bee exempted from the choice of those who are to make lawes, for him to live under, and for him, for ought I know, *to loose his life under*."[133] An "agitator" who spoke on the same day, Sexby, said, "There are many thousands of us souldiers that have *ventur'd our lives*; wee have had little propriety in the Kingedome as to our estates, yett wee have had a birthright. Butt itt seemes now except a man hath a fix't estate in this Kingedome, hee hath noe right in this Kingedome. I wonder wee were soe much deceived. If wee had nott a right to the Kingedome, *wee were meere mercinarie souldiers*."[134]

In the United States, "nearly all of the major expansions of the franchise ... took place either during or in the wake of war.... Armies had to be recruited, often from the so-called lower orders of society, and it was rhetorically as well as practically difficult to compel men to bear arms while denying them the franchise."[135] As we shall see in Chapter 4, the 1776 constitutional convention in Pennsylvania expanded the franchise to include all men who had served in the militia. At the Federal Convention, Franklin argued against restricted suffrage on similar grounds: "It is of great consequence that we shd. not depress the virtue & public spirit of our common people; of which they displayed a great deal during the war, and which contributed principally to the favorable issue of it."[136] In some cases, the extension of the franchise may have preceded military conscription and have been a condition for the willingness of citizens to serve.[137] In the Putney debates, however, the argument for extension was rights-based and backward-looking, not consequentialist and forward-looking. Sexby's

---

[132] Keyssar (2000), p. 273.

[133] Firth (1891), p. 305; my italics.

[134] Ibid., p. 323; my italics.

[135] Keyssar (2000), p. xxi.

[136] Farrand (1966), vol. 2, p. 204.

[137] See Przeworski (2009) for a critical discussion of this venerable argument. Keyssar (2000) pp. 37–38, asserts that the expansion of American suffrage after the war of 1812 was due both to backward-looking and to forward-looking considerations.

claim that many would not have enlisted had they thought they would not get the right to vote[138] does not imply that they enlisted under the expectation that they would get it.

A common, often effective but strictly speaking invalid, argument from symmetry is that of the *tu quoque*. The symmetry is not that of the arguments, but of the arguers. In the Nuremberg trials, the defender of the German Admirals Raeder and Doenitz succeeded in getting the American Admiral Nimitz to state that he, too, had engaged in sinking merchant ships without warning. Although this admission did not lead to an indictment of Nimitz, it did lead to a lesser verdict for the German admirals.[139]

Americans have often feared that the existence of American slavery and racism could provide a *tu quoque* argument to the enemies of the country. Among his reasons for hating slavery, Lincoln cited the fact that "it deprives our republican example of its just influence in the world – enables the enemies of free institutions, with plausibility, to taunt us as hypocrites."[140] In 1934, an attempt to force Roosevelt to speak out against Hitler's persecution of German Jews was stifled by the anticipation that Germany might retaliate by pointing to the lynching of blacks in the United States.[141] During the Cold War, some American historians claimed that "desegregating the [Mississippi Valley Historical Association] was an anti-Communist duty,"[142] since maintaining segregation would do a "tremendous service ... to communism in her fight against America and democracy."

Generally speaking, as I said, *tu quoque* arguments are invalid, in the sense that the accuser's own wrongdoing does not lessen the wrongdoing of the accused. In some circumstances, however, the actions of an accuser may render his accusation less credible and can legitimately be used to undermine it. In some cases, that action may be the very same as the one included in the accusation: "No, I didn't, but you did, and hence your accusation is not credible." Yet in these cases, the purpose of the defense is to weaken the case for the accusation, whereas a *tu quoque* assertion presupposes that the accusation is true. "Yes, I did, but you did too." A case in which *tu quoque* would actually constitute an *argument* is the following: "Yes I did; in fact, anyone would have done it, as shown by the fact that you did it too."

---

[138] Firth (1891), pp. 329–30.
[139] Taylor (1992), pp. 409, 554.
[140] Foner (2010), p. 66. Defenders of the peculiar institution responded in kind. In 1858, "James Hammond of South Carolina accused the antislavery movement of hypocrisy for ignoring the plight of workers at home. He hurled an explosive accusation: 'Your whole class of manual laborers and operatives, as you call them, are slaves'" (ibid., p. 112). In the 1830s, Southerners had challenged northern abolitionists by a different argumentative strategy: "who first made traffic of human flesh, and made profit by bringing the negroes here?" (Miller 1996, pp. 130–31). Since many Southerners also claimed that slavery was an unalloyed good, however, this accusation ought rather to be turned into a thanking (ibid., p. 249).
[141] Larson (2011), p. 241.
[142] Novick (1988), p. 350, citing a letter by Howard Beale.

In another use, the *tu quoque* argument might also be called the "Pandora Box argument." Once a hominem argument has been raised by one side, the other side can also use it. According to Bentham, in debates it is acceptable to impute ignorance to an opponent, but not bad motives. "In political debate as in war, you ought not to employ any means which you would wish should not be employed against you."[143] For an example, consider the debates of the Massachusetts General Court in 1786 over the proposal to use tax revenues to pay off the 1785 requisition by Congress rather than to pay interest on "consolidated notes" (state bonds).

Supporters of the scheme accused its detractors of being influenced by their ownership of consolidated notes. One opponent's riposte was revealing: "Some members had accused that side of the House with holding the notes. If this observation was made to infer that interest dictated their votes, gentlemen should recollect, that those who made the observation, acknowledged themselves not to be holders of notes, and of course were not interested in paying them." He had a point there. Taxpayers who owned no consolidated notes (the vast majority of the state's citizens) would benefit materially if the impost revenue was used to slash the sum they had to hand over to Congress.[144]

The common feature of the preceding arguments is that they involve only *conditional* moral claims. Thompson does not affirm an unconditional right to abortion in cases of rape, but uses an indirect argument that relies on a close analogy with a case in which intuition does provide an unconditional answer. Although some speakers in the Putney debates affirmed the right to vote as a birthright, the most compelling argument seems to have been based on service in the army. Many cases essentially appeal to *coherence* among moral propositions, implying that there could be several possible coherent sets of claims ("A and B" or "non-A and non-B" but not "A and non-B"). Argument then takes the form of seeking out cases in which the interlocutor is more or less rigorously compelled to choose between abandoning her position on one issue and adopting the speaker's view on another.

At the Federal Convention, Madison was a master of this argumentative strategy, as two exchanges will show. The first occurred in a debate over the representation of the states in the Senate, when Ellsworth from Connecticut appealed to the "federal pact which was still in force" and "under which each State small as well as great, held an equal right of suffrage in the General Council."[145] In his reply, Madison asked rhetorically, "Did not Connecticut refuse her compliance to a federal requisition? Has she paid, for the two last years, any money into the continental treasury? And does this look like government, or the observance of a solemn compact?"[146]

---

[143] Bentham (1999), p. 134. As he makes clear, it is not a matter of magical thinking but of "prudence" based on (as we would say today) tit-for-tat reasoning.

[144] Holton (2004), p. 291.

[145] Farrand (1966), vol. I, p. 485.

[146] Ibid., p. 497.

In this case Madison used the *actions* of an opponent's state against him. In an even more devastating reply, he used the *arguments* of an opponent regarding the role of slavery in representation to refute his opinion on the equal representation of the states in the Senate. Arguing against a proposal to include slaves in the basis for representation, William Paterson from New Jersey – a staunch defender of equal representation of the states – raised a general question: "What is the true principle of representation? It is an expedient by which an assembly of certain individls. chosen by the people is substituted in place of the inconvenient meeting of the people themselves. If such a meeting of the people was actually to take place, would the slaves vote? they would not. Why then shd. they be represented?"[147] Madison pounced immediately, by reminding "Mr. Patterson that his doctrine of Representation, which was in its principle the genuine one, must for ever silence the pretensions of the small States to an equality of votes with the larger ones. They ought to vote in the same proportion in which their citizens would do, if the people of all the states were collectively met."[148]

Even decisions seemingly made on first principles may be supported by other considerations. In trials of collaborators in countries that had been occupied by Germany in World War II, the need to respect the rule of law and in particular the principle of non-retroactivity was sometimes defended by the desire to show that "we are not like them," as Vaclav Havel put it in a similar situation after 1989. In Germany after reunification, the release from prison of convicted Communist leaders on grounds of ill health was defended by appeal to § 1 of the German constitution affirming the protection of "human dignity" as the highest value of the state. In addition, however, the court affirmed that failure to release them would show that the Federal Republic "would be as guilty of violating the human dignity of its citizens as was the GDR."[149] If the ban on retroactivity and the release of the Communist leaders had been based on first principles only, these references to the past would have been irrelevant.

The structure of the argument is this: X is the kind of thing A did to B. Since X is bad and A was bad, B has two reasons for not doing X to A. After World War II there were, however, some voices in France, Denmark, and Italy that asserted that since the Germans had not respected the rule of law, there was no reason to respect it when judging them. Rather than "since they did it, we shouldn't," the argument was "since they did it to us, they can't complain if we do it to them."[150] On this view, the badness of A cancels the badness of doing X to A. Winners will often make this claim. By contrast, in one form of the *tu quoque* argument it says that since A and B both did X, B has no moral standing to punish A for

---

[147] Ibid., p. 561.
[148] Ibid., p. 562.
[149] McAdams (1996), p. 69.
[150] Elster (2004b), pp. 235–36, 238.

doing X.[151] The badness of B doing X does not cancel the badness of A doing X but cancels the right of B to punish A for doing X. Losers will often make this claim.

I do not deny the importance of moral judgments based on first principles only. I doubt, however, that debaters often *succeed in persuading others to* adopt or abandon such judgments. Debates over security versus liberty in the age of terrorism or over pro-life versus pro-choice (in *all* pregnancies) do not seem to have produced many converts. Although some "securitarians" may have changed their mind as a result of argument, when events after 9/11 showed that severe measures were more likely to create terrorists than to capture or dissuade them, this is a far cry from being persuaded by argument that, say, torture is never acceptable. Similarly, although some pro-life advocates may have changed their minds as a result of argument on the issue of abortion after rape, this is a far cry from admitting the right to abortion in all cases.

Consider an admittedly extreme example, in which the word "convert" has a quite literal meaning, the debates in 1561 in which French Catholics and Calvinists argued over the doctrine of the transubstantiation.[152] As in some recent transitions from authoritarian regimes to democracy,[153] there were hard-liners and softliners on each side (see Figure 1.1).

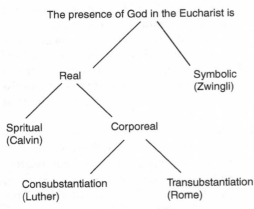

The presence of God in the Eucharist is

Real

Symbolic
(Zwingli)

Spritual
(Calvin)

Corporeal

Consubstantiation
(Luther)

Transubstantiation
(Rome)

FIGURE 1.1. Arguing and bargaining over transubstantiation

---

[151] Aristotle observes that there are "two distinct questions: Is it right that he should be treated [in a certain way]? Is it right that you should thus treat him?" (*Rhetorics* 1397b). As an example of divergent answers to these questions, he cites the son who judges that his mother should die but not that he should kill her. Aristotle also discusses *tu quoque* arguments (ibid. 1398a), but does not suggest that they could be grounds for divergence.

[152] The following draws on Bèze (1882) and Nugent (1974).

[153] Przeworski (1991).

With religious violence increasing in the country, the Queen Regent Catherine of Medici called a colloquium at Poissy to see whether an agreement could be reached. It included leading theologians on both sides, notably Cardinal Lorraine (a member of the politically influential Guise clan) and Calvin's close collaborator Theodore de Bèze. Although it seemed for a moment that the Lutheran view might be accepted by both sides, the hardliners representing Zwingli and Rome blocked this outcome. Arguing turned into bargaining, in which each side tried to make the other look responsible for the breakdown of the talks.

Catherine then convened a smaller meeting with five theologians from each side. The prelates and the ministers came up with two near-identical formulae. They differed only in that whereas the main Catholic spokesman proposed to write that "because the word and promise of God in which our faith is based, makes and renders present the things promised," the Calvinists offered the formula "because faith based on the word of God makes and renders present the things promised." The Calvinist formula is more subjective, since it is faith in God rather than God himself that makes Christ present in the blood and wine. Yet the Calvinists came a long way toward meeting the Catholics when they accepted their reference to the "true and natural body and blood of our Lord by virtue of the Holy Spirit." Although Lorraine may have liked the proposal, it does not appear that the five prelates agreed on recommending it to their fellow Catholics who were still at Poissy, occupied with other matters. When it was presented to the latter, it was first examined by a small committee, which found it riddled with heresy, and then discussed by the full group of prelates and rejected by a majority of 63 to 7.[154]

In the spring of 1593, in the process of converting to Catholicism, Henri IV engaged in discussions with Catholic and Protestant theologians, "as if the colloquium of Poissy was being reborn from the ashes."[155] On July 23, the day of his abjuration from Calvinism, he met with four bishops and debated theology with them for five straight hours. He refused to accept the doctrine of the purgatory, and expressed reservations about the *permanent* "real presence" in the sacramental bread, outside the hours of church service. A "texte modéré"

[154] While Catherine's main concern was to bring about a reconciliation over dogma, she was also pursuing more general reforms. She called a second colloquium in Saint-Germain in January 1562 to "consider images, the administration of baptism, the Eucharist, the Mass, the imposition of hands and ministerial vocations, and, if there seemed hope of accord, doctrine" (Nugent 1974, pp. 191–92). They did not get beyond the first item on the agenda. The majority of the Catholics defended the presence of images in the Church, except for immodest representations and the depicting of apocryphal miracles. The minority report generally reproved the cult of images, and recommended them to be removed from the interior of churches. The Calvinists, again represented by Bèze (1882, pp. 386–87), were willing to accept something like the minority position, although their main demand was for total abolition of images, inside and outside the Church. "The outcome of the colloquium was that each kept to his opinions without any results" (Nugent 1974, p. 388).

[155] Babelon (1982), p. 557.

was finally agreed upon.[156] This process seems, however, to have been a relatively straightforward piece of bargaining. Henri's followers would never have accepted the purgatory.

As I said, the case is extreme. Yet when people debate over *secular* first principles – consequentialist versus deontological, for example – they do not seem any more willing to change their minds upon argument. I mentioned the debate over torture. For another case, consider the 1993 decision by the Colombian Constitutional Court to strike down legislation mandating the freezing of assets of kidnapping victims, on the grounds that it violated the right to life of the kidnapped individual.[157] Whereas Congress based its reasoning on the deterrent effect on future kidnappers, the Court refused to accept the idea of "social martyrdom" implicit in the law. It is not easy to imagine what either side could have said to persuade the other.

Deciding by Aggregation

When arguing fails to bring about unanimity, the aggregation of individual votes or judgments can close the gap. (If unanimity is *required*, as in some jury systems, no decision will be made.) This procedure can take different forms. To distinguish among them, recall first that individual *policy preferences* or *policy judgments* derive from the *fundamental preferences* of the agent and from her factual or causal *beliefs*. Aggregation usually takes policy *preferences* (or judgments) as the inputs. This can be done in several ways. Suppose, for instance, that the voters rank the options and that electoral officials assign numbers to each rank, larger numbers to higher ranks. On the usual Borda count, the social choice is the option that receives the highest mean score (or, equivalently, the highest sum). On the "Borda-majority judgment method" it is the option that receives the highest median number.[158]

Aggregation can also take individual *beliefs* as inputs to produce a "collective belief," which in turn can serve as the cognitive premise for taking action. The normative premise may be either the "collective fundamental preference" of the same agents or the preference of some institutional actor, such as a judge who orders the release of the accused upon a jury verdict of not guilty. Examples to be given shortly will flesh out these remarks.

I first consider the aggregation of policy preferences and judgments, beginning with the former. As my aim in this section is to assess the goodness of collective decision-making *procedures* rather than of decisions, we need to expand the focus from intra-profile to inter-profile requirements. It is not enough to require that the social choice or ranking stand in appropriate relations, such as Pareto-optimality, to a given profile of individual preferences; we must also impose conditions on how the social choice is allowed to vary when the profile

---

[156] Jouanna (1998), p. 385.
[157] Decision C-542/1993.
[158] For the latter, see Balinski and Laraki (2010), pp. 102–9.

varies. Here, I stipulate that *all* profiles are admissible (universal domain). As we shall see later, it is possible to block some of the paradoxes of social choice, notably the existence of cyclical majorities, if we allow only preference profiles with certain properties such as single-peakedness.

I have already mentioned the uncontroversial inter-profile condition of non-dictatorship. A far more controversial requirement is that social choice should be constrained by "the independence of irrelevant alternatives" (IIA): the social preference between x and y should depend only on individual preferences regarding x and y. The condition can be spelled out in two different ways.

(IIA.1) If two profiles are identical in how individuals rank x and y relative to each other, the social ranking should be the same in both profiles even if other aspects of individual rankings (of the same set of options) change. The Borda count violates this principle. Suppose there are two elections governed by this method, one on Earth and one on Mars. In each, there are five options and three voters. On Earth, x beats y as the social choice by a margin of one point. The votes on the two planets are identical except that on Mars one voter ranks the options y > z > v > v > x, whereas her counterpart on Earth ranks them y > x > z > v > w. Because x loses three points on Mars, y is the social winner, although the voters' preferences over the pair (x, y) are unchanged. One can restate this example in terms of a single election, in which the voter who ranks the options y > x > z > v > w misrepresents her ranking as y > z > v > v > x to make her first choice be the social choice.

(IIA.2) If two profiles are identical in how individuals rank x and y, the social preference over the pair should be the same in both profiles even if some third option is present in one profile and not in the other. The Borda count violates this principle as well. Again one can construct an example involving an election on Earth and one on Mars.[159] On Earth, there are four candidates: A, B, C, D. Borda's method determines C to be the winner and C > B > A > D to be society's rank-ordering. On Mars, everything is the same except that there is no candidate D. Here, Borda's method makes A the winner and determines society's rank-ordering to be the exact opposite of what it was on Earth: A > B > C. One can restate the example in terms of a single election, in which candidate D withdraws, perhaps after pressure from candidate A.

The single-election versions of these examples raise normative questions about strategic behavior that I discuss in the next section. It is not clear, however, why the Earth-Mars versions should raise any normative issues. Why should the inhabitants of Earth worry about the fact that different social choices would be made on Mars following a difference in one voter's preferences or the absence of one candidate from the list of options? For a given profile of preferences and candidates, the Borda method has the attractive property of capturing an important *consensual* aspect of collective decision making: "a very divisive candidate, *strongly* supported by one section of the electorate and *strongly*

---

[159] For the numerical details, see Balinski and Laraki (2010), p. 52. They state the example in terms of a single election and the withdrawal of one candidate.

opposed by another section, cannot be said to be representative of the whole constituency: he is the symbol of a victory of one section over the other. The Borda count is highly effective in reducing the chance of divisive candidates."[160]

While these considerations count for nothing in selecting a wine, they matter in choosing a representative. For political choices at least, and in the absence of strategic behavior, the Borda procedure has a claim to being the best way of aggregating preferences.[161] It is not *demonstrably* the best way, however. Because of the ordinal and interpersonally non-comparable nature of the ranking, the word "strongly" has no meaning in any given case. It nevertheless seems plausible, although unprovable, that the cited claim will be roughly true on average and over time in large electorates. It has been argued, however, that the Borda method may be *too* consensual and that voter experiments show "dramatically how Borda's method and to a lesser extent Condorcet's method favor the centrist candidate and how the first- and two-past-the post penalizes him, while in contrast the majority judgment appears to be more evenhanded."[162]

With a common language, majority judgment respects the conditions of universal domain, non-dictatorship and independence of irrelevant alternatives. When there is no common language, the Borda-majority judgment method has many good properties, including (IIA.1), but it violates (IIA.2). "The reason for this failure is that the scale of grade changes when the number of candidates changes, and this induces changes in the majority ranking."[163]

I now turn to issues of belief-aggregation and joint belief-preference aggregation. The first issue might seem straightforward: a majority, supermajority, or unanimity of the members determines what will count, for decision purposes, as the "collective belief." Many jury decisions seem to take this form. With non-binary quantitative choices, one can use the median. Complications arise, however, when a given question can be addressed by two different aggregation procedures, both seemingly plausible but capable of yielding different answers.[164] In recent discussions, the problem is referred to as "the doctrinal paradox" or the "discursive dilemma."[165]

The first clear formulation of the paradox seems to be due to the 19th-century mathematician Poisson:

---

[160] Dummett (1998), p. 291; my italics. Bassett and Persky (1999), anticipating Balinski and Laraki (2010), argue in similar terms for the virtues of the Borda method based on the median rather than the mean.

[161] This is the view of, among others, Saari (1995) and Mackie (2003).

[162] Balinski and Laraki (2010), p. 125.

[163] Ibid., p. 109.

[164] Here, I understand "procedure" in an institutional sense, embodied in formal rules. One can also, however, use the term in a behavioral sense, as when juries are said to use either *verdict-driven* or *evidence-driven* procedures (Hastie, Penrod, and Pennington 1983). As noted by Bonnefon (2009), these correspond roughly to, respectively, conclusion-driven and premise-driven aggregation. To my knowledge, nothing is known about the prevalence of paradoxes of belief-aggregation in juries. In the next chapter, I conjecture that the recent Spanish jury reform may have been shaped by this concern.

[165] Kornhauser and Sager (1986); Pettit (2001).

Two individuals, whom I shall call Pierre and Paul, are accused of theft; to the question whether Pierre is guilty, four jurors say *yes*, three others *yes*, and the five remaining *no*: the defendant is declared guilty by a majority of seven votes to five; to the question whether Paul is guilty, the first four jurors say *yes*, the three others who had said *yes* against Pierre say *no* against Paul, and the five remaining say *yes*: Pierre is therefore declared guilty by a majority of nine votes to three. Next one asks whether the theft has been committed by *several* individuals, which in case of an affirmative answer entails a more serious punishment. Following their previous votes, the first four jurors say *yes* and the remaining eight who had declared either Paul or Pierre to be innocent, say *no*. Hence even though there is no contradiction in the votes of the jurors, the decision of the jury is that both are guilty of theft and that the theft has not been committed by several individuals.[166]

The jury could use two procedures to decide whether the theft was committed by several individuals. On the one hand, it could vote directly on this issue and reach a negative answer. This is usually referred to as a *conclusion-based procedure*. On the other hand, it could first vote separately on the guilt of the two individuals and then, from the finding that they are both guilty, infer a positive answer to the issue of their joint guilt. This is usually referred to as a *premise-based procedure*.

This paradox, which should perhaps be called the *Poisson paradox*, was rediscovered in 1921 by the Italian legal philosopher Vacca.[167] He presented a case in which three judges, deciding by majority vote, are faced with a case involving a question of fact as well as a question of law.

If the judges follow the conclusion-based procedure, they will vote on the verdict as shown in Table 1.1 and the accused will be acquitted. If, however, they first decide on the facts by majority voting and then on the law by majority voting, the accused will be convicted. Once "the" court has found that he did X and "the" court (in fact a different one) has decided that doing X is breaking the law, "the" court has no other option than to declare him guilty. This aggregation

TABLE 1.1. *The Poisson paradox in a court*

	Did the accused do X?	Is doing X breaking the law?	Is X guilty?
Judge 1	Yes	Yes	Yes
Judge 2	Yes	No	No
Judge 3	No	Yes	No

[166] Poisson (1837), p. 21 n. Poisson links this paradox to the secret vote, which, he says, prevents the jurors from going back on their decisions. I say "first *clear* formulation," as Condorcet (1789a), pp. 273–74, may be read as asserting that ratification of a constitution can produce different results if one requires the ratification of each clause by a majority of local assemblies and if one requires that a majority of the assemblies must approve the document as a whole. If that reading can be supported, Condorcet was at the origin of both major paradoxes in social-choice theory: the doctrinal paradox as well as the paradox of cycling majorities.

[167] Vacca (1921). I owe this reference to Horacio Spector.

paradox is not a mere abstract possibility, but, as one would expect, a problem that arises with some frequency on, for instance, the U.S. Supreme Court.[168]

The paradox of belief-aggregation can also arise when the members make non-binary quantitative judgments:

Consider a corporate board assessing the profitability of an investment project ... measured as the project's expected net present value (NPV), which per definition is the discounted cash flow (DCF) less the investment cost (IC). ... Suppose that the corporate board has three members with estimates as in Table [1.2].

TABLE 1.2. *The Poisson paradox on a corporate board*

	Discounted cash flow (DCF)	Investment cost (IC)	Net present value (NPV)
Member A	10	8	2
Member B	10	11	-1
Member C	13	12	1
Board	10	11	1

Let the members of the board vote on the size of each variable, and assume that the outcome of the vote is the median of the individual estimates. Then a vote on the conclusion variable gives NPV = 1. But this is not consistent with the majority's judgments on the two "premise-variables," since 10 – 11 = –1.[169]

As these examples indicate, the paradox can occur very easily. Moreover, in general there does not seem to be any principled reason to prefer the aggregation-based or the premise-based procedure.[170] I am not persuaded by the argument often adduced for premise-aggregation, namely, that the legitimacy of courts and other collective decision-making bodies depends on their giving *reasons* for their decisions.[171] The claim that "a bank that is incapable of explaining *why* it does what it does is failing to perform one vital aspect of its duty"[172] seems to presuppose that the *reasons* always justify the announced *policy*, as if the doctrinal paradox could never arise. In legal cases, there are no grounds for imputing the fact-finding and the legal decision to "the" same court. If we accepted the vaguely Rousseauist idea that a decision by the majority ipso facto reveals the general will and shows that the minority was mistaken, we

---

[168] Kornhauser and Sager (1993); Caminker (1999); Nash (2003).

[169] Claussen and Røisland (2010a), p. 50. For other examples relating to Central Bank decisions, see Claussen and Røisland (2010b).

[170] In the context of court decisions, Nash (2003) offers three objections to premise-aggregation and seven to aggregation of conclusions.

[171] Pettit (2001); Ferejohn (2012).

[172] Blinder (2007), p. 121. According to Blinder (discussed later), the Bank of England fails to perform that task. Philippe Maier (2010, p. 345) singles out the Bank of England, however, as following "best practice."

could indeed interpret the two premise decisions as *the* views of *the* court. The mere possibility of cycling majorities shows, however, that his claim is untenable; and even with no cycle, a majority can be wrong.

Conversely, I cannot see why aggregating conclusions would be intrinsically superior. On pragmatic grounds, however, there is something to be said for aggregating conclusions rather than premises. The fact that premise-aggregation is vulnerable to strategic voting, whereas conclusion-aggregation is not, counts in favor of the latter procedure (see the next section). Moreover, courts might find it difficult to reach decisions if they could not rely on "incompletely theorized agreements."[173] Similarly, "a highly individualistic [Central Bank] Committee may manage to reach a decision, but then find it difficult to agree on the analysis and reasoning behind [it]. . . . For example, the admirably transparent British [Monetary Policy Committee] used to find it so difficult to agree on a post-meeting statement explaining its decision that it did not even issue one."[174] In legislatures, it might be very difficult to assemble a majority if one had to include reasons for the decision.[175] This fact may explain the resolution adopted by the House of Commons on December 2, 1882, requiring that any vote on the reasons for a piece of legislation be taken *after* the vote on the law itself.[176]

Although very different from the paradox of cycling social preferences, this paradox of belief-aggregation strikes me as equally profound and perhaps more disturbing. It can be extended to cases involving preferences as well as beliefs. Table 1.3 illustrates in a very stylized form the debates over unicameralism versus bicameralism in the French Assemblée Constituante of 1789.[177] Broadly speaking, the assembly contained three roughly equal-sized groups. The reactionary right wanted to set the clock back to absolute monarchy, the moderate center wanted a constitutional monarchy with strong checks on

TABLE 1.3. *A Poisson paradox in 1789*

	Fundamental preferences	Beliefs	Policy preferences
Reactionaries	Destabilize regime	Bicameralism is stabilizing	Unicameralism
Moderates	Stabilize regime	Bicameralism is stabilizing	Bicameralism
Radicals	Stabilize regime	Bicameralism is destabilizing	Unicameralism
Majority	Stabilize regime	Bicameralism is stabilizing	Unicameralism

---

[173] Sunstein (1995).
[174] Blinder (2007), p. 114.
[175] Bentham (1999), pp. 121–23, offers several arguments and examples.
[176] Pierre (1893), p. 1007. In the American Congress, practice has often been that the vote on the preamble follows the vote on the bill. According to *Robert's Rules of Order*, "It is usually inadvisable to include reasons for a motion's adoption within the motion itself."
[177] Egret (1950).

Parliament, and the left wanted a constitutional monarchy with weak checks on Parliament. On the issue of bicameralism, the constellations were, highly simplified, as shown in Table 1.3.

In this stylized rendering, a majority made up of reactionaries and moderates *believed* that bicameralism would stabilize the regime, while a majority made up of moderates and radicals *desired* to stabilize the regime. The reactionaries desired, of course, to destabilize it.[178] The actual decision, to adopt *unicameralism*, was taken by voting over policy preferences. If instead the decision had been taken by first aggregating beliefs by (sincere) majority voting, next aggregating fundamental preferences by (sincere) majority voting, and finally taking the action that according to the aggregate belief would best realize the aggregate preference, *bicameralism* would have been the choice. In the abstract there does not seem to be any reason to prefer one procedure over the other, except, once again, for the fact that the aggregation of premises can be manipulated.

Deciding by Bargaining

When arguing fails to resolve a disagreement between two parties, they may resort to bargaining. It is not easy to determine, conceptually, what would count as a "good bargaining process." One might define it either in terms of *efficiency* or in terms of *fairness*. I shall mainly consider efficiency,[179] since fair bargaining is somewhat of an oxymoron. Let me explain.

Assuming that the bargaining does not break down, its outcome is largely a function of objective and subjective features of the bargainers.[180] On the one hand, their material assets determine their *outside options*, that is, what they will receive if the bargaining breaks down, as well as their *inside options*, that is, the resources that enable them to hold out. On the other hand, their preferences, risk attitudes, and time discounting, as well as their beliefs about the objective and subjective features of the other side, affect the impact of these objective factors on their decisions. In addition, procedural factors might affect the outcome, such as a first-mover advantage or the time interval between offers and counteroffers. Whereas the distribution of material assets may be characterized as fair or unfair, it makes little sense to characterize the bargaining constrained by these assets as fair or unfair. In bargaining over a dollar, a richer person will usually get the lion's share, because he can say, credibly, "Take it or leave it." This might seem unfair. The unfairness (if any) would, however, stem from the pre-bargaining allocation

---

[178] "[If] one argues for a certain measure that it is likely to reduce social tension, such argument will set against the measure all those who would like to see disturbances" (Perelman and Olbrechts-Tyteca 1969, p. 20).

[179] In discussing efficiency, I limit myself to what can be achieved by institutional mechanisms that do not presuppose creativity, as do for instance the practices of "integrative bargaining" and "thinking outside the box."

[180] The following draws on Elster (1989a) and the references cited therein; see also Muthoo (2000).

of assets rather than from the bargaining process itself.[181] As to the subjective factors, it does not even make sense to characterize differences between the parties as fair or unfair. A person who gets a smaller share because she is more impatient than the other bargainer may suffer from bad luck, but she can hardly claim to have been unfairly treated. *Procedure* seems to offer the only place where fairness considerations might apply. If there is a first-mover advantage, the party to make the first offer might be chosen by the toss of a coin.

As I said earlier, the assumption underlying the present section is that the participants are sincere. One might object that there is no such thing as sincere bargaining, since misrepresentation of one's preferences is of the essence of this process. In some cases, however, the parties know each other so well that misrepresentation is hard to carry out. When divorcing spouses bargain over child custody and property division, for instance, a claim by the father that he cares so deeply about custody that he would need a very favorable property settlement to give it up may not be credible to his spouse. (Since it might be credible to a judge, however, she might nevertheless act as if she believed it.) If a trade union leader suddenly claims to be so concerned with ecological issues that he will require a large wage increase to concede on the environmental dimension, management might call his bluff. Politicians engaging in logrolling may also come to know each other so well that each knows the value to the other of the concession she is making and of the concession she obtains in return.

Efficient bargaining requires, minimally, that the bargainers reach an agreement. When lack of information (or lack of an incentive to communicate it) is an obstacle to agreement, mediators can be useful. A neutral third party can enable the bargainers to communicate their possession of valuable information without actually giving it away, thus overcoming "the Arrow paradox" that one cannot offer to sell information without revealing it.[182]

In addition, efficiency requires that agreement be reached with a minimum of transaction costs, including the cost of delay. According to Leif Johansen, actual bargaining – as distinct from the merely virtual and instantaneous bargaining stipulated in many models – is often very wasteful. "*Bargaining has an inherent tendency to eliminate the potential gain which is the object of the bargaining.*"[183] A firm might, for instance, make wasteful investments in large inventories to render itself less vulnerable to strikes. The union might respond by building up large strike funds that earn low interest because they have to be very liquid. To reduce such transaction costs, the law might state that a negotiated agreement has to be reached within a certain time after a strike or lockout is called, and that the dispute will otherwise go to compulsory arbitration. This

---

[181] Thus when Habermas (1992), p. 205 argues that fair bargaining requires equalizing bargaining power, he does not refer to the fairness of the process itself.

[182] Nooteboom (1999).

[183] Johansen (1979), p. 520; italics in original. For a summary of the seven mechanisms he adduces, see Elster (1989a), p. 94.

practice is sometimes observed in Nordic countries.[184] In less institutionalized settings and notably in bargaining among nations, it may be impossible to reduce wasteful investments in bargaining power.

Finally, efficiency requires that the net gains to the bargainers be greater than losses to third parties. This issue is especially important in vote trading. One can easily construct examples where logrolling between A and B produces greater gains than the loss for C, and other examples where logrolling produces a net loss. There is little agreement in the literature on the frequency and magnitude of either effect.[185] If it could be shown that vote trading has a negative net effect in a specific domain or context,[186] it could be eliminated by the secret ballot, which would make it impossible to make the credible statements about reciprocation that are required for vote trading.

Even though obstacles to efficiency can sometimes be overcome by institutional measures, bargaining remains, for the reasons indicated by Johansen, a very imperfect procedure for making collective decisions. Yet in bilateral confrontations, when argument fails, there may not be any alternative.

VI. STRATEGIC BEHAVIOR

Strategic behavior – in one form or another – is extremely widespread. Consider the following case:

> In a candid deposition, Mr. Carney [a political adviser of Rick Perry] offered a glimpse at the [2006] Perry campaign's tactics. He said he wanted to focus the firepower on Mr. Bell, the Democratic candidate, even though few considered him a likely winner. The logic was that by attacking Mr. Bell, it would prompt Democratic candidates in [Texas] to stick with him instead of voting for Carole Keeton Strayhorn, a Republic-turned-independent who the Perry campaign saw as the main threat.[187]

Perry won the election with 39 percent of the votes, Bell receiving 30 percent and Strayhorn 18 percent. It may seem unlikely that the strategic attack on Bell could have induced as many as 22 percent of the voters to switch from Strayhorn to Bell, but the possibility cannot be discounted.

One can tell many such stories from the netherworld of politics; I recount some of them below. I limit myself, however, to strategic behavior in the context of arguing and aggregation. (I have nothing to say about strategic behavior in

---

[184] Ibid., pp. 158–59. Imposing a time limit may also have the effect of equalizing bargaining power, if the inside options of one side are more limited than those of the other.

[185] "Today, no consensus exists in the normative public choice literature as to whether logrolling is on net welfare enhancing or welfare reducing" (Stratmann 1997, p. 322); see also Mueller (2003), pp. 104–12. Riker and Brahms (1973) claim that in the long run *everybody* loses by vote trading.

[186] Logrolling between judges across cases would, for instance, seem clearly unacceptable (see Caminker 1999, pp. 2330–32, for discussion). For a rare documented case of vote trading on the Supreme Court, see Powe (2010). Decisions involving future generations may also be ill-suited for logrolling.

[187] *Wall Street Journal*, November 4, 2011, p. A6.

bargaining beyond the comments in the previous section.) I shall discuss three main forms: strategic misrepresentation of beliefs and preferences, strategic introduction or elimination of alternatives, and strategic choice of decision-making procedures. The impact is not necessarily negative, as it may have been in the example just given, but it can be. After discussing and illustrating these forms of strategic behavior, I tentatively enumerate some cases in which they may be justified and some in which they are not.

Strategic Uses of Argument

When arguing for her preferred policy choice, a speaker may find it useful to offer reasons in which she does not believe. I shall canvass some cases that show that such lies or misrepresentations may serve either the private interest of the speaker or her conception of the public good.

Returning to an earlier example, a speaker may argue that the road should pass by her house because that would be cheapest, while really caring only about her own convenience. If challenged, she might respond that it would be absurd if one were never to be allowed to favor a position that favored one's personal interest, as the implication would be that only *counter-interested* arguments are acceptable. (An equally absurd claim might be that only roads equidistant from all houses would be acceptable.) While the deliberations in the first French Constituante were to some extent shaped by the norm of counterinterestedness,[188] most debates apply a less rigorous standard (to be discussed shortly). As Paul Veyne observes, "there are so many ... intellectuals who take a position contrary to that of their class that one should credit those who don't with an equally disinterested attitude."[189]

When speakers search for public-interest arguments to defend policy proposals that are in reality motivated by their personal interests, they have *two degrees of freedom* while also being subject to *two constraints*. On the one hand, given the large number of plausible-sounding moral theories and causal theories, it would be an unfortunate or inept speaker who could not present a public-interest argument aligned with his private preferences (see the Introduction). On the other hand – this is the less rigorous standard I referred to – for the argument to be credible the alignment must not be *too* perfect (the imperfection constraint). Moreover, once a speaker has adopted a public-interest argument, he must stick to it, at least for a while (the consistency constraint).

Strategic use of argument can also occur for a different and less opportunistic reason. A speaker may support public policy P for public-interest reason X, but believe that no one would be persuaded by that argument. Instead, he argues that one should adopt P for public-interest reason Y, which he believes will be more persuasive. "Speech is like a feast, in which the dishes are made to please the

---

[188] For examples, see Elster (2009a), pp. 315, 323, 329.
[189] Veyne (1976), p. 469.

guests, and not the cooks."[190] We may take an example from the debate in the French Constituante in October 1789 over the confiscation of Church goods. In their attempts to justify this measure, Mirabeau and Talleyrand used the following argument. Instead of simply saying that the financial crisis required the confiscation, they argued that these goods in reality belonged to the nation by right.[191] If the Church had not, on the basis of its income and property, provided religious services and assistance to the poor, the state would have had to do so. Therefore, the state was the real owner of that property.[192] I conjecture that Talleyrand and Mirabeau appealed to rights because they thought this argument would be more persuasive than a straightforward utilitarian one.

To promote their cause, speakers can also make *factual* claims they believe to be false (*suggestio falsi*) and refrain from making claims they believe to be true (*suppressio veri*). The first strategy is intrinsically more risky, although the latter can also backfire if others know or find out that the speaker failed to cite a fact of which he was aware and that counted against his position. The lesser risk of being detected is not the only reason, however, why people might view *telling an untruth* differently from *not telling the whole truth*. Because people tend to view sins of omission as more acceptable than morally equivalent sins of commission,[193] debaters who would never dream of lying may not feel guilty about selective truth telling.

Speakers who are genuinely motivated to reach a good decision rather than to have *their* proposal chosen should volunteer information even if it counts against the position they defend. If speakers on all sides of a question withhold relevant information, the quality of the debates and of the decision can suffer. Assume that a hospital has to make a decision about how to treat pneumonia in patients who are hospitalized for other reasons. A committee of three doctors is asked to make a recommendation. Initially, the oncologist and the heart specialist are in favor of adopting drug X, whereas the neurosurgeon argues against it. Each of the first two believes that the drug is beneficial on balance, although he is also aware of negative side effects that are specific to his patients. If they suppress the private information about the side effects, the committee might recommend the drug by a majority vote. By contrast, if *all* side effects become common knowledge, the committee might decide that their sum total is so serious that the drug should not be adopted.

Suppression of information could, however, be justified in a second-best perspective. A participant may have reason to think that the public interest

---

[190] Perelman and Olbrechts-Tyteca (1969), p. 24, citing the 17th-century Spanish moralist Gracian.

[191] For the most explicit statements, see AP 9, pp. 639 ff., 649 ff.

[192] The best refutation of this specious argument came from Clermont-Tonnerre, based on a deep and modern understanding of the rights of corporate actors (AP 9, p. 496). But we can also follow Camus (AP 9, p. 416) and proceed by analogy (see discussion in Section IV). A father has the obligation to provide a dowry for his daughter. Assume that a friend or a relative is willing to provide it instead, thereby discharging the father of his obligation. Should we imply that the father thereby becomes the owner of the dowry offered to his daughter?

[193] See, for instance, Spranca, Minsk, and Baron (1989); Ritov and Baron (1990).

will suffer if he provides information to opportunistic fellow participants. If a deputy has private information that a prospect contrary to the public interest would have attractive private benefits for other deputies, he would be entitled to withhold it. As we shall see shortly, concern for the public interest may also induce strategic voting to counteract strategic behavior by others.

A more opportunistic reason for self-censorship of speech derives from the concern for reputation. Members of a central bank committee, for instance, may "care both about reaching the correct decision and about convincing an outside audience that they have a high level of expertise."[194] For instance, if – as is often the case – "a known expert on the committee speaks first, other members of the committee will have a greater incentive to reveal their private information truthfully if their individual statements in committee meetings *are not* subsequently made public."[195] If their statements *are* made public, the outside audience may interpret any dissent from the first speaker – especially if he is the Governor of the bank – as a sign of lower competence. The risk may be attenuated if the order of speaking varies from meeting to meeting (as in Japan) or if the Governor speaks last (as in Chile),[196] yet even in these cases the anticipation of what the expert will say may have a chilling effect on speech. Although secrecy would eliminate the risk completely by removing the concern for reputation (or rather by making it coincide with concern for the right decision), transparency of the debates is often recommended on other grounds.

As I shall argue in the next chapter, jury trials can involve "judicial lies" of various kinds. In the examples I cite there, the lies are not morally defensible but serve some more pragmatic purpose. In other cases, however, judges may have a moral obligation to lie, if the decision that would follow from their sincerely held beliefs about the facts and the law would produce what their values tell them would be an extreme injustice. Today, we believe that judges in the Old South had a duty to subvert fugitive slave legislation and that judges in Nazi Germany had a duty to subvert the Nuremberg racial laws. Although they almost never did,[197] later judges and scholars have been more willing to engage in or to recommend subterfuge.[198] The predicament of such judges has been described as follows:

The subversive judge ... believes that the outcome she desires is unsupported by law. She pretends otherwise, however. In this sense her opinion is a lie. If she is a trial judge, she makes findings of fact to insulate her decision, to the extent she can, from appellate review. If she is an appellate judge she cloaks her analysis in the language of precedent and statutory interpretation. She tries to proceed under the radar, hoping that attention will

---

[194] Stasavage and Meade (2008), p. 696.
[195] Ibid.; italics in original.
[196] Philippe Maier (2010), pp. 345, 351.
[197] Cover (1984); Müller (1991).
[198] See the catalogue of "subversive stories" in Butler (2006–07), pp. 1794–1805.

not be paid by higher courts. Subversive judges are double agents. Everyone thinks they work for law, but their true boss is justice.[199]

Strategic Behavior in Aggregation

In voting and judgment aggregation, participants can behave strategically in three ways, related to *inputs*, *options*, and *procedures*. While some of these actions are regular moves within the institution, others rely on informal persuasion, manipulation, and pressure.

When strategic actors give their inputs to the aggregation process, they do not necessarily state the option or the candidate they prefer or judge to be best. Instead, they offer the input that will maximize the chances that the option or candidate they deem best will be chosen. In the special case of vote trading, they exchange a vote against their own preference on one issue for the vote by another party against that party's preference on another issue. In addition to strategic choice of input, I shall also consider *signaling behavior*, a misrepresentation of preferences or of judgments that does not aim at increasing the probability that one's favored candidate will be chosen, but rather at sending a signal about the policies one wants her to adopt. "Every election is a signaling device as well as a government selector."[200] In this perspective, sincere behavior has *two antonyms*: strategic behavior and signaling behavior.

When strategic actors introduce a new option on the agenda or a new candidate on the slot, it is not to make that option or that candidate the social choice, but to make it more or less likely that one of the *other*, previously existing alternatives will be chosen. Conversely, if they deploy informal means to make one candidate withdraw or have one option removed from the agenda, it is not to prevent that candidate or option from being chosen, but to ensure the choice of another option. I cited an example in the discussion of IIA.2.

Finally, when strategic actors propose to establish or change a procedure, it is not because they are concerned with the goodness of the mechanism, but because they believe the procedure will produce the choice they favor. They can go about this task in two ways, either through informal means when the procedure is not fixed or by using the amendment principles to change the procedure. Earlier in the chapter I cited a possible example of the first tactic from the founding of the Continental Congress.

I consider first strategic manipulation of inputs. I shall mainly discuss voting, since neither majority judgment nor Borda-majority judgment creates an

---

[199] Ibid., p. 1792. This situation differs from cases in which judges behave insincerely or strategically in stating the *reasons* for their vote. Sometimes "a majority on the [Supreme] Court will agree on a single disposition but disagree as to the optimal legal rules justifying that disposition. Sincere voting will leave the majority disposition supported by two or more divergent rules, each championed by a minority faction of one to four Justices. Such fractured support for the Court's disposition undermines various institutional values" (Caminker 1999, p. 2317). To protect those values, "one or more Justices often deviates from her substantively preferred rule" (ibid., p. 2319).

[200] Downs (1957), p. 42.

incentive to manipulation as defined previously.[201] (Majority judgment can, however, create an opportunity for signaling behavior.) In addition to the instances of strategic voting considered here, I also offer numerous examples in the discussion of cross-voting in Chapter 5.

The basic idea behind strategic voting is simple. An agent first forms an expectation about how others will vote. She then casts the vote that is most likely to bring about the outcome she favors, constrained by that expectation. Thus in the elections of 2000, 56 percent of Nader supporters voted for Al Gore,[202] no doubt because they were confident that Nader would not receive enough votes to be elected. This behavior is extremely common.

I shall shortly return to other forms of strategic voting. First, however, I comment briefly on signaling behavior. In some cases, each of many voters may adopt a signaling strategy on the collectively self-defeating assumption that others will not. Being at the left of the Socialist Party, and confident that it will win in the upcoming elections, I vote Communist to tilt my party to the left. If many others think like me, however, the Socialists may lose. It has been argued that the failure of Lionel Jospin to reach the second round of the 2002 French presidential elections was due to a mechanism of this general kind.[203] Judgment-aggregation is no less vulnerable than preference-aggregation to this temptation.

This behavior instantiates the phenomenon of *pluralistic ignorance*.[204] In stylized form, each person in a group believes himself or herself to be the only one to act in a certain way or (in the original statements of the idea) to hold a certain belief. In less stylized form, many people intend to act in that way or hold that belief, but believe that few others will or do. Among the reasons why this phenomenon might arise is what we may call the *younger sibling syndrome:*[205] just as we tend to underestimate younger brothers or sisters, we do not easily impute to others the same capacity for deliberation and reflection that introspection tells us that we possess for ourselves. If this explanation is correct, it shows that a cognitive bias can induce signaling behavior with consequences that go against the preferences of the voters themselves.

After this digression into signaling behavior, I return to strategic voting. In national elections, strategic voting by one part of the electorate will normally not create an incentive for strategic countermoves by another part. In committees and assemblies that are less numerous than a national electorate and use more complicated voting procedures, such incentives frequently arise. One might then

---

[201] For the strategy-proofness of majority judgment, see Balinski and Laraki (2010), ch. 10.1. For the strategy-proofness of the Borda-majority judgment, see ibid., p. 108.

[202] Abramson et al. (2010), p. 71.

[203] Blais (2004), who refers to this signaling behavior as "inverse strategic voting." Later in the chapter I consider a different explanation, related to strategic behavior, of Jospin's defeat.

[204] The idea was proposed independently (I assume) by Hans Christian Andersen in 1835 ("The Emperor's New Clothes") and by Tocqueville (2004a, p. 758) in 1840. It was rediscovered by Katz and Allport (1931) and later used both in social psychology (e.g., Miller and McFarlane 1987) and in political science (e.g., Taylor 1982).

[205] Elster (2007), pp. 307–11, adapting an expression from Merleau-Ponty (1945), p. 494.

search for a *strategy-proof system*, which satisfies reasonable intra-profile and inter-profile conditions and does not lend itself to misrepresentation or manipulation. Allan Gibbard and Mark Satterthwaite proved, however, that no such system exists, at least if we restrict ourselves to deterministic procedures. If, however, we choose a voter at random and declare his or her top-ranked candidate to be elected (lottery voting), there is no incentive to misrepresent one's preferences. As noted above, lottery voting is not a collective decision procedure in the sense in which I use the term, since it is not strongly interactive: the votes cast by other voters have no impact on the impact of a given vote on the outcome. Moreover, if voters care about the election producing a consensual candidate, they may not have an incentive to misrepresent their preferences. This remark does not of course invalidate the theorem, which is proved by assuming universal domain. It may, however, attenuate its importance in practice, especially when voting is public (see later discussion).

In the unpublished dissertation where his proof was first given, Satterthwaite listed five reasons why strategic voting might be undesirable.[206] I shall add one more. His first argument effectively relies on (without naming it) the possibility of pluralistic ignorance. His second argument cites the risk that constituencies might not be able to hold their representatives accountable, or might wrongly hold them accountable, if they vote strategically. I shall shortly present an example of the latter case (misplaced accountability) related to the passage of the 1964 Civil Rights Act.

Satterthwaite's further arguments all rely on an example of voting using the Borda count. As will be clear from an example given earlier, this method is eminently vulnerable to manipulation. In a similar example, Satterthwaite shows that if a second voter anticipates strategic voting by the first and counteracts that move by misrepresenting *his* preferences, he can bring about the outcome that would have occurred if both had voted sincerely. Satterthwaite's third argument relies on the fact that individuals may be unequally skilled as manipulators. "Those members who are less skilled will, in effect, have greater weight on the committee's decisions than those members who are less skilled. This inequality of weighting may contradict whatever principle of representation – such as one man one vote – that may have guided selection of the committee."[207]

The argument I would add to Satterthwaite's list relies on the *waste* that would be generated by members who are *equally* sophisticated spending their time figuring out strategic moves and countermoves that, in the end, produce the same decision as the one that would have been taken by naive voters. The argument can be related to one of the examples I cited earlier concerning the inefficiency of bargaining. If both the firm and the union invest in bargaining power by building up inventories and strike funds, they may reach the same agreement as they would have negotiated if neither had done so, but more wastefully. These are, of course, cases of the Prisoner's Dilemma.

[206] Satterthwaite (1973), pp. 5–16.
[207] Ibid., p. 10.

Satterthwaite's fourth argument relies on what Bentham referred to as the problem of "active aptitude" (see Chapter 3). "Since a committee member can increase his influence on the committee's decision by skillfully employing sophisticated strategies, he has an incentive to concentrate his time and effort on the devising of appropriate strategies. But this means that he will have less time and effort available to consider the content of the committee's decision" and, perhaps, to discover that his "first impressions" were mistaken.[208] This important argument applies very widely to strategic behavior.

His final argument relies on the fact that manipulable procedures create an incentive for members to conceal – and not only to not express in voting – their sincere preferences. "[Each] committee member will want to prevent the other members from successfully employing sophisticated strategies. The means by which he can accomplish this goal is simple: concealment of his own preferences.... The existence of strategy proof voting procedures would provide the means to eliminate this barrier to the flow of information among committee members." As he goes on to say, the incentive to conceal their preferences may "result in committee members misunderstanding the implications of particular alternatives directly as a consequence of other committee members misrepresenting their preferences, facts, and opinions."[209] The last observation makes the important point that misrepresentation of policy preferences may require members also to misrepresent their factual or causal beliefs and hence to reduce the amount of information available to other committee members. Thus if a member of the armed forces committee in Parliament sincerely *prefers* weapon systems A, B, and C in that order but strategically *ranks* B at the bottom in order to get A adopted, he might try to justify his position by making false factual claims about B or withholding positive information about B.

Strategic reasoning can also occur in belief aggregation. Consider again the aggregation paradox in Table 1.1, and suppose that the court uses aggregation from premises. Then either Judge 2 or Judge 3 could move the decision of the court to the outcome they prefer by changing their vote to No on, respectively, the factual and the legal issue.[210] Central bank voting, too, is vulnerable to this problem.[211]

The same phenomenon could occur in joint belief-preference aggregation. Consider the constellation presented in Table 1.3, and assume (implausibly) that the assembly had decided to separate aggregation of beliefs and preferences before choosing the option that, according to the collective belief, would best realize the collective preference. With sincere voting, bicameralism would be chosen. This procedure might trigger a series of misrepresentations of either beliefs or fundamental preferences. (1) To avoid bicameralism, the reactionaries could falsely assert that they believed it would destabilize the regime, thus

---

[208] Ibid.
[209] Ibid., pp. 11–12.
[210] For discussion, see Nash (2003), pp. 133–35.
[211] Claussen and Røisland (2010b), Section 6.1.

creating a majority for that belief and hence a majority for the choice of uni-cameralism. (2) If the moderates anticipated this move, they could neutralize it and assure the choice of bicameralism by falsely stating that their funda-mental preference was to destabilize the regime. (3) If the left anticipated this move, they could neutralize it and assure the choice of unicameralism by falsely stating as their belief that bicameralism would stabilize the revolution. Although the second counterfactual is wildly implausible (not all misrepresentations are credible), the example illustrates how a situation could get out of hand by successive moves and countermoves of misrepresentation.

I next consider the strategic introduction or elimination of options or candi-dates. When there exists a common language that allows for qualitative judg-ments, majority judgment is proof against this form of strategic manipulation.[212] The Borda-majority judgment, however, is not.[213] As I cannot assess the practical importance of that problem, I move on to the clearly important issue of how aggregation of *votes* is vulnerable to such strategies.

The best-known case may be that of "killer amendments" in the American Congress. In Table 1.4 (alternatives ranked from top to bottom), assume that A is the status quo and that B is proposed as an alternative. In a pairwise vote, groups I and III will ensure that B is chosen. Assume now that group II strategically proposes C as a "killer amendment," inducing a cycle. Under the rules of Congress, C will first be held up against B. Assuming sincere voting, C will be the winner. Next, C will be held up against A. Assuming sincere voting, the status quo will be the winner. Anticipating this outcome, however, members of groups I and II may vote strategically against the killer amendment, to ensure the adoption of the original bill.[214] *Strategic introduction of a new option may induce strategic misrepresentation of preferences.* Moreover, if group II anticipates this reaction, it can refrain from proposing the amendment, a fact that may explain why killer amendments are rare.[215]

TABLE 1.4. *A Condorcet paradox*

I	II	III
B	A	C
A	C	B
C	B	A

[212] Balinski and Laraki (2010), p. 182.

[213] Ibid., p. 109.

[214] Below, I describe an example showing that, by an additional twist, they might have an incentive to refrain from voting against it.

[215] In a close study of the 103rd and the 104th Congresses Wilkerson (1999) finds virtually no examples. Finocchiaro and Jenkins (2008) uncovered only five successful instances in the U.S. Congress between 1953 and 2004.

It is possible – but unproven – that the 2002 election of Jacques Chirac as President was due to the strategic withdrawal of one candidate (Charles Pasqua) and by strategic action to prevent the withdrawal of another (Christiane Taubira). The election used the "two-past-the-post system" in which the two candidates receiving the largest number of votes in a first round are pitted against each other in a second round. Given the near-certainty that the Far Right candidate (Jean Marie le Pen) would obtain 15–20 percent of the vote, the system gave the major candidates on the Right (Chirac) and on the Left (Lionel Jospin) an incentive to encourage the proliferation of candidates in the other camp (to reduce the opponent's chance of beating Le Pen) and reduce the number of candidates in his own (to increase his chances of beating him). It is possible that Chirac prevented Jospin from getting to the second round (and won a subsequent hands-down victory against Jean Marie le Pen) by exploiting this possibility:

Had either Jean-Pierre Chevènement, an ex-socialist, or Christiane Taubira, a socialist, withdrawn, most of his 5.3% or her 2.3% of the votes would have gone to Jospin, and the second round would have pitted Chirac against Jospin. According to most of the polls, Jospin would have beaten Chirac, though by little. In fact, Taubira had offered to withdraw if the [Socialist Party] was prepared to cover her expenses, but that offer was refused. It was rumored that [Chirac's party] helped to finance Taubira's campaign (a credible strategy gambit backed by no specific evidence). But if Charles Pasqua, an aging ally of Chirac, had been a candidate, as he had announced he would be, then he might have taken away enough votes from Chirac to result in a second round between Jospin and Le Pen. In this event Jospin would surely have been the overwhelming victor.[216]

According to this analysis, the Socialists might have won if they had subsidized the strategic withdrawal of Taubira (or, less feasibly, leaned on the notoriously stubborn Chevènement). Since Jospin's defeat came as a huge surprise to all observers and (less verifiably) to all participants, the Socialists may simply not have perceived the need for this move.

I now turn to the roundabout method of trying to shape decisions by strategic manipulation of *procedures*. "Despite the substantial cost of modifying institutional constraints, experienced actors have always recognized the advantages of influencing policy output by such indirect methods."[217] If you cannot achieve your goal in one step within the rules of the game, you may try to do it in two steps by first changing the rules.

An important set of cases arises when one branch of government with the power to appoint members of another branch that is opposing its measures uses or threatens to use that power to get its way. The following examples can be cited:

[216] Balinski and Laraki (2010), p. 42.
[217] Majone (1989), pp. 96–97.

Gibbon writes about the reign of Augustus that "[the] principles of a free constitution are irrevocably lost, when the legislative power is nominated by the executive."[218]

When François II called an Assembly of Notables in 1560 to support his policies, 19 of the 54 were created "chevaliers" for the occasion.[219]

In England, during the Walpole era, "at the local level, where Whig magistrates could be relied upon to outnumber Tories ... , Whig sheriffs could ensure partisan juries in crucial cases."[220]

In England, "It had often been asserted that the British government consisted of three equal, co-ordinate parts; but the statement was not true so long as the king could always control the lords by increasing their number at will."[221] (In the 18th century, the King could also control the House of Commons by using his "influence," a practice strongly defended by Hume.)[222]

In 1911, Lloyd George threatened to pack the House of Lords to force them to give up their veto over bills.

In France, Louis XVIII and Charles X also created new members of the upper house when necessary for the passage of legislation. Louis XVIII's minister Villèle, is reported to have threatened to create so many new pairs that "it would be shameful to be among them and shameful not to be among them."[223]

In 1830, Louis Philippe created 36 new life peers known to be favorable to the abolition of hereditary peerage to create a majority in the upper house for that measure. "The text presented to the upper house three days after the creation of the 36 new peers was adopted ... by 102 votes to 68. If one subtracts the 36 from the 102, one obtains 66; hence the new batch was indeed necessary!"[224]

In 19th-century America, Congress frequently increased or reduced the number of judges on the Supreme Court to allow the President to appoint judges sympathetic to his views or prevent him from doing so.[225]

In 2011, the Hungarian Parliament, dominated by the party of Victor Orbán, adopted legislation allowing the government to pack the governing board of the Central Bank.

---

[218] Gibbon (2005), vol. 1, p. 86.

[219] Jouanna (1998), p. 70.

[220] Langford (1991), p. 119.

[221] Turner (1913), p. 252. This practice began in 1712, when Queen Anne created twelve new peers to ensure the success of the treaty of Utrecht.

[222] Hume (1742). The decline of this practice in the early 19th century provides a good example of reform in the spirit of Bentham: "the King's influence was, almost entirely, reduced ... not ... by excluding placemen from the House of Commons, but by abolishing places" (Kemp 1965, p. 103).

[223] Daudet (1834), p. 345.

[224] Antonetti (1994), p. 671.

[225] Gerhardt (2000), pp. 154–55.

Other well-known examples include opportunistic changes of the electoral law, a regular practice in contemporary France, and strategic redistricting, a regular practice in the United States since Elbridge Gerry. Concerning the former, "from 1980 to 2007, one or another part of the electoral system has been changed eight times. It is difficult to pretend that any of these modifications were motivated by the wish for a more equitable, more representative system."[226] Concerning the latter, "the old art of political gerrymandering – 'the practice of dividing an electoral district, often of highly irregular shape, to give one political party an unfair advantage by diluting the opposition's voting strength' (*Black's Law Dictionary* 2001) – has in the twenty-first century become a science."[227]

I now discuss in more detail three instances of strategic manipulations of procedure, two that were tried and failed, and one that was proposed and succeeded.[228] The first two arose at the Federal Convention, when Gouverneur Morris twice attempted to shape the proposed constitution to limit the importance of slave-holding and the power of slave-holding states. The third occurred in 1974 when President Giscard d'Estaing strategically facilitated recourse to the Constitutional Council, in the expectation – which proved correct – that if the Right were to become a minority, it would be able to use the Council as a "third chamber of parliament" against the Left.

At the Convention, Morris was by far the most adamant opponent of slavery, and very much concerned with limiting the diffusion of slavery and the clout of slave-holding states in Congress. His primary strategy was to argue that for purposes of legislative apportionment, slaves should count for nothing rather than, as the Convention decided, for three fifths of a free person. When that strategy failed, he made two strategic procedural proposals motivated by the same end. Although he presented them as aiming at strengthening the existing eastern states against future western states, their main aim was to strengthen the northern non-slave-holding states against the slave states in the South. Whereas he presented the *Southwest* as part of the *West*, he was in fact mainly concerned by its being part of the *South*. Both proposals took the form of replacing apparently impartial or non-manipulable procedures by partial or manipulable ones. While on their face his proposals seemed to violate basic principles of fairness and of prudence, they make sense in a second-best perspective.

---

[226] Ibid., p. 37.
[227] Ibid., pp. 24–25.
[228] One might ask whether the choice between premise-based and conclusion-based belief aggregation (or joint belief-preference aggregation) could be made strategically, as a function of the expected outcome of using the one or the other procedure. In Table 1.1, suppose that only Judge 1 knows the views of the other judges. To achieve his favored verdict of Yes, he might persuade a majority of the court to adopt the premise-based procedure. Bonnefon (2007, 2009) provides some evidence that preferences over outcomes can shape preferences over procedures in this way. Note, however, that if Judge 2 were able to anticipate this move, he could defeat it by changing his opinion on the factual premise to No. As in the killer amendment case, a procedural manipulation might trigger misrepresentation.

The first proposal occurred in the context of determining the terms of access of future western states to the Union. It was widely (but incorrectly) believed that population growth would occur mainly in the Southwest rather than in the Northwest, and widely (and correctly) believed that the Northwest Ordinance banning slavery in the latter territories implicitly authorized it in the former. Reasoning from these premises, Morris proposed that future states acceding to the Union should never be able to outvote the original thirteen states. In his argument, he did not cite the threat from slavery, however, but rather the uncouth behavior of people from the backcountry of Pennsylvania, which, he claimed, showed that "the Busy haunts of men not the remote wilderness, was the proper school of political Talents."[229] Although Madison and George Mason objected that future states should not be subject to "unfavorable distinctions" or "degrading distinctions,"[230] their argument did support the vastly more degrading distinction between free citizens and slaves.[231] Morris, in effect, argued for a partial rule to prevent the bad consequences of a facially impartial rule.

Morris's second procedural proposal concerned reapportionment. Randolph insisted on the need for a "permanent & precise standard" for adjusting the number of representatives as a function of demographic change, rather than leaving the adjustment up to Congress itself. As he said, "From the nature of man we may be sure, that those who have power in their hands will not give it up while they can retain it."[232] In a phrase on which I elaborate in Chapter 4, those in power should not be able to use their power to stay in power. Morris argued that Congress should be left free in this respect, perhaps with the aim of giving "Northern-dominated Congresses in the near future leeway to count the slaves at some ratio less than three fifth."[233] His argument – essentially that Congress could be trusted to do the right thing – was feeble. Madison very effectively made fun of it as inconsistent with Morris's general view of the depravity of human nature. Yet here too Morris's proposal must be seen as a second-best move in the larger context of slavery. Discretionary power can be used for good as well as for bad.

Constitutional courts exercise control over legislation that is proposed by a parliamentary majority. It follows that a current majority never has a short-term interest in creating a strong court or in strengthening an existing one. It might want to do so, however, if it takes a long-term perspective: "rational constitutional designers will prefer stronger judicial review to the extent that they see

---

[229] Farrand (1966), vol. 1, p. 583.

[230] Ibid., pp. 584, 579.

[231] Amar (2005), p. 90, suggests that this was also the *intended* effect, citing the facts that Madison and Mason were large slaveholders who did not decide that their slaves should be freed upon their death. In Chapter 4 I cite a remark (Farrand 1966, vol. 2, p. 111) by Madison at the Convention suggesting he was more impartially minded.

[232] Farrand (1966), vol. 1, p. 578.

[233] Amar (2005), pp. 89–90, who also argues that Morris was motivated by the interest of the eastern financial seaboard in counting wealth alongside with population in apportionments.

themselves being out of power."[234] This proposition seems confirmed by the creation of a Constitutional Court in the 1989 Round Table Talks between the Communist government and the opposition in Hungary: "The Communists wanted [and got] a strong court because they hoped it would protect them against reprisals if they lost power."[235] As this process remains shrouded in uncertainty, I shall not consider it here, but limit myself to a better-documented French case.

In the Constitution of the Fifth French Republic, the intended function of the Constitutional Council was to protect the executive against the legislature. Only four individuals – the President of the Republic, the Prime Minister, and the Presidents of the two legislative chambers – could bring a bill in before the Council for judicial review before its promulgation. Moreover, although the 1789 Declaration of Rights was cited in the Preamble to the 1958 Constitution, it had no *valeur constitutionnelle*. In practice, this arrangement left few opportunities to initiate judicial review. In 1971, however, the Council carried out what may be seen as a judicial coup d'état, by unilaterally incorporating the 1789 Declaration and other texts into its jurisprudence.[236] Three years later, President Giscard d'Estaing expanded the scope for judicial review even more, by promoting an amendment of the constitution that allowed any group of sixty deputies or senators to bring in a bill before the Council.

Why did he do so? A former judge on the Council, Noëlle Lenoir, told me that Giscard was inspired by liberal principles of individual rights, which he expected the Council to uphold, rather than by considerations of political advantage. That explanation certainly cannot be excluded. It is very probably how Giscard himself justified the reform. Yet there are indications that the reform was motivated by less avowable strategic considerations, and that *property rights* counted for more than rights in general. Giscard may have expected (1) that the Socialists would come into power; (2) that if they did, they would enact nationalization bills; (3) that the future right-wing minority would bring these in before a Council appointed mainly by right-wing politicians;[237] and (4) that the Council would strike them down. All these things did indeed come to pass.[238]

It seems clear that (2), (3), and (4) were widely anticipated. The fact that the Socialists were against the reform is most plausibly explained by the assumption that they thought it would be used against them. François Luchaire, a former judge on the Council and a leading member of the Left Radicals, wrote in 1974 that "the individualistic and liberal conception that is emerging from the jurisprudence of the Council is being asserted at the very moment that a coalition

[234] Ginsburg (2002), p. 5.
[235] Schwartz (2000), p. 77.
[236] Beardsley (1972) provides an accessible explanation of the murky juridical situation.
[237] The President of the Republic and the Presidents of the two assemblies each appoint 1/3 of the judges. Before 1981, none of the appointers belonged to the Socialist Left.
[238] For the details of the decisions, see Loyrette and Gaillot (1982–83).

of ... collectivist and interventionist political forces is gaining ground. From its origin as a 'cannon aimed at parliament,' has the Constitutional Council now become a minefield protecting property and the individual against the *Programme Commun* [of the Communists, Socialists and Left Radicals]?"[239] It does not seem unreasonable to assume that Giscard wanted to reinforce that minefield by enabling a future right-wing opposition to appeal to a liberal Council against a government of the Socialist Left.[240]

Although strategic behavior and, to a smaller extent, signaling behavior have a bad reputation, they are not necessarily undesirable.[241] Let me suggest three conditions under which they may be justified and even required.

First, strategic moves may be acceptable if they can stand the light of day. A voter might express and justify her preference for Nader or Chevènement and also explain, *appealing to the very same values*, why she would not vote for them. (In the elections of 2000, only 26 percent of Nader supporters voted for him.)[242] Legislative vote trading that involves no loss to third parties can also be announced publicly without any risk to the reputation of the vote traders.

Second, strategic behavior can be justified as a second-best move against an opportunistic opponent. Insincere voting against a killer amendment provides one example. The suppression of information that would create an incentive for others to promote their private interest offers another. If one voter tries to exploit the Borda count by misrepresenting her preferences, another might do the same to neutralize the effect.

Third, and more controversially, strategic behavior can be acceptable if the agent believes it will serve the public interest. As we shall see shortly, de Gaulle believed that the "national interest" (preventing a Communist takeover in 1945) could justify manipulation of the electoral law. Lloyd George was surely justified when he threatened to pack the House of Lords. The strategic moves of Gouverneur Morris were also fully justified. If one believes that respect for individual property rights is essential for economic efficiency and economic growth, Giscard's strategic expansion of the right to bring in bills before the Constitutional

---

[239] Luchaire (1974), p. 573, cited after Favoreu (1984), p. 2003. Stone (1992), p. 71, presents a more complicated picture, citing Duverger (1974) to the effect that "the Left had nothing to lose" by the change. I tend to attach more weight to Luchaire's assessment.

[240] Strategic behavior based on the anticipated decisions of a new (or strengthened) institutional actor may of course fail. "In [Norway] in 1922, the Confederation of Trade Unions (LO) [persuaded] Labor Party members in parliament to vote in favor of a proposition [for compulsory arbitration]. This behavior may be explained by the arbitration rulings of 1920. They were passed on the peak of an economic boom, fixing wages for a two-year period during which employers normally would demand wage reductions. The rulings followed the principle of 'splitting the difference,' and [LO] expected the 1922 rulings to follow the same line in spite of the now evident recession. But the rulings did not. Instead, they built on the economic situation and forecasts, largely following the employers' point of view" (Stokke 2011, p. 20).

[241] For a sustained defense of strategic behavior, see Van Hees and Dowding (2007). For a systematic survey of "arguments against giving sincere reasons," see Cohen (2010), pp. 1115–21.

[242] Abramson et al. (2010), p. 71.

Council was also justified. A judge on a court may misrepresent her views on a matter of law or fact if she believes it necessary to prevent a great evil.

In the long run, however, stratagems of this kind could undermine the respect for institutions and induce general cynicism in actors and observers. In the case of subversive judges, there is both the "'macro-concern' ... that the court's legitimacy may be eroded if the public perceives too much subversion" and the "'micro-concern' ... that if an individual judge subverts too much, she might begin to lose her power as other courts look at her decisions with more scrutiny and view her decisions with less respect."[243] The appeal to *raison d'état* is a notorious slippery slope. The dangers of act-utilitarianism are equally well known.

Let me also cite three forms of *undesirable* strategic or signaling manipulations, the first taking the form of bilateral manipulation and the other two the form of unilateral manipulation.

First, there are strategic moves that can trigger strategic countermoves by another actor. As noted previously, this behavior may benefit neither party and in fact cause an efficiency loss. In Chapter 4 I cite Richard Posner's observation that an easy-to-amend constitution may lead to wasteful investments in constitutional amendments, as the support of a political party flips back and forth between 49 percent and 51 percent. As an important special case, the manipulation of electoral law, including strategic redistricting, is in general undesirable. To prevent it, or at least to make it more difficult, one should write electoral laws and reapportionment procedures into a hard-to-amend constitution (see Chapter 4).

Only a small number of constitutions, however, specify the electoral law with enough detail to make them immune to manipulation. In addition to the obvious explanation from self-interest – politicians at the constituent stage have no incentive to "bind themselves" in ways that would restrict their freedom of action at the post-constituent stage – there can be non-opportunistic reasons for adopting electoral laws as ordinary statutes. In his conversations with Alain Peyrefitte, de Gaulle cited his experience from 1945 as a reason for not writing majority voting – ideally, his preferred procedure – into the 1958 constitution: "In '45, the communists represented one vote out of three, the other two thirds being dispersed among numerous formations. If I had adopted majority voting, the assembly would automatically have been three quarters Communist. This could be avoided only by the proportional vote.... There might be, one day, once again, reasons to *revert to proportional voting for the sake of the national interest*, as in '45."[244] This episode underlines the inevitably tentative nature of any general normative statements in this area.

Second, there is signaling behavior that is *conditional on the expectation of non-signaling behavior of others*. Citizens who vote for the Communist Party to send a signal to the Socialist Party illustrate this case. If adopted by many voters,

[243] Butler (2006–07), pp. 1820–21.
[244] Peyrefitte (1994), pp. 451, 452; my italics.

this behavior can, as we saw, be collectively self-defeating. This fact does not prove, of course, that an individual cannot have good reasons to adopt it in a given case. In general, however, it is very difficult for individual voters to determine whether others are likely to vote sincerely or not. Opinion polls are an unreliable instrument, as it is hard to know whether responders express their sincere preferences or their signaling intentions.

Third, there is the strategic *exploitation of the non-strategic behavior of others*. If the Chirac camp did in fact encourage Taubira to maintain her candidacy, it must have been on the assumption that some Socialists would "waste their vote" on her rather than vote strategically for the more credible candidacy of Jospin. The handful of Republican donors who over the years offered financial support for Nader must have operated on the same assumption. Unilateral opportunistic exploitation of the Borda count also falls in this category (see Section VII).

VII. THE BENTHAMITE APPROACH TO COLLECTIVE DECISION MAKING

In Sections IV through VI I have expounded and commented on some standard and nonstandard approaches to normative issues of collective decision making and institutional design. I have repeatedly emphasized the virtues of the majority judgment method over traditional voting procedures, and notably the fact that it is much less vulnerable to strategic manipulation. In this respect, the method fits in very well with the Benthamite approach I am advocating in the present book. Instead of looking for ways of choosing non-opportunistic politicians, we should design institutions so that opportunism has no *purchase* – or as little as possible – on the decision makers.

I shall now try to state the Benthamite approach in more explicit and general terms. I shall not advocate any specific procedures (arguing, voting, or bargaining), nor – apart from truth seeking – any particular criterion for the goodness of outcomes (Pareto-optimality, utility maximization, fairness). Rather, I shall try to identify causal factors that can have a distorting influence on decisions reached by *any* procedure and judged by *any* criterion, and discuss how one might reduce their impact by institutional design. In addition, I consider how institutions may contribute to epistemic competence. The two tasks overlap, since passion, prejudice, and cognitive biases can undermine that competence.

Let me first address some issues of epistemic competence. In designing institutions, one must not only pay attention to the content of information but also to the way in which it is presented – visual, oral, or written. In jury trials, for instance, witnesses should appear in open court so that jurors can base the judgment of their credibility on their responses under cross-examination as well as on their nonverbal behavior ("demeanor evidence"). In one jury trial, "a woman claimed that as a result of an automobile accident she continued to have severe back pain. During discussions, [a female juror] observed that she was wearing high heels, and that when she stepped off the raised witness stand after her testimony, she didn't even wince."[245] (As a man might not have noticed this discrepancy, the anecdote also illustrates the value of diversity on the jury.) If witnesses simply signed written depositions, as they did in France under the ancien régime, such sources of information would not be available.

At the same time, it is important that the information be presented in ways that do not distract from its propositional content. Bentham and Condorcet both argued, for instance, that the quality of assembly decisions would be improved if they were based on written information rather than on oral communication (Chapter 3). An inflammatory speech is surely more persuasive than the text of the same speech communicated in writing. In jury trials, gory pictures of a victim are sometimes excluded because of the disproportionate impact they can have on jurors. As I note in Chapter 2, the Athenian Areopagites deliberated in the dark to shield themselves from irrelevant and potentially distracting features of the proceedings.

Rational belief formation also requires good *processing* of information – which I again define negatively as the absence of interest, passion, prejudice, and bias. Although one might also define processing capacity positively, in terms of sheer *intelligence*, this criterion is never to my knowledge used to select decision makers. One often attempts, of course, to choose them on grounds of *competence*. Although the latter idea covers possession of information as well as the capacity to draw proper inferences from it, the capacity is never assessed separately.

To avoid prejudice, one may either try to avoid the selection of prejudiced individuals or to prevent the creation of situations that can trigger prejudice. Juries offer numerous examples of both strategies (Chapter 2). Whereas I understand prejudices as "standing" or permanent features of individuals, such as misogyny, racism, or xenophobia, the passions will for my purposes in this book be understood as episodic, situation-triggered reactions. They include all "strong feelings,"[246] intoxication as well as emotions in the narrower sense. In my opinion, the impact of emotions on information processing is uniformly negative.[247] (As I shall argue shortly, this view does not imply that emotions or passions have no positive role to play in collective decision making.) To cite two emotions that will concern me in later chapters, decision making should be structured to minimize the *vanity* of assembly members and the *fear* of jurors. The first may prevent deciders from changing their minds as the result of argument, the second from focusing properly on the task at hand.

I understand bias as a cognitive or "cold" mechanism that shapes beliefs in normatively inappropriate ways. There is little doubt that these operate in

---

[245] Vidmar and Hans (2007), p. 272. See, however, Saks (1997), p. 21, for skeptical remarks about the usefulness of demeanor evidence, notably facial cues. The two opposed interpretations of defendants' swaggering noted above also suggest the limited reliability of this evidence.

[246] Elster (2000).

[247] This is not the place to defend this controversial position; see Elster (1999), ch. 4 and Elster (2010a), ch. 6.

collective decision making.[248] Earlier, I cited the cognitive bias (the "younger sibling syndrome") that may underlie cases of pluralistic ignorance among voters. It is widely argued that jurors are deeply shaped by hindsight bias and anchoring bias when awarding compensatory and punitive damages.[249] In the presentation of evidence to a jury, the recency bias as well as the primacy bias may operate. Typically, the latter is stronger.[250] If subject either to the "sunk cost fallacy"[251] or to the "planning fallacy,"[252] members of an assembly may form unrealistically optimistic beliefs about the economic viability of projects. In addition to these individually based distortions, bias may arise through interaction, an example being group radicalization as an effect of deliberation.[253] One may also include, in this category, interactive mechanisms that, although consistent with individual rationality, can lead to unwarranted conclusions. In "rational conformism" (to be distinguished from "motivated conformism"), each person in a sequence forms a conclusion that is justified by her own private evidence and by the conclusions of those who preceded her in the sequence.[254] This process can prevent the optimal aggregation of information if the earlier signals swamp the later ones.

Among individually based distortions, one might perhaps neutralize hindsight bias and anchoring bias by transferring certain tort cases from juries to judges. However, the jury seems to be out, as it were, on the question whether judges are in fact less prone than juries to cognitive illusions of this kind.[255] A more robust finding is that understanding of statistical information – for instance, concerning DNA evidence in a murder trial – is enhanced when it is communicated in terms of natural frequencies rather than probabilities.[256] Jurors may also be less likely to be biased by their mental models if they receive instruction about the law at a pre-trial conference rather than, as is usually the case today, after the evidence phase of the trial.[257] Psychologists report somewhat successful attempts to reduce the primacy bias and, more ambitiously, "to minimize the totality of primacy and recency effects."[258] Generally, however, I concur with the following statement, which is even truer today than when it was made: "demonstrated cognitive biases have grown like weeds in a vacant

[248] Eskridge and Ferejohn (2001).
[249] Sunstein et al. (2002).
[250] For these two effects, see the essays in Hovland et al. (1957); also Perelman and Olbrechts-Tyteca (1969), p. 499.
[251] Arkes and Blumer (1985).
[252] Buehler, Griffin, and Ross (2002).
[253] Isenberg (1986). As the author notes, the effect can also result from a quite respectable cognitive mechanism, if members of a group all have different premises pointing to the same conclusion and, when sharing these premises, acquire stronger reasons to believe in it.
[254] Bikhchandani, Hirshleifer, and Welch (1998).
[255] For opposing views, see Sunstein et al. (2002), ch. 11, and Vidmar and Hans (2007), pp. 163–64.
[256] Hoffrage et al. (2000).
[257] Simon (2004), p. 552 ff. He also proposes (ibid.), p. 571 ff., to debias jurors by asking them to take some time to consider whether the opposite side has a better case.
[258] Luchins (1957), p. 71.

lot. As documented biases have multiplied, it has become harder to reach conclusions from them. In any given institutional situation, there will be several potentially applicable and potentially cross-cutting biases."[259]

I now turn to the question whether institutions might *shape preferences* in normatively undesirable ways. This can indeed happen when either *interest* or *passion* usurps the place of *reason*. (Once again, in the general negative spirit of my argument, I *define* reason by the absence of an impact of distorting factors.) Let me first offer some examples of usurpation by interest or passion, and then explain why a more elaborate answer is needed.

It is a commonplace that collective decisions often need to be shielded from the personal interests of the decision makers. Many legislatures have elaborate rules to prevent members from enacting laws or decrees for the sole purpose of enriching themselves. The 27th Amendment to the American Constitution states that "No law, varying the compensation for the services of the Senators and Representatives, shall take effect, until an election of Representatives shall have intervened." On one occasion, long before the amendment was passed, the opprobrium attached to self-dealing assembly behavior had the same effect: there was such a high "degree of citizen indignation when legislators voted themselves a pay increase in 1816 that almost two thirds of them failed to return to Capitol Hill after the next election, even though they had hastily repealed the compensation law in the meantime."[260] As a further indication of the opprobrium attached to self-serving assembly behavior, one may cite the fact that when the members of the French Constituante enacted emoluments for themselves on September 1, 1789, they were so afraid of being seen as self-interested that they did not insert the decision in the published record.[261] One reason for the anonymity of jurors and the transient existence of juries is to prevent them from being bribed. The same consideration justifies the secret ballot.

When an assembly decision could entail private benefits for some members, one might, in theory at least, disallow their voting on the issue. To my knowledge, this idea has never been carried into practice. One occasion on which it was proposed concerned debt redemption in the American states after the end of the Revolutionary War. The war effort had largely been funded by paper money and by certificates issued to soldiers and suppliers, to be redeemed in hard money (gold and silver) at some later date.[262] As these instruments quickly depreciated to 10 percent or 1 percent of their face value, they were often bought up by speculators in the hope of full redemption. After the war, several state legislatures enacted tax legislation that would compel the citizens – many of them original possessors of the certificates who had sold them to speculators, sometimes in bargains of desperation – to pay heavy taxes in hard money to fund the redemption.

---

[259] Eskridge and Ferejohn (2001), p. 633.
[260] Young (1986), p. 59.
[261] Pierre (1893), p. 1154.
[262] Ferguson (1961) is the standard work on the issue.

The perceived injustice of this procedure triggered several proposals. On the one hand, one could differentiate among the targets or recipients. "Taxpayer advocates in at least nine states proposed to treat the original recipients of bonds differently from those who had purchased them on the open market."[263] On the other hand, one could distinguish among the decision makers. In Philadelphia, Pelatiah Webster proposed that in decisions concerning the public debt, assembly members who were "directly or indirectly *possessed, interested,* or *concerned,* otherwise than as an original holder, in any *public securities*" should not be allowed to vote, any more than "a *judge* or *juryman* should sit in judgment in a cause, in the event of which he is *personally interested.*"[264]

Decisions are *automatically* insulated from interest when interest has no purchase on them, that is, when the personal interest of the individual decision maker induces no preference over the options. Once jurors have been insulated from bribery and threats, and jury selection has eliminated prospective jurors with a link to the defendant, interest has only a minor role in their decision. (A juror who is eager to get home for dinner or to go on a planned vacation might, however, agree to convict, against her conviction.) According to one scholar, the relative place of *ideas* and *interest* at the Federal Convention was exclusively a function of whether state or group interest had a purchase on a given issue.[265]

Decisions are *contingently* insulated from interest when the decision makers have an interest in the issue at hand but choose to disregard it. When such choices can be traced back to features of institutional design, they are often due to the *publicity* of the process. "Sunlight is the best disinfectant." The long-term interest of a congresswoman in being reelected may trump her short-term interest in enacting a large salary increase for representatives, if she fears that voters would disapprove of such self-serving behavior. Note that while the disapproval of the voters might be emotionally grounded, the abstention of the congresswoman from pursuing her interest is not. Her "fear" is prudential, not visceral.

The idea of adopting electoral procedures that would favor the choice or the emergence of *wise characters* is more attractive than the idea of relying on publicity to induce *wise actions* by average or ordinary characters, but also, I think, more fragile. As I explain below, I now believe I was wrong when I asserted, in some of my earlier writings, that deliberative procedures tend to foster wisdom and concern for the public interest. Although decision makers can be screened for competence, directly or indirectly, there is no reason to think that competent individuals are more disinterested than others. As we shall see in Chapter 3, Bentham insisted strongly on this point.

The direct impact of *passions* on preference and choice must be distinguished from the indirect impact mediated by beliefs. While fear of retaliation from associates of the accused might cause a juror to be distracted from her task, it

---

[263] Holton (2007), p. 55.
[264] Webster (1785), pp. 302–3.
[265] Jillson (1988), p. 16. See Chapter 4 for some critical comments.

could also provide a motive for voting to acquit. It is with the latter kind of effect I am concerned here. Frequently, it is highly desirable to reduce or eliminate the intrusion of passion on collective decisions. Two main institutional strategies can serve this end.

First, one may try to *prevent situations that might trigger passion*. Debates behind closed doors can reduce the scope for vanity; the secret ballot can eliminate the fear of being persecuted for voting against the wish of the government or the majority; ex post and not merely ex ante anonymity for jurors may ensure that they do not have to fear retaliation by associates of the accused. Also, one may use neutral go-betweens to prevent direct and possibly inflammatory interaction. Georg Simmel observed that "[In England] there are boards of conciliation where the parties negotiate their conflicts under the presidency of a non-partisan. The non-partisan shows each party the claims and arguments of the other; they thus lose the tone of subjective passion which usually provokes the same tone on the part of the adversary."[266] The use of written rather than verbal exchanges can serve the same goal. In the age of twitter and blogs, the written medium can be as fast as verbal exchanges, without generating "the tone of subjective passion."

Second, one can try to ensure that no decisions are taken *until passions have had time to cool*. Measures to this effect include bicameralism, elections at fixed times with no possibility of recalling representatives, requiring that constitutional amendments be adopted by two successive parliaments, and prohibiting amendments or the suspension of basic rights during an emergency. As we shall see in Chapter 2, the tactic of delaying jury trials has been used for the same purpose. The common practice of requiring televised debates and the publication of opinion polls to cease some time before election day is perhaps motivated in part by this concern.

I shall often return to the role of interest and passion in later chapters. Here, I want to enter two caveats. The first concerns interest. While I do not accept the general proposition that interest-based voting or bargaining will tend, as by an invisible hand, to promote the public good, I believe there are situations in which it is perfectly acceptable to vote according to one's interest. While it would be wrong for the elderly members of the municipal council to vote for a swimming pool so that they can have their morning swim, it would not be wrong for parents with children to vote for high property taxes to fund high-quality schools. *What other procedure could one use* besides interest-based majority vote? While I do not know how to characterize, in general terms, situations for which interest-based decisions are acceptable and those for which it is not, it seems clear to me that the former set is non-empty. At the same time it does not, as Bentham claimed, exhaust the whole set of collective decisions.

The second caveat, concerning passions, splits into two sub-caveats. Passions can in fact improve collective decisions in two ways. Kant reported as a common saying that nothing great was ever done without enthusiasm. In particular, the struggle against petty and partisan interest may require sustained passion, as shown by the examples of Karl Marx and Jean Jaurès. In this respect, the important but ill-understood emotion of *enthusiasm* – inducing a state similar to hypomania – can be crucial.[267] It has been said that the Norwegian framers of 1814 were characterized by "an incredible vitality and restless activity" – "enthusiasm was their normal state of mind."[268] Jed Rubenfeld makes a general claim to this effect: "constitutional provisions tend to be enacted at times *not of sober rationality, but of high political feelings....* For if the legitimate authority of constitutionalism is conceptualized in the Ulyssean terms of 'Peter sober' legislating for 'Peter drunk,' the world is turned upside down when we seem to find, in actual constitution-making, Peter drunk legislating for Peter sober."[269] I return to the issue in Chapter 4. Here I only want to note that while passion may indeed provide the motivation to overcome interest, it may also cause cognitive distortions. Once again, Marx provides an example.[270]

The second sub-caveat, which I shall now explain at some length, stems from the causal role of the *normative hierarchy of motivations* in generating good collective decisions. In any society or community, the members will bestow praise and blame not merely on actions, but also on *motivations* for acting.[271] Commenting on Coriolanus, Plutarch writes that "one great reason for the odium he incurred with the populace in the discussions about their debts was, that he trampled upon the poor, not for money's sake, but out of pride and insolence" (*Comparison of Alcibiades and Coriolanus* III.2). Some motivations are highly ranked, others are more lowly. In classical Athens, they were ranked in roughly the following order: concern for the public interest, anger, self-interest, hubris (insolent pride), and envy. In most contemporary Western societies, anger and the desire for vengeance probably occupy a lower place in the hierarchy than the pursuit of self-interest. To cite another motivation to which I shall return shortly, *snobbish preferences* are probably also ranked close to the bottom. In the 18th-century American elites, there was a cult of disinterestedness.[272] Only half a

---

[267] The emotion of enthusiasm is not discussed in standard readers on emotion such as Sander and Scherer (2009); Goldie (2010); or Lewis, Haviland-Jones, and Barrett (2010). Poggi (2007) seems to be an isolated example. Kant (1798), p. 302, offers a famous analysis of *observer enthusiasm* during the French Revolution, but does not in that context consider *participant enthusiasm*. Elsewhere, he did say, though, that "The idea of the good with affect is called *enthusiasm*. This state of mind seems to be sublime, so much so that it is commonly maintained that without it nothing great can be *accomplished*" (1790, p. 154; my italics; see also Kant 1764, p. 267, for the same statement without the qualification "it is commonly maintained"). Kant (1797), p. 536, dismisses affect, including enthusiasm, as "a momentary, sparkling phenomenon." Although emotions do in general have a short half-life, the enthusiasm of the French framers of 1789 and the Norwegian ones of 1814 seems to have been more than momentary.

[268] Steen (1951), pp. 143–44.

[269] Rubenfeld (2001), pp. 129, 130 (italics in original); see also Sajó (2011).

[270] Elster (1985), pp. 54–55.

[271] For a fuller discussion see Elster (1999), ch. 5.

[272] Adair 1998; Wood (1987).

century later, Tocqueville claimed that among the Americans he observed, the pursuit of private interest was ranked above public-interested motivations. This may remain true for contemporary Americans.[273] In the United States today, therefore, motivations might perhaps be ranked as follows: self-interest, public interest, anger, snobbish preferences, and envy. Assuming that sincere voting is associated with public-spiritedness and strategic voting with self-interested aims, the alleged disapproval in the United States of sincere voting by legislators points in the same direction.[274] In societies characterized by "amoral familism," the desire to promote the public interest might be ranked at the very bottom of the hierarchy.[275]

If a person is perceived by others as having acted on a motivation that occupies a low place in the hierarchy, he or she will be exposed to "blame and shame." From Aristotle onward, many writers have observed that being the target of the contempt of others is an intensely unpleasant experience, independent of any material sanction that might accompany it.[276] Even a deputy who is not planning to stand for reelection might be deterred by this prospect. This fact generates a strong emotionally based second-order motivation for *hypocritical misrepresentation* of first-order motivations. Because others will in general have only a rough-and-ready belief about the *distribution* of the various motivations in the population, such misrepresentation will often succeed. Crucially, the hypocrisy can also, as we shall see, affect nonverbal behavior.

In my earlier work on "the civilizing force of hypocrisy," I mostly assumed that the desire to promote the public good is at the top of the hierarchy and that individuals will be motivated to present themselves as motivated by that desire. The observations in the paragraph before the last show, however, that the effect of hypocrisy is not always civilizing. In societies with strong codes of honor, even an individual who does not want to take revenge might be forced to do so to avoid the contempt to which he would be exposed if he didn't. In the United States and elsewhere, public-spirited individuals may fear being branded as do-gooders.[277] Amoral familism might also force the general interest to go underground. I shall restrict myself, however, to societies in which the desire to promote the public good is highly ranked, with envy and snobbishness being close to the bottom. The fear of shame and blame may then keep certain non-public-spirited motivations out of public discussion.

Moreover, constraints on public argument may also create constraints on public *action*, notably on public voting. The "consistency constraint" and the

---

[273] Tocqueville (2004a), p. 611; Miller (1999).
[274] "Given social situations within certain kinds of decision-making institutions and in which exist two alternative courses of action with differing outcomes in money or power or success, some participants will choose the alternative leading to the larger payoff. Such a choice is rational behavior and it will be accepted as definitive *while the behavior of participants who do not so choose will not necessarily be so accepted*" (Riker 1962, p. 23; my italics).
[275] Banfield (1958).
[276] Elster (1999), pp. 146–47.
[277] Elster (1989a), p. 189; see also Hermann, Thöni, and Gächter (2008).

"imperfection constraint" can thwart purely opportunistic uses of public-interest arguments.[278] First, there is the phenomenon of "moral priming": once an agent has made an opportunistic use of a public-interest argument, she cannot easily abandon it if, on a later occasion, it works against her interest. Second, there is the need to avoid public-interest arguments that coincide *too well* with one's private interest. In practice, these two constraints may mimic or simulate true disinterestedness to a considerable degree. *How* considerable is of course an empirical issue.

In a given community, the real or "sincere" motivations can be highly diverse. The civilizing force of hypocrisy may, however, cause *expressed* motivations to be more homogeneous. Since voting cycles are often due to heterogeneous preferences in the population, in a sense to be explained shortly, hypocrisy might, perhaps, alleviate the problem of cycling. I shall now propose a hypothetical example – not, in my view, intrinsically implausible – to show how this might happen. First, however, I want to sketch some background.

Many years ago, I wrote, "Rather than aggregating or filtering preferences, the political system should be set up with a view to changing them by public debate or confrontation. The input to the social choice mechanism would then not be the raw, quite possibly selfish or irrational preferences ... but informed and other-regarding preferences.... There would [then] not be any need for an aggregation mechanism, since a rational discussion would tend to produce unanimous preferences."[279] To produce this happy outcome, I counted on "the psychological difficulty of expressing other-regarding preferences without coming to acquire them."[280]

As correctly observed by Christian List and his co-authors, the first statement is hopelessly naive.[281] They go on to argue, however, in the general spirit of my argument, that one might expect discussion to make preferences more *homogeneous* in the sense of moving them toward single-peakedness (explained later). Moreover, they adduce empirical evidence that supports this conjecture. Finally, they cite theorems to the effect that the closer preferences are to single-peakedness, the lower will be the probability of cycles.

The postulated mechanism in their work is that deliberation makes for more *informed* policy preferences, by changing instrumental and factual beliefs. The exact mechanism by which this effect would move preferences toward single-peakedness is not clear, to me at least. While they provide some pointers, their argument is far from conclusive.[282] Be this as it may, I want to explore an alternative way in which deliberation followed by a public vote can bring about single-peakedness. If deliberation and voting are public, the *civilizing*

[278] Elster (1999), pp. 347–49, 375–80.
[279] Elster (1986), p. 112.
[280] Elster (1983), p. 36.
[281] List et al. (2007).
[282] Dryzek and List (2003).

force of hypocrisy can reduce the heterogeneity of *expressed* preferences and, as a result, prevent cycles from arising.

In the second of the two statements from my earlier work that I cited above, I argued that deliberation might change the *intimate* or private preferences of the agents. I now make the weaker and, I think, more plausible claim that deliberation followed by public voting might change their *expressed* or public preferences. In my previous work, I misunderstood, in fact, the implications of cognitive dissonance theory on a crucial point, by assuming that the constraint of having to *state* impartial or public-interest arguments for one's position would always, over time, make one *embrace* those arguments. The theory of cognitive dissonance implies, however, that when an agent expresses an opinion that is contrary to his private view, the strength of the tendency to also adopt the expressed view privately is inversely related to the strength of the pressure on the agent to elicit the overt behavior.[283] In a typical experiment, subjects are asked to write an essay on, say, abortion that goes against their own convictions. Subjects who are paid a large sum of money to write the essay do not change their mind, whereas those who are asked to do so as a favor to the experimenter tend to adopt the view they expressed in the essay. Both types of subject need to believe they have a *reason* for what they do. For the former, the payment provides a sufficient reason. The latter, however, change their minds to justify their behavior to themselves. Hence dictators cannot rely on dissonance reduction to induce private compliance by forcing public compliance, nor can deliberative democrats count, as I did, on the same mechanism to induce public-spirited *motivations* through the need to use public-spirited *language*. In both cases, the strong *sanctions* that would be triggered were he to express his private opinion provide the agent with a sufficient reason for not doing so.

Imagine now a local community with three groups of voters: senior citizens, young couples without children, and parents with young children. They are, let us assume, equally represented in the municipal council that votes taxes. The personal benefits (utility) each group derives from low, medium, and high property taxes and from the corresponding levels of school quality are as shown in Figure 1.2.[284]

Whereas the utilities for seniors and parents are easily understood, those of the young couples without children require a brief explanation. On the one hand, they have low incomes today. On the other hand, they expect to have children later. In the light of these facts, they prefer a medium-quality school to a bad one and a bad one to an expensive one. If we now assume that the voting preferences of each group are selfish and dictated only by the personal benefits they derive from different levels of school funding, Figure 1.2 also represents

[283] Festinger and Carlsmith (1959).
[284] Although the options are discrete, the utility functions are drawn as continuous lines. We may think of the points on the horizontal axis between Low, Medium, and High as representing probability combinations of the discrete options.

Utility

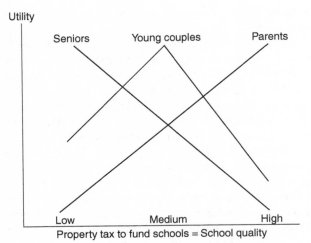

FIGURE I.2. Single-peaked preferences

these preferences. These are *single-peaked*, meaning that one can order the options such that for each group the farther to the left or the right an option is from its preferred option (or ideal point), the less it is preferred. In this case, the social preference is unambiguously for medium-level taxes. Young couples and parents prefer this option to low taxes, while young couples and seniors prefer it to high taxes.

Assume now a different scenario. Instead of the seniors, there is a group of "snobs." Since they want to place their children in a private school (which is neither better nor worse than a high-quality public school), their top-ranked option is to pay low taxes that will allow them to pay the high tuition fees. At the same time, their bottom-ranked option is a medium tax level that will neither allow them to pay the tuition fees nor ensure for their children a high-quality education. Figure 1.3 shows the ensuing private preference profile, which is not single-peaked. If people vote following their private preferences, as they would do in a secret ballot, majority voting yields a cycle.

My suggestion is that if deliberation and voting are public, the snobs will be *ashamed to express their snobbish private preferences*. They would not be willing to state publicly that they do not want their children to go to the same (high-quality) public school as children from low-income families. Instead, they would express preferences identical to those of the parents. This would illustrate the civilizing force of hypocrisy.

To recapitulate, I have offered three hypothetical examples of majority voting with three voting blocs and three options. (1) In the senior–young-parent case, private preferences are single-peaked. Under a secret ballot in which the blocs vote on the basis of these preferences, no cycle arises. It seems plausible that the same result would be observed under public voting. Although an opprobrium is

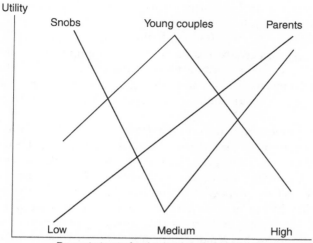

FIGURE 1.3. Snobs and young prefer L to H. Snobs and parents prefer H to M. Parents and young prefer M to L. Hence *interest-based secret majority voting* yields a cycle.

often attached to self-interested voting, I believe that in the kind of situation I have described, voters would see it as perfectly acceptable if others vote according to their self-interest, especially as it is not at all clear what the public interest would require. (2) In the snob–young-parent case with secret ballot, expressed preferences are not single-peaked, because the snobs now introduce an additional dimension to the problem. (3) In the snob–young-parent case with public voting, this dimension goes underground, as it were, and the expressed preferences are single-peaked. In case (1) as well as in case (3), expressed preferences are relatively homogeneous. There is conflict, but it is manageable. In case (2), it is unmanageable because of the greater heterogeneity of expressed preferences.

I do not imply, of course, that *all* multi-dimensional conflicts involve preferences that are "inadmissible" or "unavowable" along all dimensions except one, and that publicity of debates and votes would *always* eliminate cycling. The preferences of the snobs as shown in Figure 1.3 could also be due to motives that occupy a higher place in the normative hierarchy. Suppose that some parents believe that home-schooling provides the best education, although it would require one parent to stay at home without earning an income. They could afford and would prefer this option with low school taxes, but could not afford it with medium or high taxes. Yet because they place a high priority on a good education for their children, they would prefer the best public education to a mediocre one. In other words, the dimension of private versus public schools is here replaced by that of home versus public schooling. Unlike the views of the snobs, the preference of the home-schoolers can perfectly well tolerate the daylight of publicity. Public deliberation and voting would not suppress the cycle.

It is clearly unfeasible to assess how frequently this cycle-preventing effect of public deliberation occurs. Perhaps the phenomenon is empirically marginal. I believe nevertheless that it merits a place in the catalogue of cycle-preventing conditions and mechanisms. The civilizing force of hypocrisy can reduce the dimensionality of *overt* conflict, and cycling often arises from multi-dimensionality.

Let me conclude with some comments on the relation between *hypocritical* and *strategic* misrepresentation of preferences. In what I suppose to be the standard view, these differ in three respects: with regard to their effects, with regard to the motives that induce them, and with regard to the procedural preferences they induce. When "hypocrisy is the homage that vice pays to virtue," misrepresentation has in general good consequences, at least when public interest occupies a high place in the normative hierarchy of motivations. As we have seen, strategic voting has a more ambiguous normative status. The two kinds of misrepresentation are also assumed to arise from different motives. In the pure strategic case, the agent is assumed to have only one aim: the adoption of an outcome that is as highly ranked as possible on his preference scale. In the hypocritical case, the agent also cares about this aim, but cares in addition about how other voters assess his motivation. To avoid being assessed, the hypocritical agent will often prefer a secret ballot.[285] By contrast, the strategic agent is not assumed to have any systematic procedural preferences.

The standard view does not get it quite right, however, since *hypocrisy and strategy can operate together*. Even a strategic agent may be embarrassed to "lie in public" by expressing preferences that everybody knows she does not hold. In this case, others would sanction *the insincerity of the expressed preferences*, whereas in the pure hypocritical case they would sanction *the substance of the private preferences* were these to be expressed. In the case of the Borda count, the fact of ranking one's second choice in the last place would reveal that one *cared less about making a consensual collective decision than about having one's own candidate chosen*. When someone pointed out to Borda that his scheme lent itself to manipulation, he is reported to have answered, "My system is intended only for honest men," implying that attempts to game the system would reveal dishonesty.[286] It is possible, therefore, that publicity might be an antidote not only to cycling, but also to strategic voting.

[285] He may, however, be reluctant to propose or demand this procedure if doing so would reveal that he intends to vote in a way that, if known to others, would trigger sanctions. He might, therefore, welcome the demand *if made by others* for the purpose of enabling him to vote according to his true preferences. Thus in the Italian constituent assembly of 1946–48 the Communists demanded secret voting so that Catholics would be free to vote against the proposed indissolubility of marriage (Giannetti 2010).

[286] It would reveal this fact only if the voters' real preferences are known to others, as is in fact usually the case in ongoing bodies with a stable membership (Johansen 1977).

As I argued in Section VI, strategic voting can be desirable. It follows that the counteracting effect of publicity on strategic voting can be undesirable. A case that came close to illustrating this possibility was the passage of the Civil Rights Act of 1964, when publicity almost caused the adoption of a killer amendment:

[When] the 1964 Civil Rights Act was being debated in the House, the conservative chair of the Rules Committee (Howard Smith of Virginia) introduced what he thought of as a killer amendment: he proposed that the bill prohibit discrimination on grounds of sex as well as race and national origin. The House leadership (sharing Smith's belief that the amendment might kill the bill) tried to persuade liberal Democrats to vote against the proposal. According to some accounts, many of these members would have been personally willing to do so if only such a vote could have been held in private. But the galleries were filled with women's interest groups who were there to observe behavior on any unrecorded (teller) votes and, at least in this case, liberal members were unwilling to go along with the leadership and vote down Smith's amendment. As it turns out the Smith amendment did not lead to the defeat of the bill but rather to the inclusion of gender as one of a group of statutorily protected classes. We suspect that liberal congressmen were favorably disposed to prohibiting gender discrimination all along but that they would have preferred to follow the Democratic leadership if such work could have been done in the dark of night. That is in a secret vote, many would have had an induced preference to vote against the Smith amendment. However, the fact that the vote was to be "public" (in the sense of a standing or teller vote) and the presence of motivated interest group representatives probably induced these members to vote for the amendment.[287]

Since the liberal democrats thought that the House leaders and Smith were correct in assuming that the amendment would kill the Civil Rights Act, they would have been justified in voting against their conviction. If the assumption had actually been right, exposure to the public of feminists would have prevented the passage of the Civil Rights Act: the best would have been the enemy of the good. As it turned out, the assumption was wrong and the amended Act was passed. Publicity had a benign effect, but only by accident. Unusually, the case involved three layers of preferences: the sincere preferences of the liberal Democrats for the amendment, their strategic public-interest–based motivation to misrepresent these preferences, and their hypocritical motivation to express their sincere preferences.

[287] Brady, Ferejohn, and Pope (2007), p. 70.

2

Ignorance, Secrecy, and Publicity in Jury Decision Making

I. INTRODUCTION

The institution of the jury displays in a uniquely focused way many of the problems and challenges of collective decision making in general.[1] Because of the complexity and richness of the institution and its history, I shall mainly discuss one particular aspect: *secrecy versus publicity* in jury decision making. Actually, as we shall see, some of the choices can more accurately be cast in terms of *ignorance versus knowledge*.

The jury is an institution of great antiquity. The Athenians used juries to decide legal as well as some political issues.[2] Some Roman courts also relied on jurors.[3] I shall occasionally refer to these institutions. The jury then seems to have disappeared from Western Europe until its reemergence in England around 1200.[4] Although I shall mostly discuss contemporary jury systems in Great Britain, the United States, and a few other countries,[5] I shall also cite some cases and debates from earlier periods. I shall pay particular attention to what one might call the rise and fall of the French jury between 1789 and 1941.[6]

Jurors are laypersons, often chosen at random, and today usually on a one-off basis. Judges are professional "repeat agents."[7] When, as is the case in many

---

[1] I shall not consider *grand juries*, which raise several issues of their own, as well as some of those discussed here.

[2] MacDowell (1978), ch. 2; Hansen (1991), ch. 8; Todd (1993), pp. 82–96.

[3] Esmein (1913), p. 17 ff.; Staveley (1972), pp. 228–29.

[4] Thayer (1898), chs. 2–4; Green (1985).

[5] See notably the exceptionally detailed and valuable study by Thaman (1998) of the jury system in Spain, where it was reintroduced in 1995. As noted later in the chapter, it is virtually unique in requiring that jurors give *reasons* for their decisions. The Italian jury is also required by Art. 111 of the Constitution to give reasons for its decisions. Since it is made up of six laypersons and two judges, however, I assume the latter pen the reasons.

[6] Leib (2008) provides a worldwide but incomplete overview of 28 democracies having "pure juries," "mixed juries," or no juries. ECHR (2010) provides a complete summary for European countries.

[7] An exception was found in the Hellenistic era, when a small city sometimes invited one or several judges from other cities to decide in cases where local judges were suspected to be corrupt (Gauthier 1994), a procedure that has some of the impartiality-enhancing effects of selection of jurors by lot.

countries, jurors are supplemented by judges, the dynamics of deliberation change. In that case, the jurors cannot reserve their opinions for other jurors but must share them with the judges. In this (somewhat special) sense, these augmented courts reduce the secrecy of jury deliberations. I do not here have in mind the "mixed jury" that is used in Germany and other countries, where a few lay judges serve together with one or several professional judges. Rather, I have in mind cases in which a full jury is supplemented by one or a few professional judges.

In 19th-century France, juries were notoriously reluctant to convict in political trials and in trials involving freedom of the press. They also often refused to convict in cases of infanticide, honor killings, murders of alleged witches, or the fatal mauling of a neighbor who had let his cow wander into the fields of the accused.[8] These acquittals reflected partly local values and beliefs, partly social pressure on the jurors, partly a belief that punishment was better left to the community, and partly reluctance to convict when the required sentence was felt to be excessively severe.[9] When *and because* the magistrates were allowed to enter the room where the jury deliberated (around 1850), the percentage of acquittals fell substantially.[10]

A further change introduced by the Vichy government in 1941 is, with modifications, still in force today.[11] The number of jurors was reduced from 12 to 6, and they were supplemented by three professional magistrates. The acquittal rate fell from 24.7 percent in 1941 to 8.4 percent in 1942. It is overwhelmingly plausible that the new law was the cause of the fall. A reduction of the acquittal rate was also the principal *motive* behind the reform. Justifying it, Minister of Justice Joseph Barthélemy said that "although it does not suppress the jury, it tends to defang it" (*lui enlever son venim*). After the war, almost nobody pleaded for the elimination of the magistrates, but the number of jurors was increased to 7 and then to 9. Today the rate of acquittal is about 4 percent.[12]

Jury nullification (discussed later in the chapter) seems less likely in the presence of professional judges than in their absence. At the very least, we would expect that their presence would have a chilling effect on the use of certain *arguments*, such as "the law according to which the act of the defendant constitutes a crime is unjust" or "the sentence that would follow upon a verdict of guilty is too severe." Yet with the secret ballot used in French juries, the *votes* of the jurors might still reflect their "intimate conviction" rather than the text of the law. Thus the effect of the abolition of one kind of jury secrecy (the opening of the deliberations to non-jurors) may be counteracted, to some extent, by the

---

[8] Claverie (1984).

[9] Donovan (2010).

[10] Claverie (1984), p. 146.

[11] See Vernier (2007) for a full discussion.

[12] The difference between the pure and the mixed jury can also be assessed by comparing the rates of disagreement between jurors and magistrates. Thus in the United States juries arrive at a judgment that differs from that of the presiding judges in 22 percent of the cases, whereas in Germany only 1.4 percent of lay judges offer a verdict differing from that of the magistrates (Langbein 1981, p. 204, emphasizing, however, that selection bias leads to an overestimation of the real difference).

maintenance of another (the secret ballot). If both kinds of secrecy were abolished, it seems likely that the magistrates would dominate completely and that acquittals would become extremely rare.

The design of the jury varies a great deal in time and space. In many countries, jury reform – or abolition of the jury – is regularly on the political agenda. Many reform proposals and actual reforms are motivated by the idea that underlies the present book, namely, the need to screen jury decisions from interest, passion, prejudice, and bias. I give a few introductory examples shortly, and then many others throughout the chapter. First, however, I want to signal some significant obstacles to the assessment of reforms or proposals. As noted in Chapter 1, we have no independent knowledge of the accuracy of jury verdicts, assuming that juries are only to establish facts. Because of the possibility of jury nullification, that assumption is false; and even if it were true, there would still be no general and reliable independent criterion by which we could assess the accuracy of a jury's decisions. "There are no answers at the back of the book."[13] Also, the secrecy surrounding jury deliberations – including in some countries a ban on interviewing jurors after the trial – makes it difficult to establish the empirical premises for reform.[14] Some writers claim – echoing a dictum about legislation attributed to Bismarck – that jury decisions are like sausages: you do not want to know how they are made. The dismaying experience of the economist Ely Devons, who served as juror in two trials and had discussions with jurors in two others, made him conclude that "if the jury is to remain part of the English legal system, it is just as well that its proceedings should remain secret."[15] Others have argued that secrecy may be the bane of the jury: the prohibition on jury research "has imposed yet another layer of secrecy which handicaps those who would wish to defend the system with more than anecdotal evidence."[16]

---

[13] Gross and O'Brien (2008), p. 928. I disagree, therefore, with the following statement by Dawes (1994), p. 227: "If, for example, a certain attitudinal dimension could be shown to be systematically related to *incorrect* decisions of one type or another, then we would have very good cause to be concerned about jury selection procedures that led to a biased selection of attitudinal predispositions among the jurors. In general ... investigations of human judgment on tasks with a criterion (e.g., an actual disease, actual success or failure of staying out of jail or in graduate school) has led to greater insight about the judgmental process than have investigations of tasks without [a criterion]." Whereas with the passage of time we can learn whether predictions about recidivism or academic success *turn out to be correct*, no similar procedure (barring cases of DNA-based reassessment or a compelling later confession by the real culprit) can tell us whether a jury decision *was correct*. Moreover, with regard to sentencing and awards, the very notion of *the* correct decision does not make much sense, although some decisions may seem obviously disproportionate.

[14] Vidmar (2000a), p. 39; Lloyd-Bostock and Thomas (2000), pp. 58–59; Cameron, Potter, and Young (2000), p. 200; Duff (2000), p. 269; Sanders, Young, and Burton (2010), p. 594. Although American legislation permits much more probing questioning of jurors after the trial, the findings from such studies do not necessarily carry over to the very different English setting. Moreover, answers may not be very reliable.

[15] Devons (1965), p. 570. Some of the "reasons" offered by Spanish jurors (discussed later) confirm this impression.

[16] Robertson (1993), p. 361.

There is, however, a large body of social science that studies the issues through *mock trials*.[17] The external or ecological validity of these studies is controversial, given the absence of independent criteria against which their findings might be checked.[18] The most important objection to generalizations from these studies is that "experimental jurors [are] aware that their verdicts would not affect a real defendant's fate."[19] Dr. Johnson said, "When a man knows he is to be hanged in a fortnight, it concentrates his mind wonderfully." Presumably, the knowledge that a defendant who is physically present before them might be hanged or go to jail as the result of their decision also makes the jurors bring a degree of seriousness to their task that cannot be re-created in mock trials, unless you can make the participants believe, falsely, that they are participating in a real trial. For ethical and practical reasons, such "mock mock trials" are likely to be rare.[20] Although I tend to be skeptical toward the findings of mock trial studies, I shall cite them from time to time because they often ask interesting questions.

In *The American Jury*, perhaps the best book ever written on the jury, Harry Kalven and Hans Zeisel set out to bypass the twin obstacles of the impenetrability of real trials and the lack of realism of mock trials. They mailed questionnaires to 3,500 judges who had presided over jury trials in 1954–55, asking them how they would have decided the cases. They received answers from 555 judges who had presided over a total of 3,576 jury trials, about 6 percent of the total of such trials in that year. Their main concern was to understand the cases – about 25 percent of all – in which the judge would have proposed a verdict, charge, or sentence different from the one the jury arrived at. They were aware of the issue of realism, citing a conversation with a judge who reported in conversation "that he had wondered if he would have decided a given case as he did, had he been

[17] Usually, mock trials study decisions by mock jurors rather than mock juries. "This is done for reasons of economy of human resources (for example n = 12 individuals as independent data points versus n = 1 jury composed of 12 individuals) and time (deliberation takes longer)" (Saks 1997, p. 7 n. 15). Mock trials therefore often ignore the effect of deliberation. An important study of civil trials that focuses on this effect is Sunstein et al. (2002), ch. 3. Here, the subjects were constrained, however, to 30 minutes of deliberation. The data in Brunell, Dave, and Morgan (2009) indicate that few civil juries decide that quickly. The findings in Sunstein et al. (2002) may have been affected both by the short time limit and by the very existence of a time limit.
[18] Hastie, Penrod, and Pennington (1983), ch. 3; Bornstein (1999). The fullest discussion known to me (Kerr and Bray 2005) is unconvincing, because of its near-complete neglect of the issue of realism (see note 20 later in this chapter).
[19] Hastie, Penrod, and Pennington (1983), p. 43. Green (1985), p. 13, makes a similar point about the difference between (what are today called) grand juries and petit juries.
[20] In an experiment (Breau and Brook 2007) comparing mock trials in which participants knew they were not making a real decision and "mock mock trials" in which they thought they were, the ecological validity of the former proved quite low. Kerr and Bray (2005) claim ecological validity on the basis of the findings in Kerr, Nerenz, and Herrick (1979). In that study, however, participants in "mock mock trials" were told that the "case would be decided by the majority of the student juries participating in the project" (p. 343). Apart from the fact that no actual decisions are made this way, the dilution of responsibility in a two-step procedure (see Chapter 3) makes it difficult to generalize to real juries. Moreover, the study had little variation in the dependent variable.

exposed to the responsibilities and full pressures of the actual decision. The implication was that he might be more legalistic on paper than he would have been in a real trial."[21] They nevertheless concluded "that there are sufficient reasons for taking the hypothetical judge verdicts as reliable."[22] I have no reason to disagree with their assessment. As I discuss later, the authors also obtained permission to record deliberations of the jurors without their knowledge but had to renounce using it. In the present book (see the Conclusion), I shall pay particular attention to their discussion of "crossover" cases, those in which the jury convicted and the judge would have acquitted.

The central question that will be explored in various forms in the present chapter is, *Who knows what, and when, in a jury trial?* In many cases, the question can be spelled out as publicity versus secrecy. The publicity of the jury trial prior to jury deliberation, and the secrecy of the deliberation itself, are cornerstones of the jury system. The Sixth Amendment to the U.S. Constitution states: "In all criminal prosecutions, the accused shall enjoy the right to a speedy and public trial, by an impartial jury of the State." Whereas "speedy" and "impartial" are elastic and ambiguous notions, that of publicity leaves less scope for interpretation.[23] To my knowledge, no jury has ever deliberated publicly, that is, before an audience, although in some cases they have deliberated in a public space, that is, without retiring to a secluded room.

In other cases, the question can be spelled out as knowledge versus ignorance. In some circumstances, legislators or judges may wish jurors to be ignorant of certain facts about the law or about the defendant so that they will decide "behind a veil of ignorance," to use a phrase coined for a different context. Yet ignorance is not the same as secrecy, and the facts in question may well be in the public domain. The criminal record of a defendant or the possibility of jury nullification, to cite only two examples of a category I shall discuss at some length, are not exactly secrets. More paradoxically, judges routinely instruct jurors to ignore – that is, not to take account of – facts of which they can hardly fail to be aware, such as the fact that the defendant has been indicted.

I shall now give two examples to introduce the topic of secrecy and publicity in jury decision making, both of them involving (among other issues) the risk of

[21] Kalven and Zeisel (1966), p. 54.
[22] Ibid., p. 54; for "reliable," read "valid."
[23] In English and American jurisprudence, publicity in criminal trials seems to have been present from the beginning. In France, the Ordinance of 1670 established that witnesses "be heard secretly and separately" before the judge (Esmein 1913, p. 218). This amounts to two requirements of secrecy: testimony shall be known neither to the public nor to other witnesses. Even if the first requirement is abandoned, the second may be preserved or be kept as an option. In the United States, the Federal Rules of Evidence lay down that "[a]t the request of a party the court shall order witnesses excluded so that they cannot hear the testimony of other witnesses." In France under Napoleon, witnesses normally testified separately but the accused could demand that they testify in each other's presence (Douai 1813, vol. 6, p. 683). Whereas the first system reduces the risk that witnesses distort the truth because they are subject to conformism or intimidation, the second deters them from telling falsehoods in the presence of someone who may know the truth.

bribery. Throughout the history of the jury, fears of corrupted jurors have been prominent. In England, at an early stage, the mere assessment by the judge (or the Star Chamber) that the finding of the jury was against the evidence created a presumption for bribery – not merely perjury – that constituted a ground for punishing the jurors.[24] Later, the tendency was to prevent the jurors physically from receiving bribes rather than inferring bribery from their verdict:

> Once the presentation of evidence to the jury commenced, the trial had to be completed and the jury charged with the case in a continuous proceeding, no matter or how long the court had to sit. If necessary, the members of the jury were to "be kept without Meat, Drink, Fire or Candle, till they agree".... These rules preventing jurors from separating for meals or lodging had as their ostensible rationale that they protected against tampering by outsiders, but the effect was also to hasten deliberation.[25]

Rather than being designed as a rational system for preventing corruption, the rules may simply have reflected "callousness or disdain toward criminal business"[26] (as distinct from civil trials). In the words of Alexander Pope:

> Mean while declining from the Noon of day,
> The Sun obliquely shoots his burning Ray;
> The hungry Judges soon the Sentence sign,
> And Wretches hang that jurymen may Dine.

> (Rape of the Lock)

The second example relates to the English Criminal Justice Act of 1967, which introduced majority verdicts of ten to two. According to some observers,

> [The] official rationale for the change was to [1] prevent professional criminals from escaping conviction by intimidating or bribing individual jurors. It has also been argued that majority verdicts [2] allow the views of extremists to be discounted in jury decisions. Critics believe that the change was motivated more by [3] a desire to save the expense of retrials, and that [4] it undermines the principle that the prosecution must prove guilt beyond a reasonable doubt.[27]

Rationale [1] relies on the fact that under a non-unanimous voting rule (and assuming secrecy of the jury deliberations), no juror can make a credible promise

---

[24] Green (1985), p. 140. Juries could also find against the evidence simply because they wanted to acquit, notably in cases involving worship (ibid., ch. 6).

[25] Langbein (2003), p. 23. Since he also cites (ibid.) the fact that one jury was fined because some members had " Figs and Pippins in their Pockets, though they did not eat them," preventing the jurors from separating may not have been the only concern. A striking contrast with this sequestration without food or drink is provided by a juror in the 1968 Spock case who "described how the government took care of him during sequestration. 'We had entertainment – always the best food – always the best martinis before dinner'" (Van Dyke 1977, p. 182). The author goes on to speculate that jurors may *"feel grateful to the government* for such attention" and that their gratitude "may conceivably translate itself into a pro-government bias" (ibid.; my italics). The risk that jurors might feel *resentment toward the defendant* for causing them to be sequestered (Vidmar and Hans 2007, p. 115) is perhaps more substantial, but seems unproven (Kassin and Wrightsman 1988, p. 190).

[26] Langbein (2003), p. 25.

[27] Lloyd-Bostock and Thomas (2000), p. 86.

to acquit in exchange for payment.[28] If the defendant is convicted, a bribed juror can claim, and nobody can contradict him, that he voted for acquittal.[29] In Chapter 1, I commented on the tension between [1] and [3], as well as on the tension between [2] and [4]. There is also a tension between [1] and [4], in that both unanimous and non-unanimous juries can arguably undermine accuracy. These complexities are not uncommon in jury reform; rather, they seem to be the rule. As noted, assessment of the impact of reform is often made difficult by the black-box nature of the jury decisions.

The discussion in the rest of this chapter will be organized by the flowchart in Figure 2.1.

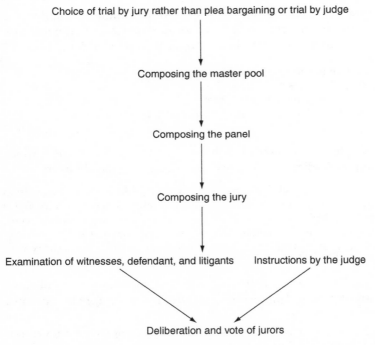

Choice of trial by jury rather than plea bargaining or trial by judge

Composing the master pool

Composing the panel

Composing the jury

Examination of witnesses, defendant, and litigants   Instructions by the judge

Deliberation and vote of jurors

FIGURE 2.1. Flow chart of jury trial

[28] Verdicts of 11 to 1 would have been sufficient to prevent such promises. As noted by Kalven and Zeisel (1966), p. 463, however, the findings of Asch (1951) suggest that the pressure to conform is much stronger when the deviant has no allies. Hung juries caused by a lone holdout juror are, therefore, somewhat unlikely. At the same time, the presence of two "rogue jurors" out of twelve seems statistically unlikely. If this line of reasoning is correct, reducing the majority from 12 to 11 may be ineffective and reducing it to 10 may be unjustified.

[29] True, the defendant might bribe or intimidate *three* jurors, as happened in a notorious British case in 2002 (Sanders, Young, and Burton 2010, p. 570). He might, for instance, tell each of them that unless he is acquitted he will hurt all of them, thus creating an incentive for each to vote to acquit.

Occasionally, I shall depart from the flowchart progression if a given mechanism occurs in several stages. My focus, in fact, is on the *mechanisms* – the repertoire of institutional devices to ensure secrecy or publicity, knowledge or ignorance – rather than on the jury trial as a whole.[30] This approach also justifies, I hope, what might otherwise be seen as incongruous juxtapositions of procedures used in different times and places.

II. COMPOSING THE POOL, THE PANEL, AND THE JURY

In some cases, defendants have the option of choosing between jury trial and being tried before a judge. In general, they will do so on the basis of their beliefs about the verdict and sentencing patterns of judges and juries in general. They may choose juries because they have higher acquittal rates, or avoid them because they tend to impose heavier sentencing.[31] If they knew who the trial judge would be, they could also try to ascertain his or her particular pattern before they make their choice. To limit such venue-shopping by the defendant, Australian law requires that the choice between jury and judge must be made behind a veil of ignorance, before the identity of the judge is known.[32]

If the case is to be decided by a jury, its composition results from the creation of a master pool of potential jurors, the selection of a jury panel from the pool, and the elimination of jurors from the panel until the required number remains. In the first and second stage, the process aims – ideally – at preventing biased, or non-representative, *juries*. The master pool should be neutral – a microcosm of the population – and the selection from the pool should be random. For this purpose, ignorance is crucial. In the third stage, it aims – ideally – at eliminating biased, or prejudiced, *jurors*. For this purpose, knowledge is crucial. The relative importance of the three stages varies greatly. I shall not try to compare the various regimes, except to note the extreme and unique importance of the third stage in the United States. As always in this chapter, the aim is to discuss mechanisms and their intended and unintended effects, not to provide a systematic overview of various regimes.

The voter register is often used as a master pool. This procedure has a potential for bias, if "the voter registration list has been chosen as the exclusive source for jurors by persons with the knowledge that the choice will lead to underrepresentation of certain groups."[33] The use of voter lists has nevertheless been defended as a selection mechanism, on the grounds that it "automatically eliminates those individuals not interested enough in their government to vote or

---

[30] For an exposition and defense of mechanism-based thinking, see Elster (1999), ch. 1, and Elster (2007), ch. 2.

[31] Lloyd-Bostock and Thomas (2000), p. 64.

[32] Chesterman (2000), p. 131. The Sixth Amendment of the U.S. Constitution aims at limiting the scope for venue-shopping by the *government* (Abramson 2000, p. 23), by requiring trial by "a jury of the State and district wherein the crime shall have been committed." In addition, local juries were justified by the personal knowledge jurors might have of the case and of the defendant (ibid., p. 27).

[33] Van Dyke (1977), p. 62.

indeed not qualified to do so."[34] The use may also eliminate some who do not want to do jury duty and therefore choose not to register as voters.[35] In Bentham's language (see Chapter 3), people who for either reason do not register to vote show only a lack of active aptitude, however, not a lack of intellectual aptitude. There is no reason to believe that their performance as jurors will be inferior to that of voters.

In the second stage, biased panels can arise through non-random selection from the master pool. Examples abound. It is often difficult, however, to *prove* intentional bias. At most, intention can be inferred from the opportunity to discriminate together with a statistically significant underrepresentation on the panel of a "cognizable group." To prevent bias, removal of the opportunity to discriminate is essential. Selectors should not, for instance, be allowed to know the race of potential jurors. In *Avery v. Georgia*, the Supreme Court of Georgia reversed a conviction in a trial where the names of white persons were printed on white tickets and the names of blacks on yellow tickets, which were placed together in a jury box. A judge then drew a number of tickets from the box, and he testified, without contradiction, that he had not discriminated in the drawing. Although blacks represented 5 percent of the master pool, not a single black was among the 60 selected by the judge. The probability of this occurring by chance is less than 5 percent, a commonly used significance level in many contexts.

Neutrality and randomness are intended to ensure that juries be representative. Judges or other selectors should not be in a position to influence the *composition* of pools and panels. In addition, randomness serves the end of preventing defendants and their associates from influencing the *decision* of the jury. In the words of the Federal Farmer, "it is quite impracticable to bribe and influence [the jurors] by any corrupt means, ... because it is not, generally, known till the hour the cause comes for trial, what persons are to form the jury."[36] In practice, ensuring this ignorance requires random selection of jurors.

To minimize the opportunities for bribery and intimidation, the trial should begin immediately once the jurors have been drawn from the pool. This requirement would obviously eliminate the third stage altogether. Alternatively, one might allow the parties a right to peremptory challenges on the spot, without giving them the advance notice that would enable them to investigate the background of the prospective jurors. As far as I know, this practice is found only in New South Wales.[37] Usually, some advance notice is given. In 1696, the English Treason Trials Act granted "the treason defendant the right to a copy 'of the Panel of the [trial] jurors . . . two Days at the least before' the trial. The purpose of

---

[34] Judge Irving Kaufman testifying in the Senate, cited in Van Dyke (1977), p. 90. For a somewhat different argument along similar lines, see Amar (1994–95), pp. 179–80.

[35] Van Dyke (1977), p. 99. For a similar practice in 17th-century England, see Langford (1991), pp. 279–80.

[36] Storing (1981), vol. 2, p. 321.

[37] Chesterman (2000), p. 139.

this measure was to allow some investigation of prospective jurors' back-grounds, in order to allow the accused to exercise his challenge rights in an informed way."[38] In contemporary legal systems, the identity of the jurors is revealed before the trial, 24 hours in Norway, 48 hours in France, 7 days in South Australia. The actual numbers, which vary greatly, do not matter. The general point is simple: there is an inevitable tension between the desire for juror anonymity (to prevent bribery and threats) and the desire for knowledge of juror identity (to allow challenges that go beyond those based on observable characteristics such as age, gender, race, facial hair, or weight).

In addition to the time allowed for background investigation, practice also varies with regard to the *kind* of information that may be disclosed. Thus in England, prior to 1973 defense and prosecution were given the names, addresses, and occupations of persons on the jury panel, but in that year the Lord Chancellor abolished the right to know a juror's occupation after allegations that the defense in trials arising from industrial picketing had used the information to deduce whether a juror might be a member of a trade union. In a later case, the courts refused to squash the conviction of a striking miner for picketing even after it was discovered that one of the jurors had been a strike-breaking miner.[39]

In England and some former Commonwealth countries, "challenges are extremely rare ... because ... the parties have so little opportunity to obtain knowledge about the jurors before trial, because the law requires that the challenge be made *before* the juror is called, and because judges are ordinarily hostile to such attempts."[40] As a result, the "jury may be more democratic, in that it is the undiluted product of random selection, but whether or not its members are biased is virtually impossible to determine."[41]

In the United States jurors have been excluded on a bewildering variety of grounds,[42] and the process of questioning them (*voir dire*) may take up as much time as the trial itself.[43] Here I focus on exclusion on grounds of what the jurors *know*. As many authors have observed, the history of the jury shows a complete reversal in this respect. "The jury in legal disputes started as a group of people called upon for their prior knowledge of the case or of the people involved. Only later did the principle emerge that, on the contrary, they should have no previous

---

[38] Langbein (2003), pp. 95–96; see also ibid., p. 51, for a possible explanation why this right was not granted in ordinary criminal trials.

[39] Robertson (1993), pp. 358–59.

[40] Vidmar (2000a), p. 33.

[41] Gobert (1997), as cited by Jonakait (2003), p. 129.

[42] Melilli (1995–96), p. 498, lists some 60 group stereotypes that have been used as a basis for peremptory challenges. Many of these are thinly disguised, facially neutral proxies for the inadmissible criterion of race (*People v. Randall* 671 N.E.2d 60). Jonakait (2003), p. 147, notes the risk of using such stratagems: "If my pretextual explanation for excluding a black candidate is that I do not trust bearded people, I may later, to preserve the pretext, have to use a peremptory on a bearded white person whom I wished to keep." This illustrates the "consistency constraint" discussed in Chapter 1.

[43] Alschuler (1989), p. 158.

knowledge."[44] The following illustrations offer a window into the varieties of knowledge that jurors are supposed not to have:[45]

- Jurors can be excluded for cause if they make it clear that they are aware of the possibility of jury nullification. As a result, the Fully Informed Jury Association not only seeks to inform jurors that they are allowed to give verdict "according to conscience," but also that they should prevent judges and prosecutors from learning that they know.[46]
- Jurors can be excluded – or whole juries canceled – if they have been exposed to extensive pre-trial publicity. The risk of bias may be assessed on the basis of media coverage or from examination of the jurors. Alternatives to juror exclusion include restricting media coverage, issuing gag orders to the trial lawyers, and postponing the trial until passions have cooled down.[47] (As the last remedy suggests, knowledge per se is not necessarily the problem.) The risk is that in selecting jurors for their ignorance about the case, one may exclude the most alert citizens.[48]
- In *Fernandez v. New York*, the U.S. Supreme Court upheld the exclusion of English-Spanish bilingual jurors in a trial with a Hispanic defendant, on the grounds that they might be unable to base their opinion exclusively on the official translation of testimonies given in Spanish.
- In the O. J. Simpson criminal trial, the defense asked prospective jurors questions such as "Have you or anyone close to you ever undergone an amniocentesis," in order to "screen the jury for those with favorable experiences with genetic testing and those with no experiences or unfavorable ones. The latter fit the profile of the pro-defense juror most receptive to doubting the reliability of DNA-evidence against Simpson."[49]

The examination of prospective jurors to determine possible interest, bias, or prejudice usually takes place in public. If the questioning is very probing, as it often is in the United States, it may cause embarrassment to the juror. One judge "reports from his own experience that jurors are more willing to admit their prejudices when questioned individually in judge's chambers, than when queried in open court in front of their peers."[50] On the other hand, "some attorneys have

---

[44] Lloyd-Bostock and Thomas (2000), p. 55; see also Esmein (1913), p. 329; Thayer (1898), p. 179.

[45] Later I discuss the question of knowledge *about* the jurors that *others* are not supposed to have. The two issues are related, since background investigations that are carried out to inform challenges may violate the privacy and security of the jurors.

[46] King (1996a); Abramson (2000), ch.2; Vidmar and Hans (2007), ch. 11.

[47] Vidmar and Hans (2007), p. 108.

[48] "Judge John Sirica asked the panel of prospective jurors summoned to consider the first Watergate indictments in 1973 whether they had heard of the case.... When a handful indicated they had not heard of the scandal, he expressed astonishment and indicated that those persons ought perhaps to be the least qualified to sit on the jury" (Van Dyke 1977, pp. 143–44). See also Amar (1994–95), p. 1180: "a juror should have an open mind, but not an empty mind."

[49] Abramson (2000), p. xiv.

[50] Kassin and Wrightsman (1988), p. 209; see also Abramson (2000), p. 163.

identified one potential advantage of the group setting. . . . When one prospective juror admits to a particular bias, it may be easier for others to follow suit."[51]

I conclude this section by considering some further aspects of juror anonymity. If, for whatever reason, the identity of jurors is not disclosed at all, the scope for challenge will be reduced by the lack of background information.[52] On the other side, it has been argued that in jurisdictions that allow challenge of jurors for cause and also allow lengthy interrogations to determine possible bias, anonymity during the selection process is in fact desirable, to encourage prospective jurors to reveal embarrassing but relevant information about themselves.[53] Like publicity, anonymity may cut both ways.

A more common argument for anonymity is based on the fear of jurors of retaliation by the defendant or his associates if he is found guilty.[54] Such fears are especially likely to arise when the defendant is accused of being involved in organized crime or terrorism. In the United States, this concern has over the last 30 years led to a steady increase in anonymous juries. The decentralized nature of American state courts makes it hard, however, to gather accurate data. The federal jury judging the four policemen accused of beating Rodney King was anonymous. The jury in the Moussaoui trial (discussed later) was anonymous, as was the jury in the 1994 trial of the four accused of bombing the World Trade Center. In the Spanish *Otegi* trial, nine jurors acquitted a young Basque nationalist accused of murdering two policemen. The extensive measures taken to ensure their anonymity "apparently did not succeed in dispelling their fear of reprisals if they convicted the defendant."[55]

If juror fears are justified, they provide pro tanto an argument for anonymity. Even critics of the practice admit that in some cases it may be used as a measure of last resort. Even if the fear is not justified, it has been argued that like any other emotion, it will have a negative effect on the quality of the deliberations,[56] independent of a tendency to acquit that might also be induced by the fear. One might also conjecture, however, that anonymity will cause jurors to take their task less seriously. Although jurors cannot be held formally accountable, the knowledge that they will have to face their fellow citizens after the verdict could focus their minds. It is hard to assess the net effect of these tendencies.

Whether the fears *are* justified is hard to tell. Although *witnesses* have often been harmed, "in the 200-year history of the American justice system, there are few if any instances in which jurors have been injured, and none in which a juror

---

[51] Vidmar and Hans (2007), p. 92.

[52] Abramovsky and Edelstein (1998–99), pp. 478–79; Jonakait (2003), p. 131.

[53] King (1996b), pp. 136–37, 147–48. Contrary to this argument, Jonakait (2003), p. 132, asserts that because jurors learn what answers will lead to removal, which they view as being censured by the judge, "admissions of bias decline significantly as the voir dire proceeds."

[54] The purpose of such retaliation would presumably be to send a signal to future juries, not to punish the convicting jurors.

[55] Thaman (1998), p. 381.

[56] King (1996b), pp. 137, 142–43.

has been killed, as a result of his service on a jury."[57] It is of course possible that some members of anonymous juries would have been harmed had they been identified; we cannot tell. It seems, however, that fear of harm to jurors in Northern Ireland during the "troubles" was very much justified. One case from 1998, "involving eight men charged with armed robbery in Belfast, was certified for jury trial despite reports that the men had IRA connections. Seven trials involving seven juries reportedly took place before the case was finally stopped, and one of the trials collapsed amid allegations of jury tampering."[58]

The Irish remedy to juror intimidation was not jury anonymity but the creation of "Diplock courts," trials by a judge rather than by jury. It was widely believed that in a small country (about 2 million citizens), one could not achieve juror anonymity. Paramilitary groups needed only to identify one juror in order to force that person to reveal the names of the others. In the United States, at least in big cities, anonymity was easier to achieve. It has been objected, however, that "this urban-areas-only limitation would mean that a defendant accused of theft in one part of the state would face a drastically different criminal trial procedure than would a similar defendant in another part of the state."[59] The objection is related to the proposal to make anonymity a regular rather than an exceptional jury feature,[60] an idea to which I return shortly.

The main objection against anonymity in high-profile cases is that it will bias the jurors against the defendant and undermine the presumption of innocence. In practice, judges have occasionally tried to meet this problem by falsely telling the jurors that anonymity was a regular practice, or that its main purpose was to protect them from the media rather than from the accused.[61] In one jurisdiction, Fairfield County in Ohio, all defendants are in fact routinely tried by anonymous juries, absent a showing of good cause for publicity.[62] To the proposal of generalizing this practice, it has been objected that "even though [routine] jury anonymity would not suggest that any one defendant is more guilty than another, it would suggest that defendants as a whole are, generally speaking, guilty of the crimes charged and that jurors need protection. This, of course, would violate a defendant's right to a presumption of innocence."[63]

An analogy-based argument (see Chapter 1) against the claim that jury anonymity would violate the First Amendment is that "one could not very well claim that the failure to provide voter identities deprives the press of the ability to cover elections and their results."[64] In modern societies, elections are in fact the only decisions in which *the identity of the deciders is unknown*. By and large, nobody except election officials knows who casts a vote, who puts a blank vote in the

---

[57] Abramovsky and Edelstein (1998–99), p. 466.
[58] Jackson, Quinn, and O'Malley (1999), p. 223
[59] Rastgoufard (2003), p. 1019; see also Abramovsky and Edelstein (1998–99), p. 481.
[60] King (1996).
[61] Abramovsky and Edelstein (1998–99), pp. 472–76.
[62] Rastgoufard (2003), pp. 1016–17.
[63] Rastgoufard (2003), p. 1020. Abramovsky and Edelstein (1998–99), p. 472, make the same point.
[64] King (1996), p. 154 n. 123.

ballot box, and who abstains by staying home. (In the next chapter I discuss how one could and perhaps should eliminate the anonymity of voters, while respecting the secrecy of their votes.) Although it is true that anonymity is not an obstacle to adequate press coverage either of elections or of jury trials, I believe the analogy is halting. The fact that an individual juror has an impact on the decision that vastly exceeds that of the individual voter seems highly morally relevant. Moreover, whereas jury service is obligatory, voting in most countries is not.

III. THE TRIAL

Jurors are supposed to make up their minds on the basis of what they hear and observe during the trial, and nothing else. In practice, this ideal is unrealistic and, in fact, far from ideal. The value of jury diversity stems from the fact that jurors come to their task with different personal experiences and different conceptions of human nature. Moreover, in high-profile trials it may be impossible to find jurors who have no knowledge about the case. Even if they are willing to change their minds upon the evidence, their knowledge affects their prior subjective probabilities and possibly the final judgment resulting from evidence-based updating of these priors.[65]

This being said, what jurors observe and hear is evidently crucial. In the following, I focus on what they are *not* supposed to observe and hear. I first consider visual impressions, then oral testimony, and then instructions from the judges. Among the last, I also include instructions about facts jurors are supposed to ignore in the sense of not taking account of them in their decisions, even though they are not literally ignorant of them.

In civil as well as in criminal cases, "juror blindfolding" is common. Before I proceed to examples and discussion, let me note some cases of (almost) literal blindfolding from a broader range of contexts. In the dialogue *Hermotimus* by Lucian of Samosata we read that

Reason insists that the owner of it must further be allowed ample time; he will collect the rival candidates together, and make his choice with long, lingering, repeated deliberation; he will give no heed to the candidate's age, appearance, or repute for wisdom, but perform his functions like the [Athenian court of the] Areopagites, who judge in the darkness of night, *so that they must regard not the pleaders*, but the pleadings. (my italics)[66]

In Plutarch's *Life of Lycurgus*, we read the following description of voting in Sparta:

---

[65] These remarks do not imply that I believe that jurors make up their minds through a strict process of Bayesian updating; see notably Lopes (1993), pp. 257–59, for some telling objections. Yet if twelve jurors are confronted with the same evidence, common sense suggests that those who enter the courtroom with a stronger belief in the defendant's guilt will on average be more likely to convict.

[66] The comment on the Areopagus may explain Aristotle's statement that this body "forbids talk about non-essentials" (*Politics* 1354a).

The manner of their election was as follows: The people being called together, some selected persons were locked up in a room near the place of election, so contrived that they *could neither see nor be seen*, but could only hear the noise of the assembly without; for they decided this, as most other affairs of moment, by the shouts of the people. This done, the competitors were not brought in and presented all together, but one after another by lot, and passed in order through the assembly without speaking a word. Those who were locked up had writing-tables with them, in which they recorded and marked each shout by its loudness, without knowing in favor of which candidate each of them was made, but merely that they came first, second, third, and so forth. He who was found to have the most and loudest acclamations was declared senator duly elected. (my italics)[67]

In a study of the effect of having a screen between audition committees and applicants for positions in an orchestra, it was found that it led to a substantial increase in the hiring of female musicians.[68] The practice is somewhat similar to double-blind refereeing in scholarly journals.

Note, however, a difference among these four cases. The Areopagites and the musical audition committee were screened from certain *perceptions* that might have an undesirable impact on their choices.[69] The Spartan voters and journal referees are screened from irrelevant and possibly bias-inducing *information* about candidates or authors.[70] Both issues arise in jury cases. Although perception-screening is unlikely to be realized, the issue merits a brief discussion.

[67] The loudness of the shouting may have expressed intensity of preferences as well as the social hierarchy among the Spartans (Flaig 1993). In the crucial decision in 432 B.C. to declare war on Athens, the Spartans substituted a vote by division for shouting (Thucydides I. 87. 2). Although the ephor who proposed this procedure claimed it was used only because the outcome of the shouting was in doubt, Thucydides implies that he used it to manipulate the decision. Specifically, the "process of voting by division will have been both longer and less anonymous than voting by shouting; any coercion, be it moral or patronal, could be applied more, not less, effectively" (Lendon 2001, p. 174). If this interpretation is correct, the episode was a remote ancestor of the practice in the Constituante to substitute roll calls for vote by standing and sitting in order to apply "moral coercion" to moderate members. In that case, too, the demand for roll-call vote was sometimes justified by spurious claims that the outcome of the vote by standing and sitting was in doubt (Castaldo 1989, pp. 348–53).

[68] Goldin and Rouse (2000).

[69] Plutarch (*Camillus* XXXVI 6) offers another example of "out of sight, out of mind" in criminal proceedings: "Manlius was brought to trial, but the view from the place was a great obstacle in the way of his accusers. For the spot where Manlius had stood when he fought his night battle with the Gauls, overlooked the forum from the Capitol, and moved the hearts of the spectators to pity. Manlius himself, too, stretched out his hands toward the spot, and wept as he called to men's remembrance his famous struggle there, so that the judges knew not what to do, and once and again postponed the case. They were unwilling to acquit the prisoner of his crime when the proofs of it were so plain; and they were unable to execute the law upon him when, owing to the place of trial, his saving exploit was, so to speak, in every eye. So Camillus, sensible of all this, transferred the court outside the city to the *Peteline Grove*, whence there is no view of the Capitol."

[70] Perceptions may, to be sure, yield information. In a study discussed later, the observation by the jurors that a defendant is under armed guard may suggest an inference that he is particularly dangerous and hence likely to be guilty. By contrast, the observation that he is dressed in prison attire does not add any information to what they already know, just as the use of gruesome pictures on cigarette packs probably does not tell customers anything they did not already know about the risks of smoking.

Two perceptual bias-triggering factors are gender and race. As juries, unlike musical audition committees, do not seem to be biased against women, I limit myself to race. Following a proposal to allow anonymity of the defendant in celebrity cases,[71] the argument was subsequently extended to minority defendants.[72] In fact, whereas the former article simply argued for *name anonymity*, the latter advocates for *invisibility*, that is, for allowing the defendant to be physically absent from the courtroom throughout the trial.[73] If witnesses had to identify the defendant, they could do so through closed circuit video technology that shields the defendant from the jury. An obvious objection arises from the likelihood of "creating an inference of guilt among jurors should a defendant choose to remain anonymous or absent. Jurors may view the absence of a defendant at a trial as an indication of guilt if it is not a practice that is often followed by defendants."[74] It seems hard to imagine, however, a reform to attenuate the anti-defendant bias created by defendant anonymity by making it mandatory.

The defendant's appearance in court may also trigger bias. In a study where subjects watched videotapes of real trials, they also saw photos of the defendant in court shown in four conditions: wearing prison attire in the presence of armed security guards, wearing personal dress in the presence of guards, wearing prison attire with no guards present, and wearing personal dress with no guards present.[75] Subjects in the second and third conditions tended to be more severe (convicting for second-degree murder rather than manslaughter) than those in the first and last condition.[76] American courts have in fact decided that compelling an individual to appear in prison attire violates his or her right to a fair trial.[77] Similarly, a "judge may decide not to allow a jury to see photographs of an accident victim, or pictures of the victim's surviving children, because it might arouse too much sympathy."[78]

I now turn to the question of *information* to be withheld from jurors. It is not here a question, as it was in the previous section, of excluding jurors who possess specific information, but of preventing already selected jurors from obtaining it.

---

[71] Morris (2003).

[72] Note (2005)

[73] If he or she has a characteristic given name or family name indicating ethnic origins, that might also have to be withheld. It is currently widely discussed whether a CV for a job application ought to be anonymized in a similar way. In France, this reform is part of the program of the Socialist Party. A recent study concludes that this measure would be counterproductive, however, since it appears that firms are more willing to overlook spelling errors and gaps in the applicant's record if they know his or her social background (*Le Monde*, August 17, 2011).

[74] Note (2005), p. 1159.

[75] Fontaine and Kiger (1978).

[76] The authors suggest that *sympathy* explains why the two biasing factors (prison attire and guards) cancel each other when both are present, rather than reinforcing each other.

[77] Kassin and Wrightsman (1988), p. 102. By contrast, the Supreme Court denied the prejudicial impact of armed guards (ibid.).

[78] Ibid., p. 108. See below for the idea that visual information might *improve* decisions.

In one case – knowledge about jury nullification – both mechanisms can come into play.

Legislators or judges may prevent jurors from obtaining information for two reasons: to induce other agents to behave in socially desirable ways, even at the expense of a good decision in the given case, or to increase the likelihood of a good decision in the given case.

Concerning the first reason, the best-known example is perhaps the ban on the fruit of the poisoned tree. In a given case, illegally obtained evidence might provide useful information to the jury, but over time banning such evidence will dissuade law enforcement agents from seeking to obtain it. Another example concerns the question whether, in an action for injuries caused by a deficient product, a subsequent improvement of the product is evidence of negligence in the original fabrication. "Evidence law ... forbids a jury from learning this information under the theory that if 'subsequent remedial measures' can be used against those who improve products after accidents occur, they will make fewer improvements."[79] Finally, "evidence that a party offered an out-of-court settlement is inadmissible to prove liability ... because ... 'individuals would be reluctant to negotiate compromises if they knew evidence about their offers could be used against them in a court.'"[80]

Concerning the second reason, I begin with information about the law. Perhaps the most important concerns nullification. In theory, Anglo-American jurors are supposed to be finders of fact only, and to leave the law to the judge. In an apparent paradox, which is at the heart of the jury system, they are also allowed to decide according to their conscience or, in France, "intimate conviction."[81] Since jurors may not be aware of their power of nullification, the question arises whether the judge is allowed to tell them, forbidden to tell them, or obliged to tell them.[82] In *United States v. Dougherty* (1972), the court found, in paraphrase, that "nullification may occasionally be a good thing, but jurors definitely ought not to be informed of this option." The court "expressed a preference for *sua sponte* nullification by the naïve jurors."[83] In the words of the court itself, the "explicit avowal [of nullification] risks the ultimate logic of anarchy." In Indiana and Maryland, however, judges are required to tell jurors about nullification upon the request of the defendant.

In Canada, "case law has established that it is a legal error to inform the jury about possible punishment prior to its verdict of guilt on any charge."[84] The

---

[79] Jonakait (2003), p. 189. Earlier reasoning on the topic was more confused, and some American states did admit subsequent changes as evidence of prior negligence (Thayer 1900, pp. 229–31).

[80] Lempert and Salzburg (1977), p. 187, as cited by Thompson and Fuqua (1998), p. 437.

[81] Green (1985) is the classical exposition of nullification in English law. Overviews of the American situation include Scheflin and Van Dyke (1979–80) and Horowitz (2007–08). The French developments are described in Esmein (1913) and in Donovan (2010).

[82] He obviously cannot instruct them not to use their power to nullify, for in so doing he would inform them that they have it.

[83] The paraphrase is that of Horowitz (2007–08), p. 434.

[84] Vidmar (2000b), p. 220.

same principle is found in a number of American states.[85] More frequently, jurors are told to ignore the issue of sentencing when deliberating on the verdict. This mental compartmentalization is probably impossible. In fact, the belief of the jurors that if found guilty the defendant would incur an unreasonably severe sentence has always been among the main causes of nullification, leading to acquittal or a reduced charge. In the United States, the problem takes the form of "death qualification" for jurors in capital cases. In *Lockhart v. McCree* (1986), the Supreme Court accepted that state courts could exclude jurors who were absolutely opposed to the death penalty, even while accepting (at least for the sake of argument) that death-qualified juries were more prone to convict than non-death-qualified juries. "In an ideal world we might be able to cope with the conviction proneness of the death-qualified jury by having one jury selected to decide guilt without death qualification questions. Then, if guilt is found, a second jury would be death qualified to decide on the sentencing."[86]

In England, "the jury is told to deliberate under a unanimity rule, but after a period of time, typically around two hours, it is informed that a majority of ten is sufficient."[87] A similar principle was used in France under the Directory,[88] except that the law (19 Fructidor of year V) did not say that the jurors have to be kept ignorant about the post-deadline majority until the deadline expires. The rationale for the ignorance is presumably that jurors will deliberate more seriously if they believe they all have to agree. Although this piece of judicial hypocrisy may seem innocent, it may undermine the respect of the jurors for the court if they see through it. It seems likely, in fact, that in many cases at least one juror out of twelve would be aware of the rule and inform the others about it.

I now turn to factual knowledge that is to be kept from the jurors. In two American states, they are not be told about a defendant's refusal to take a blood test, lest they draw a conclusion that is unfavorable to the defendant.[89] In American criminal cases, "the criminal record of the defendant who does not testify generally cannot be made available to juries as evidence of his or her propensity to commit such acts. While a defendant with such a record may be more likely to have committed the offense currently charged, the probative value of this information is seen as outweighed by its potential prejudicial effect."[90]

---

[85] Diamond, Casper, and Ostergren (1989), p. 249.

[86] Vidmar and Hans (2007), p. 255. They add, "For administrative and financial reasons, a two-jury plan is not usually feasible, but even it were, the problems of the death-proneness of the sentencing jury would persist."

[87] Vidmar (2000a), p. 31. Stephen (1883), vol. 1, p. 305, writes that "it has been often suggested that after a certain time the verdict of a minority [*sic*] should be taken, as for instance, that the verdict of eleven should be taken after one hour, and that of nine after three hours." He objects that it seems perverse to require unanimity for guilt in easy cases but not in difficult ones, and proposes that the unanimity requirement should at most be relaxed for acquittals.

[88] Esmein (1913), p. 464.

[89] Voas et al. (2009).

[90] Diamond, Casper, and Ostergren (1989), p. 249. In most Continental European jurisdictions, such evidence is admissible (Jackson and Kovalev 2006, pp. 110–11). In earlier English law, it may have not been "thought feasible to apply a rule of exclusion to past conviction evidence, since

The Federal Rules of Evidence allows, however, evidence about a prior record to be used to assess the credibility of a defendant who does testify.[91]

In civil cases, jurors are not supposed to know "(1) that a plaintiff who bears 50 percent of the responsibility for his or her losses will be barred from any recovery; (2) that the defendant carries liability insurance; (3) that the parties have arranged for payment of attorneys' fees; (4) that the award may not be subject to taxation; (5) that original parties to the suit have settled; (6) that settlement offers have been rejected; (7) that repairs were made following an accident; and (8) that a jury award in a private antitrust suit is by statute automatically tripled by the court."[92] In tort cases, one may use a "bifurcated" trial in which the jury first awards compensatory damages on the basis of evidence about the severity of the plaintiff's injury and subsequently imposes punitive damages on the basis of evidence about the defendant's reprehensibility. If all the evidence is presented at once, as it is in a "unitary" trial, the award of compensatory damages may be contaminated by evidence of reprehensibility.[93] Although bifurcated trials prevent this risk, they will not prevent punitive damages from being contaminated by evidence about severity. To avoid that risk, the decisions would have to be made by two separate juries.

In general, it is no doubt possible to keep such facts from the jurors, except if one juror accidentally happens to know them (they are usually not *secrets*). What happens, however, when jurors are *instructed to ignore* information presented to them? Jurors may be told to ignore a defendant's criminal record for the purpose of determining guilt, while being allowed to take account of it in assessing credibility. When a juror is dismissed after the jury has begun to deliberate and an alternate juror is added, California judges are required "to instruct the jury to forget their prior deliberation."[94] When "lawyers are slow to object to an improper question, allowing the witness to present inadmissible testimony before the objection is sustained," jurors are told to ignore what they just heard.[95] Intuitively, it makes little sense that jurors will abide by these instructions.

---

already-branded defendants carried their thumbs into court" (Langbein 1978, p. 304). He adds that "the judges could have devised, had they cared to, a routine that would have kept defendants' hands out of jurors' sight." It would indeed have be a routine, that is, applied to branded and nonbranded defendants alike.

[91] These two principles seem somewhat inconsistent, as the first denies and the second presupposes the existence of stable cross-situational character traits: a past robbery allows the inference to a propensity to lie, but not the inference to a propensity to commit robberies. Judges used to authorize jurors to make an inference from a past lie to a propensity to lie ("falsus in uno, falsus in omnibus"), but this practice seems to be on the wane (see endnote 2 to 239 F.3d 120, 2nd Cir. 2000). On the existence of consistent character traits, see Elster (2007), ch. 10 and the writings by Mischel, Ross, and Nisbett, and Doris cited therein.

[92] Diamond, Casper, and Ostergren (1989), pp. 249–50.

[93] See, for instance, Adams and Bourgeois (2006).

[94] Golding and Long (1998), p. 63.

[95] Thompson and Fuqua (1998), p. 440. Even if the witness is not allowed to answer, the suggestion implied by the question may bias the jurors (Kassin and Wrightsman 1988, p. 77).

Might a judge also instruct the jury to ignore the evidence of their eyes? In a recent Florida murder trial, the judge ruled, at the request of the defense, that the defendant's tattoos, including a swastika on his neck, be cosmetically hidden during the trial.[96] According to the lawyer, "There's no doubt in my mind – without the makeup being used, there's no way a jury could look at [the defendant] and judge him fairly." The director of the state attorney's office claimed that the judge could just as easily have instructed the jury to ignore the tattoos. "We believe the jurors listen to judges' instructions," he said, adding that the judge might have ruled to allow the "cosmetic assistance" with an eye to the appeals court. Thus either the judge may not have believed the jurors would obey the instructions to ignore or he thought an appeals court might not believe they had obeyed the orders.

Qualms on this score go back at least to 1786, when the counsel for the defense in an English trial told the judge, "My Lord, I am not fond of the jury hearing what they are afterwards told to forget."[97] Even earlier, Montaigne observed that "there is nothing which stamps anything so vividly on our memory as the desire not to remember it."[98] There is by now a considerable literature confirming the intuition that instructions to ignore have little effect and may even be counterproductive. The findings do not all point in the same direction, but "in most ... experiments, the judge's admonishment either did not have the intended curative effect or produced a paradoxical boomerang effect."[99]

Scholars have offered (at least) five explanations for these effects. First, and most trivially, the instructions may be unintelligible. Fearing that the decision might be reversed on appeal, judges are often talking, in highly technical language, to the appellate court rather than to the jurors.[100] Second, juries may be more concerned with accuracy than with due process.[101] Third, there is evidence that what looks like a harmless error in a trial may have effects that cannot be corrected later by telling jurors to ignore it, because the error may have excited other nodes in a cognitive network.[102] Fourth, there is the "Montaigne effect" or the "white bear effect":[103] trying to forget or to ignore something merely stamps it more vividly on your memory. Finally, being *told* to ignore something easily triggers *reactance*, the tendency to rebel against a perceived loss of autonomy.[104]

---

[96] *New York Times*, December 6, 2010, p. A18.

[97] Langbein (2003), p. 250. Citing Damaska (1997), p. 50, he refers to this problem as how to "unbite the apple of knowledge."

[98] Montaigne (1991), p. 551.

[99] Kassin and Studebaker (1998), p. 424.

[100] For the general incomprehensibility to laymen of judge instructions, see Ogloff and Rose (2005). A sample of the instructions to the jury in the O. J. Simpson criminal trial (Thompson and Fugua 1998, pp. 447–48) provides a bizarre illustration. The consequence can be "judicial nullification" of the law: "Judges who rail against jury nullification and then offer juries incomprehensible instructions are kidding someone, perhaps including themselves" (Saks 1997, p. 35).

[101] Kassin and Studebaker (1998), p. 424.

[102] Simon (2004), drawing on Thagard (1989).

[103] Wegner (1989).

[104] Brehm (1966).

Patients sometimes refrain from taking their medications because they are *told* to take them.[105] Similarly, it seems that jurors often put more weight on evidence when instructed to ignore it.[106] If one of the first three mechanisms is operating, we should expect little or no effect; if the fourth or fifth is involved, we should expect the opposite of the intended effect.

IV. JURY DELIBERATION AND VOTING

The choice between secrecy and publicity, or between ignorance and knowledge, can arise at many stages in the proceedings of a jury. Look at the following choices:

- Whether the jury foreperson is chosen by a secret or public procedure
- Whether jurors are allowed to communicate among themselves
- Whether jury deliberations are recorded
- Whether participants in a jury trial have to give reasons for their decisions
- Whether jurors are allowed to reveal their deliberations to the outside world
- Whether voting is open or secret
- When unanimity is not required, whether the number of votes is revealed
- Whether the votes of individual jurors are revealed

In some of these issues one also needs to specify the *audience* to which these facts may or may not be revealed. Thus with public voting, the jurors will know who voted how, but nobody else will know. With secret voting, no one but the juror will know how she voted. Also, the *time* (if any) at which the facts may be revealed can be important.

Choice of Foreperson

A jury foreperson can shape the outcome *directly*, by the views she expresses, or *indirectly*, by the procedures she proposes. Concerning the direct influence, several studies find a correlation between the foreperson's predeliberation award preferences in civil cases and the final decision.[107] Because the foreperson also tends to speak more than other jurors, especially in large juries that heighten the fear of talking in front of an audience,[108] this correlation may well reflect a causal influence. Concerning the indirect influence, the foreperson may propose that the jury vote by secret ballot, in jurisdictions where that procedure is neither mandatory (as it is in France) nor forbidden (as it is in Norway). Alternatively, she may propose "going around the table" (and impose the order in which the votes are taken) or a simultaneous show of hands. In some

---

[105] Fogarty (1997).
[106] Lieberman and Sales (1997), pp. 607–8; Kassin and Studebaker (1998), p. 422. Jurors may also react against judges who insist too strongly on the guilt of the accused (Gilbert 1986, pp. 103–4).
[107] Devine et al. (2001), p. 696
[108] Boster, Hunter, and Hale (1991).

cases, the foreperson decides by "apparent consensus,"[109] that is, by the absence of opposition to the decision she proposes.

The methods used for selecting a foreperson are as varied as the methods she may propose for reaching the decision. A piece of advice to the defending counsel in American jury trials lays out some options:

Methods of determining who will be the foreperson vary from jurisdiction to jurisdiction, e.g., the judge may select the foreperson, the jurors may chose one of their number as foreperson by selection or election, the first juror to enter the jury box may automatically become the foreperson. The judge will inform the jurors which method is used.... If the jurors are left to their own devices, they may nominate and select the first person, particularly if standing while the others are seated, who says, "We've got to pick a foreperson," the person who seats him/herself at the head of the rectangular table (it's usually rectangular, rather than round as it should be to promote equal and face-to-face discussion), the person who volunteers by self-nomination, or the person who has been given the single copy of the jury instructions by the court bailiff who acts as jury shepherd. [Note: Be aware of the pro-prosecution ploy of having the bailiff nominate the jury foreperson by giving the court's jury charge to a juror the bailiff, a courtroom law enforcement officer who has observed the trial, deems to be leaning toward the prosecution. Defenders should prevent this unfairness by moving the court to order that the official copy of the instructions be placed in the center of the jury table before the jurors enter the deliberation room. Another alternative is to ask that each juror be given a copy of the court's instructions, preferably at the jury instruction stage of the case.][110]

The foreperson is rarely chosen by lot, except on an optional basis.[111] Although the *diversity rationale* for random selection applies to the choice of jurors, it is obviously irrelevant for the choice of a foreperson among the jurors. By contrast, the *anti-manipulation rationale* may well be relevant, as suggested by the bracketed statement in the quoted passage. To my knowledge, Norway is the only country today that chooses the foreperson by secret ballot, with ties broken by lottery. The system was also used in Germany before World War I, with ties broken by age.[112] In the literature on foreperson choice I have not come across any references to *open and competitive* elections, with more than one candidate. The general impression is that elections are done by acclamation, often preceded by self-nomination.[113]

Self-nomination is the most common procedure. An advantage of this procedure is that it tends to promote active aptitude (see Chapter 3). Against this, an assertive and domineering self-nominated person might not allow a sufficient

[109] Urfalino (2007).
[110] Moses (2009).
[111] In France after 1848, the jury "chooses a foreman, or chef des jurés, but, in default of any such choice, the first called into the jury-box by lot acts as foreman" (Forsyth 1873, p. 304). The same optional arrangement currently exists in Belgium.
[112] Howard (1904), p. 664.
[113] Often, a person sitting at one of the short ends of a non-square rectangular table is chosen as foreperson. Since "it also turns out that jurors of higher status naturally tend to take more prominent seats" (Kassin and Wrightsman 1988, p. 178), the seating is endogenous rather than random.

diversity of opinions to be expressed. Small-group psychology indicates that groups with randomly selected leaders perform better than groups with leaders who are designated (or are believed by the group members to have been designated) on the basis of their responses to a questionnaire.[114] Yet selection by lot (or by age) might lead to an unsuitable person being chosen. A judge-appointed foreman might reflect the prejudices of the judge.[115] The Norwegian solution does not seem to have any of these flaws and arguably also favors active aptitude.

Communication Among the Jurors

It might seem obvious that jurors ought be allowed to discuss before they vote. Under a regime of voting by secret ballot without prior deliberation, jurors "would not have to construct defensible and convincing positions from the evidence.... The evidence would have less primacy, allowing extralegal factors more play."[116] A study comparing deliberating mock juries with non-deliberating mock jurors found that the former were "more likely to restrain the desire to simply ignore unpopular judicial instructions when deciding on a verdict."[117] I now survey two cases in which deliberation was not allowed.

In classical Athens, the large jury – at least 201 jurors – heard the arguments against and in favor of the accused before deciding on a verdict and (when the penalty was not determined by statute) a sentence. According to Aristotle (*Politics* 1268b), "most lawgivers" – presumably also the Athenian ones – forbade jurors to confer with one another. In his example, the reasoning applies mainly to the sentencing stage. He argues that in a very large jury it would be technically impossible to reach a compromise agreement on, say, the exact fine to be imposed. Hence the jury was constrained to a kind of "final-offer arbitration," that is, to choose between the sentence proposed by the accuser and that proposed by the defense. Yet this argument does not seem to apply to the *verdict* stage. Although it would clearly be impossible for *all* the jurors to express and exchange opinions, that would not have been an obstacle to debate. After all, in the Athenian assembly an average of 6,000 citizens did make decisions after listening to debates among (a subset of) themselves. The fear of demagoguery could hardly have been a reason for excluding debates, since, as Aristotle's

---

[114] Haslam et al. (1998); Henningsen et al. (2004). The latter authors suggest reactance as an explanation of this phenomenon. Neither study explicitly focuses on juries. Blinder and Morgan (2008) finds that "mock Central Bank Committees" with leaders selected on the basis of a good performance on a previous task similar to the one the group was to perform did not do better than groups without a designated leader.

[115] Horwitz (2004–05).

[116] Jonakait (2003), p. 232.

[117] Kerwin and Shaffer (1994), p. 159. Sunstein et al. (2002) p. 57, find that deliberating juries tend to "decide on an award that exceeds the initial judgment of its median member – and sometimes the highest predeliberation judgment of all its members." As the latter authors point out (ibid., p. 58), the effect may be due either to (presumably desirable) "informational influences" or to (presumably undesirable) "social influences," leaving it indeterminate whether on the whole deliberation improves the decision.

Rhetoric shows, the speakers for and against the accused engaged extensively in such practices.

The Athenian juries also decided by secret ballot. The only other jury regime known to me that forbids discussion among the jurors also uses the secret ballot. This is the Brazilian regime, described as follows:

At the end of the trial, the jury, the judge and the attorneys all go into the jury room. There, the judge presents the jury with narrowly drafted questions that will determine the outcome of the case. The jury votes by secretly placing small Yes or No cards in a basket. No deliberation is allowed. Indeed, in contrast to the common law's tradition of juror deliberation, *it is the height of misconduct and cause for a mistrial for one juror to make his or her voting intentions known or attempt to persuade another juror*. The questions move from the more general ("did a death occur") to the more specific ("did this defendant cause the death"), gradually guiding the process toward the final outcome. The results of each round are announced before the next round, so that the decision is built piece-meal, without deliberation but with information about the previous decisions made by fellow jurors. Like the secret ballot box, the voting method does not require jurors to identify, explain or justify their decisions, giving them full freedom to act on their individual judgments about the case – and on their prejudices and preconceptions.[118]

This regime, which has been in operation since 1822, is currently limited to cases of homicide, infanticide, and instigation to suicide. I refrain from speculating about the motivation behind the principle that an attempt to persuade another juror can give rise to a mistrial (but see Condorcet's argument against deliberation cited in Chapter 3). It does seem somewhat logical, though, that once *influence by words* has been banned, *influence by action*, in the form of seriatim voting in public, should also be prohibited. Although, as we shall see in the next chapter, public voting need not take a form in which it can influence others, the main rationale for what I shall call ex post publicity is to create pressure for consistency between words and action. If no words are allowed, that rationale fails.

Although modern jurors – outside Brazil – are always allowed to talk among themselves, they are never to my knowledge *obliged* to express their opinion. The "silent juror" certainly exists. If the vote is taken by secret ballot, the idea of silence should be expanded to include "cheap talk." In a recent trial, "only one juror stood between the death penalty and Zacarias Moussaoui and that juror frustrated his colleagues because he never explained his vote, according to the foreman of the jury that sentenced the al-Qaeda operative to life in prison last week."[119] Not only did he not explain his vote, but also, as the vote was secret, he never identified himself. Although "the other jurors were relying on the discussions to identify the holdout," they were not able to. The holdout may not have been literally silent, but any opinion he or she expressed must have been insincere. Although this example has been used to argue for nonunanimous jury verdicts,[120] it could also be used as an argument for public voting.

---

[118] Brinks (2004); my italics.
[119] *Washington Post*, May 12, 2006.
[120] Holland (2006).

Recording Jury Deliberations

From some perspectives, it might be desirable to record the deliberations of the jury. One could ascertain how well the jurors understood the instructions from the judge; whether bias, pressure, or conformism seems to have operated; and a host of other interesting matters. As I noted earlier, such knowledge might put jury reform on a firmer basis. If possible, one might also want to compare two regimes, one in which jurors knew that their deliberations were being recorded and might or would be made public, and one in which they were unaware of recording equipment. One purpose would be to verify the presence or absence of the often-alleged chilling effect, according to which jurors would be more reluctant to engage in freewheeling and sometimes productive debates if they knew they were being recorded. As noted earlier, it has been argued that this effect was observed in a unique natural experiment involving debates in the Open Market Committee of the Federal Reserve Board.[121]

For a number of reasons, a similar study of the jury system is hard to imagine.

As part of the groundwork for the pioneering book by Kalven and Zeisel, *The American Jury*, researchers at the University of Chicago tape-recorded the deliberation of juries in six civil cases, with the consent of the judge and counsel for both sides, but without the jurors' knowledge. When this fact became known, there was a general outcry, leading first to Senate hearings and later to federal and state legislation prohibiting the recording of jury deliberations. In the opinion of Senator Jenner of the subcommittee of the Senate Judiciary Committee, the knowledge that jury deliberations may be recorded "must color the thinking of all juries from now on until appropriate action has been taken to insure that this eavesdropping on jurors will not recur in any single instance."[122] In his testimony Harry Kalven denied that recording would tend to have a chilling effect: "With the consent of the attorneys and with the consent of the judge, and for scientific purposes, a few juries may from time to time be recorded. I see no reason why that should strike any fear in the heart of any juror in America."[123]

In 1997, CBS made video recordings of three criminal jury cases, with the consent of the parties (attorneys and judges) as well of the jurors. Because jurors who did not want to speak on camera were excused, the procedure introduced a self-selection bias that may have affected the deliberations as well as the verdict. Also, the fact that two of the three trials ended in hung juries "might indicate that the presence of cameras in the jury room caused jurors to harden their positions and be more reluctant to compromise."[124] As a possibly more acceptable form of publicity,

---

[121] Meade and Stasavage (2008).

[122] U.S. Senate (1956), p. 1.

[123] Ibid., p. 7. In the Senate hearings, it was implicitly assumed that the behavior of the attorneys and judges would not be affected by their knowledge that, unbeknownst to the jurors, the deliberations were being recorded. This assumption may well be justified. Yet given a well-known dictum from lawyer folklore, "in the face of a weak case, confusion is good," one can at least wonder whether a lawyer for the defense would be as willing to spread confusion if the effects of his obfuscation could be recorded for subsequent scrutiny.

[124] Abramovsky (1996).

one could make transcripts of jury deliberation available after the verdict and before appeal.[125] In an analogy with some central bank committees, one might also publish anonymized minutes rather than verbatim transcripts that name the speakers. Yet in the absence of recorded cases in which the jury not only ignored that they *were* being taped, but also that they *might be* taped, there are no empirical grounds for asserting the superiority or inferiority of the secret regime.

Giving Reasons

Under this heading, I shall discuss not only the fact that juries have usually not been required to give reasons for their decisions, but also the fact that prosecution and defense have usually not been compelled to give reasons for peremptory challenges. Although the second fact logically belongs in an earlier section of this chapter, I discuss it here because of a conjecture – far from proved – that the two facts may have the same rationale.

On a common view, accurate decision making is enhanced by *deliberation based on propositions* rather than by *intuition based on perceptions*.[126] When we have to decide whether to trust a person, we should not go by our gut feelings, prompted perhaps by his facial features or his resemblance to a fifth-grade bully, but take the time to gather and process information about his past behavior.

According to the "theory of unconscious thought,"[127] however, we can sometimes do better if we rely on perceptions rather than on evidence in propositional form, and if we leave the processing to our unconscious rather than our conscious mind. In a 2 (visual vs. written information) times 2 (conscious vs. unconscious processing) experiment, the subjects were presented with description of a real legal case and asked to give a judgment. It was found (1) that "participants in the unconscious thought condition were able to make the most accurate judgment about the legal case when asked to indicate who of the parties involved should pay for which part of the damage," independent of the kind of information they received, and (2) that "participants in the conscious thought condition made less-accurate damage judgments when they had been presented with [visual] information but not when presented with [written] information."[128] The claims are

---

[125] Ruprecht (1997).

[126] This everyday idea is akin to the distinction proposed by psychologists between System-1 and System-2 processing (see, for instance, Alter et al. 2007; Kahneman 2011). As this distinction is hard to nail down, and comes in many versions, I shall not rely on it here.

[127] The following draws on Dijksterhuis et al. (2006), Dijksterhuis and Nordgren (2006), Dijksterhuis and van Olden (2006), Hastie (2008), Ham, van den Boos, and van Doorn (2009), and Ham and van den Bos (2010). Hastie, an authority on jury decisions, is skeptical about the value of the framework in this context. My own attitude is agnostic. The issues seem worth exploring, but at this stage it would be foolhardy to base jury reform on the reported findings.

[128] Ham and van den Bos (2010), p. 185. I have substituted "visual" and "written" for their "direct" and "indirect." In the conscious and unconscious conditions, subjects were asked to give their judgments three minutes after the information was presented. (There was also a third condition in which subjects had to answer immediately.) Unconscious processing was induced by asking subjects to answer after performing a distracting task for three minutes. The visual information was

that the unconscious is superior because of its greater capacity,[129] and that "conscious thinkers will incorrectly weigh [visual] information" because of its salience.[130] In a related scholarly tradition, it has been found that people make worse decisions when they are required to give reasons for them.[131] They can obviously state only the reasons to which they have conscious access, which may be a biased subset of all the reasons they have.

These arguments, if correct, could provide a rationale for peremptory challenges. Supreme Court Justices have protected these on the grounds that they allow "the covert expression of what we dare not say but know is true more often than not" (Chief Justice Burger in *Batson v. Kentucky*) or permit "rejection for a real or imagined partiality that is less easily designated or demonstrable" (Justice White in *Swain v. Alabama*). These somewhat murky statements also suggest, however, an obvious objection to the claim of the superiority of unconscious processing. Implicit association tests show that many biases are held unconsciously.[132] As biases are often unjustified, we should beware of trusting our gut feelings.[133] *The anti-defendant bias of a prosecutor may lead her to an unjustified assumption of a pro-defendant bias in a potential juror.* This risk may offset the risk that a prosecutor or defense attorney who is limited to challenges for cause might be constrained by the fact that they have access only to their conscious reasons.

I now turn to the more central issue of reason-giving by juries or jurors. For centuries, the right (and duty) of juries to decide without giving reasons for their decisions has been uncontested. It is often linked to the fact that, strictly speaking, there can be no appeal from a jury verdict, since an "appeal, properly so called, implies a judgment on the part of the court appealed from and an argument to show that it decided wrongly, which cannot be unless the *reasons* of the decisions are known."[134] This right has not always existed, however, and has recently become less absolute than in the past.

The very idea of *the* reason for a collective decision is, as we saw in Chapter 1, inherently fragile. In the case of the jury, "it will frequently be true that not all members of the group will have reached the joint decision for the same reason."[135] For instance, in a suit for damages, "Juror A may rate pain and suffering more important than Juror B, and Juror B may take disability as more substantial

presented by photographs of appalling wounds suffered by a horse in an accident, and the written information by a veterinarian's description of the same wounds. The accuracy was assessed by comparing the judgment of the subjects with the decision by an arbitrator in the actual legal case. Given the argument of the authors, that accuracy criterion seems questionable.

[129] Dijksterhuis et al. (2006).
[130] Ham and van den Bos (2010), pp. 181–82.
[131] Wilson and Schooler (1991). Conscious thinking can presumably take place without giving explicit reasons, but not conversely.
[132] See, for instance, Greenwald, McGhee, and Schwartz (1998); Greenwald and Krieger (2006). Using this method, Eisenberg and Johnson (2004) find bias in defense lawyers and Rachlinski et al. (2008) in judges.
[133] Biased beliefs are always unjustified in the sense that they are not justified by the *evidence*. They can still correspond to the *facts*, however.
[134] Stephen (1883), vol. 1, p. 568; my italics. We shall see, however, that in contemporary legal practice appeals can also be based on the answers of juries to the questions put to them.
[135] Kalven and Zeisel (1966), p. 87.

than Juror A. They will air these differences, to be sure, in the deliberation but they will not insist on their resolution so long as by whatever route they can agree on the overall sum."[136] In a criminal trial, one juror may disbelieve one witness and another juror a different one, but if the veracity of both witnesses is essential to the case, they will reach the same conclusion. If, as in *Taxquet v. Belgium* (discussed later), the demand for reasons is grounded in the desire of a convicted defendant to know the reasons of the *jury*, it might be difficult to come up with an answer that would satisfy him. One could only offer him the reasons of the *jurors*. In that case, as we saw in Chapter 1, he might theoretically be able to claim that aggregation of these reasons should have led to his acquittal.[137]

Historically the demand for reasons came from the judge. In early English law, "the judge could ... discover the reasons for a proffered verdict when the jury returned from deliberations, because in many cases the jury either volunteered the information or supplied it under questioning by the judge."[138] When a 19th-century English jury issued a nonbinding recommendation of mercy, it was "usual to ask for the reason of the recommendation."[139] By and large, these practices seem to have been rare.

Today, the demand for reasons may either come from the defendant or be justified by the needs of appellate courts. In *Taxquet v. Belgium*, the defendant argued that his right "to be informed in detail of the nature and cause of the accusation against him ... should also extend to the cause of his conviction."[140] In Spain, the only country in which the jury has to give reasons for its decision, this requirement was motivated both by Art. 120. 3 of the Spanish Constitution ("reasons shall be given for all criminal judgments") and by the argument that the jury "has to state its reasons so that a reasonable appellate procedure can be facilitated."[141] In other European countries, both the rights of the defendant and the facilitation of appeal are thought to be safeguarded if the questions put to the jury are sufficiently numerous and specific. In *France v. Papon*, for instance, the jury had to answer 768 questions. By contrast, in *Taxquet v. Belgium*, the Grand Chamber of the European Court of Human Rights found that both the formulaic character of the questions and the laconic nature of the answers violated the right of the defendant to a fair trial. The

---

[136] Kalven (1958), p. 176.

[137] The draft of the Spanish Jury Law of 1995 "allowed for dissenting jurors to give their reasons as well.... The provision was removed following a critique ... that it would violate the secrecy of jury deliberations" (Thaman 1998, p. 364). Dissenting opinions could, however, have been anonymized. Another possible explanation is that the drafters became aware of the doctrinal paradox.

[138] Langbein (1978), p. 289. The five examples he goes on to cite all seem to involve volunteering. As he refers to "numerous case reports" (ibid., p. 290), I assume that others did involve questioning by the judge. In the "Arrowsmith case" that he discusses at some length (ibid., pp. 291–95), the jury volunteered their reasons for acquitting whereupon the judge harassed them until they returned a verdict of guilty.

[139] Stephen (1883), vol. 1, p. 562.

[140] ECHR (2010), §66.

[141] Thaman (1998), p. 365.

Court did not say, however, that the defendant had a right to learn the reasons for his conviction *from the jury*.

An important study of the "overwhelming majority of the seventy-five to eighty cases" of jury trials in Spain from May 1996 to June 1997 shows that the idea of "giving reasons" can be understood in very different ways.[142] In some cases, the reasons were perfunctory, in one case limited to a single word: "witnesses." In other cases, reasons were provided that have been "described as vacillating between the tautological and the unintelligible." Two Spanish scholars found "a restatement of conclusions in lieu of reasons" in 7 of the 17 verdicts they studied. In many cases, however, the juries gave detailed answers that, in some cases, included inferences they drew from the evidence presented in the court. Some reasons were, however, incompatible with the verdict the jury had reached. In one case where the jury found the defendant guilty, "its reasons seemed to show that it did not understand that it had acquitted the defendant." I take this to mean that the *reasons* they offered as premises implied a different verdict from the conclusion they reached (see Chapter 1)

The case material is extensive and fascinating. Rather than going into more detail, I conclude with two general observations. First, some legal scholars thought that the need to give reasons might shape the verdict in undesirable ways: "a 'yes' answer could, through its reasoned justification, turn into a qualified 'no,' or vice versa." An "intimate conviction" may prove too elusive to be spelled out in explicit terms. According to the psychological studies of unconscious thought cited earlier, that fact would not show that it is unreliable; on the contrary. Second, in many of the trials, the jury asked for the assistance of a legally trained secretary in drafting their reasons. For some observers, this fact indicates that the Spanish jury is de facto moving toward a mixed jury of laymen and magistrates.

Revealing the Deliberations

The jury secrecy rule, which prohibits courts, newspapers, or private individuals from receiving or soliciting information from jurors after the verdict, is widely adopted outside the United States. The main arguments for the rule cite the chilling effect on free deliberation that could occur if the jurors knew that their discussions might become public, the need for a finality of the verdict, and the legitimacy of the jury system. In addition, a juror might be harassed if it became known that she had argued for the guilt of the accused or, in civil cases, for or against the plaintiff. Just as random selection and one-off duty are guarantees against ex ante pressure, secrecy of the proceedings provides ex post protection. Jury nullification might also be jeopardized if the proceedings were not secret.[143]

The main argument against complete jury secrecy has always been that juries are prone to mistakes, because of incompetence, normative prejudices, or

---

[142] The following draws on Thaman (1998), pp. 364–80.
[143] On all these points and several others I refer to a Note in *Harvard Law Review* (1983), Campbell (1985), Ruprecht (1997–98), Markovitz (2000–01), Daly (2004), Hoeffel (2005), and Courselle (2005–06).

cognitive biases. If unjustified acquittals were the main danger, these mistakes might be seen as an acceptable cost of the system. Although it is hard to speak with any quantitative precision, we should not ignore that juries can also produce unjustified convictions. In England, the House of Lords has recently had the opportunity to consider the matter in the conjoined appeals of *R v Mirza* and *R v Connor and Rollock*:

In both cases, the appellants were convicted following a majority verdict. After the trial, a member of the jury sent a letter to defence counsel (*Mirza*) and the trial judge (*Connor*) alleging impropriety on the part of the jury. The defendant in *Mirza* was a Pakistani man who had resided in the United Kingdom for 13 years. He used an interpreter at the trial, and following queries from the jury, the judge gave a direction that no adverse inference should be drawn from this. The letter sent by the juror suggested a failure to follow this direction (the jury believing the use of the interpreter to be a "devious ploy") and racial bias. In *Connor*, the defendants were convicted following a joint trial. The letter suggested that the jury had failed to consider the evidence properly (they were looking for a "quick verdict") and had convicted both defendants when they were uncertain which of them was guilty. The Court of Appeal dismissed both appeals, holding itself unable to admit into evidence the terms of the jurors' letter.[144]

In a dissent to the dismissal of the appeal by the House of Lords, Lord Steyn "accepted that there must be a general rule of secrecy, but held that the Court of Appeal should have the power 'in exceptional cases' to examine material regarding jury deliberations. The effect of an absolute rule was that in the 1 per cent of cases tried by jury, the law was subordinating the risk of a miscarriage of justice to the interests of protecting the efficiency of the jury system. The safeguards in place did not deal with this problem and in the long run this would reduce confidence in the system."[145] This factual conjecture is the very opposite of the one that is usually made, namely, that the knowledge that jury secrecy can be breached would, in the long run, undermine the legitimacy of the system. As far as I know, there is no evidence to sustain either conjecture.

In the United States, there is no ban on jurors communicating what happened during their deliberations. Revelations of misbehavior may nevertheless fail to have an impact. After the trial of a defendant later exonerated by DNA evidence,

one juror came forward ... long before the DNA testing to say she did not support the guilty verdict. She had remained silent because there was a "lot of pressure" from other jurors. Two other jurors had voted to acquit but changed their minds. For hours, the other jurors told her that the defendant had their names and might rape their family members, and that this rapist could not go free on the streets. They took the "non guilty" forms away from her. The hold-out juror finally told them, "whatever you want to do, you go ahead and do it." She remained silent without signing the guilt verdict forms, but without objecting. The defense moved for a new trial based on these revelations. The judge denied the motion. [The defendant] was not exonerated until more than fourteen years later.[146]

---

[144] Daly (2004), p. 186.
[145] Ibid., p. 189.
[146] Garrett (2011), p. 173.

Open or Secret Voting

The vote cast by a juror may either be unknown to the other jurors, or be known to them but (disregarding illegal leaks) not to anyone else. When a jury uses public voting, it usually remains secret in the second sense, except if a unanimity requirement makes it clear that a verdict of guilty implies that all jurors voted for it. If less than unanimity is required, it is usually impossible for outsiders to identify which jurors, if any, dissented. The only exception known to me occurs in the polling of the jury in the two American states that allow for non-unanimous verdicts. In Oregon, the following is the rule: "When the verdict is given, and before it is filed, the jury may be polled on the request of a party, for which purpose each juror shall be asked whether the verdict is the juror's verdict. If fewer jurors answer in the affirmative than the number required to render a verdict, the jury shall be sent out for further deliberations." In Louisiana, the judge may at her discretion *either* poll the jurors orally *or* ask each juror to write on a slip of paper the words "Yes" or "No" along with his signature. If the jury votes by secret ballot, the Oregon procedure and the first Louisiana procedure will reveal to each juror how the others voted. The second Louisiana procedure will not.

As this observation suggests, one can combine secrecy ex ante with publicity ex post. The taking of votes can be arranged so that no juror can know, when casting her vote, how anyone else voted and yet so that all votes are known to all once they are cast. In the next chapter, I discuss Bentham's advocacy of this procedure. Here, let me note his observation that "neither the process of crying *Aye* or *No*, nor that of holding up hands, can be rendered so exactly simultaneous, but that, if the slave is *bonâ fide* upon the watch, he may wait to observe the part taken by the master's voice or hand, so that his may take the same."[147]

Also, show of hands is vulnerable to pluralistic ignorance: "Suppose a juror fears that her position is unpopular, or appears insensitive or stupid. Before raising her own hand, she will look around the room to see how many other hands are going up. Other like-minded jurors might be employing the same strategy. The result can be zero votes for a particular verdict, despite the fact that several jurors actually support it."[148] In principle, these obstacles could be overcome by asking jurors to sign their written ballots before handing them to the foreperson, who would then read the votes with names out loud. Although the votes might not strictly speaking be simultaneous, they would be unobservable by others at the time of voting.[149] As Bentham asserts, "The concealment thus recommended is not that which forms the inconvenience, where there is any, resulting from the secret mode of voting. It is only the will of the seducer that is concealed, for a moment, from the knowledge of the voter – not the conduct of

---

[147] Bentham (1999), pp. 107.
[148] Schwartz (2006).
[149] As explained by Urfalino (2010), the advisory committees to the FDA now use a system of public but simultaneous voting. Initially this was done by a show of hands, but later implemented by machine voting, presumably to eliminate any residue of the conformism that was thought to have been prevalent in the earlier system of sequential oral voting.

the voter that is concealed, at the long run, from the knowledge of the public."[150] Disregarding for a moment the reference to the public, my point here is that one may not want the conduct of the juror to be concealed, "at the long run," *from other jurors*.

To my knowledge, this obvious solution is not chosen in any jury system. It would have the double advantage of reducing irrational conformism *and* of forcing the jurors to take their task seriously. The loss of information that a juror might infer from the vote of those preceding her in a sequential vote (rational conformism) would not cause a serious problem, since most of that information would be contained in the discussion prior to the vote.

An example from Seneca (*On Mercy* I. 15) illustrates how ex ante publicity may induce conformism and invite pressure:

When Tarius was ready to open the inquiry on his son [who had plotted against him], he invited Augustus Caesar to attend the council; Augustus came to the hearth of a private citizen, sat beside him, and took part in the deliberation of another household. He did not say, "Rather, let the man come to my house"; for, if he had, the inquiry would have been conducted by Caesar and not by the father. When the case had been heard and all the evidence had been sifted – what the young fellow said in his defense, and what was brought up in accusation against him Caesar requested each man to give his verdict in writing, lest all should vote according to his lead.

In this hierarchical setting, the secrecy was optional. In other cases, it has been imposed as mandatory for similar reasons. In American court-martials, mandatory secret voting is justified by the need to insulate junior officers against pressure from their superiors.[151] Moreover, the votes are *collected* by the junior jurors, since if "the junior member collects the ballots, the senior member is less likely to see how each member voted; but if the senior member collects the ballots, then he can readily identify each member's ballot, raising the possibility that the junior members will defer to the senior member's opinion."[152]

In mixed or quasi-hierarchical juries, which contain a majority of jurors and a minority of magistrates, the secret vote may be the only way for jurors to retain some independence. A study based on interviews with French jurors[153] found

---

[150] Bentham (1999), p. 107.
[151] Holland (2006), p. 124 n. 126. The practice of anonymity prevents superior officers from knowing how junior officers vote. The court-martial practice of non-unanimous verdicts of guilt prevents the *accused* from knowing who voted against him. We may compare the trio consisting of a superior officer, an inferior officer, and the accused to the trio consisting of the book review editor of a scientific journal, a reviewer, and the author of the reviewed book. In the latter case, anonymity between editor and reviewer is obviously impossible. The past practice of anonymous book reviews in the *American Historical Review* (Novick 1988, p. 58) was intended to prevent authors from learning the identity of reviewers. At other times, the journal adopted the practice that no book should be "reviewed by a teacher, student, or colleague of the author" (ibid., p. 54). The equivalent for the court-martial jury would be to have it made up of officers of the same rank serving in different regiments, eliminating vertical pressure and reducing the risk of horizontal pressure.
[152] Ibid.
[153] Vernier (2007).

that their work is articulated around four concerns: to express an opinion, to defend it with arguments, to respond to the arguments of other jurors and the magistrates, and "to vote by secret ballot, given that a juror may write down a quite different conclusion from the one he has defended during the debates." Overt opposition to the magistrates was rare. "If jurors rebelled, they did so in the anonymity of their vote, as in the case of JS, an educator from Paris, who voted No to the question of guilt although she understood very well that he was guilty of the acts alleged against him."

Belgian juries present a variation on the French system. The question of guilt is decided by 12 jurors voting by secret ballot. Three courts magistrates can undo the verdict of guilty if it was voted by a simple majority (7 to 5). Sentencing is decided by a body of 15 – jurors and magistrates – who vote by a show of hands. In France, a body of 9 jurors and three magistrates make both decisions by secret ballot. In Belgium, both the presence of magistrates and the public voting are likely to make jurors go along with the sentencing proposed by the professional judges.

In *non-hierarchical* juries, secrecy may be valued as a means of protecting holdouts against horizontal pressure. The pressure may be especially strong when, as in almost all American criminal juries, unanimity is required. We might expect, therefore, hung juries to be more frequent under a regime of secret voting. One study, however, reports the opposite finding in mock juries. In the opinion of the authors, "being publicly identified with a position may force *early* commitment to that position and make it difficult to change one's position without appearing inconsistent or irresolute" (my italics).[154] Their study allowed the foreperson to propose successive (open or secret) ballots until unanimity was reached. Under those conditions, early public commitment may well have been conducive to hung juries. When there is only a single ballot, however, this mechanism would not operate.

When voting is public and sequential rather than simultaneous (or unobservable), *order effects* may arise. Although some path-dependence and informational cascades are inevitable under such regimes, one can try to reduce undesirable effects. The reason why the foreperson of a Norwegian jury is required to cast the last vote is presumably to minimize the importance of the juror who has already, by virtue of his position, a special influence. The German pre-1914 regime cited earlier imposed the same rule, while also requiring other jurors to cast their votes in the order in which they had been drawn from the jury

---

[154] Kerr and MacCoun (1985), p. 361. We may compare this statement with Madison's well-known comment on the Federal Convention: "had the members committed themselves publicly at first, they would have afterwards supposed consistency required them to maintain their ground, whereas by secret discussion no man felt himself obliged to retain his opinions any longer than he was satisfied of their propriety and truth, and was open to the force of argument" (Farrand 1966, vol. 3, p. 479). It seems clear, in fact, that the fear of appearing inconsistent may also shape debates in groups that deliberate in private, such as the Convention or a jury. Yet it seems plausible that the fear is larger when the speakers are exposed to an external audience (or when the group itself is large).

lottery. Although the contemporary German regime is not part of my universe of cases, the rules for the voting of the mixed bench are nevertheless interesting: "The order of voting is [the following]: first the youngest lay judge will cast their vote, then the older one. The professional judges vote after them, first the rapporteur, the others in the order of their length of service, the youngest first. The presiding judge is the last one to cast their vote. This is meant to ensure that the lay judges do not feel inhibited before the professional judges, or the younger judges before the older ones."[155]

Although regulating the order of voting by *lottery* might seem an attractive option, a passage from Cicero's *Pro Cluentia* shows that it can be risky:

At the trial, after the speeches and evidence on both sides had been heard, the votes of the jurors were given, not by ballot, but openly, at the desire of the accused, who availed himself of the option granted by a law at that time in force. Those to whom it fell by lot to vote first were men of notoriously bad character, and all of these gave a verdict of guilty, some of the more respectable and conscientious, feeling convinced that there was foul play somewhere, declined voting, five gave a verdict of not guilty, but when the votes were summed up, the accused was condemned by a majority of two.[156]

In this case the accused had the choice between secret and open voting. Perhaps one could say that he gambled on the order of voting and lost. The Roman jury seems mostly, however, to have used the secret ballot.[157] In some systems, notably in American state trials, the accused also has the choice between going before a jury or a judge. The fact that juries return guilty verdicts at a higher rate than judges do does not show that the defendants who prefer a jury are irrational, since they may have a weaker defense to begin with.

In the absence of ex post publicity, secrecy may be the source of suboptimal deliberation. "The rule that juries should vote by secret ballot would be a direct inducement to impatience, and fatal to any real discussion."[158] Moreover, the secret ballot might cause a discrepancy between words and actions. A juror might appear to go along with the perceived majority only to vote against it. (If the majority is only *perceived* to exist, as in cases of pluralistic ignorance, the majority itself might be reversed upon the vote.) By contrast, if jurors know that any such discrepancy will be revealed after the vote, they are more likely to *articulate their reasons* for voting against the majority and to change their minds if met with persuasive objections. Even though they would not incur any material sanctions when their insincerity was brought out, they might be deterred by the highly aversive idea that others would think badly of them.[159]

---

[155] Siegismund (2000), p. 123.

[156] The actual vote stood as follows. Nine jurors of unimpeachable character gave a verdict of guilty. (Some of these may have been influenced by the second group, who voted first.) Eight jurors, suspected of being venal, also gave a verdict of guilty. Five said not guilty and ten abstained.

[157] Staveley (1972), pp. 229–30.

[158] Stephen (1883,) vol. 1, p. 560.

[159] Dana, Cain, and Dawes (2006); Elster (2007), p. 368.

To discuss a further variation on the theme of ex ante secrecy with ex post publicity, I shall consider first a hypothetical case and then a historical one. In contemporary Norway, juries are (roughly speaking) made up of an equal number of men and women. Imagine a regime of this kind deciding by majority vote. Votes are taken by secret ballot, but in some cases (involving rape or battery, for instance) the total numbers of female and male jurors voting to convict shall be made public.

An actual historical precedent involved the Roman jury:

On the tribunal was set either one voting urn or, when as normally the jury was drawn from members of distinct social groups, as many voting urns as there were groups represented. As to the purpose of this practice of using different voting urns for different groups, we can only speculate that it was designed to minimize the chances of either *excessive bias or corruption* on the part of any one group. The verdict of each group, senators, equites, and, after 70, tribuni aerarii, was made public along with the overall verdict of the court; and any undue divergence of view would have been certain to induce suspicion.[160]

Although the Romans might have required their stratified juries to have a majority within each subgroup for conviction, this is not how they proceeded. Instead, they acted (I assume) on the belief that if jurors know that any group bias will be exposed to public scrutiny, they will curtail it. In this case, the ex post publicity extended to the world at large, not only to the other jurors.

I now turn to the use of open or secret voting by juries in different political systems. In a book on voting in the ancient world, it is stated as a general proposition that "the trend in any democratic society is towards the observance of greater secrecy in the recording of the vote rather than less."[161] The main purpose in making that claim is to discredit the idea that the Athenian assembly may have used secret ballot before passing to vote by a show of hands. To support the argument, the author refers to a passage in which Thucydides (4.74.3) asserts that the Megarians established their oligarchy by bringing their enemies before the people and "compelling the vote to be given openly, had them condemned and executed." In *Against Agoratus* (36–37), Lysias similarly claims that those accused of thwarting the plans of the Thirty Tyrants would have "escaped harm if they had been tried before the proper court," but that since "the vote had to be deposited, not in urns, but openly on tables [in front of the Thirty]," they had no chance of escape.

It seems obvious, in fact, that oligarchs and tyrants would want to prohibit secret voting on popular juries. It is less clear whether democracies tend to induce open or secret voting in juries. In the French jury reform in 1835, it was argued that juries should vote by secret ballot since voting in assemblies and elections already used this procedure. In the jury system introduced by the Revolution, each juror expressed his vote to the President of the court, in the absence of the other jurors. A reform of 1808

---

[160] Staveley (1972), p. 229; my italics.
[161] Ibid., p. 84

did not preserve these somewhat spectacular forms, but it maintained the principle of the oral verdict; *it did not even isolate the jurors from each other* as had been previously done. When they had retired into the jury room, and the discussion was at an end, the foreman of the jury questioned them one after another and took down their replies (Article 345). This method was bound frequently to put a restraint upon timid dispositions and even falsify the voting. It was changed by the Law of 9th September, 1835, establishing the vote by secret ballot. "It is asked," said the Keeper of the Seals, in the Committee Report, "why, *when everything is done among us by ballot*, it is not allowed to the courts of assizes to express one's private conviction, – the proceeding used in elections at all stages, *and in the making of the laws.*"[162]

At the time, the National Assembly did in fact adopt laws by secret ballot (see Chapter 3). The general proposition that secret voting in elections, secret voting in assemblies, and secret voting in juries tend to go together and to have a common justification is, however, based on a halting analogy. After the Italian Parliament abandoned secret voting in 1988, no elected assembly to my knowledge uses this procedure on a regular basis. The mandatory use of secret ballot in juries exists in France and in Belgium and no doubt elsewhere too, but is far from universal. By contrast, there are no exceptions today to the principle of secret voting in elections to political office. Today, secrecy rules in elections, publicity in assemblies, whereas juries can be organized on either principle.

During the Terror phase of the French Revolution, we can observe a close link between assembly publicity and jury publicity. Although the Convention (1792–95) never voted by secret ballot, it had the choice between voting by standing and sitting on the one hand and voting by roll calls on the other. On a spectrum from private to public voting, the former was closer to the private extreme and the latter to the public extreme. Neither was *at* the extreme, since full secrecy would require non-disclosable ballots and full publicity the recording and publication of individual votes. In the Constituent Assembly and during the first years of the Convention, the radical left successfully developed the rhetorical strategy of using roll calls as a weapon of intimidation (see Chapter 4).[163]

On March 10–11, 1793, the Convention debated the creation of a revolutionary tribunal. Two questions were intermingled: should the assembly vote on the establishment of the tribunal by a relatively public procedure (roll call) or by a relatively secret one (sitting and standing), and should fact-finders (the jury) on

---

[162] Esmein (1913), p. 531; my italics. This passage describes the succession of three regimes: secrecy among the jurors but not toward the President of the court, no secrecy among the jurors but (presumably) secrecy toward the outside world, and full secrecy.

[163] *After* the Terror, the Convention adopted the Constitution of 1795 decreeing (Art. V. 65) that votes should normally be by standing and sitting, unless there was a doubt, in which case one should proceed to a *secret* roll-call vote. It is clear from the debates that the aim was to protect deputies from what Legendre, a deputy from Paris, called "the daggers of the factions" which they might offend by speaking their mind (see extracts of the debates reproduced in Troper 2006, p. 424). Legendre had himself been at the receiving end of Robespierre's intimidating tactics (Aulard 1921, p. 464).

the tribunal vote publicly or by secret ballot? Although the record does not allow certainty, I conjecture that some of those who wanted secret ballot in the jury to avoid intimidation of the jurors would have preferred secret voting in the assembly to avoid intimidation of the deputies. What is certain, however, is that in the debates, the radicals did resort to tactics of intimidation. One deputy (Lépeaux) having asserted that "a degree of this kind requires a roll-call vote" ("l'appel nominal pour un pareil décret"), another (Monmayou) added that "only counterrevolutionaries can fear it."[164] Later, the deputy Vergniaud demanded "roll-call vote to make known those who always use the word of freedom in order to abolish it."[165]

These interventions took place, however, before the deputy Thuriot proposed "an amendment that will reconcile all. I demand that the jury give their vote openly (à haute voix)."[166] It is not clear from the record which opinions in the previous debate he wanted to reconcile, and why public voting would be a means to this end. It is possible, however, that the proposal was made on the background of the experiences from an earlier revolutionary tribunal, created on August 1792 and abolished on November 29 of the same year. In that tribunal, the jurors in each session were drawn at random from a pool of 96 elected by the Sections of the Paris Commune and voted by secret ballot (white and black balls). Although these features should have rendered the jurors immune to bribery, the acquittal of M. de Montmorin (a relative of the former Foreign Minister) was nevertheless widely ascribed to corruption.[167] In this perspective, the following passage from Révolutions de Paris (No. 193) takes on considerable interest:

[On March 10, 1793] one adopted a measure that at first seemed to eliminate the effects of corruption from this tribunal: no more secret voting, and they were right; in the tribunal of August 17 hypocrites used the white balls to hide themselves and to acquit the scoundrels.... Yet while this measure is good to stop a weak man, it fails before the scoundrel of character, the determined conspirator. One needs to have a conscience and a sense of shame (pudeur) to be afraid of the strict [public] opinion; but if a jury sells its conscience and its shame, how can open voting serve you? It would be better to prevent it from being sold, by merging it in a large crowd of jurors until it is drawn by lot.

The author does not seem to notice that the corrupt juries had in fact used the very regime he advocates. The general point is nevertheless interesting: if the rationale of open voting (or of ex post publicity) is to deter by means of shame, a shameless person will not be dissuaded. Yet in the context of the Terror, other deterrents were more important. Among the deputies who argued against open voting, Buzot argued that it would "hinder the freedom of the juries"[168] and Guadet that "open voting favors innocence when the judges are corrupt, but in

[164] AM 15, p. 681.
[165] Ibid., p. 684.
[166] Ibid.
[167] Monselet (1853), pp. 149–50.
[168] AM 15, p. 688.

moments when the multitude is inflamed by passion, this mode of voting will be fatal to it."[169] To put it more starkly, it was more important to prevent jurors from being massacred by the crowds if they acquitted than to prevent them from being bribed to acquit. Predictably, the radicals responded that "it is an insult to the people of Paris to claim that that would disturb the representatives of the people in their function."[170] Also, the radicals asked, since the deputies had voted publicly for the execution of Louis XVI without fear of being accused of influence, "why [did they] not think jurors capable of the same firmness?"[171]

Finally, I shall comment briefly on the mechanics of secret voting. There are several ways of delivering a secret vote. Roman jurors were given waxed tablets inscribed with the letters A (absolvo) and C (condemno) on the two sides and instructed to erase one of the letters before putting the tablet in the urn.[172] In some French courts white and black balls have often been used to vote not guilty or guilty. In other French courts, jurors have been required to write down "Yes" or "No" on bulletin votes. In all cases, they are usually asked to cover the tablet, ball, or bulletin with their hands to ensure secrecy.

I do not know how often these regimes have allowed the voluntary disclosure of one's vote to other jurors. In elections, it is generally recognized that to serve its purposes, secrecy has to be mandatory, not optional. Under many voting regimes, it is in fact technically impossible to disclose one's vote. Some assemblies that use the secret ballot have also banned disclosure, but not necessarily by making it impossible. Under the July Monarchy, the President of the assembly could invalidate a vote if a deputy intentionally made it possible to observe the color of his ball.[173] In that case, the rationale usually cited for obligatory secrecy was not so much to hide the vote from other deputies as to prevent the actors from making credible promises to outsiders (notably the King) to vote in their favor. In juries, neither open nor optionally secret voting would allow an outsider to monitor the votes. As noted earlier, it is only when verdicts require unanimity that a juror can make a credible promise to vote for acquittal.

In the case of written ballots, the identity of the juror may sometimes be inferred from the handwriting. Alternatively, the handwriting may be unintelligible. In a bizarre and revealing episode from 1822, the President of a court in Amiens described one case as follows:

We have learned from positive and definite information that we have received from eight of the jurors that the jury, upon a proposal from them, voted by secret ballot. As a result there were eight positive votes for conviction [the minimum required], or with regard to one of them so at least it seemed. One of the bulletins, written by an untrained hand and probably by an illiterate, presented a number of letters in excess of what is needed to express OUI or NON. The first letters were V.O., suggesting that the person had the

---

[169] Ibid., p. 689.
[170] Lamarque, ibid., pp. 688–89.
[171] Prieur, ibid., p. 689.
[172] Staveley (1972), p. 229.
[173] Connes (2009), p. 95.

intention of writing OUI but spelled it as VOUI, which is how some people pronounce it. As the foreman of the jury could not see how this concoction of meaningless letters could stand for either "oui" or "non," he thought it his duty to ask the juror who had written this bulletin which of these two words he had intended to write. But since none of the jurors wanted to admit to the vote or to reveal his ignorance, the bulletin was interpreted in the favor of the accused as a NON, thus producing the simple majority [7 out of 12] to which the accused owed his life.[174]

This event took place during the period where the foreman was supposed to question the jurors one by one. It seems that they just ignored the law and arrogated to themselves the right to use a secret ballot. Moreover, the secrecy also made it impossible to resolve the ambiguity created by the illiterate juror (and by his shame to admit his illiteracy). The episode also tells us that the strict tax-payments requirements for being a juror, satisfied by only 100,000 French citizens in a population of 30 million, were no guarantee for literacy. As noted, this gentry elite also believed that killing a witch was legitimate self-defense.

Revealing the Number of Votes and the Identity of Voters
According to § 17 of the English Jury Act of 1974, "The Crown Court shall not accept a verdict of guilty ... unless the foreman of the jury has stated in open court the number of jurors who respectively agreed to and dissented from the verdict." There is no similar requirement for a verdict of not guilty. (I conjecture but have not been able to verify that the foreperson is *forbidden* from stating the numbers in this case.) Hence neither the accused nor the public at large will know whether the acquittal was based on a unanimous decision or whether a minority (of one or two) voted to convict. If the foreperson is not required to state the number of jurors who agreed to or dissented from the verdict of not guilty, the reason is presumably that the taint of suspicion associated with a non-unanimous acquittal would be a greater burden than the suspicion of a taint associated with a number-free acquittal. In Scotland, "the foreman must state, or be asked, whether [the verdict] is unanimous or by majority, but should not asked for the size of the majority."[175] As a Scottish jury of 15 decides by simple majority, the answer "majority" might reflect any number from 8 to 14. I have not been able to think of a rationale for this rule.

In 19th-century France, there was an absolute ban on making known the number of votes on each side of the questions put to the jury.

The mode in which the jury vote in coming to a decision, is regulated by a law of the 13th of May, 1836, and is as follows. Each juryman receives in turn from the foreman a slip of paper, marked with the stamp of the court, and containing these words; "On my honor and conscience my verdict is ..." He is then to fill up the blank space with the word Yes! or No! upon a table so arranged that none of his colleagues can see what he writes, and afterwards hand the paper closed up to the foreman, who is to deposit it in a box kept for

---

[174] Claverie (1984), p. 148.
[175] Duff (2000), p. 269.

the purpose. A similar operation must be gone through on the questions of whether there are extenuating or aggravating circumstances or not; whether the fact admits of legal excuse; and whether the prisoner was competent to distinguish right from wrong when he committed the act. The foreman must next draw out the slips of paper and write down the result, *without, however, stating the number of votes on each side.* . . . The slips of paper must then be burnt in the presence of the jury.[176]

I do not know the reasons behind this procedure either. Since the decision only required simple majority during most of this period, one may have wanted to avoid creating the doubts associated with a 7–5 vote for guilty. Although I have no grounds for asserting a causal influence, the practice conforms to the ideology of the revolutionary period. In the Constituent Assembly, there was a general ban on publishing the exact number of votes that had been cast for or against a proposed law, not only because the knowledge that it had passed by a bare majority might weaken its legitimacy, but also because the deputies were – or claimed to be – under the sway of a metaphysical theory of the general will. According to a contemporary text, "the minority was supposed to merge its will with that of the majority as soon as it was known."[177] Whether the ban on publishing the number of juror votes on the two sides is an echo of this idea is conjectural.

In contemporary Norway, too, the law states that the number of votes cast for and against is not to be made public outside the jury room. Since the vote itself is public, however, the members of the jury know how many voted to convict. In the French system just described, only the foreman of the jury knew the numbers. As it seems that the foreman was usually the oldest juror,[178] his identity could presumably be known outside the jury room. If he had been elected by the jurors or chosen by lot among them, this would not be the case. Hence in theory the French system could be vulnerable to bribery. At the very least, as we saw, it could lead to mistakes.

The jury system that was used in Denmark until 2008 presents a special case. Whereas the verdict was decided by the jurors alone, the sentence was set by jurors and judges voting together. "The penalty is decided by a simple majority vote, the milder result prevailing in case of deadlock. If there are more than two possible results, the most severe opinion is averaged with the next less severe etc., until a majority is reached. Whereas the vote of the jury as to guilt must remain secret [i.e., the actual numbers are not published], the number of votes given for the different penalties is published, but the identity of the votes of the judges/jurors is not divulged."[179]

The last feature of the Danish regime needs underscoring. Even when (as is usually the case) the identity of the jurors are known and the number of votes for and against conviction is known, the identity of the jurors who voted for and

---

[176] Forsyth (1873).

[177] Castaldo (1989), p. 351. This statement was made in reaction to a proposal by Mounier to have votes written down in two columns, with the names of those who voted for and against. As I discuss in Ch. 4, considerations of the general will were not the only source of objections to this proposal.

[178] Esmein 1913, p. 413. He refers only to the grand jury and says nothing about how the foreman of the petit jury was selected. I conjecture that the same method was used.

[179] Garde (2001).

against need not be known. Under secret voting, it will not be known, but even with open voting the information need not be formally recorded and released to a wider public. We might thus want to distinguish between the secrecy of the juror and the secrecy of the jury.[180]

V. CONCLUSION

No other issue of institutional design has been so relentlessly pursued to "prevent the prevention of intelligence" as the organization of the jury. In earlier centuries, there have also been efforts to select jurors on positive grounds of competence or "quality," including the local knowledge possessed by jurors from the "vicinage."[181] These efforts have always gone together with the negative effort of screening the information of the jurors, insulating them from the external world, and the many other practices canvassed in this chapter. Today, however, the negative efforts dominate completely. It used to be the case, for instance, that at least "some members of the jury should speak the defendant's language."[182] Today, as we saw, linguistic ability that is not shared with the jury as a whole can provide a ground for disqualification.

The study of the jury suggests, however, a refinement of the distinction between positive and negative aims in institutional design. In many contexts, a positive aim is defined by positive qualities, as in the effort to select competent jurors. In the United States and to a much smaller extent elsewhere, legislators, judges, prosecutors, and attorneys also set themselves the positive task of eliminating jurors who have a *preexisting* bias, prejudice, or personal interest in the outcome. I call this a positive task, since it aims at shaping the jury rather than insulating it from informational and perceptual cues, as well as from social norms, that can *trigger* bias, prejudice, and interest. In Bentham's spirit, only the latter is strictly speaking a negative task.

The positive task of eliminating jurors with preexisting bias, prejudice, or interest is very difficult, except for obvious cases of personal relationships. A prison officer who may have met the defendant should not serve on the jury, nor a close relative or a business associate. Beyond this, "scientific jury selection" is a dubious enterprise. It is essentially impossible to validate it. Even though practitioners may claim that their experience shows that "it works," a large number of studies of expert decision making should undermine our confidence in their self-confidence.[183] Reportedly, one author based "his strong belief in the effectiveness of jury selection on the rise in the earnings of firms that do such work and on virtually nothing else."[184] We would hardly assess the effectiveness of astrology

[180] Ruprecht (1997–98), p. 246.
[181] Oldham (1983) has a full discussion.
[182] Ibid., p. 169.
[183] See notably Dawes, Faust, and Meehl (1989) and Kahneman (2011), ch. 22, for summaries of these findings.
[184] Saks (1997), p. 10, commenting on Adler (1994).

by the income of astrologers or that of mathematical finance by the income of its practitioners.[185] More seriously, the scientific consensus seems to be that jury selection is not scientific in any meaningful sense.[186] To the extent that it is based on gut feelings, it may reflect prejudice rather than eliminate it.

For this reason, I believe that Bentham's truly negative method is more appropriate. Rather than screening the jurors, we should screen the information on which they base their decision, as well as insulate them physically from bribes and threats. We should guarantee the secrecy of their deliberations to prevent chilling effects due to the fear of subsequent publicity. At the moment of voting, a juror should be ignorant about how others vote (to limit conformism), while also knowing that her vote will subsequently be revealed to the other jurors (to focus attention and limit bias and hypocrisy). In some cases, information about the case, the defendant, and the law that might cause prejudice should be kept from the jury, except if there are good reasons to believe that an ignorant jury will make its own guesses that are even more prejudicial.

In many ways, the American jury system has gotten out of hand.[187] I am referring not only to the bizarre system of jury selection but also to the way in which the system invites judicial hypocrisy or worse. Judges lie to the jurors about the reasons to maintain their anonymity. They instruct the jury in incomprehensible language that addresses a possible appellate court rather than the jurors. They tell the jurors that they should ignore facts of which they are fully aware. They do not tell them about the possibility of nullification. They accept challenges based on obvious proxies for race with a straight face. To the (unknowledgeable) extent that these and other pathologies, reinforced by bogus statistical analyses, lead to more death penalties and executions, they come with a heavy cost.

---

[185] Myron Scholes "counterpunches [to criticism of the efficient market hypothesis] that the usefulness of this empirical analysis is proven by the fact that demand for it continues to grow. At [the] 50th-anniversary symposium [of the Center for Research in Security Prices (CRSP)] plans were unveiled to publish new indices for large-cap and small-cap shares, as well as for growth and value stocks. These indices, CRSP claims, will be more academically rigorous and cheaper than existing ones. For believers in the efficiency of markets, that should be enough to ensure CRSP's continuing success" (*The Economist*, November 18, 2010). The success is equally consistent, however, with the views of disbelievers in market efficiency.

[186] Vidmar and Hans (2007), pp. 99–100; Lieberman and Sales (2007); Posey and Wrightsman (2005), ch. 9; Jonakait (2003), ch. 12; Abramson (2000), ch. 4; Kassin and Wrightsman (1988), ch. 3; Hastie, Penrod, and Pennington (1983), ch. 7. If jury selection were becoming increasingly scientific, the more recent works should reflect a higher degree of confidence in the methodology. This does not seem to be the case.

[187] Amar (1994–95) offers a devastating and mostly compelling indictment. The main point on which I disagree with him concerns his advocacy of less-than-unanimity for verdicts in criminal trials. In particular, I disagree with the argument that "most of our analogies tug toward majority rule – legislatures generally use it; voters use it; appellate benches follow it" (p. 1189). As I noted in the discussion of jury anonymity, there are morally relevant differences between jurors and voters.

3

A Dialogue with Bentham

I. INTRODUCTION

Since Bentham is the guiding spirit of the present book, it is appropriate to devote a chapter to the exposition and discussion of his views on institutional design.

I shall mainly rely on two bodies of his writings. The first consists of *Political Tactics* and other texts written around the time of the French Revolution and formulated in part as advice about how to organize the Estates-General. *Political Tactics* is an especially important text. It "seems to be the first attempt ever made to theorize broadly about parliamentary procedures."[1] In his introduction to the 1816 edition of that work, the editor Etienne Dumont also affirmed that "The internal rules of a political assembly is a branch of legislation, and even an essential branch. Until now, no political writer has discussed them explicitly."[2]

The second body of texts, written from 1820 onward, proposes and justifies a constitutional code, by which Bentham simply meant a legislative code. (As I explain below, he was opposed to constitutions that fetter majority rule.) At that time, he also made detailed proposals for a constitutional code for Libya (Tripoli). Over these thirty years, Bentham's political views changed radically, and in a radical direction. He discarded, for instance, his earlier proposal of economic qualifications on voters. As my main task is to bring out the intrinsic interest of the causal mechanisms that Bentham proposed at various times, I shall not attempt to trace the evolution of his thought in any detail.[3] I am self-consciously and unapologetically engaging in cherry-picking, not in intellectual history.

While Bentham's early writings are relatively accessible, over time they became more forbidding. They are characterized by extensive use of special terminology and neologisms, baroque irony, extreme attention to minute details

---

[1] Burns (1966), p. 98.

[2] Bentham (1999), p. 5. Some passages in the published text, including a defense of bicameralism, were actually written by Dumont, a close collaborator of Mirabeau as well as of Bentham. I discuss some of Dumont's contributions later in the chapter.

[3] A task for which I am in any case unequipped and which has been admirably undertaken by Rosen (1982) and Schofield (2006).

of procedure, and convoluted nested sentences.[4] These features of his style, together with the sheer mass of his writings, create a formidable obstacle to a full grasp of his ideas. Bentham is not obscure, and almost always has interesting things to say, yet it is not always clear whether the benefits of a close reading will be commensurate with the necessary intellectual investment. Hence there may well be cherries – nuggets of analytical insights – that I have overlooked.

The guiding line in Bentham's writings on politics was to determine the procedures most conducive to the greatest happiness of the greatest number, a phrase he repeats endlessly. To this end, one should *maximize official aptitude and minimize expense*.[5] Strictly speaking, this program is incoherent, since it is only by accident that one and the same action will maximize one function and minimize another. (Bentham should have appreciated the fact that one cannot serve two masters.) Publicity, for instance, is an important but sometimes costly means toward ensuring official aptitude. Similarly, considerations of costs might suggest a smaller assembly size than the one that maximizes aptitude. To my knowledge, Bentham never raises the issue of a possible trade-off between these two factors.[6] In this chapter, I focus only on aptitude.

Bentham distinguishes among three aptitudes that are desirable in voters, deputies, and officials. In addition to the obvious desiderata of moral and intellectual aptitude, the latter further divided into knowledge and judgment, Bentham emphasizes the less frequently mentioned – but crucial – quality of *active* aptitude. This somewhat elusive idea can be understood as dedication, application, energy, exertion, or industry. Bentham may have read and applied to legislators Gibbon's observation that "the time of a prince is the property of his people."[7]

Although the conjunction of all three aptitudes is desirable, they are not always so taken in isolation. Distrust of elites has often been rooted in the perception that "[great] abilities have generally ... been employed to mislead the honest, unwary multitude."[8] If moral aptitude is low, high intellectual and active aptitude may be positively harmful,[9] and low aptitude in the latter two respects is then to be welcomed.[10] Gibbon cites the poet Claudian (fourth century A.D.) as comparing "in a lively epigram, the opposite characters of

---

[4] In his biography of Etienne Dumont, Selth (1997), p. 158, cites similar characterizations by Samuel Romilly and John Stuart Mill.

[5] The verbs "maximize" and "minimize" were invented by Bentham, so his neologisms were not all useless.

[6] True, Bentham does claim that the best way of selecting officials for active aptitude is to offer positions to those who make the lowest bid for them (e.g., Bentham 1983, p. 297 ff.). This idea belongs, however, to the more eccentric part of his doctrine.

[7] Gibbon (1995), vol. 2, p. 52, commenting on the fact that "the virtuous mind of Theodosius was often relaxed by indolence." I do not know whether Bentham's thinking about active aptitude was shaped by Gibbon, but given this passage as well as the one quoted later, an influence does not seem too implausible.

[8] *Cato's Letters*, cited in Storing (1981), vol. 4, p. 244.

[9] Bentham (1989), pp. 103, 139, 178.

[10] The characterization of some dictatorships as "despotism tempered by incompetence" offers an example (Elster 2007a, pp. 439–40). Although there may have been dictatorships tempered by

two præfects of Italy; he contrasts the innocent repose of a philosopher, who sometimes resigned the hours of business to slumber, perhaps to study, with the interested diligence of a rapacious minister, indefatigable in the pursuit of unjust, or sacrilegious gain. 'How happy . . . might it be for the people of Italy if Mallius could be constantly awake, and if Hadrian would always sleep!'"[11]

Writing "H" for high and "L" for low moral, intellectual, and active aptitude (in that order), there are cases in which LHH is to be preferred to LLL. In some cases, however, we may prefer LHH to HLL:

By the mere care of ministering to his own happiness, a man possessed of a certain degree of intellectual talent or active talent would be led to make better provisions for the happiness of his fellow citizens than could or would be made by a man in whom intellectual aptitude or active talent were to a certain degree deficient, although he were at the same time endowed with the highest conceivable degree of appropriate moral aptitude.[12]

Bentham offers Napoleon[13] as an example of the first case, and Louis XVI[14] and Alexander I as being closer to the second.

The interaction between intellectual and moral aptitude is also at the core of Bentham's rebuttal of the claim that the people at large does not possess the wisdom needed for choosing deputies:

[Objection.] Taken in the aggregate, the people neither do any where possess, nor are capable of being made to possess, appropriate knowledge sufficient, nor thence appropriate judgment sufficient, to qualify them, respectively each of them, for contributing by his vote to the location of a Member of the supreme operative body, in which provision shall be made for the promotion of his (the Elector's) share in the universal interest.

Answer. The objection applies not, unless the case be, that in some other quarter indication has been given [of] a person or set of persons in whom there has [sic] place appropriate intellectual aptitude to a greater degree, in conjunction with appropriate moral aptitude in an equal degree: or at any rate in so high a degree superior in appropriate intellectual aptitude, and in so low a degree inferior [in] appropriate moral aptitude, as to be superior in the aggregate of appropriate aptitude. Of no such person or set of persons can indication have been or can be ever made.[15]

---

laziness, I do not know of any. Hitler may have been a "lazy dictator" in his early career, but this was largely offset by the tendency of others to "working toward the Führer" (Kershaw 1998, ch. 13).

[11] Gibbon (1995), vol. 2, p. 162.
[12] Bentham (1989), p. 179.
[13] Bentham affirms obliquely (ibid., p. 180) that Napoleon was aware, through the intermediary of Talleyrand, of Bentham's own "all-comprehensive body of law, having for its end in view the greatest happiness of the greatest number," but that his "want of appropriate moral attitude made him put it aside."
[14] Louis XVI was certainly deficient in active aptitude. Two crucial and (at least from his own point of view) fatally mistaken decisions concerning the location and the possible relocation of the Estates-General may have been due to the fact that he preferred hunting to dealing with matters of state (see Chapter 4).
[15] Bentham (1989), p. 142.

Bentham offers a large array of mechanisms that, he thought, might remove obstacles to moral, intellectual, and active aptitude. Especially important are *publicity* in assemblies and *secrecy* in the election of their members. He also proposes *sanctions* for inaptitude, whether issued in the "Tribunal of Public Opinion" or by administrative measures. Moreover, the *size* of electorates and of assemblies is an important determinant of active aptitude. He also discusses possible criteria for active and passive suffrage, notably property, payment of taxes, literacy, age, race, and gender. He discusses and rejects *indirect elections, bicameralism, supermajorities, entrenchment, judicial review,* and *prorogation* as remedies for inaptitude.

Some of Bentham's claims, although often ingenious, are implausible, with only antiquarian interest. Others, such as his advocacy of female suffrage, were progressive at the time, but are now accepted as a matter of course. Still others remain fertile and controversial sources of insight and discussion. His relentless majoritarianism and rejection of counter-majoritarian devices corresponds to an important strand in contemporary political thought.[16] He offered an important objection to the currently much-discussed idea of the "wisdom of crowds." His scheme of what I shall call secret-public voting would, in many committees and assemblies, provide a superior alternative to the standard forms of secret and public voting. From a theoretical point of view, I focus on his idea that the goal of institutional design is essentially *negative*. In particular, elected assemblies debating in public prevent elites from pursuing what he called their "sinister interests."

Over the years, Bentham described these interests in ever stronger language. An example from *Securities Against Misrule* may illustrate the cast of his mind. He first observes that the members of the all-important Tribunal of Public Opinion (discussed later) can be divided into four classes: those who are merely speaking; those who are speaking and reading; those who are speaking, reading, and writing; and those who are also printing and publishing. He then goes on to explain how the ruling classes would suppress the means of communication and expression of the members of the Tribunal if it were not for the side effects of doing so:

The class of merely speaking members forms the basis of the several others: it can not any where at any time be extinguished. If it could be extinguished, European governments are not wanting in which it would be most assuredly be extinguished. For example by cutting tongues out it might be extinguished, and would of course be extinguished. But tongues and the use of them are indispensable to the performance of the labour without which the stock of the external instruments of felicity, by means of which the felicity of the ruling one and the subruling few is reaped could not be brought into existence.[17]

---

[16] See notably Waldron (1999). Although Waldron discusses Bentham in various places, he does not (in this book) mention the extent to which Bentham's criticism of judicial review anticipates his own.

[17] Bentham (1990), p. 58. Later (ibid., pp. 72–73) he argues that the British government would have closed down all newspapers were it not for the loss it would incur of £500,000 annual revenue from the tax on newspapers.

The remainder of the chapter will be organized as a running dialogue with Bentham. Exposition of and comments on the text will be distinguished typographically from comparisons with other writers and discussion of historical episodes that confirm or sometimes contradict his ideas. The excursions are indented. The relevance of the dialogue is enhanced by the fact that Bentham's early contributions were written at the time of what were arguably the two greatest constitutional moments in history, the making of the American and French constitutions in 1787 and 1791. Whereas Bentham was remarkably well informed about France, his knowledge about American politics was more erratic. In his later period, his frequent references to the United States were characterized by "enthusiasm and, in many ways, indiscriminate admiration."[18] Yet, as we shall see, his earlier comments on the Continental Congress or on George Washington are not without interest.

I shall proceed as follows. In Section II, I consider the aptitudes of voters as a function of their individual qualifications, the voting procedure, and the size of electoral districts. In Section III, I discuss the aptitudes of deputies as a function of (among others) eligibility criteria, publicity, assembly size, forced attendance, voting procedures, and the ban on plurality of offices. In Section IV, I discuss Bentham's views on constitutionalism and rights. In Section V, I offer a brief and selective comparison of Bentham and Condorcet. Section VI offers some concluding comments.

II. APTITUDE OF VOTERS

In Bentham's terminology, the constitutive power is "that by the exercise of which it is determined who the person or persons are by whom the operative power shall be exercised."[19] Operative power, in turn, is divided into legislative and executive powers. Bentham argues that the people at large ought to be the constitutive power, since "on the part of the people appropriate aptitude in the shape of moral aptitude is at all times at a maximum."[20] His argument is as follows:

For giving to the supreme constitutive power the best form possible, for placing it in a set of hands better disposed than any other set can be, nothing more is requisite than the placing it in the hands of individuals disposed each of them to take that course which in his judgment is most conducive to his own individual interest: so disposed, he will be disposed to take that course which is most conducive to the universal interest, for the universal interest is nothing else but the aggregate of all individual interests.[21]

> Tocqueville made a related argument for the moral aptitude of the people: the majority of citizens "may be mistaken but cannot be in

[18] Hart (1982), p. 54.
[19] Bentham (1989), p. 6.
[20] Ibid., p. 143.
[21] Ibid., p. 133; see also Bentham (1990), p. 56, along similar lines.

conflict with themselves."[22] He had a lower opinion of the intellectual aptitude of the people. Harrington makes similar assessments: "the debate of the few, because there be but few that can debate, is the wisest debate, and the result [decision] of the many (because every man hath an interest what to choose, and that choice which suiteth every man's interest excludeth the distinct or private interest or passion of any man, and so cometh up unto the common and public interest or reason) is the wisest result."[23] The people, he claimed, would not "cast themselves into the sea" as a mad prince might do.[24]

In an earlier text, Bentham had distinguished two objections to universal suffrage: "Some contest that the voter has the capacity to know what would be to his advantage: others that he possesses the capacity to act on this knowledge, assuming he has it."[25] The second objection is based on the possibility of influencing the vote through bribes and threats. Bentham notes that the constant references in the English debates to the danger of the dependence of the voters on others who could influence them reveal a "strange blindness," since it could easily be eliminated by use of the secret ballot.[26]

The text in which this argument occurs was written shortly after the Federal Convention in 1787 and before the opening of the French Assemblée Constituante in May 1789. The argument to which Bentham objects was made in both assemblies. In Philadelphia, Gouverneur Morris argued that "Give the votes to people who have no property, and they will sell them to the rich who will be able to buy them."[27] Madison asserted that if the propertyless had the right to vote, "they will become the tools of opulence and ambition."[28] Neither mentions the remedy of the secret ballot. In Paris, many argued that an unrestricted suffrage would create an unholy alliance between the very rich and the very poor, the former using their wealth to buy the votes of the latter. This point was clearly

---

[22] Tocqueville (2004a), p. 265.

[23] Harrington (1977), p. 416.

[24] Ibid., p. 429.

[25] Bentham (2002), pp. 70–71.

[26] Before women got the right to vote France in 1944, "the left had been, by and large, opposed to granting the vote to women: its members claimed that priests would dictate their votes" (Balinski and Laraki 2010, p. 36 n. 9). If that form of dependence did in fact exist, the secret ballot would not have neutralized it. Moreover, the secret ballot itself could have been neutralized by the confessional (Kalyvas 1996, p. 98).

[27] Farrand (1966), vol. 2, p. 202.

[28] Ibid., p. 204. He also mentions, as a less probable outcome, that the propertyless might "combine under the influence of their common situation, in which case the rights of property & the public liberty will not be secure in their hands" (ibid.). This remark corresponds to Bentham's first objection, further discussed later.

made by Prugnon,[29] and more obscurely, but also more eloquently, by Barnave.[30] According to one scholar, this was actually a progressive argument. "Excluding the poor was a revolutionary act by the Constituante."[31] It seems to me, however, that Bentham's objection is compelling: if the *constituants* had really been concerned with preventing vote-buying and with ensuring the real independence of the vote, they could have enforced the secret ballot.

In his early writings, Bentham took the first objection more seriously, notably with regard to economic qualifications. He first defines the propertyless as "those to whom it must appear that they would benefit from a redistribution among everyone of the mass of properties"; affirms that they would not in fact benefit from an egalitarian redistribution of wealth; but adds that it would be impossible to convince them of that fact.

> Similarly, Tocqueville writes that "it is idle to object that the self-interest properly understood of the people is to spare the fortunes of the rich because they must soon feel the effects of the financial difficulties they create. Is it not also in the interest of kings to make their subjects happy and of nobles to know when to open their ranks? If long-run interests had always trumped the passions and needs of the moment, there would never have been tyrannical sovereigns or exclusive aristocracies."[32] As I have argued elsewhere, Tocqueville's argument has two prongs: the people may lack the cognitive capacity to assess the future consequences of their present behavior, or the ability to be motivated by those consequences.[33] Bentham refers only to the cognitive deficiency. Later, he changed his opinion on this point, citing the example of New York State and Pennsylvania to show that property could be secure in voting regimes with virtually no economic qualification.[34]

With regard to the specific form of economic qualification for suffrage, the early Bentham preferred "quota of imposition" to "the value of property." "If a citizen feels injured by this substitution, it can only be because he has obtained an undue advantage in the tax assessment. When joined to this condition, the right to vote will serve as a counterweight ... to the influence of motives which lead the taxpayer to reduce the amount he owes."[35] For Bentham, then, using payment of taxes as a suffrage criterion has the additional benefit of creating a

[29] AM 9, p. 372.
[30] Ibid., pp. 376–77.
[31] Guennifey (1993), p. 48, citing Michelet and Jaurès in his support; see also Fitzsimmons (1994), p. 190 n. 54. Although Michelet did in fact offer this argument, he was criticized by Jaurès (1968), p. 593. See also Rosanvallon (1992), p. 80.
[32] Tocqueville (2004a), p. 240.
[33] Elster (2009b), pp. 80–81.
[34] Bentham (1843a), pp. 612–13.
[35] Bentham (2002), p. 81.

disincentive to tax avoidance or evasion. Alternatively, the criterion might create an incentive to work hard and earn enough to be allowed to vote. This idea is affirmed in an anonymous notice inserted in *Le Moniteur* as a response to a claim that "France now has citizens that are *passive* or *subject*." The author of the response claims that in contradistinction to countries where some individuals are condemned to lifelong subjection, "there is no French citizen who by a few years of work and saving cannot make himself competent to fill all public functions."[36] Guizot's slogan, "Enrichissez-vous," is also often but wrongly understood in this sense.[37]

The texts I just discussed were written as a response to 20 questions that Necker had put to the Assemblée des Notables which had met in the fall of 1788. In a project for a constitutional code for France, written in the fall of 1789 in response to the first laws adopted by the Assemblée Constituante, Bentham proposed that "The Right of election shall be in every French citizen, male or female, being of full age, of sound mind, and able to read."[38] Concerning the last criterion, the following statement shows both his concern for detail and his insistence on creating manipulation-proof procedures: "The fact of being able to read shall be ascertained by reading at the Church in the face of the Congregation a page to be chosen by lot in the collection of laws."[39] As he did with the tax-payment criterion, he also defends the literacy criterion by its desirable side effects: "So far as the pressure of it is at all felt it will operate as a spur to the desire of instruction and as an instrument of civilization."[40] Moreover, since the criterion is based on achievement and not on ascription, it is not discriminatory: "An exclusion which every man has it in his power to free himself from whenever he thinks proper, and not to his detriment in other respects, can scarce be looked upon as the invasion of the rights of any one."[41]

Arguably, making the right to vote conditional on a non-manipulable and not excessively demanding test of literacy does not violate basic democratic tenets. Rights can be universal and yet conditional on some action by the citizen. The action will have to be universally feasible, however. Because a disabled person may have no earning potential, economic qualifications are unacceptable. Literacy tests can be acceptable, if one adopts a scheme like the one proposed by Bentham. As an example of an unacceptably difficult test, one can cite one of the questions put to voters in Alabama before the passage of the 1964 Civil Rights Act: "At what time of day on January 2nd each four years does

---

[36] AM 8, p. 514.
[37] Elster (2006a).
[38] Bentham (2002), p. 231. He valued literacy highly: "You can never read too much or listen too little" (ibid., p. 55). Unlike some literacy tests that have been used for voting or serving on juries, he placed little emphasis on the ability to *write*.
[39] Ibid., p. 231.
[40] Ibid. p. 249.
[41] Ibid., p. 248.

the term of the president of the United States end?" At the same time, the test has to pass Bentham's implicit criterion of being unpredictable, a criterion not satisfied, for instance, by the English practice of citing memorized lines from the Bible to obtain benefit of clergy.[42]

Let me cite two other arguments that have been made for conditional rights. In 1968, the United States House Judiciary Committee defended the practice of drawing jurors from voter lists by the following argument: "In a sense the use of voter lists as the basic source of juror names discriminates against those who have the requisite qualifications for jury service but who do not register to vote. This is not unfair, however, because anyone with minimal qualifications ... can cause his name to be placed on the list simply by registering or voting."[43] At the Federal Convention, Gouverneur Morris defended the limitation of the suffrage to freeholders against the objection that merchants and manufacturers also deserved the right to vote, by saying that "As to Merchts. & if they have wealth & value the right they can acquire it. If not they don't deserve it."[44] As we saw in Chapter 2, the "desert" part of Morris's argument was also used to defend the use of voter lists for selecting jurors.

Bentham was a staunch defender of the right to vote for women. To the question whether any good can arise from admitting women to the supreme constitutive power, he answers "Yes. The affording increased probability of adoption to legislative arrangements placing sexual intercourse upon a footing less disadvantageous than the present to the weaker sex."[45] Among his other arguments for female suffrage, and refutations of objections to it, the following is worth citing: "The fact [of the inferior intellectual faculties of the female] is dubious, but were it ever so certain, it would be nothing to the purpose, unless in the best endowed of the one sex they were inferior to what they are in the worst endowed of the other."[46] Yet the statistical discrimination that Bentham objects to here underlies the age-based restrictions that he accepts: there are surely some individuals 20 years of age who are intellectually superior to some 21-year-olds.

Ability to read is an aspect of intellectual aptitude. Whereas Bentham thought the people's moral aptitude was at the maximum, its intellectual aptitude "is at all times naturally on the encrease"[47] when the people forms the constitutive power. By contrast, in monarchies and aristocracies "the object towards which on this occasion the endeavours of government have actually been directed has been to diminish on the part of the people the degree of appropriate intellectual aptitude"[48] and to "implant in their minds the persuasion that, instead of that

---

[42] Green (1985), p. 146.
[43] Cited after Abramson (2000), p. 128.
[44] Farrand (1966), vol. 2, p. 203.
[45] Bentham (1989), p. 99. On Bentham's rational views in sexual matters, see Boralevi (1983).
[46] Bentham (2002), p. 247.
[47] Bentham (1989), p. 143.
[48] Ibid., pp. 143–44.

minimum which really has place, the heart of the ruling one is the seat of maximum moral aptitude."[49] Elsewhere Bentham refers to the "interest-begotten prejudice"[50] which multiplies the sinister interests of the few by creating the illusion, in the many, that the few are the best fit to rule. If Marx had read these passages, he might not have been as critical of Bentham as he was.

I conclude this section by some comments on active aptitude. To introduce the topic, let me cite an English proverb: "What's everybody's business is nobody's business."[51] It harks back to Aristotle's criticism of Plato's ideal of communal property: "that which is common to the greatest number has the least care bestowed upon it" (*Politics* 1261 b). In one of his many discussions of the vices of *boards* – in which several individuals are jointly responsible for a task – Bentham uses this proverbial phrase, adding "what is everybody's fault is nobody's fault: by each one the fault is shifted off upon the rest."[52]

> Alexander Hamilton made the same point: "Lately Congress ... have gone into the measure of appointing boards. But this is in my opinion a bad plan. A single man, in each department of the administration, would be greatly preferable. It would give us a chance of more knowledge, more activity, more responsibility and of course more zeal and attention. Boards partake of a part of the inconveniencies of larger assemblies. Their decisions are slower their energy less their responsibility more diffused. They will not have the same abilities and knowledge as an administration by single men. Men of the first pretensions will not so readily engage in them, because they will be less cospicuous, of less importance, have less opportunity of distinguishing themselves. The members of boards will take less pains to inform themselves and arrive to eminence, because they have fewer motives to do it."[53] Although the argument is in some ways remarkably similar to Bentham's, the reference to "eminence" and "men of first pretensions" is in general foreign to Bentham's spirit (see later discussion).

In his writings on France, Bentham argued that in the opening sessions of the Estates-General the task of proposing an address of thanks to the King should devolve on the Principal Minister rather than on a deputy. "Why a Minister rather than another member? ... Everybody's business is nobody's business. Any assembly needs someone whose task it is to lead it."[54] More generally, "the success with which the public is served depends upon the use

[49] Ibid., p. 144.
[50] Ibid. p. 180 ff. In addition to interest-begotten prejudice, Bentham also diagnosed "authority-begotten" prejudice as a source, for instance, of the mindless adoption of bicameralism in the United States (ibid., pp. 106–7). See also his observations on Scotch Reform discussed later.
[51] I might also have cited Gilbert and Sullivan : "When everybody is somebody, nobody is anybody."
[52] Bentham (1843a), p. 571.
[53] Hamilton (1780). For the inefficiency of these boards, see also Jillson and Wilson (1994), pp. 106–12.
[54] Bentham 2002, p. 45.

which each man makes of his own powers, and not upon the reliance he places on those of other men."[55]

Although Bentham asserts that "In the case of the people in their quality of Electors, no demand for active aptitude has place,"[56] I believe this statement is inconsistent with the general argument I am reconstructing. There are at least two possible devices for enhancing the active aptitude of voters – to make them show up and to inform themselves. First, one could fine absentee voters or at least publish their names. Bentham endorses these ideas for representatives, and I can see no reason not to extend them, at least the second of them, to voters. Second, one could reduce the number of voters through an "enfranchisement lottery," which would both enhance the motivation of voters to inform themselves and make it possible to provide them with information at low cost.[57]

It is an interesting and puzzling fact that almost no society, to my knowledge, has availed itself of the option of publishing the names of non-voters or identifying them in some other way. (In small communities where people can observe who votes and who does not, informal social sanctions, the Tribunal of Public Opinion, as Bentham calls it, may shame people into voting.) The comedy *The Acarnians* by Aristophanes implies that in the fifth century B.C. one tried to shame people into attending, by staining the coats of abstainers or latecomers with red paint. "In some of the manuscripts in which the play has come down to us there is a marginal note saying that any citizen who got red paint on his coat was liable to a fine."[58] If fines were in fact imposed, the Athenian system was similar to contemporary practices of compulsory voting, which also operates by fining non-voters.

Aristotle (*Politics* 1297 a) has a long and interesting discussion of polities that fine citizens who do not attend the assembly. He notes that "In some states a different device is adopted in regard to attendance at the assembly and the law courts. All who have registered themselves may attend; those who fail to attend after registration are heavily fined. Here the intention is to stop men from registering, through fear of the fines they may thus incur, and ultimately to stop them from attending the courts and the assembly as a result of their failure to register." In the context of the jury, it has been argued, similarly, that "some people fail to register to vote because they want to avoid jury duty, and thus the exclusive use of the voter list as a source for jurors is in some sense a tax on the right to vote."[59] Unlike the case Aristotle discussed, however, I have not seen any claim that this effect was an intended one.

55 Bentham (1999), p. 74.
56 Bentham (1989), p. 142 n.
57 López-Guerra (2011a).
58 Hansen (1991), p. 5.
59 Van Dyke (1977), p. 91.

What these observations suggest is that *the free-rider problem is an obstacle to an active aptitude in the voters.* In the next section, we shall see how this problem also arises in assemblies. In elections, it arises because "the larger the Districts, the more numerous the voters in each district, and the less the value which a voter will be disposed to set upon his vote."[60] Other things being equal, this effect provides an argument for small districts. At the same time small districts imply large assemblies, with their attendant free-rider problems.

III. APTITUDE OF DEPUTIES

To continue the immediately preceding discussion, I begin with the question of the active aptitude of deputies. This dimension of aptitude has two components: motivation and attendance. I begin with the motivational free-rider problem.

We know that Bentham was aware of Condorcet's jury theorem by 1808, when he refers to it ironically in a work on "Scotch reform,"[61] an attack on the Scottish practice of having courts with multiple judges. Bentham first argues that this system was deeply pernicious, among other reasons for its tendency to dilute individual responsibility. He then asks:

At its institution, anno 1532, why was the court so crowded as we see it? Because France was the model for everything, and in France, judicature was thus crowded. In France, how came judicature to be thus crowded? From this sinister interest [of the judges] came the custom; from the custom, the prejudice: and that prejudice so strong, that it became a sort of axiom – that if any instance the ends of judicature failed of being fulfilled, it was for want of a sufficiently great multitude of judges. We have a book, my Lord, on this subject, by *Condorcet*: a quarto volume with 460 well-filled pages in it: all algebra, all demonstration, and this axiom (preface, p. 24) a basis of it.[62]

This statement is of course a caricature, since Condorcet's jury *theorem* is not an *axiom*, although, like any theorem, it is derived from axioms. As we shall see shortly, Bentham seems to have accepted that other things being equal, the theorem was valid, yet strongly asserted that other things were *not* equal. I say "*seems* to have accepted," as the two texts I shall cite date from 1789. I have no direct evidence that Bentham had read Condorcet's 1785 essay at that time, yet I believe that the words in these texts that I italicize here strongly suggest that he had.[63]

Bentham argued that the proposed size of the Estates-General, with 1,200 deputies, was excessive.

It is certain that with a more numerous assembly there will be an increased probability of a wise decision rather than a bad one, an increased probability against any decision being made at all, and an increased slowness in coming to a decision, assuming that one is

---

[60] Bentham (2002), p. 243.
[61] I am indebted to Philip Schofield for this reference.
[62] Bentham (1843b), p. 19.
[63] Contrary to the assertion by Guidi (2010), p. 587.

made.... The example that approaches most closely [to a body that numerous] is the House of Commons in England. In appearance, the number of members is 550. But this never has never been reached.... Often it does not even equal the 40 members needed for a quorum.... *The reason is that the larger the number of voters, the smaller is the weight and value of each vote and the smaller its price in the eyes of the voter, and the less does he care about its conformity to the true end, and even about casting it at all.* From the devaluation of the right results negligence in using it and great fluctuations in the number of those who use it: fluctuations which make the outcome for the interested parties a matter of chance.[64]

In the opening sentence, Bentham appears to accept the jury theorem, with the qualifications that a large assembly might not be able to reach any decision at all, or do so very slowly. These qualifications are due, presumably, to the sheer complexity of organizing the vote of 1,200 deputies. Toward the end, however, Bentham questions the theorem itself. To prove it, Condorcet had assumed some degree of what Bentham called "intellectual aptitude." More precisely, he assumed that the probability of each voter "getting it right" in a binary decision exceeded 50 percent. It is far from clear what meaning one can give to this condition in real assembly decisions, but I shall ignore that issue. If we also assume that voters form their opinions independently of each other and that they vote sincerely, the theorem asserts that as the number of voters increases indefinitely, the probability of a majority vote "getting it right" approaches 100 percent.

Let me assume with Bentham that intellectual aptitude depends on "appropriate knowledge" as well as on "appropriate judgment" of the voters.[65] These can also be expressed as (1) *possession of information* and (2) *information-processing ability*. The first breaks further down into (1a) information that the deputies possess before they start deliberating and (1b) information that they acquire in the process of deliberation itself. Whereas (1a) and (2) are exogenous to the deliberations, (1b) is endogenous. As Bentham argues, the incentive for deputies to inform themselves about the matter they are to decide is diluted in large assemblies. Hence, as he observes, increasing the number of deputies has two opposite effects:

[Claim:] *With the number of members increases the chance of wisdom.* So many members, so many sources of light. Answer: the reduction which that same cause operates in the strength of the motive to bring out this light ... offsets this advantage.[66]

Assume now that as the number of deputies increases indefinitely, the likelihood of each of them "getting it right," while remaining above 50 percent, decreases steadily. Aanund Hylland has shown (personal communication) that if p_N is the probability that each of N deputies will "get it right," the probability of a

[64] Bentham (2002), p. 35.
[65] Bentham (1989), p. 77.
[66] Bentham (2002), p. 122. Guidi (2010), p. 590, takes the first statement to express Bentham's view, contra Condorcet, whereas I believe the second statement makes it clear that Bentham is arguing against the view expressed in the first statement.

majority vote "getting it right" converges to 100 percent only if $(p_N - 1/2)$ goes to 0 more slowly than the square root of N goes to infinity.[67] If that is not the case, the dilution of active aptitude may offset the increase in "lumières."[68]

An assembly can overcome this collective action problem by setting up a separate informational gathering structure staffed by officials who are paid to determine the facts. An example is provided by the Unfunded Mandates Reform Act of 1995, which obligates Congress to determine the obligations that a federal law would impose on states, municipalities, and tribes, and indicate which of them would not be funded by the federal government.[69] The decision by the Belgian Parliament in 1875 that no proposition of law could be signed by more than six members[70] can be interpreted in the same spirit.

Bentham's argument anticipates recent debates about informational free riding in committees and assemblies.[71] I believe that Bentham, toward the end of the first of the two passages, also anticipates the absence of a unique equilibrium in pure strategies in strategic decisions whether to vote or not. If others vote, my vote is worth little, so I might as well abstain. But if others think along the same lines and abstain, my vote increases in value to make voting worth my while. Roughly speaking, under simplifying assumptions this game has a very large number of equilibria in pure strategies, in each of which exactly M out of N citizens decide to vote, and a mixed-strategy equilibrium in which each citizen votes with probability M/N. Rational voters will never be able to converge to any of these. Instead, they will follow their "animal spirits," second-guessing each other more or less successfully, with turnout fluctuating randomly.

The following clarification may be needed. From a rational-choice-cum-self-interest perspective, the electorate or the assembly has to be quite small to make voting or making an effort objectively worthwhile. Subjectively, however, individuals seem to be sensitive to differences that, objectively, should be irrelevant. Election turnout is higher when stakes are high or when elections are expected to be close, regardless of the fact that, in national elections at least, the probability of being the pivotal voter remains too small to justify the cost of voting. Similarly,

---

[67] The same result obtains if the competence of the deputies diminishes for exogenous rather than endogenous reasons, that is, if an expanding group has to enroll less competent members (Berend and Paroush 1998).

[68] Grofman and Feld (1989), p. 1338, also noted this weakness in Condorcet's argument.

[69] Vermeule (2007), pp. 228–31.

[70] Pierre (1893), p. 724. The four other European countries he cites require a *minimum* number of signatories.

[71] Karotkin and Paroush (2003); Mukhopadhaya (2003). Grossman and Stiglitz (1980) show that *markets*, as well as *assemblies*, can induce suboptimal investment in information. In all cases, the problem is caused by the free riding problem first identified by Bentham.

citizens or deputies may be more motivated to participate in smaller groups than in larger groups even when rational self-interest would tell them to abstain in both cases. *That* people are somewhat but not fully consequentialist seems clear; *why* that is the case remains a mystery.

Bentham goes on to make three further claims.[72] First, he affirms that "light" increases with the numbers of "proposans et plaidants" (proposers and pleaders) – including contributors such as Bentham himself – rather than with the number of judges. Second, he affirms that there might be a stronger argument for the Condorcet jury theorem (or the wisdom of large bodies) in secret assemblies. Third, in "times of ignorance," when there are few written and no printed documents, an Athenian or Roman assembly of 2,000 members might in fact have more lights than one of 1,000 members.

> The first claim (and perhaps the third) suggests that Bentham attached little importance to the impact of deliberation among the deputies on the quality of the outcome. For a good decision, what matters is that the deciders all have access to information, the more the better, and make up their minds on that basis, not that they deliberate among themselves. It is useful in this respect to consider Condorcet's essay on "Whether it is useful to divide a national assembly into several chambers." In addition to his objections to bicameralism (discussed later), Condorcet offered a criticism of deliberation. Although through discussion "one learns facts that one ignored and is made aware of objections one had not foreseen, ... one is also seduced and worked up by the voice of an orator, led into error by clever sophistry without having the time to detect the trap; one is subject to the empire of those sudden movements which excite the assembly." He claims that unless there is a need to inform oneself concerning recent events, "it would be easy to prove that spoken discussion harms the truth more than serving it, and that the preference [*voeu*] of the majority would more often conform to the truth if one deduced it, without discussion, from votes given separately." In fact, he adds, the same result could be obtained if the vote took place after a "written discussion, which would perhaps be less impractical, long and costly than usually believed."[73] Obviously, Condorcet could not literally prove anything of the kind. Whether the good effects of deliberation dominate the bad or inversely depends on a myriad of details of institutional design, and notably on the secrecy or publicity of the proceedings.

Although Bentham does not draw attention to the fact, his arguments about district size and assembly size generate a dilemma. Large electoral districts exacerbate the free-rider problem for voters, whereas small districts produce large assemblies that exacerbate the free-rider problem for deputies. He might

[72] Bentham (2002), pp. 122–23.
[73] Condorcet (1789b), pp. 344–45. Today, deputies might discuss issues in a blog before voting.

have proposed to resolve the first problem with an appeal to the Tribunal of Public opinion – for instance, by publishing the names of non-voters. As we shall see shortly, this was one of the solutions he proposed to the problem of deputy abstentions. Yet, as I said, he did not propose to have the people judge itself.

Thus deputies may either not show up in the assembly for debates and votes, or they may show up and pay little attention. Both behaviors exemplify free riding. Bentham makes several proposals about how to address the first problem. As he believes that fining absentee deputies would create needless complications, he proposes instead the following scheme: "requiring of each member a deposit, at the commencement of each quarter, of a certain sum for each day of sitting in the quarter; this deposit to be returned to him at the end of the term, deduction being made of the amount deposited for each day he was absent."[74] Since wealthy deputies will not be affected by this scheme, he proposes to supplement it by coercive measures: "one day of arrest for each contravention."[75] Finally, he argued for a register of non-attendance, to be published at the end of each session.[76] As he observes with characteristic astuteness, these measures should be mechanical and automatic. The English practice of requiring in each case a vote of the House to punish an absentee member is unlikely to be efficient, "when all the judges are interested in the contravention of the laws."[77]

In France, the publication of the names of absent members has also been a controversial issue. On June 10, 1789, the Third-Estate at the Estates-General adopted a motion by Sieyes that invited members of the two other estates to join them, adding that "the assembly has an interest in noting the refusal of these two classes of deputies, in case they persist in their desire to remain unknown."[78] In the 19th century, the practice was discretionary. "The publication of the names of absent members has been requested several times; it was refused by the Chamber of Deputies on November 1, 1831; it was authorized for the names of the present only on December 28, 1834, and for the names of the absent on February 22, March 6 and March 8, 1832."[79] On March 1, 1878, the President of the National Assembly ruled that because there was no quorum, the assembly could not vote the publication of the names of absent members who had prevented the quorum![80] Yet with roll-call

---

[74] Bentham (1999), p. 58. As he goes on to note, this scheme "belongs to that class of laws which execute themselves," eliminating collection costs and the like. I do not know of any general study of fines and other sanctions on parliamentarians who are absent without leave. In France practice has sometimes been to deprive them of their emolument (Pierre 1893, p. 542). This seems inadequate. Without going as far as Bentham proposed, jailing them one day for each day of absence, one might perhaps fine them a week's salary for each day of absence.

[75] Ibid., p. 59.

[76] Ibid., p. 60.

[77] Ibid., p. 61.

[78] Pierre (1893), p. 479.

[79] Ibid., p. 480.

[80] Ibid., p. 988; see also p. 1034.

votes, the publication of the names of absent and present members had to be published, even without a quorum.[81] The overall impression is that in France, as in England, deputies did not want their absence from the assembly to be known to their constituents.

Just as the active aptitude of any elected or appointed official is diluted if he *shares his task* with others, it suffers when he *divides himself* among different tasks. Bentham asserted that "No one invested with [legislative] office shall during his continuance there in execute any other,"[82] arguing that "All the time and exertion a man can possibly muster can never be too much to dedicate to such a service. If to this most important of all functions a man adds any other, the consequence is infallible: the duty of one or other must be neglected."[83] Although Bentham himself does not synthesize his two claims, they can be summarized as "One person, one task."

In a passage that was inserted by Dumont, and which is fully in Bentham's spirit, it is argued that the President of an assembly should not have the right to vote or to participate in the debate.[84] In another inserted passage, Dumont proposed a ban on written speeches in Parliament,[85] a British practice also admired by Mirabeau,[86] Benjamin Constant,[87] and Mme de Staël.[88] Equally in Bentham's spirit is the 19th-century claim that "the desk on the floor [in the American Congress] encouraged members to sit there attending to personal business instead of listening: the House, it was said, ought just to have benches, like the House of Commons."[89] One might also promote active aptitude by defining an absentee deputy by her absence from the debates rather than from the vote. Except for the practice in Belgium prior to 1874, quorum rules invariably refer to presence at the moment of voting.[90] In many contemporary assemblies, the speakers address themselves to an empty room (or to C-Span). Bentham might have approved the pre-1874 Belgian practice, since it would force other

---

[81] Ibid., p. 1036.

[82] Bentham (2002), p. 231.

[83] Ibid., p. 251.

[84] Bentham (1999), pp. 68–69.

[85] Ibid., pp. 132–33.

[86] Pierre (1893), p. 899. He adds that at the beginning of the July Monarchy the commission in charge of revising the procedures of the assembly proposed a ban on written speeches; the proposal was not adopted, but written speeches became more and more infrequent.

[87] Constant (1815), pp. 124–25.

[88] Mme de Staël (2000), p. 179.

[89] Miller (1996), p. 46; see also Goodsell (1988). This defect may have been offset by another difference: the American representatives "sit in the House instead of running out into the lobbies as people do in the House of Commons" (Bryce 1995, vol. 2, p. 130). When the desks were removed in 1913, "benches were substituted for the comfortable swinging chairs which invited members to loll at ease or doze during dull debates" (ibid., p. 131).

[90] Pierre (1893), pp. 986–87.

deputies to pay attention to the speaker rather than devoting themselves to private matters or to their reelection.

These issues have a long ancestry as well as acute contemporary relevance.

Plutarch cites many institutional devices from ancient Greece and Rome for encouraging active aptitude:

He asserts (Lycurgus VI.5) that Lycurgus ordered the Spartan assemblies to be held in open air, since he "was of the opinion that ornaments were so far from advantaging them in their councils, that they were rather an hindrance, by diverting their attention from the business before them to statues and pictures, and roofs curiously fretted, the usual embellishments of such places amongst the other Greeks."

In the Comparison of Solon and Publicola (XXV.5) he asserts that Publicola's reason for appointing "quaestors over the public moneys . . . was that the consul, if a worthy officer, might not be without leisure for his more important duties and, if unworthy, might not have greater opportunities for injustice by having both the administration and the treasury in his hands" – thus ensuring active aptitude in the best-case scenario and moral aptitude in the worst case. I do not know any other statement from Antiquity that is more in Bentham's spirit.

In Aemilius Paulus (XIII.7) he cites a more curious device: Aemilius "ordered the night watchmen to keep watch without their spears, with the idea that they would be more on the alert and would struggle more successfully against sleep, if they were unable to defend themselves against their enemies when they approached."

In Cato the Younger (VIII.4) he cites another amazing device: the Aurelia law "forbidding candidates for office to be attended by nomenclators" (attendants whose duty it was to tell the candidate the names of those he was going to meet, that he might appear to be acquainted with them).

In the same spirit, he asserts that Cato (ibid., XLIX.5) persuaded "the senate to pass a decree that candidates for office should canvass the people in person, and not solicit nor confer with the citizens through the agency of another going about in their behalf."

Contemporary French politics is beset with the problem of the "cumul des mandats."[91] There are far more politicians holding more than one elected office in France than in any other European country. In the European Parliament, French members are much more likely than others to hold a concurrent national office.[92] The regime is unlikely to be abolished anytime soon given that members of Parliament have an interest in retaining it. There is little doubt that it generates negative externalities: "When calculating the costs and benefits of the *cumul des*

---

[91] As shown by Debré (1955), it is a long-standing tradition.
[92] For data, see the special issue on *cumul des mandats* of *French Politics* 2007 (No. 3), as well as the very full analysis in Bach (2009).

mandats for themselves, voters do not take account of the costs it might impose on the rest of the population. While a voter might consider that in electing a mayor as deputy, the costs of his absence from the assembly will be offset by his targeted interventions or more important subsidies in his favor, members of another electoral district suffer only the costs of the election, in the form of a less informed discussion in the assembly, a distortion of the debates towards local matters, and finally an inefficient allocation of public funds."[93] A related problem arises when deputies can vote by proxy.

In the United States, the problem takes a different form. Senators and especially representatives spend an inordinate amount of time on activities geared to reelection, at the expense of their work for the public. To counter this tendency, one might either impose a ceiling on the aggregate campaign contributions any deputy might receive or have campaigns fully funded by the state. (Because of the unequal access to funding there is also a fairness argument for a ceiling on aggregate contributions.) Since a cap on aggregate contributions or public funding would reduce the time congresspersons spend on raising them, they would have more time to do what they are supposed to be doing. Like the issue of the cumul des mandats, that of campaign financing is a collective action problem. One cannot solve it by imposing a ceiling on individual contributions, since this cap would only induce officeholders to spend more time seeking out contributors. The individual ceiling might nevertheless be useful to promote *moral* aptitude, by making deputies less beholden to important donors.

Bentham also points to another source of "motivational fatigue" in assemblies. When deputies speak in a pre-established order, as was sometimes the case in the French ancien régime,[94] a "man who finds himself low upon the list, may, in ordinary cases, naturally expect to find his arguments forestalled; and the lower he is, the less will it appear to be worth his while to be at pains of studying the subject, for so small a chance distinguishing himself, or being of use."[95] He notes that the problem is magnified when, as was usually the case in the ancien régime, members of the privileged orders spoke before the members of the third estate, and approves the adoption of the reverse order by the Assemblée des Notables of 1788 as "the least bad of all fixed orders."[96]

Bentham devotes considerable attention to the optimal system for allocating speaking time in assemblies. He first presents the British system, suggests a possible flaw, and promises to show how it can be remedied:

[93] Bach (2009), p. 41.
[94] Bentham (1999), pp. 95–96.
[95] Ibid., p. 101.
[96] Ibid., p. 106.

The order in which members speak, is that in which they happen to present themselves for that purpose; which they do by rising from their seats. In case of doubt which person, out of a number, was up at first, it is the province of the Speaker to decide; that is to say, provisionally; for ultimately nothing can be decided but by the House. Upon each occasion, the race, if so one may term it, is renewed; by starting up second, on any occasion, a man does not acquire the right of being heard first upon a succeeding one.

This mode is liable to inconveniences, which a person not rendered insensible to them by habit, will not find it difficult to divine; and which will be considered, and a remedy endeavoured to be found for them, farther on. But these inconveniences are nothing in comparison of the advantage gained by the avoidance of those which, we have seen, are the inevitable result of every kind of fixed order whatever.

In the British practice, the fundamental principle is equality: and here, in prescribing equality, public utility concurs, as we have seen, with justice. In the particular course taken to enforce and apply the principle, injustice, or at least the danger or appearance of it, as we shall see hereafter, have insinuated themselves. But under the greatest practicable degree of injustice, its efficacy on this head can never fail of meeting with a powerful controul in *the influence of chance – that incorruptible power, which in this, as in so many other instances, is the best guardian and firmest protector that equality can have.*[97]

The proviso that the race should be renewed on each occasion ensures the active aptitude of the deputies, since if the second to rise from his seat was certain to be the next speaker, he could allow his attention to wander. Although Bentham does not spell out the "inconveniences" of the system, we can perhaps infer them from the remedies he proposed. In "electing debaters" in an assembly with 600 deputies, one should "elect in the first instance, twenty-four orators by name; 2dly, To choose one hundred other persons by lot, in order to give a chance to all parties; 3dly, To permit each of these to waive his right in favour of any other member of the assembly at pleasure. Those who did not possess the talent or inclination to speak, would then voluntarily surrender their places to such members of their own party as seemed best fitted to fill them."[98] The scheme of having the assembly voting on who should speak was perhaps motivated by the idea that deputies would prefer speakers who were expected to have something valuable to say. The idea seems impracticable, and has probably never been practiced. The idea of allocating speaking time by the "incorruptible power" of lot may have been motivated by the risk of the Speaker being swayed by corrupt preferences.

In *allocating time*, then, an assembly may use four distinct methods: a preset arrangement, a demand to be recognized by the speaker, lottery, and voting. In *allocating space* – in seating the deputies – there is also a choice between several methods – free choice, preset arrangement, and lottery. Citing and disapproving the Dutch practice of fixed and predetermined places, Bentham argues for the first option: "Every one ought to take his place as he arrives" because "the members of the same party ought to possess every facility for concerting their operations and distributing their parts."[99]

---

[97] Ibid., p. 103; my italics.
[98] Ibid., pp. 137–38.
[99] Ibid., p. 52.

In the Constituante, by contrast, "there was a convention among all the deputies that was always respected: not to place oneself by groups or by deputations."[100] According to one historian, this convention had a crucial effect: although "the deputies had a natural tendency to seek the nearness of their colleagues from the same province, the wisdom of the patriots avoided, from the first days of May 1789, the federalist shoals on which the Revolution would have foundered."[101] In the Convention, seats were allocated formally by lottery once a month, to prevent "the dangers of fraction."[102] The American Congress and state legislatures have at various times adopted all three systems.[103]

Active attitude in deputies has to be fostered by eliminating undesirable opportunities in the assembly, not by including this quality among the criteria for eligibility. It is hard, in fact, to imagine observable indices for active aptitude. By contrast, there have been many proposals and attempts to promote moral and/or intellectual aptitude by appropriate criteria of eligibility. Generally speaking, Bentham is skeptical toward this idea.

In an early discussion of eligibility criteria, it is not clear whether Bentham relates them to (what he was later to call) moral or to intellectual aptitude. Whichever he has in mind, he rejects such criteria in toto: "From the capacity of being elected no human creature whatsoever shall be excluded."[104] To the question "Would you admit for example an ideot, a child in arms, a woman, a negro, or a convicted murderer," he replies

If they did, what would be the consequence? The ideot would remain in the hospital, the child in arms would remain in arms, the convicted murderer would be dealt with like other convicted murderers. As to the Negro and the Woman, were they by some strange accident to overcome the body of prejudice which combats their admission with so much force, there could not be a stronger proof of a degree of merit superior to any that was to be found among whites and among men.[105]

The last argument might also apply to the prospect of electing a fifteen-year-old person to the assembly. It would be proof of his superior merit if the majority of the citizens were to elect a person of that age. Bentham does not make that extension of his argument, however.

Thirty years later, he offered two different and rather curious objections to the use of age as a criterion for intellectual aptitude. The context is a discussion of bicameralism, which is supposedly justified by greater degree of *active aptitude in the lower chamber* and of higher *intellectual aptitude in the upper house*, by

---

[100] Bailly (1804), vol. 1, p. 330.
[101] Aulard (1882), p. 60.
[102] Pierre (1893), p. 829.
[103] Patterson (1972).
[104] Bentham (2002), p. 231. Since he excluded the illiterate and those not of sound mind from the electorate, his scheme is more restrictive for active than for passive suffrage. As I noted in Chapter 1 and discuss in more detail in Chapter 5, some actual electoral systems have had this feature.
[105] Ibid., p. 250.

virtue of the higher age qualifications for the latter.[106] Bentham first seems to argue that any inferior intellectual aptitude of the young might be offset by their greater moral aptitude: "youth has much better pretension to being regarded as the seat of appropriate moral aptitude – of *virtue* if that is to be the word – than a more advanced age has. In a ratio which is the inverse of the degree of altitude in the scale of age, the mind is susceptible of that degree of excitation, in the French phrase *exultation*, of which self-sacrifice, sacrifice of immediate self-regarding to social interest, is the result."[107]

The argument is, as I said, curious, given what Bentham elsewhere has to say about the social benefits of people acting out of self-interest, and the possibly ruinous effects of altruistic motivations.[108] In an uncharacteristically function-alist passage, Bentham also argues that exultation may be an effect of circum-stances: "more than one time the very difficulty of a project has been the cause of its realization. The time of great crises is also the time of great virtues: virtue is a good that like any other is multiplied by demand."[109]

> On this last point, Tocquevillle is more convincing: "It has been observed that a man facing danger rarely remains as he was: he will either rise well above his habitual level or sink well below it. The same thing happens to peoples"[110] – and, we may add, to assemblies. During the French Revolution, the abolition of feudalism on the night of August 4, 1789, and the Terror of 1793–94 illustrate the two reactions. As these two episodes suggest, passion can both enable individuals to overcome inter-est and make them blind and deaf to reason.
>
> Returning to the issue of age limits, in light of the main argument of the present book it is worthwhile noting that minimal age restrictions can be understood as motivated by the desire to prevent mischief rather than by the desire to promote wisdom. Thus without a minimum age rule for senators in the American constitution, "voters and legislatures in each state might be tempted to send the state's favorite scion, such as the governor's son, to Congress as young as possible."[111] The minimum age limitation for the President may also have been inspired by the desire to have candidates "evaluated on the basis of their individual merits and vices, as revealed by a long record of personal accomplish-ments and failures" rather than favorite sons unfairly benefiting "from their high birth status and distinguished family name."[112] Although the textual basis for these interpretations of the Constitution is slender, the logic is clear enough.

[106] Bentham (1989), p. 103.
[107] Ibid., p. 104.
[108] Ibid., pp. 233–34.
[109] Bentham (2002), p. 31.
[110] Tocqueville (2004a), p. 228.
[111] Amar (2005), p. 71.
[112] Ibid., p. 160.

Next, Bentham offers a dubious argument to show that even if some voters are intellectually deficient because of their age, they cannot do any harm:

Take any age for the age short [of] which deficiency in the article of wisdom is to be regarded as preponderantly probable: say for example 21 years of age. *By no such deficiency can any sensible evil be produced otherwise than in the case in which the individuals labouring under it compose a majority.* But that in any number approaching to a majority, these supposed unripe minds should have a place in any body constituted as that in question is here proposed to be, is altogether improbable.[113]

The statement I have italicized seems wrong. Even if intellectually inept members should form only a minority in the assembly, they could do harm by joining forces with some individuals who are deficient in moral aptitude. Although, as we shall see, one can enhance the moral aptitude of deputies by institutional means, it begs belief to assume that it could be brought to perfection.

By and large, Bentham devotes much more attention to moral aptitude than to intellectual aptitude. As I shall explain shortly, he viewed moral aptitude mainly as a negative quality. I suggest that one could promote intellectual aptitude through positive design, by forcing decision makers to reflect more closely on the alternatives before them. The constructive vote of no confidence may be seen in that perspective. Although this mechanism owed its origin to the experience of the coalitions of extremes that brought down the governments of the Weimar Republic, it could have been a stabilizing factor in fragmented multi-party regimes such as the Second Polish Republic or the Third and Fourth French Republics. When deputies have to compare candidates for the office of Prime Minister rather than simply assess the incumbent, they will be forced to look more carefully. "To throw off the burden of a present evil is no cure unless the general condition is improved."[114] Titus Livius offered a classical example of a constructive procedure in his account of how Pacuvius Calavius offered the citizens the opportunity to depose the senators:

He called an assembly of the people and addressed them thus: "You have often wished, citizens of Capua, that you had the power to execute summary justice on the unscrupulous and infamous senate. You can do so now safely, and none can call you to account.... I will put you in a position to pass sentence of life and death so that each of them in turn may pay the penalty he deserves. But whatever you do see that you do not go too far in satisfying your feelings of resentment, make the security and welfare of the State your first consideration. For, as I understand it, it is these particular senators that you hate, you do not want to go without a senate altogether; for you must either have a king which is an abomination, or a senate, which is the only consultative body that can exist in a free commonwealth. So you have to do two things at once, remove the old

---

[113] Bentham (1989), p. 104.
[114] Montaigne (1991), p. 1085.

senate and choose a fresh one. I shall order the senators to be summoned one by
one and I shall take your opinion as to their fate, and whatever decision you
arrive at shall be carried out. But before punishment is inflicted on any one
found guilty you must choose a strong and energetic man to take his place as
senator." He then sat down, and after the names of the senators had been cast
into the urn he ordered the man whose name was drawn first to be brought out
of the Senate-house. As soon as they heard the name they all shouted that he was
a worthless scoundrel and richly deserved to be punished. Then Pacuvius said:
"I see clearly what you think of this man, in place of a worthless scoundrel you
must choose a worthy and honest man as senator." For a few minutes there was
silence as they were unable to suggest a better man. Then one of them, laying
aside his diffidence, ventured to suggest a name, and a greater clamour than ever
arose.... A still more violent demonstration awaited the second and third
senators who were summoned, and it was obvious that while they intensely
disliked the man, they had no one to put in his place.... So the crowd dispersed
saying to one another that the evils they were best acquainted with were the
easiest to bear.[115]

Strictly speaking, this constructive procedure goes against the negative
Benthamite approach. I would argue, nevertheless, that it is somewhat
in Bentham's spirit. It is not an incentive-based procedure, only a device
to force decision makers to take account of a broad range of considerations. It may be compared to the idea of promoting active aptitude of
deputies by seating them on benches rather than at desks, to force them
to listen to the speakers.

The moral aptitude of a deputy, as of any official, is a negative quality: "it is
constituted by the absence ... of the propensity to sacrifice all other interests to that
which at each moment appears to him to be his own preponderant interest."[116]
It is not a question of deputies being motivated by the public good, but of
structuring their situation so that self-interest has *no purchase* on their decision:
"By moral aptitude is therefore here meant but practical innocuousness; ... such
innocuousness not having any other cause than impotence [to do wrong] in the
station of each functionary."[117] Moral aptitude equals impotence to do harm – it
is hard to imagine a view further removed from ideas of republican virtue.

As I argue in the next chapter, constituent assemblies are perhaps more
likely than ordinary legislatures to create this impotence. The decision by
a constituent assembly whether to require a 2/3 or a 3/4 majority for
Congress to override a presidential veto, for instance, is hardly likely to be
affected by material interest or by an interest in reelection. By contrast,
ordinary legislators often make decisions on the basis of their personal

[115] *History of Rome*, ch. 23.
[116] Ibid., p. 13.
[117] Bentham (1989), p. 15. An example that would have amused Bentham was the practice in the
French ancien régime that the "chauffe-cire" – the person who applied the seals on official
letters – should be unable to read (Olivier-Martin 2010, p. 501).

interest, such as the maintenance of the *cumul des mandats*. Yet constitution makers can impose constraints on legislators that limit their opportunity to act on their self-interest, as illustrated by the Twenty-Seventh
Amendment to the American constitution cited in Chapter 1: "No law
varying the compensation for the Senators and Representatives shall take
effect until an election of Representatives shall have intervened."[118]

Whereas appointed officials can be kept in line by minimizing their powers[119]
and the funds at their disposal[120] as well as by holding them responsible before
legal tribunals[121] and before the Tribunal of Public Opinion,[122] elected officials
are subject only to the last of these four checks. The importance of publicity and
transparency in all political matters, except in the election of deputies, is a
constant theme in Bentham's writings. Anticipating Judge Brandeis's dictum
"Sunlight is the best disinfectant," he refers to "the grand antiseptic effect of
publicity"[123] and asserts that calumny "is destroyed by the light of day."[124] He
acutely notes *two mechanisms* by which publicity can produce its desirable
effects on deputies: by the "dread of shame" and, more important, by "the
fear of being removed in an assembly liable to change."[125] In a passage written
much later, he also suggests that by losing the estimation of the Public Tribunal
the offender might "be deprived ... of their good offices, and upon occasion even
be exposed to ... positive ill offices at their hand."[126] He might, in other words,
risk both ostracism and punishment.

At one point, Bentham suggests two components of "respect for public
opinion – dread of its judgment – desire of glory."[127] Usually, however,
he only cites the first, dread. It seems that among the moral
psychologists of the 17th and 18th centuries, "those who were keenly
aware of the potency of the 'love of praise' were rarely equally sensible
to the potency of the fear of blame, and vice versa."[128] Bentham was
more sensible to the latter, Alexander Hamilton to the former.

---

[118] For a discussion of such veil-of-ignorance devices and the conflict they may create between moral
and active aptitude, see Vermeule (2007), Part I.
[119] Bentham (1989), p. 30 ff.
[120] Ibid. p. 40 ff.
[121] Ibid., p. 53 ff.
[122] Ibid., p. 56 ff.
[123] Bentham (1999), p. 149.
[124] Ibid.
[125] Ibid. , p. 30.
[126] Bentham (1990), p. 63.
[127] Bentham (1999), p. 37.
[128] Lovejoy (1961), pp. 135–36. Baumeister et al. (2001) find that people with low self-esteem are
more concerned with avoiding a bad self-image and those with high esteem with achieving a good
self-image, but that the latter also have the first concern. Hamilton, for one, was certainly not
lacking in self-esteem. While Bentham's greater emphasis on shame-avoidance than on glory-
seeking would be consistent with his having a low self-esteem, other aspects of his writings and
behavior suggest the opposite.

The importance Hamilton attached to his reputation is reflected in the fact that after his fellow-delegates from New York, Yates and Lansing, left the Federal Convention, "he felt free to make motions and offer suggestions but – though neither the rules of the convention nor his instructions from the state prevented it – he felt bound by propriety not to vote in behalf of New York."[129] His respect for his reputation had consequences. We know he dined in Philadelphia on July 13;[130] if he was present on July 16 and had been willing to cast the vote of New York, he could have sunk the "Great Compromise."

Many of the American framers were obsessed with their reputations. George Washington, for instance, "was compulsive about his disinterestedness," as shown by how he sought advice when the Virginia assembly offered him a gift of shares in canal companies: "'How would this matter be viewed in the eyes of the world [?],' he asked. Would not his reputation for virtue be tarnished? Would not accepting the shares 'deprive me of the principal thing which is laudable in my conduct' – that is, his disinterestedness."[131] From an electoral episode in 1761, it appears, however, that he was sometimes more concerned with the appearance of virtue than with its substance. While encouraging the sheriff to manipulate the order of the (public) voting, by having the first votes cast for Washington to create a bandwagon effect, he also made it clear that this had to be done sub rosa. "If Washington took an ethical shortcut here, he wanted to keep up appearances and pretend he wasn't."[132] At the same time, Washington did not want to appear "too solicitous for reputation."[133] As Gordon Wood remarks, "It was not easy to make decisions when a concern for one's virtue was viewed as unvirtuous."[134]

Bentham, too, commented on Washington's disinterested behavior.[135] Generally speaking, Bentham espoused Hume's assumption that in the design of

---

[129] McDonald (1982), p. 106; my italics. Riker (1987), pp. 12–13, Ackerman and Katyal (1995), p. 481, Chernow (2004), p. 237, Finkelman (1996), p. 473, Vile (2005), p. 823, and Ellis and Wildavsky (1989), p. 33, all assert incorrectly that Hamilton *could* not vote, either because of the rules of the convention or because of the instructions from the New York state legislature. There were no rules: on important occasions Luther Martin and Jenifer cast a vote as the sole delegate of Maryland. All the delegations except those of Maryland, Connecticut, and New York had a quorum for their delegation of two or more (Farrand 1966, vol. 3, pp. 559–86). These authors may have been misled by the fact that Art. V of the Articles of Confederation says that "No State shall be represented in Congress by less than two, nor more than seven members."

[130] Farrand (1966), vol. 3, p. 58.

[131] Wood (1987), pp. 90–91. See also Adair (1998).

[132] Chernow (2010), p. 128.

[133] Washington to Henry Lee, September 22, 1788.

[134] Wood (1991), p. 209.

[135] I note in passing his claim that in "the United States, Bonaparte might have been a Washington: in France, a Washington might have been no more than a Bonaparte" (Bentham 1989, p. 213).

political institutions, "every man must be supposed a knave."[136] "Is it objected against the regime of publicity, that it is a system of *distrust*? This is true; and every good political institution is founded upon this base."[137] Also, "in the framing of laws, suspicion can not possibly be carried to too high a pitch."[138] He fashioned the slogans "minimize confidence" and "maximize control."[139] Yet this suspicious attitude did not generate any "hermeneutics of suspicion" with regard to individual behavior:

Whatever position the King [Louis XVI] takes, whatever sacrifices he makes, he will never succeed in silencing these slanderers: they are a vermin that bad temper and vanity will never fail to nourish in even the most healthy political body. It is first and foremost vanity that is the most prolific source of this injustice. One wants to deal subtly with everything ... and prefers the most contrived assumption to the shame of having suspected that the behavior of a public person might have a laudable motive. If Washington persists in his retirement, it can only be a means to use the road through anarchy to open up the path to despotism. If Necker instead of accepting payment for his services like anyone else pays with his own funds for being allowed to render them, it can only be a sophisticated means to satisfy his greed. If Louis XVI abdicates the legislative power in favor of his people, it can only be as the result of an elaborate plan to take it all back and even more in a favorable moment.[140]

This text, written according to the editors between December 1788 and January 1789, is both insightful and misleading. Washington retired twice from public life, first in 1783 at the end of the war and then in 1787 after the closure of the Federal Convention. He reentered public life twice, to accept the presidency first of the Convention and then of the country. The decision to attend the Convention was motivated by the fear that people might impute to him the very motive Bentham describes: "What finally convinced Washington to attend the convention was the fear that people might think he wanted the federal government to fail so that he could then manage a military takeover."[141] Yet this cannot be the episode that Bentham, referring to the future more than two years after the Convention, had in mind. Rather he must be referring to Washington's post-Convention retirement. There is no indication, however, that Washington's decision to enter the Presidential elections – which also took place between December 1788 and January 1789! – was motivated by this concern. Although Washington may have been swayed by Hamilton's argument that a refusal on his part to become President

---

[136] Hume (1742).

[137] Bentham (1999), p. 37.

[138] Bentham (1989), p. 15.

[139] Hart (1982), p. 68. MacCunn (1913), p. 167, observes that Edmund Burke's slogans would rather be "minimize control" and "maximize confidence."

[140] Bentham (2002), pp. 17–18. For the idea of the "hermeneutics of suspicion," see Ricoeur (1969), p. 149.

[141] Wood (1991), p. 208.

"would throw everything into confusion,"[142] nothing indicates that he feared people might think he would exploit this confusion to stage a coup.

Bentham's remark on Necker is amusing, but I shall not pursue it, except to observe that Necker's monumental vanity, together with his wealth, is sufficient to explain his sacrifice of a salary for his services.[143] The comments on the suspicions regarding Louis XVI are more interesting. Again, Bentham's timing seems wrong. Nothing suggests that Louis XVI was contemplating "la politique du pire" – deliberately fostering anarchy to prepare the grounds for a counterrevolution – in late 1788 or early 1789. Nor have I seen any indications – apart from Bentham – that he was suspected of doing so. According to one of his ministers, this strategy came to the forefront only with the transfer of the Assembly from Versailles to Paris after the violence on October 5–6, 1789: "Everything was now decided by decrees of the Assembly, and the King did not refuse his sanction to any. He was persuaded that the Assembly would fall into disrepute through its errors and bad decisions. The weakness of this prince let him to embrace this idea, which relieved him from the needs of a daily resistance that would have been too much for his character."[144] In other words, Bentham objected to the hyper-suspicious imputation to Louis XVI of plans that were not in fact imputed to him at the time, but which the King actually formed shortly thereafter.

As noted, Bentham argued that fear of not being reelected would be an even stronger motive than the dread of shame before the Tribunal of Public Opinion. The mechanism is somewhat fragile, however. One of Bentham's own examples of the tyranny of the present over the future, the Long Parliament[145] points to an inconsistency in his position. Being – as Bentham thought it should be – omnipotent,[146] Parliament can prolong its own life indefinitely without calling new elections. The Septennial Act was perfectly legal.[147] Moreover, in this case the Tribunal of Public Opinion is not very strong. The deputies need not fear non-reelection if they can extend their tenure indefinitely. The weaker mechanism of naming, blaming, and shaming – an important part of the unwritten constitutional conventions – may not be sufficient to keep them in line.[148] Contrary to

---

[142] Chernow (2010), p. 549.

[143] John Adams thought *Washington's* refusal of a salary as a commander in chief was an act of self-promotion (Wood 1991, pp. 289–90).

[144] Saint-Priest (1929), vol. 2, pp. 24–25.

[145] Bentham (2002), p. 279.

[146] Ibid., p. 265 ff.

[147] Dicey (1915), p. 9.

[148] The "remedy for alleged convention-breaking is generally recognized to be, in the main, political. Either the government can be shamed by publicity and political debate into conceding error or changing its course of action, or its misdeeds can be made the subject of argument at the next General Election" (Marshall 1986, p. 17). If, however, the misdeed is the non-calling of election, we are left with shame (or perhaps revolution).

Bentham's often-stated opinion, written (and enforceable) constitutional constraints might be needed. As Tom Paine wrote, "Were a Bill to be brought into any of the American legislatures similar to that which was passed into an act by the English parliament, at the commencement of George the First, to extend the duration of the assemblies to a longer period than they now sit, the check is in the constitution, which in effect says, Thus far shalt thou go and no further."[149]

Moreover, the Tribunal of Public Opinion is "not infrequently divided against itself."[150] To illustrate this case, Bentham offers the example of a place-man: "Continuing to give speech or vote in favour of the King from whom he has received his place, he remains exposed to and suffering under the imputation of corruption and want of patriotism. But in so doing he preserves himself from the joint imputation of perfidy and ingratitude."[151] Bentham goes on to argue that the placeman will in general be more strongly blamed for ingratitude than for corruption. In the eyes of the Tribunal, breaking a promise he should not have given is worse than having given it. The fact that desirable behavior can be punished by the Tribunal would seem to limit its efficacy.

Among the four objections to publicity that Bentham discusses and tries to refute, the last is perhaps the most interesting: "In a monarchy, the publicity of the proceedings of political assemblies, by exposing the members to the resentment of the head of the State, may obstruct the freedom of their decision."[152] Bentham dismisses the objection as specious: "the proceedings of the assembly would always be known to the sovereign."[153] While this may well be true with regard to assembly *debates*, the secret ballot can prevent the sovereign from acquiring knowledge about the *votes*. Bentham acknowledges this fact in his approving remarks on secret voting by the Polish assembly when Poland was under the dominant influence of Russia.[154]

In this context, he also makes this perceptive remark: "In secret voting, the secrecy cannot be too profound: in public voting the publicity can never be too great. The most detrimental arrangement would be that of demi-publicity – as if the votes should be known to the assembly, and should remain unknown to the

---

[149] Paine (1791), vol. 2, p. 4. De Lolme (1807), p. 223, claims, however, that except for the Triennial Act, which was replaced by the Septennial Act, "we shall not find that any law, which may really be called constitutional, and which has been enacted since the Restoration, has been changed afterwards." De facto, that is, parliament was capable of binding itself. See also Langford (1991), pp. 155–56.

[150] Bentham (1989), p. 259.

[151] Ibid.

[152] Bentham (1999), p. 37.

[153] Ibid.

[154] Ibid., p. 147. Under Stalin, the secret ballot did not offer much protection. When he found out that between 160 and 260 delegates out of 1,225 had voted against him at the 1934 Party Congress, Stalin later had 1,108 of them liquidated (Taubman 2003, p. 78). Later, however, the secret ballot protected the Academy of Science, which used it to resist the election of two disciples of Lysenko whom Khrushchev wanted to impose on them (ibid., p. 607).

public."[155] The last regime would, for instance, allow legislators to trade votes (because their promises to reciprocate would be credible), but not allow their constituents to observe and possibly punish them for the deals. Whereas this particular "mixed" regime of secrecy and publicity is undesirable, I have argued that the mixed regime combining ex ante secrecy with ex post publicity is highly desirable. If applied to jury decisions, however, the regime would have to be one of demi-publicity: other jurors, but no one else, should know how each juror voted.

Secret assembly voting can be a tool in the struggle between the executive and the legislative branches. In contemporary Colombia, secret voting in Congress has been embedded in an ongoing conflict between the two branches.[156] Under the Restoration and the July Monarchy (until 1845), the French National Assembly voted by secret ballot.[157] The practice was defended by the need to ensure the independence of the chambers vis-à-vis the King.[158] Tocqueville wrote, however, that "One should not be fooled if a political assembly preferred the secret régime by citing the need to avoid the surveillance by the head of the State: it would only be a pretext. The real motive for this behavior would rather be the desire to submit oneself to his influence without exposing oneself too much to public blame."[159] As a parliamentarian himself from 1839 onward, Tocqueville knew the system and detested it. He approved, though, of the secret ballot in French elections, "to protect the electors against the influence of that almost omnipotent individual whom we call the Government."[160]

The use of the secret ballot in parliaments can also be a tool in the struggle between political parties and individual deputies. Between 1948 and 1988, the rules of procedure in the Italian Parliament required that the final vote on any bill be taken by secret ballot. "Factions within the governing coalitions often voted with the opposition, under the protection offered by the secret ballot, in order to promote their own agenda. This strategic use of secret voting was most strongly evident in the termination of Italian governments where success in open confidence votes was nullified by defeats in subsequent secret votes [on the same bill]."[161] The secret ballot was abolished by a secret vote in 1988.

---

[155] Bentham (1999), p. 148.
[156] Kugler and Rosenthal (2005), p. 86.
[157] Pierre (1893), pp. 1018–19.
[158] This cannot have been the motivation of William Penn, when he laid down in the 1682 Charter for Pennsylvania (his personal property) that all votes in the assembly should be made by secret ballot. In the 1683 Charter, this procedure was retained only for the election of officers.
[159] Tocqueville (1985).
[160] Tocqueville (1968), p. 217. He also asserted that in the United States, where the government is weak, secret voting is a protection against the tyranny of the majority (ibid., pp. 233–34).
[161] Giannetti (2010).

By contrast, when the French Parliament abolished the secret ballot in 1845, it did so by a public vote.[162]

Before I present Bentham's views about the objects and means of publicity, let me note that he is not at all opposed to a deputy promoting the interest of his electoral district: "the interests of the inhabitants of all the other Districts being adverse, this endeavour of his will be to no effect: the arrangements which are favorable to the interests of all the Districts, or at least to the majority of them, [will] on each occasion be adopted and carried into effect."[163] Deputies should not try to second-guess the general interest, but rely on its realization by the aggregation of group interest through majority voting.

As is well known, things are not quite that simple. First, in addition to interests we might have to consider rights and other concerns. I consider Bentham's discussion of rights in Section IV. Second, the fact of interpersonal variations in preference intensity breaks the link between the interest of the majority and the greatest happiness of the greatest number. Third, majority voting can take the form of *logrolling*, which can arguably work against the general interest. Finally, of course, there is the problem of cyclical or indeterminate majorities. Whereas Bentham was aware of Condorcet's Jury Theorem, nothing to my knowledge suggests that he was acquainted with the voting paradox that Condorcet exhibited in the same work. Apart from the first, these are anachronistic comments, and I shall not pursue them further.

In *Political Tactics* Bentham lists the "Objects to which Publicity ought to extend"

1. The tenor of every motion
2. The tenor of the speeches or the arguments for and against each motion
3. The issue of each motion
4. The number of the votes on each side
5. The names of the voters
6. The reports &c. which have served as the foundation of the decision.[164]

These objects serve different ends. Whereas publicity regarding (1) and (3) are essential for *the rule of law*, publication of (2), (5), and (6) are required for *democratic accountability*. Although publication of (5) implies that of (4), some assemblies have debated whether to publish (4) without (5). As for (6), it may serve to bring out the *reasons* behind the decision. We have seen, however, that Bentham was opposed to a formal vote on the reasons.

The publication of (1) and (3) seems a minimal demand. In 17th-century England, "the practice of publishing the Votes of the house – meaning

---

[162] Pierre (1893), p. 1019 n. 2. The question whether a vote on abolishing secret voting shall be secret or public is somewhat similar to the question whether the prospectively enfranchised shall be allowed to vote on an extension of the suffrage (see Chapter 5).

[163] Bentham (1989), p. 135.

[164] Bentham, (1999), p. 38.

decisions taken each day, not divisions – [was] often the only way [the people had] of finding out about intended measures that might affect their livelihood."[165] By contrast, in China until recently many laws and regulations remained secret, and independent publication of laws and regulations was a punishable offense. Since the law could not perform its function of "guiding the behavior of its subjects,"[166] the rule of law did not obtain. Partly due to pressure from the World Trade Organization, China has been moving toward greater transparency, "to cure a long-established tradition in the Chinese legal system ... that promulgation of law sends the wrong message to the subjects so that they would know the bottom line of the discipline and would not pursue *li* – the virtues."[167] The tradition is encapsulated in a Chinese proverb, "For each new law, a new way of circumventing it will arise."[168]

Even when decisions are published, defeated motions need not be. In October 1774, the Continental Congress decided to expunge any reference to the British-friendly Galloway plan, rejected by a mere six states to five, from the Journal. At the Pennsylvania convention to ratify the constitution, a motion and an amendment by an antifederalist delegate were not recorded in the convention's journal. His request that they be inserted was refused. "The convention's journal would record a Federalist triumph unclouded by the criticisms of dissenters."[169]

For Bentham, publication of (5) was essential for the ability of the public to punish deputies for their votes, either through "blame and shame" or by non-reelection. Being the principal, the public has to be able to monitor the actions of its agents. Generally speaking, members of a constituency will hold its deputy accountable any time he votes for a bill they dislike. The blame will be vastly heightened, however, when his vote is pivotal in getting the bill passed. In 2009, the House of Representatives voted 220 to 215 for the historic health care bill. Prior to the vote, it seemed that the majority might be even slimmer, 218 to 217. In that case each member of the majority might have risked the blame of his or her constituency for being personally responsible for the passage of the bill. This prospect apparently generated a frenzy of pressure on members of the minority. One Republican, Joseph Cao, cast

---

[165] Pole (2008), pp. 104–5.
[166] Raz (1979), p. 214.
[167] Wang (2007), p. 204.
[168] Needham (1956), p. 522. Tacitus's dictum "Corruptissima republica, plurimae leges" (*Annals*, vol. 3, p. 27) suggests the opposite causal connection. While at the level of society multiplicity of laws and corruption may go together, at the level of the individual *knowledge* of the law may be seen as suspect. In ancient Greece, "a litigious man ... needed to know the law well, and the less honest he was, the more attention he was likely to pay to the operation of legal traps" (Dover 1994, p. 189).
[169] Pauline Maier (2010), p. 120.

his vote only after the majority of 218 had been reached. Once more than the minimum majority had been achieved, each member could tell the constituency that the bill would have passed in any case.

Bentham also discusses (4) separately, and cites the Continental Congress during the War of Independence as "accustomed, if I am not deceived, to represent all its resolutions as unanimous."[170] Although the enemies of the Confederation "saw in this precaution the necessity of hiding an habitual discord," the assembly "chose rather to expose itself to this suspicion, than to allow the degrees of dissent to the measures it took, to be known" He justifies this procedure by assuming that "Congress, secure of the confidence of its constituents, employed this stratagem with their approbation, for the purpose of disconcerting its enemies."[171]

On this point, Bentham was in fact deceived, at least in part. After 1777, the Congress published its Journal with votes recorded (except in military matters that required secrecy) as the result of "pressure from the Maryland assembly, which was anxious to know how its own and other delegations were voting on questions involving the disposition of western lands."[172] One may add that the Articles of Confederation "had not required that Congress allow public spectators, and in practice the Confederation never did so, even after the war ended."[173] For Bentham, as we shall see, admission of spectators was a crucial element of publicity.

Other assemblies have on occasion decided to suppress information about the number of votes on the different sides. The decision by the Federal Convention to keep its votes secret not only during its sitting but afterwards may have been motivated by the desire of a nationalist majority to prevent the minority from making disagreements public.[174] The French Assemblée Constituante voted to keep the size of majorities secret so as not to undermine the expression of the general will.[175] The decision not to publish individual votes was probably overdetermined by this consideration and by the fear on the part of some deputies that their lives might be endangered if the public knew that they had voted against popular issues.

Assemblies have sometimes decided to publish the aggregate numbers for and against without publishing the votes of individual deputies. When the voting units are state delegations, as in the Continental Congress and the Federal Convention, we would expect ignorance about individual votes. Yet in the former assembly, considerations of

---

[170] Bentham (1999), p. 39.
[171] Ibid.
[172] Rakove (1979), p. 248.
[173] Amar (2005), p. 82.
[174] Anderson (1993), pp. 8–12.
[175] Castaldo (1989), pp. 272–73, 351.

costs often induced the states to send delegations composed of the minimal number of two delegates. If a two-person delegation was recorded as casting a vote for a proposal, one could infer that both delegates had voted for it. With regard to the latter, historians have shown remarkable ingenuity in triangulating the votes of individual framers. Yet because the Convention decided that the votes of the states were to be kept secret, contemporaries could not use them to infer which delegates had voted how. One cannot, therefore use principal-agent theory to explain delegate votes at the Convention.[176]

In some assemblies, members have claimed the right to have dissenting votes published. In England, this option was for a long time a privilege of the House of Lords. Members of the House of Commons could do so only with the consent of the whole House. In 1641, a royalist MP who proposed to allow any member who opposed the Grand Remonstrance against Charles I to have a protestation entered in the Journal of the House triggered a huge outcry and was punished to spend twelve days in the Tower of London.[177] To explain this reaction, one historian argues that "[the] word party had not yet become a description of political organization and structure; it had no ideological connotations. There was no accepted terminology for adversary politics since there was no regular experience of them. Thus factions and parties were synonymous to contemporary minds with 'cabals' and 'juntos.' The very use of such terms implied a corruption of the traditional political system in which the public good came before private or sectional interests."[178] It is perhaps not entirely far-fetched to compare this attitude to that of the French revolutionaries.

The *means* of publicity should include not only transcripts of the debates and records of the votes, but also admission of the public to the sittings of the assembly, to "inspire confidence in the reports."[179] Bentham also claims, surprisingly, that "the presence of strangers [will be] a salutary restraint upon the different passions to which the debates may give rise" and that "the publicity of debates has ruined more demagogues than it has made."[180]

The conventional wisdom is the very opposite, as indicated by the cliché "playing to the gallery." Clichés can be wrong, of course. Bentham's argument would require that deputies either be ashamed if the public in the galleries could observe their passions and demagoguery, or believe that knowledge of these propensities might deter their constituents from reelecting them. Since these are matters of demeanor rather than of words, only the first mechanism seems plausible. Its efficacy would presumably depend on the composition of the

[176] As does McGuire (2003), p. 36.
[177] Woolrych (2002), p. 202.
[178] Fletcher (1981), p. 156.
[179] Bentham (1999), p. 40.
[180] Ibid., pp. 40–41, 36.

audience. With characteristic attention to detail, Bentham devotes several pages to a discussion of how visitors should be admitted. He does not explicitly argue that categories of visitors before whom the deputies might be most reluctant to engage in demagoguery should have priority. He proposes that visitors should pay for admission, partly to reflect the "value attached to this enjoyment" and partly to ensure "a condition of life which guarantees a respectable class of spectators."[181] The second reason may reflect the priority of visitors most likely to shame demagogues.

Bentham makes, however, one striking exception. For reasons that rely on the weakness of men rather than of women, he thought the latter should be refused access to the galleries:

Ought females to be admitted? No. I have hesitated. I have weighed the reasons for and against. I would repudiate a separation, which appears an act of injustice and contempt. But to fear is not to despise them. Removing them from an assembly where tranquil and cool reason ought alone to reign, is avowing their influence, and it ought not to wound their pride. [In the House of Commons] it has been found that their presence gave a particular turn to the deliberations – that self-love played too conspicuous a part – that personalities were more lively – and that too much was sacrificed to vanity and wit.[182]

Although the non-admission of female *spectators* might seem perfectly in line with Bentham's general idea of removing distorting factors from the debates, the argument would also, contrary to his professed opinion, seem to count against the election of female *deputies*. If women were to become eligible, men would presumably also have to be denied access to the gallery, to prevent them from distracting female deputies. Yet clearing the gallery altogether would be to overemphasize active aptitude at the expense of moral aptitude. As the example shows, Benthamite fine-tuning could lead to absurdities.

Bentham made several observations about the institutional features that can heighten or reduce the sensitivity of deputies to the Tribunal of Public Opinion, while also protecting their independence of mind. First, he claimed that in *large assemblies*, members will be more concerned with their reputation among their fellow deputies than with their reputation before the Tribunal:

[A numerous assembly] is less subject to the influence of public opinion. It constitutes itself a small united public whose opinion can have greater interest for its members than this remote, colorful, dispersed and weak public out of doors. Why are so-called debts of

---

[181] Ibid., p. 63.
[182] Ibid., p. 64. Burke thought, by contrast, that the gallery should be kept open "for the instruction of young men; and for the information and entertainment of the ladies" (Lock 1998, p. 426). In the French Convention, women were barred from admission except when accompanied by a "citizen," because the notorious "tricoteuses" (knitters) were reputed to be trouble-makers (Coniez 2008, p. 89). The role of women has also been presented in a favorable light. In the *Constituante*, Duquesnoy (1894), vol. 1, p. 100, reports that on the decisive debates on June 17, 1789, "young and very beautiful women, made for other pleasures, animate by their speech and their gaze the patriotism of those who might need to be excited by something else than the importance of the matter."

honor regularly paid, whereas debts to merchants are not? It is because in one case the debtor is constantly meeting his creditors face to face: in the other, he hardly sees them.[183]

This claim seems wrong. The larger the number of deputies, the smaller the chance of face-to-face meetings between any two of them. The small American Senate has a notorious club-like nature, governed by strong social norms.[184] They are reinforced by the long tenure of the members, a variable that Bentham neglects in this context. Although he was in favor of annual elections, he did not to my knowledge use the argument that they would increase turnover and hence make deputies less susceptible to pressure by their peers.

Second, Bentham argues against *indirect elections* because they break the link between voters and their representatives. In this respect, the American Senate was doubly pernicious. An intermediate assembly "withdraws the Members of the National Assembly entirely out of the reach and influence of the body of the people.... Conceive a breach of trust ever so enormous: the traitor is perfectly out of the reach of any thing they can do: the only person they can punish is an innocent man whom the traitor has deceived."[185]

As we shall see later, Bentham claimed that bicameralism de facto imposes supermajorities. Indirect elections can have the same effect. "Suppose that in each of seven ... districts the vote was 60% in favor of the representative wanting to choose candidate A and 40% in favor of the representative wanting to choose candidate B. In [three other] districts, 20% of the voters favored the representative wanting to choose candidate A and 80% the representative wanting candidate B. When the ten representatives meet, they will vote 7–3 in favor of candidate A. But in terms of the wishes of their constituents, a majority of 52% ($0.7 \times 40\% + 0.3 \times 80\%$) preferred candidate B."[186] Although the argument is very much in Bentham's spirit, it is not, to my knowledge, to be found in his writings.

Third, Bentham argued that what one might call *secret-public voting* allows one to combine the autonomy (lack of pressure-induced conformism) of the deputies vis-à-vis each other with their accountability to their constituents. While votes ought to be *public*, they should also be cast *simultaneously*, "to lessen the efficacy of undue influence." At the moment of casting his vote, no deputy would know how others were going to vote; having cast it, his fellow deputies as well as his constituents would learn it.[187] If deputies do not put their vote where their mouth is, they can be exposed to the blame of their fellow deputies and to that of their constituents. In my view, this is one of Bentham's

---

[183] Bentham (2002), p. 121.
[184] Matthews (1973), ch. 5.
[185] Bentham (2002), p. 245.
[186] http://www.zcommunications.org/parpolity-and-indirect-elections-by-stephen1-shalom, corrected for a typographical error.
[187] Bentham (1999), p. 106.

most valuable institutional proposals, which deserves to be widely adopted. Although Bentham thought the system imperfect, since "neither the process of crying *Aye* or *No*, nor that of holding up hands, can be rendered ... perfectly simultaneous,"[188] this problem could be overcome by using secret ballots signed by the deputies, with subsequent publication of their names. The secret-public effect is achieved by the system of electronic voting used in some parliaments.

With regard to the Tribunal of Public Opinion, Bentham's constant concern was with the *mechanics of publicity*, as illustrated in his writings on a constitutional code for Tripoli. Because he viewed newspapers as the "only constantly acting visible" organ of the Public Opinion Tribunal,[189] he offered suggestions about how to ensure them a wide diffusion and appropriate content. To attract a large readership, newspapers should mix matters of public interest with more particular matters (births, deaths, commodity prices) so that "taking up the Newspaper, each person is upon the look-out for the matter of that sort in which he takes a more particular interest. But while he is on the look-out for that, matter of all sorts is continually offering itself to his eyes."[190] Newspapers should also try to ensure "impartiality without diminution of pugnancy."[191] Whereas an insipid impartiality could be achieved by omitting controversial matters on both sides, a more vigorous effect would be achieved admitting them on both sides. To this end,

[The] most effectual course ... would be for the proprietor of the Newspaper to employ two Editors, one whose affections were on one side, the other whose affections were on the opposite side: the number of days in the year allotted to each being the same. There should not however be any regular course of alternation: in particular the most obvious course, each conducting the paper every other day, should not be employed. Why not? the answer is – lest in that case there should be a correspondent alternation and division among the customers: one set buying the paper on the government day and not on the opposition day: the other on the opposition day and not on the government day.[192]

The passage is vintage Bentham in its combination of the acute awareness of problems that arise in informing the public and the impracticality of the proposed solution.

IV. CONSTITUTIONALISM AND RIGHTS

Bentham thought Parliament should be omnipotent. Constitutional constraints on the legislature were pointless or harmful; talk about natural rights was nonsense and harmful as well. His most general statement on constitutionalism is

---

[188] Ibid., p. 107.

[189] Bentham (1990), p. 45.

[190] Ibid., p. 47. Along similar lines, one might hold elections on market-days to "nudge" the citizens to vote; conversely one might prohibit assemblies from meeting on market-days to "keep away from an assembly large numbers of rustics other than 'those whom the political leaders in Rome had summoned to the city to cast their votes'" (Finley 1983, p. 87, citing Michels 1967, p. 105).

[191] Ibid., p. 49.

[192] Ibid.

perhaps the following: "The doctrine of fundamental unrepealable laws, the contrivance of graduated majorities, and that of the division of assemblies in such way as to convey to the minority the power of the majority, are all grounded upon the same weakness and the same irregular affection."[193] I shall focus on his criticism of *bicameralism* (a word he coined). As noted, Bentham thought the American Senate was the result of "authority-begotten prejudice," a blemish on an otherwise admirable political system. If he knew that Pennsylvania, which he also admired, had discarded its unique unicameral assembly in 1790, he must have deplored it.

Bentham's most extensive discussion of bicameralism occurs in a section on *Economy as Applied to Office* entitled "False security for appropriate aptitude, moral, intellectual or active. Division of the supreme operative power into two or more bodies." Here he singles out three evils of bicameralism: "1. Delay. 2. Complication. 3. Expence."[194] Usually, of course, delays are seen as a central argument *for* bicameralism. For Bentham, they represent a pointless and potentially harmful waste of time. His argument is almost syllogistic in form:

Let there be but one body, whatever can be found by any one to be said on the subject will be said in that one body – let there then be two bodies, either the same things will be said in both, or of those things which are to the purpose some will be said in one only, others in the other only; or while in one of them every[thing] is said, in the other nothing will be said. Evils are in the first case, useless repetitions and time lost: in the second case, in each of the bodies judgment deduced from partial and insufficient data: in the last, delay produced by transition from body to body and back again, and no other effect, therefore no good, is produced.[195]

This argument is somewhat artificial, as it seems to presuppose a mere division of one assembly into two houses – for instance, by random assignment of members to the one or to the other. This kind of arrangement is virtually never found in reality. Until recently, Norway had what one might call a quasi-bicameral system of this kind, with Parliament as a whole electing the members of the upper and smaller house. In the first years after the adoption of the constitution in 1814, the upper house, which was to approve the laws proposed by the lower one, may have functioned as a kind of Senate. In later periods the division was a pure formality. In genuinely bicameral systems, the two chambers might represent different aptitudes (active aptitude in the lower, intellectual in the upper) or different interests (agrarian interest in the lower, commercial in the upper). Although there are good arguments against these regimes, Bentham's objection does not apply to them.

Bentham also objected to quasi-bicameralism on the grounds that it imposes supermajorities: "The division of the legislative body . . . will often have the effect of giving to the minority the effect of the majority. The unanimity even of one of

---

[193] Bentham (2002), p. 186 n.
[194] Bentham (1989). p. 101.
[195] Ibid., pp. 101–2.

the two assemblies would be defeated by a majority of a single vote in the other assembly."[196]

In a near-contemporary essay, Condorcet made the same point, with a welter of numerical illustrations.[197] He first observed that with three chambers with 400 deputies each and the requirement of a majority of votes in a majority of the chambers, 402 members could impose their will on 798. If one chamber had 800 members and each of the others 200, a minority of 202 could block the wishes of 998. Although these numbers do not reflect the composition of the Estates-General that met in May 1789 (600 + 300 + 300), similar problems could arise in that case. If a majority in two of the three orders was required, 302 members could block the wishes of 998. If each order had a veto, things would be even worse. At the opening of the Estates-General, an unnamed deputy of the third estate argued in fact the absurdity of a system in which 151 deputies could block the wish of 1,049.[198]

Surprisingly, there was and is no consensus on what "voting by order" would have meant in 1789. Some contemporaries and historians believe it would have required majority voting, so that two estates could outvote a third (not necessarily the "third estate").[199] Others assert that it would have required unanimity, so that each estate would have a veto.[200] To my knowledge, no proponents of either view have explicitly addressed the alternative option to refute it. In all likelihood, the question has no unambiguous answer: the French kings "were careful not to decree rules that could be used as arguments for a regular convocation of these assemblies."[201] As noted earlier, procedures were up for grabs each time.

Condorcet goes on to consider the argument for bicameral assemblies that an upper house is needed to "prevent the people from attacking, by unjust laws, the rights of the noble and the rich." Nobility apart, this argument was made repeatedly at the Federal Convention. Nobody in that assembly, however, considered Condorcet's compelling objection to the argument: "the injustices that might be feared from the legislative body must be prevented by an article in the declaration of rights, and not by a negative right which may prevent justice as well as

---

[196] Bentham (1999), p. 24. Strictly speaking, I have no evidence that this passage refers to a quasi-bicameral system rather than an ordinary bicameral one, as the text is silent on the mode of election. Yet Bentham's simple quantitative objection on grounds of supermajorities does not carry over immediately to genuinely bicameral systems. For the latter, see Przeworski (2010), p. 141.

[197] Condorcet (1789b), pp. 341–44.

[198] AP 8, p. 47.

[199] These include Lefebvre (1988), p. 59; Michelet (1998), p. 106; Jourdan (2006), pp. 24, 25; Wikipedia, art. "Révolution française."

[200] These include Young (1794), vol. 1, p. 117; Droz (1860), vol. 2, p. 79; Brassart (1988), p. 45.

[201] Tanchoux (2004), p. 24.

injustice."²⁰² (Bentham, as we shall see, was opposed to that remedy as well.) Condorcet nevertheless argued for an upper house with a two-term suspensive veto, which would give to the lower house "a means to become aware of the errors into which it might have been led."²⁰³ Bicameralism can obviously serve a cooling-off function even if the upper house does not have an absolute veto. By virtue of the power it would confer to delay legislation, a suspensive veto would also, however, be a powerful bargaining tool for the upper house and enable it to prevent justice as well as injustice.

Bentham's second objection to quasi-bicameral systems, *complication*, rests on its tendency to reduce transparency and hence accountability. The deputies themselves easily get lost in the "secret and successful operation of sinister interest" encouraged by that system.²⁰⁴ Moreover, "if the texture of the business is thus more or less rendered obscure and indiscernible by [to?] those to whom by office it obtains, much more effectively it is concealed from the eye of the people at large in their character of members of the Public Opinion Tribunal."²⁰⁵ The third objection, *expence*, follows from the first.

In passages I cited earlier, Bentham discusses whether bicameralism might be justified by different age qualifications for members of the two houses, and concludes that it cannot. He then returns to the effects of delay, to answer an argument for bicameralism based on the alleged "evils of precipitation":

> As to the *good* [that a second chamber could do], the only case that affords an inlet to it is that in which a pernicious measure, which would have passed had there been but one chamber for it to pass, is prevented from being thrown out by the Second Chamber. To be on sufficient grounds assured that in this case preponderant good has been the result of the operation..., two distinguishable points must be established: viz. 1. that the law or measure, if carried into effect, would have been pernicious: 2. that had there been no Second Chamber, it would not have been thrown out in the First. For as to this latter point, a state of things not incapable of being realized is – that, on being assured that the measure will not pass the Second Chamber, many of those who would otherwise have opposed it in the First Chamber, are by one consideration or another kept back from meddling with it.²⁰⁶

Bentham's counterfactual, although speculative, is not intrinsically implausible. If members of the first chamber are opposed to a bill favored by their constituents, they may propose it with the expectation that it will be vetoed by the second chamber (or struck down by judicial review).²⁰⁷ Yet had there been no second chamber (or no judicial review), their opposition to the bill might have

---

²⁰² Condorcet (1789), pp. 94–96. *Federalist* No. 73 addresses this issue, with the feeble argument that "Preventing bad laws will make up for defeating a few good laws."
²⁰³ Ibid., pp. 101–4.
²⁰⁴ Bentham (1989), p. 102.
²⁰⁵ Ibid.
²⁰⁶ Ibid., p. 106.
²⁰⁷ See Diller (2008), p. 297 ff., and for a formal model, Fox and Stephenson (2011).

overridden their desire to please their constituents. The general mechanism does not presuppose bicameralism, however. In unicameral systems, too, a minority party may propose bills it does not want and does not expect to pass (or oppose bills it wants and expects to pass) in order to please its constituents.

Bentham was opposed to the *mandatory* delays in legislation that would be created by bicameralism. He was also opposed to *imposed delays* in the form of discretionary prorogation of Parliament by the government. In his advice to the French framers on how to design their constitution, he writes,

One can cite only one reason in favor of [prorogation], and even that one is only apparent. The assembly may, some will say, be momentarily carried away: it would be useful if the King by means of a brief prorogation could give it time to calm down, as is the practice in Poland: this will only be the power to appeal from the uninformed assembly to the same assembly but better informed, from the tumultuous assembly to the calm assembly.... This motive rests on the assumption that the Government is wiser than the assembly: and I do not see from which data one can infer this superiority. The fact that the assembly has been chosen by the people does not allow us to think of it as if it were itself the people.[208]

Yet Bentham accepts the possibility of *self-imposed* delays when the assembly finds itself in a state of passion:

What may happen to an individual may happen to an assembly. The individual may feel that, in the actual conjuncture he is not sufficiently master of his passion, as to form a prudent determination, but he may be sufficiently so, not to form any. "I would beat you," said the philosopher to the slave, "if I were not angry." This faculty, of doubting and suspending our operations, is one of the noblest attributes of man.[209]

The problem, as with the advice of counting to ten, is that in an excited state one may not perceive the transient nature of that state.[210] On the night of August 4, 1789, those who wanted immediate action said that "an élan of patriotism does not need three days" and "since one cannot vary in such sentiments, the three days would be a pointless waste of time." Yet many of them did change their minds.[211]

The episode illustrates a general phenomenon: he that can bind can also unbind. Hence, "the legislative ... , in order to its being restrained, should absolutely be divided. For, whatever laws it can make to restrain itself, they never can be, relatively to it, any thing more than simple

---

[208] Bentham (2002), pp. 133–34. The implicit reference to the saying "appeal from Philip drunk to Philip sober" is explicit in Bentham (1999), p. 145.

[209] Bentham (1999), p. 142. In the immediately preceding sentence, he affirms that in individuals, precipitation may also arise from ignorance. Yet since one may be ignorant and be unaware of one's ignorance (Kruger and Dunning 1999), ignorance does not necessarily motivate delay.

[210] In other words, Bentham's argument ignores the "hot-cold empathy gap" (Loewenstein and Schkade 1999) that makes it difficult for individuals in an emotional state to imagine that it will eventually subside.

[211] See references in Elster (2007b).

resolutions: as those bars which it might erect to stop its own motions must then be within it, and rest upon it, they can be no bars."[212]

In the earlier editions of *Political Tactics*, Bentham's collaborator and popularizer Etienne Dumont inserted a long passage, perhaps inspired by the passage just cited, in favor of bicameralism. He, too, observes that a unicameral assembly is unable to precommit itself to orderly procedures: "A single assembly may have the best rules, and disregard them when it pleases. Experience proves that it is easy to set them aside; and urgency of circumstances always furnish a ready pretext, and a popular pretext, for doing what the dominant party desires. If there are two assemblies, the forms will be observed; because if one violate them, it affords a legitimate reason to the other for rejection of everything presented to it after such suspicious innovation."[213] His observation may have been inspired by the events of the night of August 4, 1789, when he was present in the galleries.[214] On that occasion, the National Assembly violated the rule it had adopted a few days before, to the effect that "Any proposal in legislative or constitutional matters must be brought to discussion on three different days."[215] Another famous episode illustrates the same point. Although the constitution of Pennsylvania "prevented the assembly from approving even 'trifling' measures without time-consuming delays," that unicameral body completely ignored this constraint when, on September 29, 1787, it forcibly dragged back members who had left the assembly to prevent a quorum for the vote on calling a state convention to ratify the constitution proposed by the Federal Convention.[216]

On these two occasions, the procedural violations were certainly explained and perhaps justified by the urgency of the decision.[217] Dumont seems to acknowledge the latter claim when he goes on to say "that at all times the division of the legislative body, presents great obstacles to the reform of abuses. Such a system is less proper for creating than preserving. This shows that it is suitable to an established constitution."[218] He may have had in mind the memorable statements by Clermont-Tonnerre, who argued against the idea of separation of powers or checks and balances within the constituent assembly itself: the "three-headed hydra" – king, first chamber, and second chamber –

---

[212] De Lolme (1807), p. 219. The French edition of this work had a great influence on the French *constituants*.

[213] Dumont, in Bentham (1999), p. 26. Lally-Tolendal made the same point in the French Constituent Assembly in a speech on August 31 (AP 8, p. 516).

[214] Dumont (1832), p. 119.

[215] For discussions, see Elster (2003, 2007b).

[216] Pauline Maier (2010), p. 65.

[217] For a discussion of situations where urgency explains but does not justify hasty decisions, see Elster (2009c).

[218] Dumont, in Bentham (1999), p. 27.

that the constitution should create could not itself create a constitution.[219] He recognized the need to avoid precipitate decisions in ordinary legislatures,[220] but not in the constituent assembly.

Dumont tried to justify bicameralism in ongoing political systems by what came to be called "the law of anticipated reactions":

> If it were asked what good has resulted in England from the House of Lords, it would not be easy to cite examples of bad laws which it has prevented by its negative; it is possible, on the contrary, by citing many good ones which it had rejected, to conclude that it was more hurtful than useful. But this conclusion would not be just; for in examining the effects of an institution, we ought to take account of what it does, without being perceived, by the simple faculty of hindering. An individual is not tempted to ask for what he is certain beforehand will be refused.[221]

This objection to an argument against bicameralism is, in a way, the converse of Bentham's objection to an argument for it. Whereas Dumont asserts that many bad laws would have been proposed had it not been for the upper house, Bentham claimed that bad laws that were proposed might not have been put forward had there been no upper house.

In the last of Bentham's objections to bicameralism I shall cite, he argued that a chamber whose only function is to veto will use its power excessively, to justify its existence: "in reference to personal interest – the only motive in which we can constantly reckon – that body which is reduced to a single negative, will be opposed to everything. It can only show its power by rejecting: it appears as nothing when it accepts."[222] Elsewhere he imputes this obstructionist behavior to "vanity, jealousy, laziness."[223]

> That upper houses tend to embody Goethe's "Geist der stets verneint" (the spirit of perpetual negation) is a plausible proposition of political psychology.[224] Similar claims can be made about several other institutions:
>
> In the debates in the Constituante on the procedures for amending the constitution, the deputy Salle argued against having conventions at regular intervals: "if they were declared to be periodical, they would believe themselves necessary by the very fact of existing;

---

[219] AP 8, p. 574.

[220] Ibid.

[221] Dumont, in Bentham (1999), p. 28.

[222] Bentham (1999), p. 25. To the extent that this last perception is held, it must be because the public ignores the law of anticipated reactions. Of course, if the upper house *always* accepted what the lower house proposed, the perception would be justified.

[223] Bentham (2002), p. 43.

[224] Little (2000) is a rare study of the psychology of interbranch relations. Although she does not raise the issue I discuss here, she finds evidence of judicial self-aggrandizement.

they would want to act even when they have nothing to do; they would finish by upsetting everything."[225]

In his report to the Constituante on the organization of the judiciary, Bergasse, a deputy from the third estate, asserted that "it is in the heart of any person who has some power at his disposal to want to make use of it."[226] Judges, he claimed, might be excessively eager to convict if conviction were left in their hands.

In a comment on prior restraint, Thomas Emerson argues that "it is necessary to keep in mind not only the character structure of the licenser, but the institutional framework in which he operates. The function of the censor is to censor. He has a professional interest in finding things to suppress."[227]

As a final example, "pure" constitutional courts may be insufficiently deferential to the legislature because their only function and raison d'être is to strike down unconstitutional laws.

This generic problem can be attenuated or overcome. It has been argued that the American Supreme Court is more deferential to the legislature than pure constitutional courts, because it has other tasks besides striking down unconstitutional laws.[228] Conjecturally, the important non-legislative functions of the American Senate might also make it more deferential to the popular house than "pure" Senates. Bergasse argued that decisions in criminal cases should be left to a jury "so as not to put the judge in a position where he is free to multiply the occasions to exercise his function."[229] The problem raised by Salle would disappear if assemblies of revision were convened on the demand of the legislature.

In an essay entitled "The necessity of an omnipotent legislature" written a few months after the adoption of the French Constitution in September 1791, Bentham was also very critical toward the wish of the French National Assembly to tie the hands of its successors. The essay is hilariously funny, in the vein of Pascal's *Provinciales*, highly rhetorical, and difficult to summarize. I shall attempt to present some strands of the argument.

Addressing himself to the constituants, he claims that they lacked the authority to bind: "Either the mode of representation which you have substituted to that which seated you is a better one than that which seated you, or it is not: if it is not, why did you give it them? if it is, where is the pretence for setting your will and wisdom above theirs?"[230] Next he argues that a rigid constitution is both pointless and ineffective: "If the people continue to approve of the constitution,

[225] AP 30, p. 108.
[226] AP 8, p. 443.
[227] Emerson (1955), p. 649.
[228] Ferreres (2004), p. 1730 ff.
[229] AP 8, p. 443.
[230] Bentham (2002), p. 272. As we shall see, Robespierre made the same point (see note 150 to Chapter 4).

will they for want of such a steadiment to it overthrow it? Should the constitution ever become unacceptable to them, is it the sentiment of the lightness of the yoke thus attempted to be imposed on them that will reconcile them to its pressure?"[231] What Bentham calls "the nullifying clause" of the constitution, by which he must refer to the extreme difficulty of amendment, will always provide a pretext for "the enemies of liberty and good order, the plotters of disturbances":

[Thanks] to the cloud-compelling operation of this clause, petition for redress will be accompanied or rather superseded by protestation of invalidity: instead of complaint will come resistance: the whisper of complaint will give way to the outcry of rebellion: and disobedience to authority will be proclaimed (for so authority has proclaimed it) not a right only but a duty.[232]

Along somewhat similar lines, Tocqueville observed that "I have long thought that, instead of trying to make our forms of government eternal, we should pay attention to making methodical change an easy matter. All things considered, I find that less dangerous than the opposite alternative. I thought one should treat the French people like those lunatics whom one is careful not to bind lest they become infuriated by the constraint."[233] Montaigne affirmed that "We thought we were tying our marriage-knots more tightly by removing all means of undoing them; but the tighter we pulled the knot of constraint the looser and slacker became the knot of our will and affection. In Rome, on the contrary, what made marriages honoured and secure for so long a period was freedom to break them at will. Men loved their wives more because they could lose them; and during a period when anyone was quite free to divorce, more than five hundred years went by before a single one did so."[234] Tocqueville and Montaigne argue that the very fact of being tightly constrained – even constrained to remain in a situation one approves – might cause rebellion. Psychologists refer to this mechanism as reactance (Chapter 2). Bentham's point is simpler: rebellion may be triggered if it is very hard to change by simple majority a law of which the vast majority strongly disapproves.

Whereas Bentham argued that a rigid constitution is likely to provoke rebellion, its defenders claimed that it was needed to *prevent* rebellion. They argue that

had not the perpetuity of the constitution been thus solemnly proclaimed, the malecontents, the aristocrates, would have been continually attempting to bring about a change. The aristocrates attempting to bring about a change! as if this or any thing else could add

---

[231] Ibid.
[232] Ibid., p. 267.
[233] Tocqueville (1987), p. 181.
[234] Montaigne (1991), p. 698. Gibbon (1995), vol. 2, p. 815, reaches the very opposite conclusion: "the facility of separation would destroy all mutual confidence." Most likely, neither writer had much factual evidence for his assertion (Dixon 2011).

any thing to their zeal! We have seen what advantages the ill wishers to the constitution derive from the perpetuating clause – what advantages could they have deriven from the want of it?[235]

The following passage captures, I think, both Bentham's acknowledgment of the good intentions of the constituants, and the futility of their effort:

What was the real object of [the attempt to tie the hands of the future] – to guard this or that detail from alteration? – no: but to prevent fundamental alterations: to protect the whole fabric against the opposite currents of contending parties: from a relapse into aristocracy and despotism on the one hand, or from being precipitated into republicanism . . . , division and anarchy, on the other: to protect it in a word not against the corrections of reason, but against the assault of passion. Such was the object in view: what is the natural tendency and effect? against passion, against the assault of passion, it is impotent: against the corrections of reason it shuts the door: . . . opposed to the tide of popular passion it is a sheet of paper: opposed to the hand of reason it is a wall of brass.[236]

The paradox is that the constitution itself, notably the Declaration of the Rights of Man and the Citizen, will trigger passions against which it is powerless. In a passage cited earlier, Bentham notes that according to the Declaration, resistance to authority is not only a right but also a duty. In Bentham's virulent attack on rights as "Nonsense upon stilts," he asserts that "In the Codes of other countries, the great end of government is to quiet and repress the dissocial passions: in France the great study is to inflame and excite them: it does so when it talks of declaring rights."[237]

Referring more specifically to the right of resistance to oppression stated in Art. 2 of the French Declaration of the Rights of Man and the Citizen, Bentham describes its incendiary effects as follows:

Whenever you are about to be oppressed, you have a right to resist the oppression: therefore, whenever you conceive yourself to be oppressed, conceive yourself to have a right to make resistance, and act accordingly. In proportion as a law of any kind, any act of power supreme or subordinate, legislative, administrative or judicial, is disagreeable to a man, especially if, in consideration of such its unpleasantness, his opinion is that such act of power ought not to have been exercised, he of course looks upon it as oppressive. As often as any thing of this sort happens to a man, as often as any thing happens to a man to inflame his passions, this article, for fear his passions should not be sufficiently inflamed, sets itself to work to fan the flame, and urges him to resistance. Submitt not to any decree or other act of power of the justice of which you are not yourself perfectly convinced. If a Constable calls upon you to serve in the militia, shoot the Constable, and not the enemy.[238]

In the Constituante, several moderates (the *monarchiens*) had also argued that a bill of rights might give the people exaggerated, confused, and dangerous ideas about their liberties. The main concern they

---

[235] Bentham (2002), p. 274.
[236] Ibid., p. 273.
[237] Ibid., p. 386.
[238] Ibid., p. 337.

expressed was that the adoption of the Declaration in August 1789 was premature. Lally-Tolendal warned against the promulgation of "natural rights without immediately linking them to positive rights."[239] Malouet asserted that "there is no natural right that is not modified by positive rights.... If we do not indicate any restriction, why present to the people, in all their plenitude, rights which they should only use with the limitations demanded by justice ("justes limitations").[240] They would probably have preferred to enact positive rights only, but in the atmosphere of the time the most they could ask for was postponement of the Declaration until the Constitution itself had been adopted.

I shall not pursue Bentham's further discussions of the Declaration of Rights of 1789, including his comments on a draft by Sieyes, and of the Declaration of Rights and Duties of 1795. They are characterized by his usual combination of insight and pedantry. I do want to offer, however, some comments on Bentham's views on judicial review. In "The necessity of an omnipotent legislature" he takes a strong negative stance on the issue. If judges in several French jurisdictions disagree on the question whether an article is "conformable to the constitutional code,"

Who shall terminate this dissention? who shall put a period to this scene of confusion? the tribunal of Cassation? then is the tribunal of cassation not the rival only but the superior of the supreme legislature: then has the tribunal of cassation, a branch of the judicial power, a veto, a negative, on the laws? Should this judicial body and the legislature disagree, as by supposition they do disagree, what arbiter is there between them? None but the body of the people to whom no mode of suffrage is given but insurrection and civil war.[241]

The argument seems illogical, setting out from a dissension among judges and ending with a disagreement between the judiciary and the legislature. Be this as it may, Bentham's hostility to judicial review is clear. On this particular point, he was in full agreement with the French framers. The memory of the parlements of the ancien régime had created a deep-seated aversion to judicial review as a form of "government by judges," an aversion that was overcome only in the 1970s. In France, for two centuries, the fear of the government by judges was much stronger than the fear of violations of the constitution by Parliament or by the executive.

Dicey argued that public opinion offered the only control of the constitutionality of French laws: "Reliance may be placed upon the force of public opinion and upon the ingenious balancing of political powers for restraining the legislature from passing unconstitutional enactments. This system opposes unconstitutional legislation by means of moral sanctions, which resolve themselves into the influence of public

[239] AP 8, p. 222.
[240] Ibid., p. 322.
[241] Ibid., pp. 267–68.

sentiment."[242] If Bentham had accepted constitutionalism, he might have said that written constitutions are enforced by the Tribunal of Public Opinion, and added fear of non-reelection to the moral sanctions. As, however, he thought the only means by which the Tribunal could express itself in this case was by "insurrection and civil war," he rejected constitutionalism. On this empirical question, he may have been wrong. Voters do not seem to care much about unconstitutionality (or even legality) independent of the substantive issues involved.[243] When de Gaulle in 1962 proposed to amend the constitution by the blatantly unconstitutional means of referendum, a large majority of the voters voted for the proposal rather than voting against it to punish him for the choice of procedure. Those who voted No mostly did so on grounds of substance, not of procedure.[244]

In "Fragment on government" (1776), Bentham had already stated his opposition to judicial review, but in less strong terms. The essay refers to the English context, in which he decries review by judges appointed by the Crown because it would strengthen the already great power of the latter at the expense of the people. Yet he tempers his objection by stating that there is a "wide difference between a *positive* and a *negative* part in legislation. . . . The power of *repealing* a law even for reasons given is a great power: too great indeed for Judges: but still very distinguishable from, and much inferior to that of *making* one."[245] In this context, he did not make the argument he used with regard to bicameralism, that the power to repeal may induce a propensity to repeal.

V. BENTHAM AND CONDORCET

To risk a sweeping generalization, the major political thinkers of the late 18th century were Madison, Condorcet, and Bentham.[246] Although Madison had a deep understanding of politics, as shown by his "Vices of the political system of the United States" and his contributions to the *Federalist*, he was perhaps more important as a master tactician and strategist than as a theorist. The *Federalist* No. 10 and No. 51 continue to be highly cited, but do not, in my opinion, amount to a distinct Madisonian doctrine. That assessment is of course controversial, and in any case tangential to my concerns.

---

[242] Dicey (1915), p. 70. Schmitt (2008), p. 162, cites an episode from June 1849 when leftist parties unsuccessfully called the population of Paris to arms when President Louis Napoleon had violated the constitution by invading Rome.

[243] Diller (2008), pp. 334–35; Schauer (2010).

[244] Goguel (1963); Guillaume (2004).

[245] Bentham (1776), p. 162.

[246] In their Introduction to an English translation of Condorcet's major political writings, McLean and Hewitt (1994), p. 73, cite the trio of Madison, Condorcet, and Rousseau. They do not mention Bentham. As we have seen, Bentham was familiar with Condorcet's *Essai*; conversely, Condorcet (1792), p. 379, cites approvingly Bentham's proposal that speaking time in an assembly should be allocated by a lottery in contested cases.

By contrast, Bentham and Condorcet both offered distinct theoretical analyses of political institutions that command our attention even today. With an important exception to which I shall return, their contributions were mainly *negative*, although not of course negative in the same sense. I need not dwell on the negative aspect of Bentham's views. What is arguably Condorcet's main contribution to social theory – the paradox that bears his name – is also essentially negative: majority voting does not always yield a determinate outcome. If we read him as the originator of the doctrinal paradox (Chapter 1), that achievement is also a negative one.

Condorcet's negative result "destroyed the foundations of Rousseau's political theory."[247] At the same time, one can argue that it prepared the ground for the negative Benthamite approach to institutions. To recapitulate from Chapter 1: Condorcet showed that we cannot coherently define a good institution as one that tends to produce good outcomes if the latter are defined in terms of majority voting. Although Bentham thought that properly organized majority voting would track independently defined good outcomes, we need not, and should not, follow him on this point. Instead we should just focus on the proper organization of political institutions, without expecting them to track anything.

The "Jury Theorem" was Condorcet's main positive contribution to institutional design. As it deals with the optimal way of deciding between two options, such as Guilty or Innocent, it is not vulnerable to the Condorcet paradox, which can arise only when one has to choose among three or more options. As Poisson discovered, dichotomous majority voting is vulnerable to the doctrinal paradox. This fact does not, however, constitute my main reason for being skeptical of the practical or empirical relevance of the theorem. Rather, my skepticism rests on the fact that we cannot determine, in practice or even in theory, whether the conditions for the theorem to hold – individual competence, independence, and sincerity – obtain. This is not simply an empirical difficulty, but a logical one. Although the competence and the independence conditions may be simultaneously true, they cannot simultaneously be *shown* to be satisfied.[248] In addition, the independence condition in itself seems questionable. While it prevents bad interactions effects that arise through conformism and social pressure, it also excludes good interaction effects from information-pooling.

As noted, Condorcet did not really believe in the Jury Theorem applied to assemblies, because of the need to admit less naturally competent individuals as the assembly size increases. Hence he consistently argued for two-stage elections[249] – a system to which Bentham, as we have seen, was violently opposed. Presumably, though, Condorcet would have argued that a jury of twelve was more likely to arrive at the truth than a jury of six. If it is possible to select six jurors with the requisite competence, it should be possible to select twelve.

---

247 McLean and Hewitt (1994), p. vii. As noted earlier, this claim holds only if the general will is identified with the outcome of majority voting.
248 Dietrich (2008).
249 McLean and Hewett (1994), p. 36.

Bentham could have responded that even if the exogenously given ability of all jurors were the same in juries of unequal size, large juries would suffer from endogenous defects caused by informational free riding. On this point, Bentham's argument is more general and more compelling.

The comparison between Bentham and Condorcet could no doubt be pursued further, exploring similarities as well as differences. They were both major figures of the Enlightenment, with advanced (that is, rational) views on issues such as female suffrage and the abolition of slavery. As noted, they had partially similar views on the design of assemblies, being opposed to bicameralism and preferring written exchanges to oral debates. Bentham's concern with these issues was, however, vastly more focused. As a result of his legal training and his knowledge of British politics, Bentham was highly attuned to apparently minor yet often crucial institutional details. As a result of his training as a mathematician and, until 1791, lack of practical political experience, Condorcet took a much more abstract approach. In a strange way, as I suggested, they complemented each other.

VI. CONCLUSION

To an unusual degree, for his time and for ours, Bentham thought that the public interest could be promoted by institutional design that would induce ordinary people to act in socially desirable ways. The people at large, in its double capacity as possessors of the supreme constitutive power and as judges in the Tribunal of Public Opinion, could be trusted to realize its own interests.

In the situation of possessors of the supreme constitutive power with relation to the possessors of the supreme operative power, those whose interest composes the universal interest were brought to view in the character of legislators: in the situation here in question [the public opinion tribunal], the same persons, the same functionaries if such they may be stiled, are presented to view in the character of judges. Neither of the one power nor of the other, though lodged in the same hands, is there in any case any danger of abuse: in the case of [each] power, making the most of it for the advancement of their own interest is in this case the very course that is most desirable.[250]

Instead of *selecting* voters or deputies for preexisting moral, intellectual, or active aptitudes, one should *foster* these virtues in all citizens. As I have explained, the virtues are essentially negative and consist in the absence of an opportunity to promote one's self-interest when doing so would be socially undesirable. At least this holds for active and moral aptitude; for intellectual aptitude, Bentham recognizes the importance of education, but adds that "even without any such endeavours it has been found sufficient."[251]

As I noted, Bentham does not ask the people to judge itself, as in theory it could do by the publication of the names of non-voters. (Nor does he suggest a system of compulsory voting.) Only the representatives of the people were to be

[250] Bentham (1989), p. 241.
[251] Ibid., p. 143.

exposed to the antiseptic force of publicity. This limitation has in fact been almost universally respected. In *Doe v. Reed*, however, the U.S. Supreme Court found, 8 to 1, that those who had signed a petition against legalizing same-sex marriage had no right to anonymity. In the hearings before the Court, Justice Scalia said that "running a democracy takes a certain amount of civic courage." In France, the candidate of the far right in the Presidential elections of 2012, Marine Le Pen, demanded that the 500 elected officials who would have to endorse her candidacy to make it valid should be allowed to do so anonymously. The Constitutional Council denied her request. What would Bentham have thought about these two cases?[252]

---

[252] An interesting argument that the Council discussed and rejected was based on the principle that if a candidate is endorsed by more than 500 persons, only the names of 500 among them, chosen by a lottery, will be published. Hence a person endorsing a candidate who receives 10,000 endorsements has only a 5 percent chance of seeing his or her name published, whereas in the case of Marine Le Pen, who might not receive more than the bare minimum, publication was a near certainty. The Council affirmed that this arguably unfair inequality among the *endorsers* "had a direct relation to the legislator's intention of ensuring the greatest possible equality among the *candidates*" (my italics). In other words, it was more important to ensure that no candidate could claim a greater number of endorsers than to ensure that all endorsers had the same chance of seeing their name published.

4

The Optimal Design of Constituent Assemblies

I. INTRODUCTION

Bentham did not see the need for a constituent assembly to produce a document that would constrain the legislature. He thought Parliament should be omnipotent, as the English Parliament was already at his time (the last time the Monarch had refused to sign a bill was in 1707) and as the House of Commons would become in 1911.[1] There are, however, strong arguments for placing constitutional constraints on the legislature. In the previous chapter I cited Paine's observation that only a written constitution could have prevented the Parliament from adopting the Septennial Act. Earlier, the lack of any such document had enabled the Long Parliament to maintain itself in existence for two decades.

We must ask, however, why a written constitution would have prevented Parliament from extending its tenure indefinitely. In a speech justifying what is arguably the first written constitution in the modern sense of the term, the 1653 *Instrument of Government*, Cromwell argued that a "single person," such as the Lord Protector (himself), was needed. His argument (with Carlyle's editorial comments in parentheses) identifies with precision the need both for a constitution and for a mechanism to enforce it:

It is true, as there are some things in the Establishment which are fundamental, so there are others which are not, but are circumstantial. Of these no question but I shall easily agree to vary, to leave out, "according" as I shall be convinced by reason. But some things are Fundamentals! About which I shall deal plainly with you; These may *not* be parted with; but will, I trust, be delivered over to posterity, as the fruits of our blood and travail. The Government by a Single Person and a Parliament is a Fundamental! It is the esse, it is constitutive. In every Government there must be Somewhat Fundamental, Somewhat like a *Magna Charta*, which should be standing, be unalterable.... *That Parliaments should*

---

[1] The omnipotence rested only, however, on an unwritten convention. Burke argued that "a right normally unexercised may prove a valuable latent power in some future crisis of the constitution," citing as an example "the king's power to veto legislation" (Lock 1998, p. 405). In 1940, the Americans overruled the unwritten two-terms-only convention for the Presidency.

not make themselves perpetual is a Fundamental. [Yea; all know it: taught by the example of the Rump!] *Of what assurance is a Law to prevent so great an evil, if it lie in the same Legislature to unlaw it again?* [Must have a single Person to check your Parliament.] Is such a law like to be lasting? It will be a rope of sand; will give it no security; for *the same men may unbuild what they have built.*[2]

Cromwell's solution to that classical problem was to enforce the constitution, and limit legislative omnipotence, by an executive veto. In the Constituante, Mounier made a similar proposal.[3] Sieyes proposed to give *both* the legislature and the executive the right to call for an assembly to revise the constitution if they believed the other party was encroaching on its constitutional rights.[4] In 1795, he proposed "a *jurie constitutionnaire* that would ensure that the constitution was obeyed by annulling acts of the legislature and the executive that were contrary to it."[5] In the 19th century, the French and Swedish presidents of the national assemblies arrogated to themselves the right to declare a proposed bill unconstitutional.[6] Contemporary democracies rely on judicial review, a mechanism already implicit in *Federalist* No. 78.

The Septennial Act and the Long Parliament illustrate the need to write an enforceable electoral law into the constitution, which in turn is only a special case of the idea that constitutions are *needed to prevent those in power from using their power to keep their power.*[7] The independence of state-owned media, of the central bank, or of the National Bureau of Statistics is another implication of this idea. If measures constraining Parliament are to have any effect, however, the constitution has to be relatively rigid, that is, difficult to amend; otherwise a simple majority in Parliament will simply do in two steps what it is forbidden to do in one.[8]

Moreover, the greater difficulty of amending the constitution, compared to ordinary legislation, can also be justified independently:

If the vote of a simple majority could change the basic form of the government or expropriate the wealth of a minority, enormous resources might be devoted to seeking and resisting such legislation. In a sense, a supermajoritarian constitutional provision confines legislative discretion to matters that do not matter all that much; the stakes are not large enough to evoke a disproportionate expenditure of resources on redistributing wealth or utility.[9]

[2] Cromwell (1845), pp. 120–21; my italics. In his reading of *The Instrument of Government*, Schmitt (2008), p. 92, ignores, as Cromwell did not, the issue of enforceability.
[3] AP 8, pp. 585–86.
[4] AP 9, p. 219.
[5] Bell (1994), p. 21. See Troper (2006), ch. 8, for a full discussion.
[6] Pierre (1893), p. 65. He also reports that in Sweden, the constitutional committee in parliament decided when a doubt arises.
[7] Elster (2007), ch. 26.
[8] As recent developments in Hungary show, however, rigidity may not be enough. When Fidesz won the 2010 elections with a 2/3 majority, which is the supermajority required for amending the constitution, it "grab[bed] power over supposedly independent outfits such as the media regulator, the judiciary, the central bank and the budget and audit watchdogs" (*The Economist*, January 7, 2012).
[9] Posner (1988), p. 9. To my knowledge, the stipulated correlation between potential gain from rent-seeking and the difficulty of amendment has not been verified empirically at the level of individual

The constitution is to provide a stable framework for political struggle, not to be the object of the struggle.

Rent-seeking is not the worst thing that could arrive in the absence of a stable framework. If we generalize the argument to unwritten constitutional norms, notably regarding succession to a throne, they are essential to prevent civil war According to Pascal,

> The most unreasonable things in the world become the most reasonable because men are so unbalanced. What could be less reasonable than to choose as ruler of a state the oldest son of a queen? We do not choose as captain of a ship the most highly born of those aboard. Such a law would be ridiculous and unjust, but because men are, and always will be, as they are, it becomes reasonable and just, for who else could be chosen? The most virtuous and able man? That sets us straight away at daggers drawn, with everyone claiming to be most virtuous and able. Let us then attach this qualification to something incontrovertible. He is the king's eldest son: that is quite clear, there is no argument about it. Reason cannot do any better, because civil war is the greatest of evils.[10]

By contrast, the Roman Empire was torn by civil strife because it did not have any focal-point principle: "There was not, as there was in the Middle Ages and under the *ancien régime*, a dynastic superstition that made the throne into the property of a determinate family, always the same and an object of faith over the centuries; a superstition that from the Merovingians to the Bourbons prevented innumerable civil wars."[11]

Whereas unwritten constitutional norms or conventions *evolve*, in ways that no one understands very well, written constitutions are *made*, usually in a one-shot event. (Israel's basic laws, which were adopted over a period of 40 years, may or may not count as a constitution, depending on how we define the term.) While the task of the assembly is to *design the constitution*, I shall address the normative issue of how to *design the assembly* itself.[12]

One may question whether the task of constitution-making should be entrusted to an assembly. A good constitution is a complex piece of machinery, a set of interlocking parts that are finely adjusted to each other. A priori, one might think that the task of writing it is best entrusted to a single individual who can weigh all the relevant considerations without having to accept the compromises that are inevitable in any collective decision-making process. In stylized form, whereas both [A, B] and [A?, B?] might be viable institutions, the compromises [A, B?] or [A?, B] might not be. The first reasonably well-documented

provisions. Broadly speaking, though, the idea of stability gains from a rigid constitution seems compelling.
[10] Pascal, *Pensée* 786, ed. Sellier. Olivier-Martin (2010), p. 355, affirms that France was one of the few European countries in which there was no ambiguity in this respect, a fact that discouraged intrigues.
[11] Veyne (2005), p. 19; see also Veyne (1976), p. 718. Griffin (2000), ch. 12, has an illuminating discussion of this issue.
[12] D. Horowitz (2007–08) offers a useful discussion of the relation between the substantive task of designing a good constitution for severely divided societies and the procedural task of designing a good process.

constitution, that of Solon, was in fact the accomplishment of a single individual. Although many details are shrouded in obscurity, it seems to have been remarkably successful. Similarly, Descartes claimed that "if Sparta was in earlier times very prosperous, that was not on account of the goodness of each of its laws in particular, seeing that several were very strange and even contrary to good morals, but on account of the fact that they were devised by only a single man and thus they contributed towards the same end."[13]

Other examples of constitutions essentially handed down by a single person include the French Charter of 1815, the "octroyed" Prussian constitution of 1848, and the constitution of the Fifth French Republic (based in most essentials on de Gaulle's Bayeux speech in 1946). I do not see, however, how one could lay down reliable *procedures* for selecting a single founder who will combine moral, intellectual, and active aptitudes superior to those of a collective body.

Rather than considering a *single founder*, I shall consider in the abstract how a *single omnipotent designer of a constituent assembly* ought to structure the selection of delegates, the organization of the assembly, the definition of its tasks, and the mode of ratification (if any). Although the practical relevance of this abstract normative approach is obviously limited, it can at least point to dilemmas and pitfalls that actual constitution-makers need to be aware of. A simple example, discussed later, concerns the inadvisability of holding the constituent assembly in a large city. Even that implication, I shall argue, is highly context-dependent.

In practice, the design task will be divided between the convener of the assembly and the framers themselves. The convener may try to influence the proceedings of the assembly as well, often to no avail. Constituent assemblies usually have what in German jurisprudence is called *Kompetenz-Kompetenz* – the power to determine their own powers. If they were not omnipotent once they came into being, they would be a *pouvoir constitué* rather than a *pouvoir constituant*.[14] Although this statement seems to be widely true, I can cite a couple of French exceptions. In the third French Republic, the Senate and the Chamber of Deputies acting together could form an "assemblée de révision" charged with amending the constitution. The question sometimes arose whether an assembly created for a partial revision of the constitution could assume plenary constituent powers. Clémenceau asserted that one partial revision might lead to others and unforeseen ones, for "all parts of an organism are tightly interdependent."[15] Others recognized the unlimited powers of a constituent assembly but affirmed that when the two chambers voted a mandate of limited reform, they were bound by "honor" to respect it once they were united

---

[13] Descartes (1637), § 2, no doubt relying on Plutarch, *Lycurgus* V. 3. For other examples from the classical world and a general discussion of the possible virtues of single-founder constitution, see Lanni and Vermeule (2011).

[14] Elster (1993). Hoar (1917), ch. 9, provides numerous examples from American state conventions, as well as a few exceptions.

[15] Pierre (1893), p. 28. See also Saleilles (1895), p. 10.

in an assembly of revision.[16] When the parliamentarians of the Fourth French Republic authorized de Gaulle to draft a new constitution, they excluded an American-style presidential system. This was "the only time in [French] constitutional history that the constituent organ was not vested with unconditional competence."[17]

More important exceptions arise when a country defeated in war is adopting a new constitution. I shall consider four cases: the constitutions adopted by Germany in 1919, by Japan in 1947, by Italy in 1947, and by Germany in 1949. I shall pay particular attention to the post-1945 Japanese and German cases, not because of their considerable intrinsic interest, but because they constitute important instances of mixed vertical and horizontal decision making. The making of the Bonn constitution is especially instructive.

In 1919, the German constitution-makers had to take account of the fact that Germany was defeated, and that the constitution had to be written with the victorious enemy in mind. Although many of the drafters were far from democrats at heart, "they adopted democracy as a means of persuading the Allies to grant Germany lighter peace terms."[18] Along the same lines, in December 1918 Max Weber asserted (in debates on the new constitution that took place in the Ministry of the Interior) that "The making of a new constitution must rely as little as possible on juridical and all the more on practical considerations. Germany is for the time being under foreign domination. As a consequence, monarchy as well as excessive radicalism are excluded. The facts on the ground require a large degree of federalism, however much a unitary solution might be preferred."[19] To my knowledge, the victorious powers did not interfere actively in German constitution-making after World War I. Their influence on the democratic and decentralized form of government seems to have operated according to "the law of anticipated reactions."

The making of the 1947 Italian constitution was almost free from foreign influence. "The attempts to influence the solution of the Italian political crisis at the end of the war (sometimes trying to save the monarchic government) were made (in different directions from the English, the Russian and the American government) in the period between 1943 and 1946. But after the decision of the Italian government to call a referendum on the choice between Monarchy and Republic and the election of the Constitutional Assembly, those moves ended."[20] The German and Japanese post-1945 constituent processes were subject to considerably more pressure from the victorious powers. In the Japanese case, the constitution was essentially imposed. In Germany, it was written under constraints that, in the end, proved relatively weak.

---

[16] Ibid., p. 27 n. 31.

[17] Burdeau, Hamon, and Troper (1991), p. 449.

[18] Craig (1981), p. 415.

[19] Weber (1988), p. 57. He goes on to say that he prefers the model of the 1849 German constitution to that of 1867, since the latter gave too much power to the Länder.

[20] Olivetti (2004).

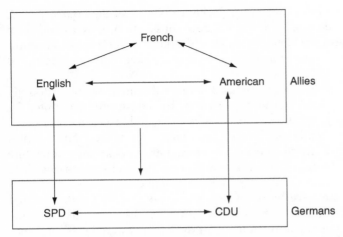

FIGURE 4.1. The making of the Bonn constitution. SPD = Socialists; CDU = Christian Democrats.

The German process had a complex structure, shown in simplified form in Figure 4.1.[21] The diagram omits all the German parties except for the Christian Democrats (CDU) and the Socialists (SPD), which between them had 54 of the 65 members of the Parliamentary Council that drafted the constitution, as well as intra-party differences among the three occupational zones. Most important, it omits the potential for tension between the Allied military governors and the Foreign Ministers. As we shall see, in the final weeks of the process overt conflict erupted between Americans on the ground and the Department of State.

Collective decision making took place among the Allies as well as among the Germans. In principle, the output of the first process was supposed to constrain the second. In practice, three factors conspired to weaken the constraints: time pressure, division among the Allies, and the need to make the constitution appear to be an indigenous product of the occupied country rather than imposed by the occupier. These features were also observed in the making of the Japanese constitution.

Before I enter into (some of the) details of the process, a brief overview of the substance may be useful. As in 1919, the main issue was the degree of decentralization or federalism, notably with respect to tax policy.[22] One question was whether the federation or the *Länder* should have power to legislate on custom duties, direct taxes, and indirect taxes. Another was whether the administration and collection of taxes should be centralized or decentralized. The Allies initially

---

[21] Standard histories of the making of the 1959 German constitution include Golay (1958), Merkl (1963), and Feldkamp (1998). Studies that focus on the influence of the Allies on the process include Grabbe (1978), Hahn (1995), Wilms (1999), and the very useful blow-by-blow account in Spevack (2002).

[22] Golay (1958), pp. 74–91, provides an excellent overview.

wanted a high level of decentralization on both counts, allowing the federal government to raise revenues only for its own obligations. Their demands would notably have excluded transfers from the richer to the poorer Länder. It would also have produced the kind of inefficiencies familiar from the American Confederation between 1783 and 1787.

Whereas the German framers were in no particular hurry to finish, the Allies, especially the Americans, were. "Adenauer and Schumacher [the leaders of CDU and SPD] both knew that the Americans badly needed the West German constitution as a weapon in the Cold War."[23] A Department of State memorandum of February 10, 1949, on "Effects of postponement of the Western German State" stated that "Communist circles would herald postponement [of the constitution] as a triumph of Soviet diplomacy and power."[24] As in other cases, this asymmetry offers a leverage to the less impatient party.[25] When Carlo Schmid (the SPD leader in the Parliamentary Council) was reported to have said that "because of the serious international situation, the Allies would never dare to turn down a German-made Basic Law," a French liaison officer responded by saying that the Allies would never allow themselves to be blackmailed in this way. Other liaison officers threatened to adopt a harsh Occupation Statute.[26] As we shall see, the Allies blinked first.

The Germans could also play on division among the Allies. These were not homogeneously motivated, nor did their motives remain constant during the constitution-making period. Initially, they all opposed a strong central government for Germany, fearing, in the words of American Secretary of State George Marshall, that "it could be too readily converted to the domination of a regime similar to the Nazis" (speech of April 28, 1947). After the Prague coup in February 1948, the British and Americans changed their attitude. Their fear of a Communist takeover acted as a brake on their decentralizing tendencies: "if a Western German government were so handicapped [by decentralization] that it could not deal with pressing economic and social problems effectively, a situation might develop that would be ripe for exploitation by Soviet power."[27]

The French, however, continued to insist on decentralization: "If the Soviets had set themselves up as champions of German unity, the French said, it was only because the centralization of power in Germany would afford to the Communists the easiest means of penetrating the government and seizing control."[28] De Gaulle said to John Foster Dulles that "the establishment of a central government [in

[23] Spevack (2002), p. 323.
[24] FRUS (1949), vol. 3, p. 197.
[25] To the examples cited in Chapter 1 one can add the recent Iraqi constitution-making process, in which the Kurds were able to obtain concessions from the Americans because President Bush "had to have results quickly if he wanted to be reelected" (Arato 2009, p. 173).
[26] Spevack (2002), p. 369.
[27] Golay (1958), p. 8.
[28] Ibid. This is a classical dilemma. While more difficult to capture by internal or external enemies of democracy, a decentralized system is also less capable of energetic action to defend itself against capture.

Germany] could only lead to a government by Stalin and von Paulus."[29] As we shall see, the American military governor was also sympathetic to this view. Eventually, however, the French became less obsessed with protecting France against German power and more concerned with economic recovery. They were not willing to follow de Gaulle when he said he was "willing to give up the benefits of the Marshall Plan, if this was the price France would have to pay" to prevent its zone from merging into a state with the British and American zones.[30]

The American military governor Lucius Clay took a very strong stance against centralization. In February 1949, he wrote that since the Germans would not listen, the Allies had to impose their will: "If that means no Western German government, then there would be no Western German government."[31] In late March, he proposed if necessary, to have a decentralized constitution adopted by a "Kampfabstimmung" (a closely contested vote), relying only on the Christian Democrats in the Constitutional Council.[32] He stressed that "the main disagreement lay in the field of finances. The CDU was willing to go along with US wishes, while the SPD held out and resisted US demands. Clay said that although he did 'not have any substantiating evidence,' he did believe that 'a part of our difficulties are rumored to come from British encouragement to SPD to hold out until Foreign Ministers meeting, as this meeting may result in acceptance of SPD views.'"[33] He was right on both counts.

When the Department of State expressed its desire to have a consensually adopted constitution, Clay replied in strong (if ungrammatical) terms:

> To accept German proposal on Basic law means that open defiance by SPD [Socialist] leader Schumacher has won. It makes him greatest figure in Germany and repudiates CDU/CSU which loyally stood by and which represents great majority in our zone. It accepts what I know to be a fact. British back door promise to SPD and assures socialist Germany. Do not let [Department of] State claim SPD only democratic force as it is close to a totalitarian party in operation and lacks the democracy which comes from local pride. We would truly establish the centralized and dangerous structure which Molotov wanted as facile to communist touch.[34]

---

[29] Roussel (2002), p. 551. (Von Paulus was a German general who surrendered at Stalingrad and later joined the Communists.) In August 1948, C. J. Friedrich, acting as adviser to the American military governor, stressed the need to adopt the constitution quickly. "One reason was that John Foster Dulles might become Secretary of State in the United States. His policies were known to be pro-French, and this would hurt the Germans. Secondly, Charles de Gaulle might gain power in France at the end of 1948, and he was known to categorically oppose the formation of any kind of German state" (Spevack 2002, p. 276).

[30] Spevack (2002), p. 337.

[31] Cited after Grabbe (1978), p. 397.

[32] Wilms (1999), pp. 253–54.

[33] Spevack (2002), pp. 435–36.

[34] Cited in Wilms (1999), p. 290 (verbatim text). Earlier, Clay had claimed that the Socialists had electoral rather than substantive motives when arguing for a centralized policy, citing "the very great dangers which will result from permitting [Schumacher and the small group of party bureaucrats sitting around him] to make a success of defiance of the occupation authorities on an issue of major policy, particularly as it is done to gain political popularity in the following election" (ibid., p. 257).

Although CDU had earlier accepted the "great compromise" that allowed for financial transfers among the Länder, it declared, on March 30, that it was indeed willing to give in to the American demands. When the Foreign Ministers met on April 4–8, they adopted one statement urging the Germans to comply with the requests of the military governors, and, in case these were not accepted by the SPD, another statement expressing willingness to give in to the SPD demands. Once the SPD had expressed its defiance on April 20, the second statement was released. The Allies blinked first, not only because of the time pressure, but also because of their desire to have the constitution adopted with a high degree of consensus.

In Chapter 2 I referred to the psychological mechanism of *reactance* – the tendency to reject, even at the expense of personal welfare, any perceived attack on the autonomy of a decision maker. A person who initially prefers A over B might undergo a preference reversal if a person in authority tells her to choose A. According to one analysis, that is the story of the Bonn constitution: "Considering the actual over-all modifications effected in the Basic Law by the heavy-handed interference of the Allied governors, the result seems not to have been entirely to their advantage.... The cause of federalism in Germany had been much stronger before the military governors discredited it with their constitutional engineering."[35]

The last statements seem impossible to verify. The Americans were, however, aware of the problem. They "tried everything in order not to let the new constitutional order of West Germany be perceived as an imposed constitution" and to avoid "the public impression of a dictated constitution."[36] Specifically, the Americans did not appear in uniform at the opening session of the Parliamentary Council.[37] Also, when Adenauer and the British military governor Robertson "discussed the handling over of an *aide-mémoire* to the Germans informing them of various Allied policies on the basic law ..., Robertson said that since the Allies did not wish to create the impression that they were trying to pressure the Parliamentary Council, they would not hand over an *aide-mémoire*, but rather they would read a note very slowly to Adenauer so notes could be taken on the German side."[38] With regard to the constitutions of the Länder, an American memorandum of July 20, 1946, to the experts stated that "informality should be the key note of their contact and the efforts should always be to elicit the necessary changes on the initiative of the Germans, and not to impose them."[39]

It is hard to imagine that these naïve if well-meaning efforts made much of a difference. General Clay claimed, however, to have succeeded in the effort to avoid what one might call "reactance formation" (not to be confused with Freudian reaction formation). In a later interview with his biographer, he stated

---

[35] Merkl (1963), p. 126; see also Spevack (2002), p. 387.
[36] Spevack (2002), pp. 124, 261.
[37] Ibid., p. 363.
[38] Ibid., p. 384.
[39] Cited in ibid., pp. 95–96.

that "indirectly we influenced the Basic Law, far more than we would have if we tried to dictate it. If we had tried to dictate the Basic Law, the convention would have adjourned. There wouldn't have been any constitution."[40] The statement is somewhat self-serving, however, since if Clay had had his way in April 1949, the SPD might have left the convention and there might indeed not have been any constitution. Hard bargaining under time pressure and the need for a large consensus rather than tact and informality made the constitution possible. The Allies achieved one of their aims, a decentralized tax collection.

In Japan, the main constitutional issue concerned the person and the office of the emperor. Before Japan's capitulation, Dean Acheson argued against a proposal to open the door for the preservation of the dynasty in the Potsdam declaration: "the usefulness of the emperor in arranging surrender must be weighed against the long-term dangers of the institution."[41] Hirohito did indeed turn out to play a valuable role in the surrender, but that is not why General MacArthur engineered to have the constitution include the person and the institution of the emperor, albeit in a purely symbolic role. Rather, it was because he thought Japan without the emperor would be a hotbed for Communist agitation (p. 48) and that one would need, in his words, to maintain "a minimum of a million troops ... for an indefinite number of years" (p. 291).

The time pressure in this case was due to the division among the Allies. The Moscow Agreement adopted by the victorious Allies on December 26, 1945, stated that "Directives which prescribe fundamental changes in Japan's constitutional structure ... shall be issued only after consultation and agreement has been reached in the Far Eastern Commission" (p. 88). Each of the big four would have a veto. Some countries represented on that commission, notably Australia and the Soviet Union, wanted to abolish the imperial institution or at least try Hirohito as a war criminal (p. 261). MacArthur successfully conspired with the Japanese to preempt any decision along those lines. In early February 1946 he told his collaborators to prepare a draft constitution within a week, which they did. He then enlisted the Japanese in a conspiracy to present his text as theirs:

MacArthur's concern ... was not only to save the emperor but to defend his own authority as supreme commander against the Moscow Agreement. His goal was to have a draft constitution ready before the commission began its meetings in Washington, one he could pass off as the work of the Japanese government. The commission scheduled its first meeting on February 26. As the date approached, [MacArthur] increased the pressure on the Japanese quickly to convert the American draft into a Japanese document. MacArthur was playing a complicated game. Having a draft constitution "initiated by the Japanese through a revision process that predated the Moscow Agreement might block the [Far Eastern Commission] from assuming direction of constitutional reform (p. 119).

---

[40] Smith (1992), p. 541.
[41] Moore and Robinson (2002), p. 27. In the following discussion of Japan, all page references in parentheses are to this outstanding study.

As in Germany, it was important to present the draft as an authentic national document rather than as an imposed one. "Both sides needed secrecy: the Japanese cabinet to maintain the appearance of being the initiators, [MacArthur] to avoid the appearance of violating the Moscow Agreement" (p. 110). The audience for their deception was not domestic, however, but international. The strong "odor of translation" (p. 141) was so obvious that no Japanese citizen could be fooled. Yet when the newly elected Diet debated the constitution in the summer of 1946, the main Japanese defender of the draft "never permitted members of the House to treat the Japanese text as a translation" (p. 242). The pretense was dropped only in a subcommittee working behind closed doors (ibid.).

The Diet adopted the draft in all essentials.[42] On its own initiative, it obtained the substitution of a bicameral legislature (as had traditionally existed in Japan) for the unicameral one proposed by the Americans. The main drafter, Colonel Charles Kades, "expressed the opinion that, whether the Japanese legislature would be unicameral or bicameral could be used as 'an effective bargaining lever' to negotiate with the Japanese government so that 'a more important issue' could be kept in the Draft."[43] On the initiative of the Far Eastern Commission, the constitution requires the Prime Minister and members of the cabinet to be members of the Diet. These two changes are somewhat incongruent, the second suggesting a Westminster system not usually associated with bicameralism. The constitution was not written with a view to coherence.

The Japanese and especially the German episode illuminate collective decision making quite generally as well as constitution-making more specifically. In a broad sense, both involved joint decision making by the occupier and the occupied rather than top-down imposition of a decision. The writing of the Soviet-style constitutions in Eastern Europe illustrates the latter case. These constitutions, however, were never meant to matter. They slowed down the machinery of legislation, but (with the partial exception of Poland) did not constrain the outcomes. By contrast, in Germany and in Japan the victorious powers wanted to set in place an enduring constitution that would constrain future national governments, a goal that constrained their own freedom of action and required them to enlist the defeated powers as co-deciders.

In the remainder of this chapter I shall consider normative issues that arise in designing a constituent assembly. I do not believe that an *optimal design* can be defined by its tendency to produce a *good constitution*, one that conforms to independently defined criteria of goodness. Instead I shall focus on the negative task of removing passion, interest, bias, or prejudice from the process, or reduce

---

[42] It has been argued (Inoue 1991), however, that the American and Japanese versions of the document express entirely different constitutional ideas, reflecting the different values and traditions of the two countries.

[43] http://www.ndl.go.jp/constitution/e/ronten/04ronten.html; see also Moore and Robinson (2002), p. 354.

the influence of these distortions on the framers. In addition, I shall consider the desirability of diversity among the members of the constituent assembly.

Generally speaking (see Chapter 3), the assembly ought to be organized to promote the moral aptitude, intellectual aptitude, and active aptitude of the framers. By moral aptitude I shall understand *impartiality* (in the negative form of disinterested and dispassionate decision making). By intellectual aptitude, I shall understand *absence of cognitive bias* at the individual level and *diversity* at the collective level. By active aptitude, I shall understand the *full attention and concentration* of the constitution-makers to their task, by making it seem worthwhile and by eliminating other charges that might occupy them. Although I have argued that these are general desiderata of collective decision making, they need to be modulated by the constitution-making context.

Constitutions and their individual articles are intended to *endure*, not indefinitely and not without change, but with a greater expected life span than ordinary legislation. This feature of constitutions follows immediately from what I said about the need to make it difficult to amend them. It also follows that *intergenerational impartiality* becomes an important consideration. Although the remote future is to a large degree shrouded in uncertainty, that fact can generate advantages as well as obstacles. Concerning the latter, the sheer intellectual difficulty of predicting the development of society a few generations in the future might seem almost paralyzing. As George Mason wrote to his son in the first days of the Federal Convention, "to view, through the calm, sedate medium of reason, the influence which the establishment now proposed may have upon the happiness or misery of millions yet unborn, is an object of such magnitude as absorbs, and in a manner suspends the operation of the human understanding."[44] How could measures to counteract climate change, for instance, be entrenched in a constitution?

At the same time, in the debates at the Convention Mason stressed how a veil of ignorance could *facilitate* decision making:

We ought to attend to the rights of every class of people. He [Mason] had often wondered at the indifference of the superior classes of society to this dictate of humanity & policy, considering that however affluent their circumstances, or elevated their situations, might be, the course of a few years, not only might but certainly would distribute their posterity through the lowest classes of Society. Every selfish motive therefore, every family attachment, ought to recommend such a system of policy as would provide no less carefully for the rights and happiness of the lowest than of the highest orders of Citizens.[45]

---

[44] Farrand (1966), vol. 3, p. 33.
[45] Farrand (1966), vol. 1, p. 49. For other more or less sincere uses of the argument at the Convention, see ibid., vol. 1, p. 531, and vol. 2, p. 3. On impartiality-mimicking mechanisms in general, see Elster (2004a, 2006b, 2009a).

In other words, behind a veil of ignorance, the long-term self-interest of families can *mimic impartiality*. That mechanism only works, however, if framers have children[46] (or collateral descendants) and have a long time horizon.[47]

The general framework also needs to be modulated with regard to *passion*. Compared with other collective bodies, constituent assemblies stand out because of the turbulent environment in which they operate. "No liberal democratic state has accomplished comprehensive constitutional change outside the context of some cataclysmic situation such as revolution, world war, the withdrawal of empire, civil war, or the threat of imminent breakup."[48] To this list of triggering factors we can add the occurrence of an acute financial crisis, as in France in 1789 and Iceland in 2011. All these situations are likely to create a high emotional temperature. In some cases, passion has affected the decisions of constituent assemblies in arguably undesirable ways.

Although *Federalist* No. 85 refers to the "[prodigious] establishment of a Constitution in time of profound peace," the reality was quite different.[49] Shays's Rebellion had strongly impressed many of the framers in Philadelphia. Writing to William Smith on November 13, 1787, Jefferson asserted that "Our Convention has been too much impressed by the insurrection of Massachusetts: and in the spur of the moment they are setting up a kite [hawk] to keep the henyard in order." He was clearly implying that the framers were acting under the impulse of visceral fear and not merely out of rational or prudential fear.[50] Although some scholars minimize the importance of Shays's Rebellion for the proceedings of the Convention,[51] I am inclined to believe that Jefferson knew what he was talking about. The highly exaggerated statements by many

---

[46] George Mason had ten children. He also proposed that every father of a household with three children receive the right to vote; for others he wanted to impose strict property requirements (Pole 1966, p. 287). The argument from the long-term self-interest of families does not imply, however, that childless individuals are less likely to be motivated by the long-term public interest. Some 30 years ago I heard a later Nobel prize–winning economist assert that Keynes's allegedly disastrous lack of concern for the future ("In the long run we are all dead") had to do with the fact that, as a homosexual, he had no stake in the welfare of future generations. Apart from the absurdity of the argument when applied to Keynes, "whose inspiring devotion to the public good . . . finally killed him" (Cairncross 2004, p. 497) and who was *skeptical* about our ability to anticipate long-term consequences of present actions rather than *unconcerned* with the future, it ignores the fact that family interests can be mediated by collateral descendants. In the Catholic Church, for instance, prelates have often favored the ecclesiastical careers of their nephews.

[47] Vermeule (2007), p. 47.

[48] Russell (1993), p. 106. The Swedish constitutional reform of 1974 and the Hungarian reform of 2011 are exceptions.

[49] Elster (2012); also Sajó (2011), ch. 3. It is not always clear, however, whether the passages adduced by Sajó reflect visceral or merely prudential fear.

[50] For this distinction, see Gordon (1987), p. 77. When Montaigne (1991), p. 83, wrote that "It is fear that I am most afraid of" or Franklin Roosevelt asserted that "The only thing we have to fear, is fear itself," they probably referred to a prudential fear of visceral fear (Ken Shepsle, personal communication).

[51] Feer (1966), and, relying on him, Ackerman and Katyal (1995). Brynner (1993) offers a persuasive refutation of Feer's views; see also Richards (2002), ch. 6.

delegates about the dangers of democracy, leveling, and agrarian laws reveal the influence of visceral fear.[52]

Several French constitution-making episodes also demonstrate the impact of passion – more specifically of *fear* – on framers. At Versailles, the abolition of feudalism on August 4, 1789, indubitably owed something to the visceral fear of the constituants that their castles might be burned and their families slaughtered.[53] The debates on bicameralism and the royal veto one month later also took place in the shadow of violence. If we compare the two drafts made by the Committee of Constitution of the French constituent assembly of 1848, before and after the June insurrection of the Parisian workers, the second was considerably less radical than the first.[54] The constitution of the Fifth French Republic was adopted when the parliamentarians of the Fourth Republic granted full powers to de Gaulle under the pressure of events in Algeria. In his inimitable telescoping, "In 1958 I had a problem of conscience. I could just let things take their course: the paratroopers in Paris, the parliamentarians in the Seine, the general strike, the government of the Americans: it was written on the wall. Finally a moment would have arrived when everybody would have come looking for de Gaulle, but at what price? Thus I decided to intervene in time to prevent the drama."[55] It makes sense to assume that some parliamentarians feared for their lives and that their visceral fear affected their decision to abdicate from power.

Other exogenous emotions can have a more constructive role. La Bruyère asserted that "Nothing is easier for passion than to overcome reason; its great triumph is to conquer interest."[56] One might add, as a corollary, that nothing is easier for interest than to overcome reason, except when reason allies itself with passion.[57] Some decisive episodes in the first French *constituante* had a strong basis in passion. The abolition of feudalism on August 4, 1789, was due not only to fear but also to enthusiasm.[58] In September 1789, when the assembly debated the new division of the country into *départements*, which would replace the old division into provinces, Clermont-Tonnerre, said that "Anarchy is a frightening yet necessary passage, and the only moment one can establish a new order of things. It is not in calm times that one can take uniform measures."[59]

[52] Elster (2012).
[53] Ferrières (1932), p. 109 ff.; Elster (2011, 2012).
[54] Bastid (1945), vol. 1, p. 234; Coutant (2009), p. 91. Among other changes, the second draft abolished the right to work and substituted proportional for progressive taxation. According to Coutant (2009), pp. 241–54, other constitutional choices were shaped by the actions of the radical workers in Paris in May 1848 and notably by their invasion of the assembly on May 15.
[55] Peyrefitte (1995), p. 262.
[56] La Bruyère (2007), p. 98.
[57] Rubenfeld (2001) offers a sustained argument to that effect.
[58] Tocqueville (2004b), p. 593; see also Elster (2007b, 2009a, 2011).
[59] AP 9, p. 461. It is amusing in this context to see Madison at the Federal Convention objecting to a reconstruction of the Union in 13 equal-size states by citing Necker's unsuccessful efforts in France "to equalize *in some points only* the different usages & regulations of the different provinces" (Farrand 1966, vol. I, p. 321; my italics). Madison ignored, as did Necker, that the aim could be achieved only by a revolution *across the board*. It is not true that he who cannot do the less cannot do the more.

These passions were mainly exogenous to the constitution-making process, but to some extent also a result of institutional design. In his *Mémoires*, Bailly, the normally sober President of the Constituante in June 1789, explained why he went back on his initial proposal to ban applause:

I observed that silence, being a sign of reverent contemplation (*recuillement*), would be more dignified. I was interrupted by general applause. The rule was once again violated, and the Assembly was much amused by this disobedience, of which I could not really complain. What one had asked for was too much, and it was not possible. Gravitas, contemplation and silence no doubt constitute the majesty of the representatives of the nation. The legislative body must arrive at this point some day; but at that time all was danger, exhaustion, discouragement, all proposals were fraught with difficulty, all options had their inconvenient side; it was necessary to feel approved, animated, electrified. All men are men, that is, they are weak. The wise, the legislators for the nation were new and as it were like children in politics; and we all needed the *macte animo*.[60]

This being said, the net effect of enthusiastic feelings is not necessarily positive. While emotions may cause an agent to be motivated by the common interest rather than by self-interest, they may also reduce his capacity to determine the appropriate means to realize his goal.[61] In Bentham's language, if emotions enhance the "exultation" and hence the moral aptitude of the actors, they can also undermine their intellectual aptitude, by two distinct mechanisms. First, enthusiasm tends to inspire wishful thinking. Second, the *urgency* of emotion tends to induce suboptimal investment in information.[62]

I shall now consider the following design choices: the task of the constituent assembly (II), the location of the assembly (III), the size and duration of the assembly (IV), the elections to the assembly (V), the secrecy or publicity of debates and votes (VI), and ratification of the document produced by the assembly (VII).[63] These

---

[60] Bailly (1804), pp. 314–15. The deputy Bouche used the same metaphor to argue for transferring the locus of debate from the committees to the assembly, where "souls become strong and electrified, and where names, ranks, and distinctions count for nothing" (AP 8, p. 307). Although both arguments are consistent with the debates being closed to non-deputies, the radicals wanted an even larger resonance chamber.

[61] Kant (1790), p. 154, claimed that enthusiasm, like any other affect, is "blind, either in the choice of its end, or, if this is given by Reason, in its implementation; for it is that movement of the mind that makes it incapable of engaging in free consideration of principles." If we understand Reason as the conjunction of impartial ends and the choice of rational means (Elster 2006c), we can understand Kant as saying that in enthusiasm the first component is present, but not the second. Allouche-Pourcel (2010), p. 105, hits the nail on the head when she affirms that enthusiasm illustrates the proverb that "The best is the enemy of the good."

[62] Elster (2010c).

[63] Let me briefly mention two other design elements that I could also have discussed, but that seemed too marginal. First, one might consider the choice of a unicameral versus a bicameral assembly. In 1789, some actors called for the transformation of the Estates-General into a bicameral constituent body, but it never became a live option. Although there are examples of bicameral constituent assemblies (Japan 1946, Turkey 1961, Spain 1978, Romania 1991, Poland 1992), the only argument in their favor (see Chapter 3) would seem to be that a bicameral assembly is less likely to disregard its internal rules of procedure. Second, one might consider the voting and quorum rules of the assembly. Although many assemblies have aspired to a high degree of consensus, the

instrumental variables will be considered with regard to their capacity to enhance active aptitude and epistemic quality, and to reduce the impact of interest and passion. Section VIII offers a brief conclusion.

II. THE TASK OF THE CONSTITUENT ASSEMBLY

Some constituent assemblies are elected only to write or propose a constitution, and in fact only perform that task. Examples include the Federal Convention, the Norwegian assembly of 1814 (with a minor exception mentioned later), the German assembly of 1948–49, and many American state conventions. Overall, however, these "pure" assemblies or, as I shall call them, *conventions* are in a minority.[64] The more common mixed assemblies take three forms: legislatures elected with a dual legislative and constituent mandate (*mandated constituent legislatures*), legislatures that arrogate the constituent power to themselves (*self-created constituent legislatures*), and assemblies elected to write a constitution which then also assume legislative powers (*self-created legislating assemblies*). I shall argue that conventions are superior to the three mixed regimes in several respects.[65] I first characterize the various regimes, then discuss and reject arguments purporting to show the superiority of mixed regimes to conventions, and conclude by arguing directly for the superiority of conventions.

A convention usually needs to be supplemented by another organ to handle current affairs. The Federal Convention ran in parallel with the Continental Congress.[66] In Colombia (1991) and Venezuela (1999), the Presidents essentially

formal voting rules have almost always been vote by simple majority (South Africa 1996 is a partial exception). In the frequently occurring situation where there is no status quo that can serve as a default option, this choice is almost inevitable. At the Constituante, where many feared that a high quorum would allow the privileged orders to obstruct the proceedings (Castaldo 1989, p. 130), a low quorum of 200 (out of 1,200) was chosen. At the Federal Convention, a quorum of seven states (out of twelve) was necessary; also, nine states imposed a quorum on their delegations. While the diversity desideratum (discussed later) points in the direction of a high quorum, the risk of obstruction by a minority points in the opposite direction.

[64] Ginsburg, Elkin, and Blount (2009), p. 205, classify 406 constitutions adopted between 1789 and 2005, and find that only about 100 were written or proposed by a pure assembly. Their data are unreliable, however, as they also include Soviet-style sham constitutions. In addition to being overinclusive, they are also underinclusive, in not taking account of state constitutions in federal systems. As shown by Hoar (1917) and Kruman (1997), constitution-making in the American states has been an extremely rich laboratory for institutional design.

[65] Bryce (1995), vol. 1, pp. 606–8, is one of the few writers on the subject to offer a comparative analysis of the merits of conventions and other constituent assemblies. In addition to several arguments in the favor of conventions that overlap with the ones offered later in the chapter, Bryce claims that self-selection will lead to a greater proportion of public-spirited individuals, that is, with greater moral aptitude. He also asserts, without argument, that conventions will induce people of greater ability (intellectual aptitude) to stand for office. Miller (2010), pp. 611–15, discusses the pros and cons of pure conventions in 19 recent constitution-making processes.

[66] In parallel, but also interacting with one another in what might, perhaps by a stretch, be called a single encompassing decision-making process. James Madison's secretary recounted, "This brings to my recollection what I was told by Mr. Madison, and which I do not remember ever to have seen in print. The Old Congress held its sessions in 1787 in New York while at the same time the

declared war on their legislatures by calling elections to constituent assemblies in ways not provided for by the existing constitutions. The "cohabitation" of the two assemblies proved to be highly unstable. In Colombia, the constitutional convention ordered the dissolution of the legislature and elected an interim legislature from within its own body.[67] In Venezuela, the constitutional convention "seized the constituted power" in what amounted to a coup d'état.[68] These events would seem to validate Robespierre's analysis in a speech from 1793, in which he said that "A double representation contains the germ of civil war.... One assembly would appeal to the existing constitution and the other to the keener interest that a people takes in new representatives; the struggle would be engaged and the rivalry would excite hatred."[69] The American case does not support this claim, however.[70]

The handling of current affairs can also be managed by a non-legislative body. In Italy, the decree-law of March 16, 1946, assigned most legislative powers to the government. De Gaulle also wanted a solution of this kind for the constituent assembly in 1945, but it was rejected by the provisional consultative assembly that had been established in Algiers in 1943 and transferred to Paris in 1944.[71] When the German Parliamentary Council elaborated the 1949 Bonn constitution, current affairs were handled by the occupational powers.

A mandated constituent legislature is explicitly elected with the double task of adopting a constitution and performing the task of an ordinary legislature. Thus in the election of the first French Parliament after 1945 the voters were asked, "Do you want the assembly elected today to be a constituent assembly?" and 96 percent of the voters answered Yes. In 1776, John Scott argued that the existing Provincial Congress in the state of New York "had the power to [frame] a government, or at least, that it is doubtful whether they have not that power."

convention which framed the constitution of the United States held its sessions in Philadelphia. Many individuals were members of both bodies, and thus were enabled to know what was passing in each – both sitting with closed doors and in secret sessions. The distracting question of slavery was agitating and retarding the labors of both, and led to conferences and inter-communications of the members, which resulted in a compromise by which the northern or anti-slavery portion of the country agreed to incorporate into the Ordinance and Constitution the provision to restore fugitive slaves; and this mutual and concurrent action was the cause of the similarity of the provision contained in both, and had its influence in creating the great unanimity by which the Ordinance passed, and also making the constitution the more acceptable to the slave holders" (Coles 1856, pp. 28–29). See also Lynd (2009), ch. 8.

[67] Fox, Gallón-Giraldo, and Stetson (2010), p. 474.

[68] Brewer-Carías (2010), p. 514.

[69] Cited after Le Pillouer (2003), p. 127. In 1790, the constituant Salle claimed that two parallel assemblies would soon merge into one bicameral body (AP 30, p. 106).

[70] In the context of constitution-making in Turkey, Arato (2010) proposes the simultaneous election of an ordinary legislature with the current 10 percent threshold for representation and of a constituent assembly elected without any threshold. As may happen in the current Icelandic process, the legislature would have to approve the constitution proposed by the convention, with the right to amend it. In my view, that procedure would involve an unacceptable delegation of *pouvoir constituant* to a *pouvoir constitué*. Parliamentary self-dealing would be highly likely.

[71] Bougrab (2002), pp. 270–71. As noted by Le Pillouer (2003), p. 282, the solution proposed in France and adopted in Italy amounted to "avoiding the confusion of constituent and legislative powers by creating the accumulation of executive and legislative powers."

Gouverneur Morris argued strongly, however, for calling a constitutional convention, and a compromise was reached in the election of a mandated constituent legislature, which took care of Morris's concern for the legitimacy of the new constitution.[72] In Delaware, by contrast, the need for a new constitution was seen as more important than the need for a mandate.[73]

A self-created constituent legislature is elected as an ordinary parliament and then turns itself into a constituent assembly. This was a very common pattern among the American states during the Revolutionary years. Among the constituent assemblies convened in this period, eight fell in this category.[74] The Second Continental Congress, too, was a self-appointed constituent body when it enacted the Articles of Confederation.[75] The French National Assembly of 1871 offers another, albeit more ambiguous case. Although elected only to conclude the peace negotiations with Germany, the assembly took it upon itself, by "force of circumstance," to fill the constitutional vacuum created by the abdication of Napoleon III.[76] The Hungarian Parliament of 1989–90 was also self-appointed. It had been created under Communist rule, but took it upon itself to destroy that regime by piecewise constitutional amendments that amounted to a wholly new constitution.[77]

The making of the French constitution of 1958 offers an interesting case. The day before the National Assembly on June 3, 1958, delegated the constituent power to de Gaulle, the proposition was debated in the Constitutional Committee of the Parliament. The following exchange seems worth reproducing at some length, both because it raises important issues and, more anecdotally, because it reveals the utter historical ignorance of some of the debaters.

M. Chaintron [deputy, the Communist Party]. Our fathers and our teachers in democracy judged that only a constituent assembly was empowered to offer a constitution to the people. Although the people possesses the constituent power, it cannot establish the necessary texts, but must put its trust in representatives mandated to this effect. What, however, is the situation today? The substitution of an areopage, made up, we do not know how, of one man, for these mandated representatives. The referendum is no doubt democratic, but under the conditions in which it will take place, it will de facto be a plebiscite.

M. de Marcilhacy [senator, independent]. Dear Colleague, let me remind you, since we are doing history, that the *Constituante* [of 1789] was never designed to make a constitution. I am surprised that I have to remind you that it elevated itself into a constituent assembly. The making of the constitutions of other great democracies is another matter.

---

[72] Kline (1978), pp. 54–56.
[73] Kruman (1997), pp. 28–29.
[74] Hoar (1917).
[75] Rakove (1979), ch. 8.
[76] Bastid (1956), p. 216.
[77] This is not a fully accurate description. Formally, the Communist parliaments always had both legislative and constituent power. Yet in the "unwritten material constitution of all communist regimes" (Arato and Miklósi 2010, p. 364), the party had all power. Thus what happened in Hungary in 1989–90 was that parliament turned its de jure powers into de facto powers.

Can you tell me, for example, how the constitution of the United States was drawn up? And that of the Soviet Union?

Edgard Pisani [senator, the Democratic Left]. As regards the United States, it is very simple. It was written by a secret committee of five wise men. These five persons were sworn to secrecy. All the papers arising out of their work were burned, and they took an oath never to reveal the secrecy of their deliberations. This is how the American constitution was drawn up.

M. de Marcilhacy. This shows that there are no good or bad ways of making a constitution. There are only good or bad constitutions.[78]

On the anecdotal level, it it is surprising to see a non-Communist senator characterizing the Soviet Union as a "great democracy" and more than surprising to see a senator with a B.A. in the humanities (*licence de lettres*) offering a completely fabricated version of the making of the American constitution. Substantively, Chaintron's observation that the people should speak *first* (in electing a mandated constituent assembly) and not only *last* (in ratifying the constitution) seems right on target. The final claim by Marcilhacy is, of course, an outright denial of the central idea of the present chapter.

The Spanish assembly of 1977 constitutes a unique case: elections to a constituent body under a veil of uncertainty:

Arguably, the most "democratic mode of handling constitution-drafting is through the creation of a constituent assembly. In the Spanish case, however, much confusion and vagueness surrounded the subject. Nobody quite knew whether the June 15, 1977 elections would result in a "regularly" elected parliament (or Cortes) or an "extraordinarily" created constituent assembly. The political parties were divided on the issue. Liberal and leftist parties strongly favored the constituent option. The UCD [Union of the Democratic Center], as the party in transitionary power, much preferred a regularly elected parliament, with its potentially longer lifespan. The UCD's view prevailed. Their victory would permit them to remain in power once the new constitution was adopted.[79]

A self-created legislative assembly is elected as a constitutional convention and then assumes legislative powers, following either of two maxims: "He who can do more can do less,"[80] and "He who can create a power can also exercise it."[81] Examples include the Norwegian constituent assembly of 1814, which took it upon itself to create a finance committee, a task that "normally would have belonged to a regular parliament";[82] the self-created Frankfurt Parliament of 1848, which dissolved the Assembly of the German Confederation and arrogated its powers to itself; and the Indian constituent assembly of 1946. In the

---

[78] Comité National (1987), vol. 1, p. 192; my italics.

[79] Bonime-Blanc (1987), pp. 35–36.

[80] Le Pillouer (2003), pp. 98, 130, 133. Conversely, it has been argued that "one could not admit that the [the French Estates-General] had the constituent power, since they never had possessed the legislative power" (Olivier-Martin 2010, p. 422).

[81] Le Pillouer (2003), p. 143; see also Hoar (1917), p. 65.

[82] Steen (1951), pp. 156–57.

19th century, a number of American states called conventions that authorized themselves to legislate.[83]

I shall argue that conventions are superior to mixed assemblies on three grounds: they promote active aptitude, they prevent path-dependence, and they reduce the impact of personal and institutional interest on the decisions. First, however, let me consider some objections to this claim.

The two Latin American cases and Robespierre's questionable authority do not prove that dual assemblies are disastrous. After all, the Federal Convention and the Continental Congress did coexist and in fact cooperated, apparently without friction. One might argue, perhaps, that constituent legislatures are desirable because of the scarcity of competent legislators. If a country opts for the concurrent operation of a legislature and a constitutional convention, the quality of debates and decisions in each will suffer. Against this argument one may cite the claim that "experience has shown ... in the United States, the country in which this method [conventions] has been largely used for redrafting, or preparing amendments to, the Constitutions of the several States, that a set of men can be found for the work of a Convention better than those who form the ordinary legislature of the State."[84] Hamilton argued (Chapter 3) that the glory of performing an important task might attract superior individuals.

In Canada, the Beaudoin-Edwards Special Joint Committee argued that constituent legislatures are superior because the framers can be held accountable at the next election.[85] It is certainly desirable that self-created constituent legislatures should be held accountable in some way, either by reelection or by downstream ratification of the constitution. If these were to arrogate the constituent power to themselves without being accountable to anyone, it would amount to a legislative coup d'état. It is less clear why conventions (or constituent legislatures with an upstream mandate) would also need a downstream approval. If this should be thought desirable, ratification can obviate the need to hold the (blunt) ax of reelection over the head of the framers.

One might argue, furthermore, that conventions are inferior to constituent legislatures because, in their inability to legislate, they might write matters into the constitution that ought, by the nature of the subject matter, to be left to statute. This practice has, in particular, been common in many American state conventions. Although "this subterfuge of including legislation in the constitution has not always gone unchallenged by the courts," still "many of our State constitutions today [1917] consist for the most part of legislative details which ought to have been left to the ordinary legislature."[86] Yet this temptation is matched by the temptation of a majority in constituent legislatures to constitutionalize clauses that by their nature belong to statute, to make it more unlikely

---

[83] Hoar (1917), pp. 140–48.
[84] Bryce (1905), p. 62; also Hoar (1917), p. 113.
[85] Government of Canada (1991), p. 48.
[86] Hoar (1917), pp. 143–44.

that future majorities or a constitutional court will overturn them.[87] Along similar lines, as soon as the Assemblée Constituante had imposed the principle that ordinary laws but not constitutional provisions were subject to the royal veto, the deputies had a clear incentive to present each of their decisions as a constitutional one.[88] Louis XVI complained that "the Assembly has completely excluded the King from the Constitution by refusing him the right to approve or veto the articles which it declares to be constitutional by reserving for itself the right to include in this category the articles that it finds expedient."[89]

Strictly speaking, mixed assemblies do not suffer from the problem of *cumul des mandats*. They siege in a single body. Yet because that body exercises two powers and sometimes three, mixed assemblies are likely to undermine active aptitude in a similar way. As Madison wrote in his preamble to the Virginia resolution calling for the Federal Convention, it would be "preferable to a discussion of the subject in Congress, where it might be too much interrupted by ordinary business." When one reads the records of the Assemblée Constituante, it is hard to imagine how the framers could pursue any kind of sustained and focused discussion. On any given day, the assembly might consider constitutional issues, legislative questions, petitions and addresses, and executive decisions, with priorities largely determined by the urgency of current affairs. When Clermont-Tonnerre proposed that the Assembly set aside one day a week to receive petitions and demands from the provinces, Robespierre replied that in the context of civil war and conspiracies a delayed response "could upset the public order."[90] The Assembly did not vote on the proposal. The debates in the Continental Congress and in the mixed American state constituent assemblies in the Revolutionary period operated in the same way. In all these cases, the framer legislators were also distracted by events taking place *outside* the assembly. I am not making the anachronistic claim that these mixed assemblies ought to have been replaced by a dual system, but only claiming that when multitasking and distractions are avoidable – as they were not in those cases – they should be avoided. In this respect, the Federal Convention provides a good model. Although some individual framers were distracted by their personal affairs or by their role as delegates to the Continental Congress, their focus on their task was remarkably good.

A second argument against mixed regimes is that decisions made by the assembly wearing its legislative hat may unduly affect the decisions it makes wearing its constitutional hat (a form of path-dependence). An example from the Assemblée Constituante will illustrate the problem.

---

[87] In Austria, "the Constitutional Court had overruled a 'necessity evaluation' for new taxi companies as interfering with the freedom of occupation. The constitutional legislator, however, simply re-issued the same regulation in the rank of constitutional law" (Ackerer 2008, p. 458).

[88] De Staël (2000), p. 243; she also ascribed this practice to the Assembly's "illusion d'auteur" on the perfection and durability of its work.

[89] AP 27, p. 379.

[90] AP 9, p. 469.

In the fall of 1789, Mirabeau twice addressed the issue of the relation between the King's minister and the assembly. In September, his proposal that ministers chosen from the assembly should be able to retain their seat (or stand for reelection) might have been adopted had it been put to a vote, which for technical reasons it was not.[91] When the issue came up again in November, he argued for the more limited proposal that the ministers be allowed to have a "consultative voice" in the assembly until "the constitution shall have fixed the rules which shall be followed with regard to them."[92] Had the vote not been postponed until the next day, the proposal might have been adopted. As the delay gave Mirabeau's enemies time to gather their forces, it was defeated. Among the arguments offered against it, the most relevant for my purposes was made by Pierre-François Blin, a deputy for the third estate: "The issue may seem detached from the constitution and to be merely provisional; but the authority of the past on the future binds the facts at all times."[93] Although the appeal to the danger of precedent setting was probably a pretext for excluding Mirabeau from the ministry, the argument itself is plausible and, in fact, applies directly to Blin's own successful motion that "No member of the National Assembly shall from now on be able to enter the ministry during the term of the present session." It is likely that the article in the constitution of 1791 banning members of any assembly from the ministry during their tenure and in the two years following it can be traced back to his motion. Although it was mainly adopted for the purely tactical purpose of stopping the ascent of Mirabeau, the assembly could then hardly disavow the lofty principle on which it pretended to rest.

A mixed assembly may also be subject to a self-enhancing bias, in the sense of creating an excessively strong legislative branch with correspondingly weak executive and judicial branches. The bias might stem from one of two sources.

First, if the framers expect or hope to be elected to the first post-constitutional assembly, they have a direct interest in being able to promote their interest – or just to exercise power – at that later stage. The people at large, or even the constituent assembly itself, may then take steps to prevent this confusion. In 1780, the voters in Massachusetts turned down a constitution proposed by a constituent legislature. One of their objections had been eloquently stated in 1778 by the committee to which a town meeting in Boston had entrusted the task of writing instructions to the delegates of the city in the state assembly:

You are hereby instructed by the Town of Boston to inform the Honorable General Court [the state legislature], that after mature Deliberation in a very full Meeting, consisting of Nine hundred & Sixty eight, we Voted unanimously, to Reject the Form sent out by the Convention, & proposed by them for the Government of this State in future, & to assure them, that a full Conviction of the Impropriety of this Matter's Originating with the General Court, was the Reason which induced us, the last Year, to instruct our Representatives, on no Terms to consent to any Proposals for this Purpose; & we are free to declare, the Specimen we now have, in the Form proposed, has confirmed us fully,

[91] Ibid., p. 212.
[92] Ibid., p. 711.
[93] Ibid., p. 716.

even to Demonstration, that we were right in our Conjectures of *that Honorable Body's being improper for this Business* : – A Convention for this, & this alone, whose Existence is known No Longer than the Constitution is forming, *can have no Prepossessions in their own Favor*, while it is hard for the General Court, upon a Matter of this Kind, to divest themselves of the Idea of their being Members; & the probability that they may continue such, may *induce them to form the Government with peculiar Reference to themselves* : – To this we suppose it is owing, that the Legislative & Executive Branches are so blended, & that nothing appears, but that the Members of the Court may monopolize to themselves a Variety of Offices, which we are fully persuaded, the best Form of Government will ever keep these Branches intirely distinct, & the Members confined to their particular Duties, without Incumbrance.[94]

The constitution proposed by a subsequent convention was ratified.

Even when constitution-makers do not form a body devoted to "this, & this alone," they may adopt a self-denying ordinance that removes their incentive to "form the Government with peculiar Reference to themselves." When Robespierre proposed the famous (and disastrous) decree that the French framers adopted on May 16, 1791, making the constituants ineligible for the first legislature, he justified it by the need to ensure their disinterestedness, and especially the appearance of disinterestedness.[95] At the Federal Convention, Franklin seconded Pinckney's proposal that senators be unpaid: "If lucrative appointments should be recommended we might be chargeable with having carved out places for ourselves."[96]

Second, as legislators, the members of a mixed assembly might naturally come to think that the institution to which they belong is a particularly important one, partly because they have more intimate knowledge about it than about the other branches and partly because there is a natural human tendency to enhance one's own importance in the scheme of things.[97] "One maxim, which will be found to predominate, more or less, in the minds of individuals in every corporation, consists, in an overweening opinion and extravagant zeal for the interest of that body, to which, as it is often expressed, they 'have the honor to belong.'"[98] Hence a mixed assembly might tend to create a legislative-centric constitution, as happened in Poland in 1921 and in France in 1946. In both cases, constituent legislatures created weak executives that the strong wartime leaders, Pilsudski and de Gaulle, disdained occupying. The unruly parliamentary systems that resulted were in part responsible for the breakdown of these constitutions.

---

[94] *Report of the City Commissioners of the City of Boston* (1895), p. 31; my italics.

[95] Elster (2009a), pp. 327–29.

[96] Farrand (1966), vol. 1, p. 427. The proposal was voted down by six states to five. Pinckney's reasons were different, as shown by the fact that he also suggested $100,000 in property qualifications for the President (ibid., II, pp. 248–49).

[97] For the difference between the first (cognitive) and the second (motivational) tendency to over-estimate one's own contributions, see Nisbett and Ross (1980), ch. 10. Either tendency could, for instance, account for the fact that in a couple, each of the two spouses typically believes that he or she does more than 50 percent of the housework.

[98] John Judd (1787), cited in Longford (1991), p. 210.

Generalizing the view I attributed to Bentham, one might require that constitution-making obey the principle "One organ, one task." Although my main objective in this section has been to argue against multitasking by the assembly, it is also appropriate to warn against interference of other organs, notably the executive, in the process. Commenting on this issue will also allow me to explain how a constituent assembly might produce a disastrous constitution for reasons other than non-respect for Benthamite principles.

Whether or not he expects to persist in office, an executive who is involved in drafting the constitution might favor an executive-centric one.[99] While it is possible to take precautions against that situation, it is more difficult to prevent deputies who see themselves as potential heads of the executive from giving the constitution an executive-centric bias, or from promoting a mode of electing the executive that would favor their chances. In the French constituent assembly of 1848, General Cavaignac – head of the executive and candidate for the presidency – argued for direct election of the President, despite the fact that he would have been certain to win in an election by the assembly.[100] Although the outcome of direct popular election was more uncertain, it would have given him greater independence vis-à-vis the assembly.

Cavaignac lost the gamble. He overestimated his own popularity and, like many of his fellow deputies, refused to acknowledge the rise of Louis Napoleon Bonaparte and the likelihood that he would be chosen in direct elections. Tocqueville recognized that danger, but hoped to avert it by requiring an absolute majority. If nobody reached that proportion, he would let the Assembly choose among the three candidates who had received the largest numbers of votes. Although his proposal was adopted in slightly modified form, it did not prevent Louis Napoleon from being elected with 75 percent of the votes.

The French deputies of 1848 could have used a law from 1832 to exclude the election of Louis Bonaparte to Parliament as a member of a reigning dynasty. His past record as a political adventurer (he staged two unsuccessful coups against the July Monarchy) would seem to provide an abundant justification for that measure. Instead, the deputies rejected it as undignified: the socialist Louis Blanc said that "to give the impression of fearing for the Republic is to insult it."[101] In an extraordinary and apparently decisive speech on October 6 on the mode of electing the President, the poet-politician Lamartine declared:

Even if the people should choose that [candidate] that my perhaps uninformed foresight fears it might choose, what does it matter? *Alea jacta est.* Let God and the people speak! We must leave something for Providence. That will be the light for those, who like ourselves,

---

[99] Ginsburg, Elkins, and Blount (2009), p. 213, affirm that their data confirm the executive bias of executive framers but not the legislative bias of legislative framers. Given the problems mentioned in note 64 in this chapter, I am not confident they are right. Also, the fact that they count executives as involved in the process even if their only task is to sign the final document (ibid., p. 206) casts some doubts on their findings.

[100] Bastid (1945), vol. I, p. 53.

[101] Ibid., p. 230.

cannot read in the darkness of the future. Let us appeal to Providence, pray that it will enlighten the people, and submit ourselves to its decree. Perhaps we ourselves shall perish at the task? No, No, and in fact it would be beautiful to perish in initiating the people to freedom!

So what if the people errs, if it lets itself be blinded by the splendor of its own past glory; if it withdraws from its own sovereignty after the first step, as if frightened by the greatness of the edifice we have opened for it in the republic and by the difficulties of its institutions; if it wants to abdicate its safety, its dignity, its liberty into the hands of a reminiscence of Empire; if it says: bring me back to the chains of the old Monarchy (*ramenez-moi aux carrières de la vieille Monarchie*); if it disavows us and disavows itself; oh well, so much the worse for the people (*eh bien! tant pis pour le peuple*)! It will not be ourselves, but the people that shall have been lacking in perseverance and courage.[102]

By its behavior, the constituent assembly of 1848 justifies Marx's harsh comparison with 1789: history repeats itself, the first time as tragedy, the second time as farce. Although some failures of the 1848 assembly can no doubt be traced back to suboptimal design, not even an omnipotent institutional designer could have neutralized the *amour-propre* of the framers or their refusal to face facts. Moreover, no override mechanism could have prevented the election of Louis Napoleon.

Attempts to block the way for a contender to executive office by constitutional design are rare. Although one can probably find many constitutions designed to *favor* the choice of a specific person as executive, besides France in 1848 I know only of one effort, equally unsuccessful, to *prevent* a given individual from presenting himself or to reduce his electoral chances.[103] In May 1814, the Norwegian framers attempted to exclude the French General Bernadotte, the crown prince and de facto ruler of Sweden, from the Norwegian throne by inserting a clause in the Constitution requiring that the King "confess *and always have confessed* the Lutheran religion."[104] When they had to negotiate a new constitution with the victorious Bernadotte a few months later, the words I have italicized were taken out.

III. LOCATION OF THE ASSEMBLY

If the proceedings of the constituent assembly take place behind closed doors, it does not matter much where it meets. Although, as mentioned in Chapter 3, Philadelphia was torn by violence when the Pennsylvanian assembly voted to call for conventions to ratify the constitution, the closed proceedings by the Federal Convention in the same city were entirely undisturbed.[105] If, however,

---

[102] *Moniteur Universel*, October 7, 1848, pp. 685–86.

[103] There have been efforts to reduce the power of the Presidency in the expectation that a specific person endowed with a strong personality was likely to be elected, as with de Gaulle in 1946 (Bougrab 2002, p. 460) and Pilsudski in 1921 (Jedrzejewics 1982, p. 140). Both refused to stand for the emasculated office, and returned 10–15 years later with a vengeance.

[104] Steen (1951), p. 165.

[105] Even so, in calling the closed Annapolis Convention, the Virginia Assembly thought it "prudent to avoid the neighborhood of Congress and the large Commercial towns, in order to disarm the

the debates are open to and reported in the press, and even more if they are open to visitors, location can matter a great deal. Once individuals with strong interests in one or another outcome of the process know which solutions seem to be emerging, they may try to influence the votes by bribes or threats. The constituent assemblies in Versailles/Paris (1789), Paris (1848), and Frankfurt (1848) show that this is not simply an abstract possibility but a real and sometimes decisive factor in shaping the outcome. Under such circumstances, "the uncoerced force of the better argument" may not stand much of a chance. To reduce the risk, one may choose to locate the assembly in a small town remote from any major urban agglomerations. Thus in 1919 the Germans deliberately chose to hold the constituent assembly in Weimar, well away from the street rioting in Berlin. During the 2007–08 constituent process in Ecuador, framers were sequestered in a small village. They could leave it, but visitors needed a special permit, which was hard to get, to pass the police roadblocks.[106]

In the discussions leading up to the Estates-General of 1789, the danger was only dimly understood. In 1788, there were several options on the table: Paris, Versailles at 13 km from Paris, or a more distant town such as Soissons at 100 km or Compiègne at 80 km.[107] The Queen and the Garde des Sceaux (Minister of Justice), Barentin, preferred the more distant locations because they feared the influence of the Parisian agitators on the deliberations of the assembly. The King's principal minister Necker preferred Paris, because he thought the proximity to the capital market in Paris would have a moderating influence on the assembly.[108] He also made the ingenious argument that the choice of a location at a great distance from Paris would create the impression that the King distrusted the Parisians, and hence might trigger the very unrests that were to be avoided.[109] The King apparently preferred Versailles because he did not want interference with his hunting habits. A more pragmatic and probably decisive argument for this location cited the costs of moving the royal retinue of about 15,000–16,000 persons.[110]

After July 14, however, it became impossible to ignore the dangerous presence of Paris. In September, an ill-assorted deputation of moderates and

---

adversaries to the object of insinuations of influence from either of these quarters" (Madison to Jefferson, March 16, 1786).

[106] Adam Przeworski (personal communication).

[107] Kessel (1969), pp. 74–76; Egret (1975), pp. 249–50.

[108] Necker's argument may seem surprising. We are used to thinking that assembly proceedings can be shaped by the presence of popular elements, not by the presence of creditors. Yet the case is not unique. In the Continental Congress, "Hamilton and James Wilson demanded federal taxes collected and administered by Congress [to repay the public debt]. They tried to open Congress's sessions to the public, so the creditors of Philadelphia could influence the proceedings" (Ferguson 1961, p. 165). When Congress subsequently moved to Princeton, "The adversaries of … the Nationalists welcomed Congress's delivery from the clamors of public creditors and the sinister influence of wealth and aristocracy. Stephen Higginson said that at Princeton he could carry motions in which but one man would support him in Philadelphia" (ibid., pp. 171–72).

[109] Necker (1791), pp. 52–53. I am reading a bit more into the text than what it explicitly says.

[110] Brette (1902), p. 289. The number is a telling indictment of the ancien régime.

royalists, with the approval of Necker and the Foreign Minister, Montmorin, proposed the transferral of the assembly to Compiègne or Soissons. The moderates wanted to remove the assembly from the threat of popular interference, and the royalists to remove the protection against military threats that Paris had just shown it could offer.[111] When the ministers put the proposal to the King, he refused. He was drowsy after hunting and slept or feigned sleep through most of the council. Again, his lack of active aptitude was blatant.

As implied by the comment on the motives of the royalists, popular crowds are not the only threat to an assembly: troops can be equally dangerous. The events leading up to July 14 underline the importance of this fact. As Sieyes reminded the Assembly on July 8, the provincial estates in Brittany did not deliberate if there were troops within 40 km. The assembly had not forgotten the lessons from July 13–14 (and from the events on October 5–6) when it laid down, in the constitution of September 3, 1791, that "The executive power [i.e., the King] cannot cause any body of troops to pass or sojourn within thirty thousand toises [60 km] of the legislative body, except upon its requisition or its authorization."

To digress briefly on this point, the "separation of powers" can have a literal physical meaning as well as its usual institutional meaning. The French Constitution of 1791 stipulates that the High Court that was to judge political crimes had to be located at least 60 km from the site of the National Assembly. Robespierre pleaded unsuccessfully for its location in the capital, where the pressure of public opinion could fortify its courage and energy.[112] The Convention proposed that assemblies to revise the constitution had to meet at least 200 km from the capital.[113] Tocqueville claimed that "Americans are so afraid of centralization and the influence of capitals that they almost always take care to place the seat of legislative and executive powers far from the chief cities."[114] When Congress decided to remove the federal capital from Philadelphia, it was partly to "separate the national government from intimate involvement in the society."[115] When the Central Bank of Norway was created in 1816, it was located in Trondheim, several hundred miles from the capital, to ensure its independence from the government.

More recently, similar reasoning led to a preference for Bonn over Frankfurt in 1948 and for Frankfurt over Bonn in 1956. "After a controversy about whether the Parliamentary Council [for drafting the constitution] should meet in Frankfurt or Bonn, the group favoring Bonn finally prevailed.... Part of the reason was that Frankfurt was the site of the American military headquarters, and the German members of the Parliamentary Council wished to maintain their distance from the American-dominated atmosphere of Frankfurt."[116] Eight

---

[111] Mathiez (1898), p. 272.
[112] AP 23, p. 46.
[113] Pierre 1893, p. 12.
[114] Tocqueville (1991), p. 236.
[115] Wood (2009), p. 289
[116] Spevack (2002), p. 361.

years later, preferences were reversed: in "September 1956, the chancellor [Adenauer] stirred alarm in Frankfurt by suggesting that the Bundesbank should be set up in Cologne to place it closer to Bonn. In the end, the Bundesbank stayed in Frankfurt, at arm's length from the government."[117] Several countries have also located their constitutional courts outside the capital: the German court is located in Karlsruhe, the Czech court in Brno, the Estonian court in Tartu, and the Slovakian one in Kosice. I do not know whether the reason, in any of these cases, was an explicit desire to insulate the court either from other branches of government or from the population in large cities.

When both are present, crowds can neutralize soldiers. As Mirabeau said in a speech on July 9, 1789, addressed to Louis XVI, "French soldiers, who are close to the center of discussions and share the passions as well as the interests of the people, may forget that a contract made them soldiers and remember that nature made them men."[118] The troops did remember. Although they had been called in from the provinces because they were supposedly more reliable than the French Guards in Paris, they soon melted into the population and became utterly unreliable as an instrument of repression. The conspirators did not master the most elementary techniques of a coup d'état:

Instead of dispersing the troops in Paris and around Paris and exhibiting them everywhere, which had the triple disadvantage of fragmenting the forces, exciting the spirits and exposing the soldiers to demoralizing influences, one should have assembled them some distance from Paris in a compact body, fed them well, had the King visit them, ensured their cohesion, fortified their military spirit, impose – if necessary by some severe examples – a strict discipline, take them in full charge; then, once all the troops were in place, strike quickly and strongly.[119]

Exactly 200 years later, constitution-making in Bulgaria was also shaped by the reaction of crowds to the threat of military intervention:

On [December 16, 1989] the National Assembly began discussions about the abolition of the first article of the then-acting Socialist constitution (the article promulgated the leading role of the Communist party). The members of parliament voted unanimously for its abolition but the amendment procedure required a month's delay. Some twenty thousand men [sic] waited outside the building for the results. The crowd was so upset that the amendment procedure was not changed, that it was ready to storm the building. A group of members of parliament, including the head of state, Mladenov, tried to address the protesters, but they refused to listen. The nervous president was filmed saying "Let the tanks come," perhaps addressing the minister of defense.[120]

When the tape of his statement was authenticated by experts, the President had to step down and was replaced by a reformist.

[117] Marsh (1992), p. 167
[118] AP 8, p. 213. This speech was already cited in Chapter 1. In both passages, Mirabeau presents as a warning what is in reality a threat.
[119] Caron (1906–07), pp. 657–58.
[120] Kolarova and Dimitrov (1996), p. 201.

The examples from 1789 and 1989 suggest that in the turbulent circumstances of actual constitution-making, the presence of crowds may be necessary to overcome an ancien régime, be it feudalist or Communist. They also underline the difficulty of any attempt to generalize about the optimal design of constituent assemblies. Historians will debate to the end of time whether France would have been better off had the Estates-General met far from both crowds and soldiers, or whether the tension between these two elements was necessary to create the energy needed to overcome the vested interests of the ancien régime. Clermont-Tonnerre's ambiguity is characteristic: while praising anarchy (as discussed earlier), he also advocated the removal of the assembly to the provinces.[121]

IV. THE SIZE AND DURATION OF THE ASSEMBLY

The number of delegates to constituent assemblies varies considerably, the 2011 Icelandic Constitutional Council with 25 delegates and the Assemblée Constituante (1,200 delegates) being at the two extremes. The Federal Convention with 55 delegates and the Parliamentary Council in Bonn with 65 delegates are close to the lower extreme, whereas the French and German assemblies of 1848, with respectively 800 and 649 members, are close to the upper extreme. The optimal number is clearly related to the size and homogeneity of the country. The larger and the more diverse the population, the more delegates are needed to ensure a broadly representative assembly. For the time being, I bracket that issue, which I discuss in Section V.

The question of optimal assembly size does not have an unambiguous answer. Bentham, proposing six arguments for small assemblies and three against, thought the solution was "arbitrary in a considerable degree" (Chapter 3). Let me first briefly comment on some classical discussions of the topic.

Gibbon observes that the synod of 80,000 priests summoned by Artaxerxes "could not have been directed by the authority of reason" and hence was reduced, by successive steps, to a council of seven.[122] In *Federalist* No. 55, Madison writes,

Sixty or seventy men may be more properly trusted with a given degree of power than six or seven. But it does not follow that six or seven hundred would be proportionably a better depositary. And if we carry on the supposition to six or seven thousand, the whole reasoning ought to be reversed. The truth is that in all cases a certain number at least seems to be necessary to secure the benefits of free consultation and discussion, and to guard against too easy a combination for improper purposes; as, on the other hand, the number ought at most to be kept within a certain limit, in order to avoid the confusion and intemperance of a multitude. In all very numerous assemblies, of whatever character composed, passion never fails to wrest the sceptre from reason. Had every Athenian citizen been a Socrates, every Athenian assembly would still have been a mob.[123]

---

[121] AP 8, pp. 513–14.

[122] Gibbon (2005), vol. 1, pp. 215–16.

[123] Madison seems to ignore that on the occasion when the Athenian assembly was at its most mob-like, the illegal trial of the generals after the battle of Arginusae, Socrates was the only one among the prytanes who refused to act against the law (Xenophon, *Hellenica*, I.7).

At the same time, in small assemblies *interest* can wrest the scepter from reason. A lower limit is imposed by the need to prevent "elected oligarchies" who would be able to use the "given degree of power" to promote their private interests. More generally, a lower limit is needed to prevent bargains and logrolling, at least if we can assume that these are undesirable activities in the constitutional context (see Chapter 1). Since unborn generations do not have any delegates who can bargain on their behalf, that assumption seems reasonable.

Before the rise of the modern political party it was in any case very hard to strike bargains among large numbers of unregimented *individuals*. The experience from the French Assemblée Constituante, with its shifting alliances formed around this or that leader, offers an example. The best-known attempt of logrolling, proposed by the "triumvirate" (Barnave, Duport, and A. Lameth) to Mounier in August 1789, came to nothing. By contrast, at the much smaller Federal Convention, hard bargains between the slave-holding southern states and the seafaring northern states were struck and kept. (But see note 48 to the next chapter for a bargain between the small and the large states that was not kept.)

Assuming, controversially (see Chapter 1), that strategic or sophisticated voting is undesirable, small assemblies would also be undesirable. The reason is that as the number of voters "grows large the likelihood of a voter's knowing the preferences of the others grows small, and thus so do the chances of successfully manipulating the outcome."[124] Once again, this argument holds only for the period preceding the rise of political parties.

Madison's argument that an upper limit is needed "to avoid the confusion and intemperance of a multitude" may seem to be confirmed by the Assemblée Constituante, which did indeed at times exhibit an utterly chaotic style. In a related argument, Condorcet claimed that "the inconveniences which result from interruptions ... increase in much larger proportion than the number of deputies,"[125] perhaps because the interrupters might themselves be interrupted. It is not clear, however, whether the chaos in the French Assembly was due to the large number of delegates or to the public character of the debates (discussed later). Although a numerous assembly debating behind closed doors could in principle enforce some discipline on itself, there is a near-certainty that some delegates would leak the contents of the debates and create public commotion that would prevent calm discussion.[126] A judicious choice of location for the assembly might to some extent reduce this problem.

---

[124] Mueller (2003), pp. 155–56.

[125] Condorcet (1785), p. 365.

[126] The Spanish constituent assembly of 1810 deliberated partly in secret sessions "to assure the triumph of the democratic system, by evading censorship and the influence of public opinion" (Antonetti 1994, p. 400, apparently citing Louis-Philippe but not giving his source). Many of the secret sessions were, however, leaked to the press (Crawley 1939, p. 184). Even the supposedly waterproof Federal Convention leaked, as is clear from a letter by the well-informed French chargé d'affaires Otto dated July 25, 1787 (Farrand 1966, vol. 3, pp. 61–63), in which he refers to two specific proposals debated at the Convention one month earlier.

Condorcet's Jury Theorem might seem to offer an argument for large assemblies, assuming that the conditions for the theorem (independence, individual competence, sincere voting) are empirically validated. As I noted in Chapter 3, Bentham observed that a further condition must obtain, namely, that the endogenously determined active aptitude of the delegates does not fall too quickly when their number increases. I shall not return to the question, except to repeat that it is not clear that the theorem has any empirical relevance.

Condorcet was aware of the weakness of large assemblies. In addition to the problems stemming from interruptions, he observed that his theorem does not hold for "a very large assembly, where the [individual probability of being right] can fall to about 1/2, and in which those [with the lowest probability] will be the most numerous."[127] Unlike Bentham, however, he did not see the lower individual competence in large assemblies as the endogenous outcome of assembly size, but as an exogenous fact due to the need to admit less naturally competent individuals as the assembly size increases ("scraping the bottom of the barrel"). The remedy, in his opinion, consists in two-stage elections, since members whose individual probability of being right is low "will be sufficiently enlightened, probably not to state with any probability which individual among many has the greatest merit, but to choose as the most enlightened one of those who have a high probability [of being right]. Thus a very large assembly composed of members who are not very enlightened could be usefully employed only in choosing the Members of a smaller assembly, to which the decisions ... would then be confided."[128] The argument seems to require that competence varies with the issue to be decided. Even though most individuals will not have the *issue competence* required to make good substantive decisions, they will have the *voting competence* required to choose individuals with issue competence (see also Chapter 5).

Instead of delegating all its tasks to a smaller assembly, a constituent assembly could delegate some tasks to *committees*. In Chapter 1, I distinguished among three committee models. Whereas the first two are the norm today, the third was common in the two 18th-century assemblies. The ephemeral Grand Committees at the Federal Convention were chosen by secret ballot to examine specific issues and make proposals to the full body. The *bureaux* in the first French Constituante, consisting of randomly chosen and frequently rotating members, were supposed to work in parallel and give their opinions on all bills to be debated in the assembly. The constituants preferred this model to the more specialized types because of their desire "to prevent the formation of permanent groups, which might come to dominate the deputies taken as individuals."[129] As became increasingly clear over the next years, they were obsessed with the idea of preventing intermediary groups from coming between the nation and the individual. Nevertheless, because of their perceived inefficiency the *bureaux* were rapidly replaced by standing committees.[130]

---

[127] Condorcet (1785), p. 167.
[128] Ibid., pp. 167–68.
[129] Castaldo (1989), p. 120.
[130] Ibid., p. 202; Tackett (1996), p. 220.

Because of the mixed nature of the Constituante, many of the tasks of the bureaux and later of the committees were legislative rather than constitutional. On July 8, 1789, the assembly did, however, create a more specialized "Committee of the constitution." Each of the thirty bureaux chose one of its thirty members by secret ballot. Probably because of the perceived inefficiency of this large body, the assembly created a new committee with eight members on July 14. In an amazing and ironic coincidence, on the very same day that the estate-system collapsed, the assembly decided that the committee should follow the representation of the three estates in the assembly, with four members from the third estate and two from each of the privileged orders. They were chosen by secret ballot, but the records do not show by whom they were chosen. Since the two members from the nobility belonged to the minoritarian liberal faction of that order, it seems plausible that they were chosen by the assembly as a whole rather than by the order to which they belonged. If that conjecture is correct, it would have been a unique instance of cross-voting (Chapter 5) in the assembly.

Whereas the mode of election to the Committee of the Constitution in 1789 is shrouded in uncertainty and does not seem to have been the subject of debate, on May 12, 1848, the French constituants had a long and confused, or at least confusing, discussion of this topic. Some deputies wanted the members (or some members) to be either directly nominated or indirectly elected by the bureaux, allegedly to give a chance for unknown talents to reveal themselves but in reality to avoid the dominance on the committee of well-known politicians from the July monarchy. A compromise proposal to have 18 members nominated by the bureaux and 18 elected by the assembly gathered considerable support. Although the assembly first prepared the ground for this solution when "a large majority" voted that the committee should have 36 members, it later undermined this position by reversing its decision and voting by "near-unanimity" that there would be only 18 members. It seems likely that the desire to avoid splitting the committee in two factions with different pedigrees and legitimacy was more important than the desire to keep it small, but the latter concern may also have counted. In 1789, the decision to move from a committee of 30 to a committee of 8 was probably dictated by efficiency concerns.

The *duration* of constituent assemblies is also subject to considerable variation. The Norwegian assembly of 1814 sat for five weeks, and the Indian Constituent Assembly of 1946 for almost three years. Between these extremes we find the Federal Convention (three months), the 1948–49 German Parliamentary Council (six months), the 1848 Paris assembly (six months), the 1848–49 Frankfurt assembly (one year), the 1988 Brazilian constituent assembly (two years), and the 1789 Assemblée Constituante (more than two years).

There are two relevant normative issues: Should the assembly be subject to a time limit? If so, what is the optimal duration? To my knowledge, there are few cases of firm and credible time limits, perhaps because constituent assemblies ignore the constraints that upstream actors try to impose on them. The Icelandic Constitutional Council was instructed to deliver its proposal within two months, but spent almost four months on the task. External events may create a pressure to finish quickly, but – like the passions they trigger – these can hardly be included in an institutional design. One example of a firm time limit is nevertheless offered by the 1994 interim South African constitution, which laid down that the final constitution had to be adopted within two years.

If the constituent assembly is not subject to a firm time constraint, some actors may be able to benefit from dragging their feet. Thus in the work on the 1949 Bonn constitution, "the major parties had different attitudes with regard to the time schedule of the work of the Council. . . . The sooner the elections took place the better for the SPD [Socialists], whereas the CDU [Christian Democrats] hoped to gain time until the new economic policy and the seasonal upward turn in employment might produce a shift to the right."[131] The more patient actor can obtain a substantive concession from the impatient party in exchange for an early adoption of the document. From a normative point of view, this effect can be undesirable (see Chapter 1). Bargaining of this kind may occur even with a time limit, unless the assembly is under the constraint that the constitution has to be adopted by time *t and no earlier*. Yet the relevance of this observation is somewhat reduced by the general tendency in time-constrained negotiations for the final agreement to be reached only under the pressure of the deadline.[132] Assuming, then, that time limits will in fact be binding constraints, they ought to be part of the optimal design.

There is not much one can say on the question of the optimal duration of the assembly. If secrecy is a desideratum, a short-lived assembly may be necessary. A small assembly will usually be able to write the constitution more quickly than a large one (the case of Iceland is emblematic). The Federal Convention illustrates both ideas. The issue is also related to the optimal length of the constitutional document. If the plan is to write a short and general constitution, it can be done more quickly; conversely, a short time limit may be a way of inducing conciseness (although we know the apology of the letter-writer: "I am sorry I did not have the time to be brief").

V. ELECTIONS TO THE ASSEMBLY

The optimal mode of election to any assembly depends on the task it has to perform. In electing a legislature that is to vote a government into power, a system that tends to give a clear-cut majority to one party is often preferable to one that will produce many small parties. This criterion of "governability" favors majority voting or proportional voting with a high threshold. In electing a constituent assembly, a system that tends to reflect, in miniature, the diversity of the nation is preferable to one that risks excluding significant groups. This criterion of "representativeness" favors proportional voting with a low threshold or no threshold. A mixed assembly that is to perform both tasks may therefore fail in one of them.

[131] Merkl (1963), p. 96.
[132] Roth, Murnighan, and Schoumaker (1988).

Whereas high turnout is not per se a requirement for deputies to be representative, representativeness may suffer if some social groups have below-
average turnout in the elections. In the elections to the Icelandic Constitutional
Council in 2011, for instance, voter turnout was lower in the countryside than in
the Reykvavík area.[133] To my knowledge, there are no systematic studies of this
issue, but it is reasonable to assume that the factors – notably education – that
can bias voter participation in elections to legislative assemblies also affect
elections to constituent assemblies. In countries where this bias is important,
one might want to use mandatory voting when choosing framers. The argument
that voting in elections to a constituent assembly is a *function* rather than a *right*
also supports mandatory voting.

The argument for representativeness rests on epistemic rather than on
interest-based grounds. In this respect constituent assemblies differ from ordinary legislatures. It is not a question of *the individual's right* to have his or her
interests represented, but of *the community's need* for the individual's *knowledge*. With regard to constituent assemblies, voting should be seen as a *function*,
not as a right. In that respect, electing framers is similar to performing jury
service.[134] The delegates do not represent interest, but the knowledge of interest
(where the shoe pinches). Between them, they might even have knowledge of
how to satisfy those interests (how to make better shoes). At the Federal
Convention, where the delegates had experiences with 12 very different state
political systems, they could *pool solution proposals* with, in some cases,
remarkable results.[135] By contrast, because of the poor representation of the

[133] Gylfason (2012).
[134] In England, the right for women to do jury service was guaranteed by the Sex Disqualification
(Removal) Act of 1919. In my view, the inclusion of women in panels for jury service can be
justified by two arguments. First, since there is no reason to believe that women are defective in
moral, intellectual, or active aptitude, their exclusion would be arbitrary and stigmatizing.
Second, because of the epistemic value of diversity their exclusion would be inefficient. Neither
argument is grounded in a positive right of citizens to do jury service (although the second might
be grounded in the rights of the *defendant*). The same considerations apply to the elections to a
constituent assembly. By contrast, the right to vote in legislative elections is grounded in the
positive right to choose those by whom one shall be governed. Barnave (AM 9, pp. 376–77)
claimed that while active citizens had a right to choose electors and to be chosen as deputies by
them, the high property qualifications for electors were justified by the fact that being an elector
was a function to which no one could claim a right. Pierre (1893), p. 151, cites a decision by the
French Cour de Cassation from 1876 stating that voters to the electoral college for the Senate (see
Chapter 1) exercise a "public function," whereas voters in ordinary elections exercise a right. As
space does not allow me to consider the distinction between rights and functions more fully, let
me only point to two questions that might be considered in this perspective. Do deaf people have
a right to serve as jurors (Lee 1989)? Do Israeli Arabs have a right to serve in the army (Smooha
1990)?
[135] See Adams (2001), ch. 14, for a survey of the impact of the state constitutions on the federal
constitution. Bryce (1995), p. 31, asserts that "It has been truly said that nearly every provision of
the federal Constitution that has worked well is one borrowed from or suggested by some state
constitution; nearly every provision that has worked badly is one which the Convention, for want
of a precedent, was obliged to devise for itself." This, it seems to me, is to overstate the case.

backcountry at the Convention – the average distance from the place of residence to navigable water was 16 miles[136] – the framers may not have felt all the places where the shoe pinched.[137]

In the contemporary French assembly, the utter lack of practical political experience of most delegates made them inept as shoemakers. Tocqueville's scornful comment on the philosophes also applies, with some modifications, to the constituants:

> The situation of these writers fostered in them a taste for abstract, general theories of government, theories in which they trusted blindly. Living as they did almost totally removed from practical life, they had no experience that might have tempered their natural passions. Nothing warned them of the obstacles that existing reality might pose to even the most desirable reforms.... They therefore grew bolder in their innovations, much more enamored of general ideas and systems, much more contemptuous of ancient wisdom, and much more confident of individual reason than one commonly sees in authors who write speculative works about politics.[138]

The constituants might be better at telling where the shoe pinched. In 1789, Louis XVI (or his minister) devised electoral rules that made the priests rather than the bishops the main representatives of the clergy to the Estates-General. He did so, he asserted in the electoral rules announced on January 24, 1789, because "the good and useful pastors, who assist the people in their needs on a close and daily basis ... know their sufferings and apprehensions most intimately."[139] The lower clergy "thus were to represent the peasantry as well as the clerical assemblies that had elected them."[140] The reason cited for doubling the representation of the third estate was also that "it would gather together all knowledge that might be useful for the good of the State, and one cannot contest that this diversity of knowledge belongs above all to the third estate, since there are numerous public matters that only this order is informed about."[141]

Along somewhat similar lines, the "economic interpretation" of the American constitution proposed by Charles Beard does not amount, as is often said, to a claim that the delegates to the Federal Convention were influenced, in casting their votes, by their personal economic interests. Rather the question was, "Did they represent distinct groups whose economic interests they understood and felt in concrete, definite form through their own personal experience with identical property rights, or were they working merely under the guidance of abstract

---

[136] McGuire (2003), p. 69. The maximal distance was 200 miles. See Elster (2012) for a general discussion of how the underrepresentation of the backcountry in the state legislatures shaped the events (including Shays's Rebellion) that led to the calling of the Federal Convention, how a similarly skewed representation at the Convention shaped the text of the Constitution, and how a similar bias in the ratifying conventions was crucial for the adoption of the text by nine states.

[137] McDonald (1992), p. 37.

[138] Tocqueville (2011), p. 129. The effects of ignorance were magnified by enthusiasm (see note 59 to this chapter).

[139] AP 1, p. 544.

[140] Necheles (1974), p. 427.

[141] AP 1, p. 492.

principles of political science?"[142] In opting for the former answer, he looked to the qualitative experience of the framers rather than to their quantitative interest:

That is, [Beard] makes no distinction between, say, a planter who had land of $20,000 and incidentally a few dollars in securities, and a financier who had invested most of his resources in securities. Each is classified as a security holder, and no weight is attached to the relative importance of the securities of each. This practice is consistent with Beard's explicit concentration on the significance of holdings of various forms of property as giving the delegates experience with the tribulations of each, rather than as inspiring them to act in certain ways out of self-interest.[143]

This argument, to be sure, is not quite the same as the one I made with regard to Louis XVI. One thing is to *justify* an electoral system ex ante by its knowledge-representing (rather than interest-aggregating) effects; another is to *explain* the proposed document by the knowledge (rather than the interests) of the delegates. I am only making the point that from the normative perspective of optimal design, the composition of the delegations at the Federal Convention may have served a desirable epistemic function.

The decision by Louis XVI to give a preponderant influence to the lower clergy turned out, from his perspective to be disastrous. The defection of the parish priests to the third estate in June 1789 was perhaps the crucial event in the transformation of the Estates-General into a National Assembly that, voting by head, would bring down the old régime and ultimately the King. Let me cite two other episodes in which the conveners of a constituent assembly opted, to their detriment, for representativeness rather than governability. For the election of delegates to the 1919 Weimar assembly, the provisional Socialist government under the leadership of Friedrich Ebert adopted proportional voting together with female suffrage, consistently with long-standing positions of the SPD. These two features "prevented the Majority [section of the] Socialists from gaining an absolute majority in the national assembly."[144] It is not clear whether the Socialist leaders would have been able to impose majority voting or whether they predicted the likely outcome of the law. Be this as it may, the outcome was disastrous. "While it is clearly unjust to lay the parliamentary defeat of the Republic at the feet of the Social Democrats alone, the *failure of the Reichtag's largest party to secure its own electoral self-interest* between 1918 and 1928 was indisputably a major contribution to the comprehensiveness of that defeat."[145]

In 1990, Vaclav Havel imposed a similarly counterinterested proportional system, to allow a place for his former Communist enemies in the constituent

[142] Beard (1986), p. 73.
[143] McDonald (1992), pp. 12–13. By contrast, a study that claims to be "a resurrection of Charles A. Beard's economic interpretation" (McGuire 2003, p. 32) uses (among many other variables) the *amounts* of real and personal property of the framers to explain their votes.
[144] Huber (1978), p. 1067.
[145] Hodge (1987), pp. 186–87; my italics.

assembly.[146] One of Havel's close associates told me in 1993 that "this decision will be seen either as the glory or the weakness of the November [1989] revolution: we were winners that accepted a degree of self-limitation." As Louis XVI and the German Socialists before him, Havel paid a high price for his impartiality.[147] The Communists, notably the deputies from Slovakia, ended up as constitution-wreckers rather than as constitution-makers.

These cases provide some useful reminders. There is no reason to think that the choice of proportional representation for the two 20th-century assemblies was motivated only (if at all) by a desire for a broad representation of *knowledge*. As both assemblies were mixed constituent-legislative bodies, the desire for an even-handed representation of *interests* is a much more likely motive. Moreover, there is no reason to think that even pure conventions, elected by proportional represen-tation and without clear majorities, would have been sufficiently disinterested to consider the adoption of majority voting into the constitution to ensure govern-ability. In practice, proportional representation involves representation of parties, which rarely vote themselves out of existence. Except if deciders are chosen by lot, as were the Athenian *nomothetai* or the members of the Citizens' Assembly on Electoral Reform in British Columbia in 2003–04, it is hard to see how to achieve diversity without a list system. And even in those two cases, self-selection may have reduced diversity to some unknown degree.

Independent of the choice between proportional and majority voting, an extended suffrage (active or passive) is desirable on grounds of legitimacy. When the fundamental rules of a polity are laid down, there is a normative pressure to attenuate the distinction between active and passive citizens. (A similar principle may apply to associations.)[148] In the United States, there has been a tendency to use a wider suffrage in electing deputies to constitutional conventions or to ratifying conventions than in choosing representatives to legislatures. In the elec-tions to the 1780 constituent legislature in Massachusetts, the general court (lower house) "enfranchised all free adult male town inhabitants for the duration of the constitution-making process."[149] The enfranchisement was in force from the election of delegates to a constituent legislature up to – but not beyond – the ratification of the document.[150] In the election of delegates to the 1776 state

---

[146] Elster (1995).

[147] Rapaczynski (1991), p. 617, affirms that in the Constitutional Committee of the Polish parlia-ment after 1989, "some groups expressed [a preference for proportional representation] despite a potential party interest to the contrary." He explains this fact by a general preference for ideology over *Realpolitik* among the Polish framers.

[148] In Britain, the 1964 Trade Union (Amalgamations) Act is usually taken to imply that apprentices, who do not have the right to vote in ordinary union matters, can vote on a merger with another union (Grunfeld 1964).

[149] Kruman (1997), p. 30.

[150] In fact, taking one step forward and then two steps backward, the constitutional convention chosen under the extended suffrage decided to impose *stricter* property qualifications compared to those that existed *before* the extension. Normally, however, constituent assemblies do not curtail the suffrage rules under which they were themselves elected. As Robespierre acutely pointed out (AP 29, p. 361), the attempt by the French Constituante to impose high economic

convention in Philadelphia, it was "decided that in addition to those who already had the vote, adult militia members were to be given the franchise and the right to be candidates for the convention."[151]

In many cases, either the legislature that called a convention or the convention itself has extended the suffrage for ratification.[152] In the elections to the conventions to ratify the Federal Constitution, Connecticut, New York, and North Carolina relaxed or waived the property qualifications required for electors to the state legislatures.[153] (The apportionment, though, was in many cases highly skewed,[154] reducing the claim of the conventions to be representative.) Similarly, conditions on eligibility were relaxed in many states, at least compared to those used to elect state senators.[155] In New Hampshire, even former loyalists who were normally ineligible could serve as convention delegates – just as Havel allowed a place for Communists in the first constituent elections!

Although these scattered instances seem to reflect an intuition that constituent assemblies require a broader basis for representation than ordinary legislatures, the reasons behind that intuition are hard to grasp. They were probably mainly related to a belief in the *individual's right* to participate in shaping the future of their state, but the idea of the *community's need* for a diversity of inputs to the process may also have played a role. Closer historical studies might throw light on that issue.

VI. SECRECY AND PUBLICITY – INTEREST AND PASSION

Bentham's arguments for publicity of debates and votes do not carry over immediately from ordinary legislatures to constituent assemblies. There are two differences, the first related to the one-off nature of the assembly and the second to substantive differences between constitutional provisions and ordinary laws.

Bentham's arguments about the two effects of publicity – dread of shame and fear of non-reelection – apply directly to mixed constituent assemblies. In pure conventions, the first effect is still at work, but the second need not be. Although one cannot expect all framers to be like jurors (or the *nomothetai*), who go back to the plow once they have made their decision, some of them may leave politics. In their case, fear of non-reelection will not have any purchase on what they say or on how they vote in the assembly. When the French constituants declared themselves

---

qualifications on the electorate would retroactively undermine the legitimacy of the framers themselves. A related issue was at stake in the debate between Mirabeau and his arch-reactionary younger brother (AP 9, pp. 43, 46). The German framers in 1848 faced a similar dilemma (Eyck 1968, pp. 244–45, 367–68, 382), as did the 1848 French framers when on May 31, 1850, they curtailed the suffrage under which they had been elected (Tréanton 1909–10). An elected king might also find it difficult to make the office hereditary (Olivier-Martin 2010, p. 242).

[151] Adams (2001), p. 76.
[152] Hoar (1917), pp. 206–7. In a few cases, "electorates have also been *reduced* by oaths of allegiance required by reconstruction acts" (ibid., p. 207; my italics).
[153] Amar (2005), p. 503.
[154] Roll (1969).
[155] Amar (2005), pp. 503–4.

ineligible to the first legislature, they ensured in fact that *all* would be in this position. At the same time, many votes for that very declaration were shaped by the dread of shame – or of what Bentham called "positive ill offices." Although some framers may have been "drunk with disinterestedness" or were happy to be prevented from running in an election they might lose,[156] others were probably swayed by Custine's intervention *ad terrorem*: "I demand a roll-call vote. In that way, we shall know who wants to be reelected."[157] The deputies had good reasons to fear that lists with names of those who voted against non-reelection would circulate in Paris, and that they might suffer violence as a result.[158]

The observation about a lack of purchase of an interest in reelection on decisions can be generalized. By and large, constituent assemblies differ from ordinary legislatures in that the former are called upon to make fewer decisions that affect the members or groups directly. One question debated at the Federal Convention about the majority required in Congress to override a presidential veto – 2/3 or 3/4 – provides an example. One could also cite the choice between unicameralism and bicameralism,[159] the right of the executive to dissolve Parliament, and the frequency of elections. In such cases, the preference for one solution over the other could be determined only by ideology or political philosophy, not by tangible and identifiable interest. At the Convention, "[this] was not because the constitution-makers disregarded their personal interests in favor of broader social interests when considering questions at the 'higher' level of constitutional choice, but because they were unlikely to see what difference choices concerning such broad structural questions would make to them as individuals, or to their states and region."[160] On this view, the public interest mattered for the American framers if and only if personal and group interest was silent.

Generally speaking, neither the "if" part nor the "only if" part of that claim stands up to scrutiny. With regard to the Federal Convention, they have a larger portion of truth than in other cases, but even here there were exceptions. The "if" part ignores the role of passion (see the earlier comments on Shays's rebellion) and the "only if" part ignores the capacity of reason to override interest even when the latter *does* have a purchase on the issue. Even though we do not find many instances of counterinterested reasoning or voting at the Convention, some cases can be cited. In the debates on the Presidency, Madison at one point considered the option of direct election by the people, which "with all its imperfections he liked . . . best," and went on to consider and answer some

---

[156] Mirabeau (1851), pp. 146–47.

[157] AP 26, p. 112; AM 8, p. 120 (naming Custine).

[158] On this tactic, see generally Lally-Tolendal (1790), p. 12; Mounier in AP 9, pp. 558, 562; Duquesnoy (1894), vol. I, p. 104; Egret (1950), pp. 72, 132, 154, as well as the comments on Legendre in Chapter 3.

[159] Let me mention some exceptions. The establishment of the Czech Senate in 1992 was made not on grounds of principle but to create a place for the Czech deputies to the Upper House of the dissolved Czechoslovak Confederation (Pehe 1993). For reasons explained in Section II, one might also expect a bicameral constituent assembly to write bicameralism into the constitution.

[160] Jillson (1988), p. 16.

objections to this idea. Although direct election would be disadvantageous to the South since slaves would not count, he thought that "local considerations must give way to the general interest. As an individual from the [southern] states he was willing to make the sacrifice."[161] Also, a substantial number of delegates who held either federal or state debts voted against their interest regarding the assumption of these debts by the future government.[162]

There is no doubt that many votes at the Convention did reflect the interests of individuals, states, or regions. If the proceedings had been open to the public, some of these concerns might have had to go underground or seek some plausible proxies, in the way race-based challenges to jurors are disguised by racially neutral proxies. More plausibly, as Madison is reported to have said, *"no Constitution would have been adopted* by the convention if the debates had been public."[163] In the well-known immediately preceding statement, cited in note 154 in Chapter 2, he asserts that publicity would have made the delegates less "open to the force of argument" because of their desire to remain consistent with their publicly stated positions. Because of amour-propre, it is always unpleasant to change one's mind;[164] because of vanity, it is even more difficult to do so before an audience. Moreover, the desire to make the right decision may be replaced by the desire to please the public, or the fear of displeasing it. In politics at least, publicity can be the enemy of reason.

That statement does not imply, however, that secrecy will be a friend to reason. Behind closed doors, *arguments will be better, but also fewer*, since the argumentative stance will often be replaced by a negotiating stance. Whereas bargaining in public over the public interest is almost an oxymoron, there is less opprobrium attached to interest-based bargaining behind closed doors. At one point the opportunistic Gouverneur Morris conveyed that he was – in the immortal words of Captain Renault, "shocked, shocked" – that any delegate at the Convention might "suppose that we were assembled to truck and bargain for our particular states."[165] Later on, he had no qualms in suggesting that the issues of slave imports and navigation acts "may form a bargain among the Northern and Southern States."[166] It is probably inevitable, in fact, that constitution-making in federal countries will involve some bargaining. In addition to the Federal Convention, one may cite the Meech Lake and Charlottetown accords in Canada, which were rejected in referendums precisely because they were perceived to emerge from bargaining in "smoke-filled back-rooms."[167] Federal compromises that were possible in the late 18th century may be much more difficult to achieve in a world where politics is increasingly subject to the norm of transparency.

---

[161] Farrand (1966), vol. 2, p. 111. As noted in Chapter 1, this passage casts doubt on Amar's interpretation of Madison's view. It also goes against that offered in Holton (2007, p. 188).
[162] McDonald (1992), p. 106.
[163] Farrand (1966), vol. 3, p. 479; my italics.
[164] La Rochefoucauld, Maxime 51.
[165] Farrand (1966), vol. 1, p. 529.
[166] Ibid., vol 2, p. 374.
[167] Russell (1993), pp. 134–45, 191, 219–27.

Earlier, I cited an intervention by Custine implying that anyone who voted against non-reelection of the constituants would do so out of a personal interest in reelection. In the unanimous opinion of later historians, the public interest would have been better served by allowing reeligibility. Yet in the heated atmosphere generated by the audience, a disinterested attitude could only be proved by counter-interested behavior. A deputy voting for a measure that would serve his interest could not conceivably be motivated by the general interest.

Two further examples can illustrate this variety of the hermeneutics of suspicion. After the night of August 4, 1789, Abbé Sieyes lost much of his huge prestige because he objected to the abolition of the tithe, arguing that it would benefit the large feudal landowners rather than the peasants. Although his argument was perfectly valid,[168] it was discredited by the fact that it matched his own interests as a tithe-holder. Later, Mirabeau tried to get around a similar problem, when the Assembly debated the proposal that deputies could serve as ministers. To defuse the suspicion that he only wanted to open the way for himself, he made an ironic motion to "limit the exclusion [of deputies from the ministry] to M. de Mirabeau, deputy of the third estate from Aix."[169]

In the Constituante, as in many assemblies of the ancien régime, the committees or bureaux were neither specialized nor permanent.[170] The assembly was divided into thirty bureaux, with the members chosen initially in alphabetical order and reassigned every month by a procedure that assured that the members of a bureau would not serve together again. The bureaux debated the same motions in parallel, without voting, as a preparation for the plenary discussions. It was initially envisaged that the assembly would meet in plenum two days a week, and work in the bureaux on the other days. However, the moderates and the patriots had very different opinions on these two modes of proceeding. For Mounier, leader of the moderates,

The bureaux were a great resource. It was there – detached from anything that can excite vanity, without any desire for the applause of the spectators or any fear for what might be printed, with no speeches to pronounce for publication in the newspapers – that one prepared with the most scrupulous attention the various questions to be treated in the Assembly and that many modest men opposed cool reason and experience to the heat of so-called philosophical ideas.[171]

---

[168] At least in the opinion of Tocqueville (2004b), pp. 594–95. Jaurès (1968), p. 468, agrees in substance with Sieyes, but adds that the suppression of the tithe was a necessary first step toward the expropriation of the property of the Church. While Lefebvre (1963, p. 151) may be right when he asserts that Sieyes was motivated by the loss of revenue he would suffer personally, that fact does not undermine his argument.

[169] AP 9, p. 718.

[170] The decision by the Assemblée des Notables in 1788 to work in bureaux rather than in committees was apparently motivated by the fear of discontent among members assigned to committees dealing with less important matters (Castaldo 1989, p. 55). This detail is revealing of the spirit of the ancien régime.

[171] AP 9, p. 564.

The patriot Bouche opposed the bureaux because they tended to weaken the revolutionary fervor. As noted, he preferred the large assemblies, where "souls become strong and electrified, and where names, ranks and distinctions count for nothing."[172] On his proposal, it was decided that the assembly would sit in plenum each morning and the bureaux meet in the afternoon. The importance of this move, which constituted the beginning of the end for the moderates, was perfectly understood at the time.[173]

Consider finally the issue of public versus secret voting in the assembly. In an ordinary legislature, votes are often cast in public so that the electorate can hold their representatives accountable. As a by-product, publicity makes logrolling possible. If one decides that vote trading is undesirable on normative grounds, one can block that option simply by enforcing the secret ballot. In that case, accountability would suffer.

This question is independent of the issue of the secrecy or publicity of *debates*. In theory, one might envisage any of the four possible combinations of public or secret debates and votes. (In fact, there are six combinations, since votes might either be kept secret from other voters or from the public at large.) If the debates in a constituent assembly are public, perhaps because the need for diversity requires a large assembly that will not be able to maintain the secrecy of the debates, one might in fact impose secret voting both to eliminate interest-based logrolling and to make the delegates unafraid of voting the wrong way on popular proposals. Note how, in the previous sentence, *size, diversity, publicity, secrecy, interest, and passion interact* in a way that illustrates the interlocking nature of the elements of the optimal constituent assembly.

VII. RATIFYING THE CONSTITUTION

At the end of the last section I mentioned some ways in which secrecy and publicity may be combined within the constituent assembly. Here, I suggest that they may also be combined at the broader national level. A closed assembly may be supplemented by upstream and downstream public consultations, generating an overall "hourglass-shaped" procedure.[174] There may also be room for properly designed midstream influences, broadening as it were the middle of the hourglass.

The convening of a constituent assembly and the election of delegates may go together with a public debate over the main constitutional issues. In 1789, the French people expressed their grievances and proposed remedies for them in the *cahiers de doléances* that take up 4,000 double-column small-print pages of the *Archives Parlementaires*. Before the adoption of the South African constitution in 1996, the constituent assembly invited suggestions from the citizens and received 1.2 million responses. In neither case, however, is there any evidence

---

[172] AP 8, p. 307.
[173] Egret (1950), p. 120. Later, Mounier (AP 9, p. 564) strongly reproached himself about his inactivity on this occasion.
[174] Russell (1993), p. 191.

that the opinions expressed in this way made much of a difference to the constitution that was finally adopted. In South Africa, the most influential upstream process was probably the debate among the candidates to the assembly rather than direct citizen involvement. In France, remarkably and perhaps disastrously, there were no debates in the electoral assemblies.[175]

Midstream influences on the constituent assembly can, as I have argued, be dangerous if they are expressed by an audience that is physically present. The 2011 Icelandic process suggests, however, that communication on the Internet may avoid these dangers. According to one member of the Constitutional Council, it "received 323 formal proposals that the three committees of the Council discussed and answered. More than 3,600 written comments were posted on the [Council's] website by visitors; the Council representatives answered many if not most of them. Nearly all the proposals and comments proved useful in one way or another, not only what was said, but also the things left unsaid. If no one objected to the provision articles posted on the website, then perhaps we were on the right track."[176] Bentham and Condorcet, who preferred written communication over oral discussion (Chapter 3), might have approved.

The *downstream* process of ratification by the citizens, also accompanied by a national debate, can be important. Generally speaking, one would think that most constitutions submitted to referendum would be approved, simply because members of the assembly will be sufficiently rational and well-informed to anticipate the views of the electorate. The debates at the Federal Convention are very revealing in this respect, with their constant references to what might or might not be approved by the ratifying conventions. Perhaps because they anticipated that these conventions would be elected with a broad suffrage, the framers proposed a constitution that was more democratic than the one they would have chosen in the absence of ratification.[177] Moreover, the anticipation of ratification probably caused the framers to *internalize each other's concerns*. A delegate from state A might vote for a proposal to which he was opposed because the ratifying convention in state B might otherwise reject the document, with the possible consequence that the required number of nine ratifying states would not be reached. In the process of arguing and bargaining at the Convention, the *warning of non-ratification* was probably as effective as the *threat of leaving the convention*.[178]

In ratifying their document, the American founders wisely bypassed the state legislatures. These might not have approved of Article I. 10, which deprived them of many of their powers. In 1949, the occupying powers wanted the German constitution to be ratified by referendums in the Länder, but on German insistence the

[175] Cochin (1979), pp. 81–83.
[176] Gylfason (2012).
[177] Amar (2005), pp. 279–80.
[178] Thus King from Massachusetts defended the 3/5 clause because he feared that the southern states "would not league themselves with the Northn. unless some respect were paid to their superior wealth" (Farrand [1966], vol. 2, p. 562). For my distinction between threats and warnings, which differs from that made by Schelling (1960), see Elster (2001).

ratification devolved on the state legislatures. Only Bavaria turned it down on the grounds that the constitution did not grant enough power to the Länder; however, the state assembly also decided that the constitution would come into force in Bavaria if 2/3 of the other Länder accepted it. In October 2012, the Icelandic proposal for contitutional reform was approved by 2/3 of the voters in a consultative referendum with a turnout of 50 percent. Unusually, the voters were also asked to express their opinion on five specific points in the proposal, including the abolition of malapportionment. The favorable vote on that issue – 66 percent – corresponds very closely to the percentage of the population that lives in the underrepresented Reykjavik area. At the time of writing, it is unclear whether the parliament, to which the proposal has to be submitted, will make substantial changes. Generally speaking, having a constitution ratified by a parliament – a *pouvoir constitué* approving a document produced by the *pouvoir constituant* – is clearly anomalous. Because of the occupational context, the German case does not provide a clean counterexample.

The ratification of the American constitution was a very close call. It could easily have derailed. In quite a few cases, proposed subnational, national, or international constitutions have in fact been turned down by the ratifiers. The Australian constitution of 1898 had to be revised after it failed a referendum in New South Wales. In France in 1946, voters turned down the first proposal for a new constitution, probably because it was perceived to give too much power to a parliament that might be dominated by the Communists. In 1992, a proposed constitution for Canada was turned down by voters in Québec because they thought it gave too little to Québec, and by voters in other provinces because they thought it gave too many concessions to Québec. In 1994, Albanian voters turned down a proposed constitution. In 2005, a new constitution was voted down in Kenya. More recently, the proposed European Union (EU) constitution was turned down by voters in France and Holland (for multiple reasons). At the subnational level, one can cite the remarkable fact that among the twelve constitutions submitted by conventions (not mixed assemblies) to referendum in the American states in the 1960s and 1970s, *seven* were rejected, in two cases with a high margin (4 to 1 in Rhode Island and 3 to 1 in New York State).[179] These are striking and puzzling findings, which are hard to reconcile with "the law of anticipated reactions" or with the idea that politicians have rational expectations.

The hourglass model is a theoretical construct, which has not been tried in practice. It may be incompatible with the norm of transparency, which could impose an irresistible pressure for full publicity at all stages, not only in the upstream and downstream phases. The citizens may well ask, in the spirit of Bentham, "Why should they hide themselves if they do not dread being seen?"[180] A possible remedy might be *ex post publicity*, in the form of full publication of debates and votes *after* the constitution is proposed but *before* it is put up for ratification.

---

[179] Lenowitz (2007).
[180] Bentham (1999), p. 30; personal pronouns changed.

VIII. CONCLUSION

Many collective decision-making bodies are ongoing institutions. They are not created to make a single decision and dismantled when they have performed their task. Grand juries, legislatures, constitutional courts, and central bank committees make many separate decisions. Even though some of their decisions may form precedents for or constraints on others, they are made seriatim.

Trial juries and (pure) constituent assemblies are one-off bodies. In Ancient Greece, jurors as well as *nomothetai* were chosen (by lot) for a day. In the contemporary world, some deliberating assemblies are also chosen by lot for the sole purpose of making policy recommendations. Members of constituent assemblies in the modern form, however, have always been elected. Since they are likely to be well-known public figures, they do not always follow the example of Cincinnatus and return en masse to the plow once their task has been done. The French constituants who declared themselves ineligible to the first ordinary legislature seem to provide the only example. Although the result was disastrous, the solution might be appropriate when there is a concurrent ordinary legislature.

Constituent assemblies and juries have another common feature, the relative unimportance of individual interest. In this respect, the Federal Convention was an outlier. Although the importance of individual interests in shaping the document remains controversial, these interests did affect individual votes on some occasions. It is of course not controversial that group interests – small versus large states, southern versus northern – had a decisive influence on the outcome. In modern constituent assemblies, the most important group interest is that of political parties. The most important way that interest can influence the constitution is by constitutionalizing electoral law. If a large party has more than 50 percent of the members in the constituent assembly, it may lock in the electoral system in ways that, because of the difficulty of amending the constitution, may enable it to stay in power even when it becomes a minority. This consequence is obviously undesirable. At the same time, as I noted earlier, leaving the design of electoral laws to the legislature can also "enable those in power to use their power to keep their power." Since this effect is also undesirable, one could perhaps leave the design to an independent electoral commission whose members are chosen by lottery among the citizens. The experience from British Columbia in 2004 and 2009 does not, however, strongly support this model.

Be this as it may, constituent assemblies ought as far as possible to *remove from their agenda issues on which interest has a purchase*. To the extent that they do so, there are no strong arguments for publicity of debates or for ex ante publicity of voting. Even if the assembly debates behind closed doors, argument will not be replaced by bargaining since there will be nothing to bargain about. Also, as I have argued, the quality of argument will be better than if the debates were public. Once again, the negative effects of the ex ante secrecy of voting will be counteracted by the ex post publicity.

5

Cross-Voting: A Study in Failure

I. INTRODUCTION

In this chapter I discuss *cross-voting* as an electoral device for promoting what Bentham called "moral aptitude" in deputies. More specifically, the device is intended to *prevent the election of extremists* and *favor that of moderate candidates*. In recent discussions, the term "centripetal" is often used about institutions designed for that purpose.[1] For instance, members of group A may delegate to another group B the power or some of the power to choose the representatives of group A. The process can also involve more than two groups. As we shall see, there are many other variations on the same general theme. The main variation is quantitative, in the following sense: in the election of representatives for group A, the proportion of voters who belong to group A may vary from 0 (Brittany 1576, 1614) through 1/6 (Maryland 1789), 1/3 (Georgia 1789, France 1484, 1789), to some number between 1/2 and 1 (proposed scheme for Belgium).

This general idea has been adopted or proposed independently at many times and places, ranging from the foundation of Rome to Belgian politics in the 21st century. The idea seems to be intrinsically attractive, especially – but not only – in societies divided along the lines of estate or ethnicity. In the words of one scholar, "the fact that so many different countries and conflicts have made recourse to the basic ideas of cross voting, often without reference to or apparent knowledge of the experience of others, is a testament to the recurring appeal of this idea."[2]

The question I discuss in this chapter is whether cross-voting reliably produces moderate representatives. If it did, the procedure would provide an instance of positive institutional engineering and hence a counterexample to the Benthamite thesis I defend in this book. We do not know enough about the ancient cases that I shall cite shortly to tell whether the procedures achieved their intended aim of conflict resolution or reconciliation. With regard to the more recent cases, from the

---

[1] Reilly (2011).
[2] Reilly (2011), p. 61.

15th century onward, the evidence is somewhat ambiguous. Overall, however, I believe there are general reasons to be skeptical, notably because of the fragility of institutional engineering based on incentive schemes. Needless to say, even if my argument is correct, it will not prove that other centripetal schemes could not work. One cannot prove a negative.

Let me first cite two ancient cases, to indicate the perennial appeal of the general idea. The first is taken from Plutarch's *Life* of the second King of Rome, Numa, who strived to appease the conflict between two ethnic groups, Romans and Sabines. The historical accuracy of the account is questionable, as Plutarch himself states, and in any case does not matter for the purely conceptual use I shall make of it. For my purposes, the existence of Plutarch's account written in the second century A.D. is as relevant as the purported facts of the eighth century B.C.:

After the death of Romulus senators from the two groups ruled on alternate days.

But although in this way the senators were thought to rule constitutionally and without oppression, they roused suspicions and clamorous charges that they had changed the form of government to an oligarchy, and were holding the state in tutelage among themselves, and were unwilling to be ruled by a king. Therefore it was agreed by both factions that *one should appoint a king from the other*. This was thought the best way to end their prevailing partisanship, and the king thus appointed would be equally well-disposed to both parties, being gracious to the one as his electors, and friendly to the other because of his kinship with them. Then, *as the Sabines gave the Romans their option in the matter, it seemed to them better to have a Sabine king of their own nomination, than to have a Roman made king by the Sabines*. They took counsel, therefore, among themselves, and nominated Numa Pompilius from among the Sabines, a man who had not joined the emigrants to Rome, but was so universally celebrated for his virtues that, when he was nominated, the Sabines accepted him with even greater readiness than those who had chosen him.[3]

As we shall see, the memory of Numa as the originator of cross-voting was well and alive in Maryland in 1789, spanning twenty-five centuries. My claim of independent reinvention is not, therefore, quite accurate. As many educated people in France knew Plutarch in Amyot's translation from 1565, it is possible that some cases of cross-voting at the Estates-General were also inspired by *The Life of Numa*. This influence remains conjectural.

It is puzzling why the Sabines offered the Romans the choice between having a Sabine king chosen by the Romans and a Roman king chosen by the Sabines. In fact, it is unclear whether things happened this way at all.[4] If we choose to believe Plutarch's account, we may note nevertheless that the citizens did not chose cross-voting in a more literal sense by electing two kings (as later there were two consuls), each chosen by one group from the other.

We are on somewhat firmer ground with a bronze inscription from the third century B.C. documenting cross-voting in Sicily.[5] The so-called fraternization

[3] *Life of Numa* III; my italics.
[4] Dionysius, *Roman Antiquities*, II, 57, tells a very different story.
[5] I rely on the terse translation in van Effenterre and van Effenterre (1988), as well as on the more expansive interpretation in Gabba (1984), p. 86 n. 21.

decree in Nacona states that each of two groups which had recently been in conflict should *elect thirty persons from the other group*. With their names put in two urns, the archons should draw one name from each urn and adjoin to the two people thus chosen three other persons chosen by lot. These five individuals would form a fraternity. Later, groups of five were chosen by lot from all the other citizens. It seems that further conflicts were to be resolved within each fraternity. The details are obscure, controversial, far beyond my competence, and fortunately irrelevant. What matters is the documented practice of having members of one group in a conflict choose the representatives for the other with the purpose of attenuating hostilities.

I shall now proceed as follows. In Section II, I consider the relation between active and passive suffrage (the right to vote and the right to be elected). In Section III, I discuss cross-voting in the elections to the French Estates-General between 1484 and 1789 and cross-verification of credentials at the Estates of 1789. In Section IV, I discuss three separate episodes or proposals of cross-voting in the United States between 1787 and 1789. In Section V, I consider some contemporary practices or proposals. Section VI offers an overall evaluation of cross-voting and a general discussion of incentive schemes in institutional design.

II. VOTERS AND ELIGIBLES

Before moving on to the historical and contemporary instances of cross-voting, I shall explore the implications of the following two facts. In cross-voting, some votes for a candidate for a given group are cast *by voters who are not themselves members of that group*. In some cases (including some but not all cases of cross-voting), some votes for a candidate to represent a given group may be cast *for individuals who are not themselves members of that group*. Today, these situations are relatively uncommon, but historically they have been quite important.

In modern political systems, representatives are usually chosen *by and from* those whom they represent. The "by" condition can be justified in several ways. It is a form of anti-paternalism. Whereas a child cannot choose its guardian, adult citizens will not tolerate an imposed representative, even if he is taken from their midst. Also, the condition ensures that the representative will be responsive and accountable to his constituency and not to some third party or larger group. The "from" condition makes it likely that the representative will have some knowledge of the situation of those whom he represents. People from Nebraska know more about Nebraska than do people from New York. Also, there is likely to be some commonality of interest between the representative and members of his constituency. These effects of the "from" condition are enhanced if the "by" condition is also satisfied. If the senator from Nebraska were to be chosen randomly from the citizens of Nebraska, the lot might fall on someone who knows and cares little about the situation of the typical citizen of Nebraska. Yet the "by" condition by itself is also unlikely to suffice. It might be hard to find a citizen of another state who knew as much about Nebraska as the voters would want their representative to know, and even harder to find someone who identifies with their interest. The mere interest in reelection might not suffice. It is the conjunction of "by" and "from" that creates the peculiarly intimate relation between citizens and their representatives in modern democracies: *we choose one of us to represent us*.

These truisms are, I believe, widely shared. They belong to the core of the modern idea of political representation. Yet they were not always held to be self-evident. In fact, even today some practices violate the principle that representatives shall be chosen by and from those whom they represent. To organize the discussion of these deviant cases, let us assume the existence of two groups: V (voters) and E (eligibles). An eligible who is elected by the voters is called a *deputy*. Voters and eligibles require different kinds of competence. Eligibles must have *issue competence*, that is, the ability to choose substantively good policies. In Bentham's language, they should have the moral aptitude needed for the choice of ends and the intellectual aptitude needed for the choice of means. Voters must have *voting competence*, that is, the intellectual aptitude to recognize issue competence in others. As we shall see in a moment, the ability to recognize voting competence in others may also be relevant.

For the bulk of the discussion I shall assume that the qualifications for voters and eligibles are exogenously given. They could, however, also emerge endogenously. A given body of voters might decide that only some of them shall be allowed to represent them. They might also decide that only some of them shall be allowed to vote in future elections or, on the contrary, extend the right to vote to a larger body.

I begin with the first issue. At a meeting of all "free planters" that adopted a proto-constitutional *Agreement* for Connecticut on June 4, 1639, the assembly first adopted a number of relatively vague and inconsequential measures unanimously and without any expression of opposition. When it came to the fifth proposition, however, some dissent emerged. The question was

WHETHER free burgesses shall be chosen out of the church members, they that are in the foundation work of the church being actually free burgesses, and to choose to themselves out of the like estate of church fellowship, and the power of choosing magistrates and officers from among themselves, and the power of making and repealing laws, according to the word, and the dividing of inheritances, and deciding of differences that may arise, and all the businesses of like nature are to be transacted by those free burgesses. This was put to vote and agreed unto by lifting up of hands twice, as in the former it was done. Then one man stood up and expressed his dissenting from the rest in part; yet granting, 1. That magistrates should be men fearing GOD. 2. That the church is the company where, ordinarily, such men may be expected. 3. That they that choose them ought to be men fearing GOD; only at this he stuck, that free planters ought not to give this power out of their hands. Another stood up and answered, that nothing was done, but with their consent. The former answered, that all the free planters ought to resume this power into their own hands again, if things were not orderly carried. Mr. Theophilus Eaton answered, that in all places they choose committees in like manner. The companies in London choose the liveries by whom the public magistrates are chosen. In this the rest are not wronged, because they expect, in time, to be of the livery themselves, and to have the same power. Some others intreated the former to give his arguments and reasons whereupon he dissented. He refused to do it, and said, they might not rationally demand it, seeing he let the vote pass on freely and did not speak till after it was past, because he would not hinder what they agreed upon. Then Mr. Davenport, after a short relation of some former passages between them two about this question, prayed the company that nothing might be concluded by them on this weighty question, but what themselves were persuaded to be agreeing with the mind of GOD, and they had heard what had been said since the voting; he intreated them again to consider of it, and put it again to vote as before. Again all of them, by holding up their hands, did show their consent as before. And some of them confessed that, whereas they did waver before they came to the assembly, they were now fully convinced, that it is the mind of GOD. One of them said that in the morning before he came reading Deut. xvii. 15, he was convinced at home. Another said, that he came doubting to the assembly, but he blessed GOD, by what had been said, he was now fully satisfied, that the choice of burgesses out of church members and to intrust those with the power before spoken of is according to the mind of GOD revealed in the scriptures. All having spoken their apprehensions it was agreed upon.

Thus all free men agreed, apparently under some pressure, to be governed by the subset among themselves who were also church members.[6] The argument from analogy offered by Theophilus Eaton is manifestly halting. Although apprentices or "freemen" in the London guilds could expect to become "liverymen" with full voting rights at some time, the relationship between these two groups is entirely different from that between non-members and members of the Church.

Consider now the second issue. There are two subcases. In one, the given body of voters decides that only some of them will be allowed to vote in the future. This could clearly be a risky business. In Virginia, in 1901, a constitutional convention refrained from submitting its proposal to the people, as it was obliged to do, "largely, it would seem, out of fear of its being defeated by the elements to be disenfranchised."[7] Yet sometimes the move succeeded. In Chapter 4 I noted that in 1780 the voters in Massachusetts ratified a constitution that limited their suffrage compared both to the wide suffrage used in electing deputies to the constitutional convention and to the narrower suffrage in force before the convention (one step forward, two steps backward). Another example is offered by the French constitution of 1795, which has been called "an aristocratic constitution adopted by democratic means."[8] The draft constitution, which imposed strict economic qualifications on members of the electoral assemblies, had to be approved by the electoral assemblies as defined by the constitution of 1793. In that document all citizens, defined as adult males, had the right to vote. The constitution was approved by an overwhelming majority in an election with a very low turnout.

In the second subcase, we assume that a proposed *extension* of the suffrage is to be decided by referendum. Let us call those who have the right to vote

[6] For the similarly conflicted relations between freemen and church members in the Massachusetts Bay colony at about the same time, see Seidman (1945).
[7] Hoar (1917), p. 194.
[8] Troper (2006), p. 89.

prior to the referendum the "existing electorate," and those who will have the right to vote if the extension is adopted the "extended electorate." Who shall have the right to vote in the referendum? The existing electorate or the extended electorate? In two cases the competence to judge voting competence was assigned to the extended electorate. The 1830 Virginia constitution was "ratified in an election open to all who were prospectively enfranchised by it."[9] The same procedure with the opposite result was observed in 1953 when revisions in the Danish constitution were submitted to referendum.[10] Each voter cast two votes, one for or against the proposed constitution and one for a change in the voting age. The alternatives for the latter vote were to lower the age from 25 to 23 or to 21 years. In the first vote, only citizens older than 25 could cast a vote. In the second, everybody above 21 could vote. The result of the referendum was that the extended electorate refused a corresponding extension of the electorate. A majority of the voters older than 21 decided to lower the voting age from 25 to 23 rather than to 21. Both the turnout and the majority were around 55 pecent.[11]

A remarkable – but failed – attempt to make the prospectively enfranchised vote on their own enfranchisement occurred in 1848, when a member of the House of Representatives, Joshua Giddings,

> presented [a] bill, which called for a plebiscite in slavery's future in Washington [DC] in which "all male inhabitants" would cast ballots marked either "Slavery" or "Liberty." When Patrick Tompkins of Mississippi asked if he meant to allow slaves and free blacks to vote, Giddings replied that he did. If Tompkins, he continued, wished to exclude slave-holders as well as slaves from the referendum, he would agree, but he "never would submit to give one man control over another man's liberty." The House quickly tabled Giddings's bill.[12]

The case, to be sure, differs from the Virginian and Danish ones, since the slaves were to be granted freedom, not necessarily voting rights. It also differs in that the (probably ironic) proposal to also exclude slaveholders from the vote if slaves were to be denied the right to vote on their enfranchisement has no analogue in the other cases. Yet the conundrum is similar.

I shall assume that either E is a proper subgroup of V or V is a proper subgroup of E. (In many modern systems, E = V.) I shall ignore cases, interesting as they might be, in which E and V are non-overlapping or only partially overlapping. I shall distinguish four cases.[13]

---

[9] Pole (1966), p. 332.

[10] The lowering in 1961 of the voting age to 21 was decided in a referendum in which only those older than 23 had the right to vote. (For the 1953 referendum, the age of the youngest voters is given as 21. Since it is not mentioned for the 1961 referendum, it was presumably the legal voting age of 23.)

[11] López-Guerra (2011b) offers a general discussion, with additional examples, of what he calls the "second-order enfranchisement problem."

[12] Foner (2010), p. 56.

[13] Neither Pitkin (1967) nor Manin (1997) addresses cases (2), (3), or (4).

1. E is a proper subgroup of V. Deputies represent V.
2. E is a proper subgroup of V. Deputies represent E.
3. V is a proper subgroup of E. Deputies represent V.
4. V is a proper subgroup of E. Deputies represent E.

The cases differ along two dimensions. Is eligibility more restricted than suffrage (cases 1 and 2) or is suffrage more restricted than eligibility (cases 3 and 4)? Are deputies supposed to represent the voters (cases 1 and 3) or the eligible (cases 2 and 4)? The answer to the second question may be "neither." When there are restrictions on both suffrage and eligibility, one might claim that the deputy represents the community at large, of which both V and E are proper subgroups. I shall ignore this issue. I shall now give some examples of cases (1) through (4). In later sections cross-voting, a subcase of (2), is considered in greater detail.

(1) E is a proper subgroup of V. Deputies represent V. This is the most familiar case. It obtains when there are stricter conditions (income, property, tax payment, age, gender, length of residence, etc.) on eligibility than on suffrage. In France, legislation from 1889 rendered bankrupt individuals ineligible for public office, but preserved their right to vote.[14] After the Restoration, voters had to pay 300 francs in direct taxes, which limited the suffrage to 100,000 out of an adult male population of 9 million. To be elected, one had to pay 1,000 francs in direct taxes, a condition satisfied only by 17,000 individuals. There are also many contemporary examples. In the United States, the threshold for eligibility to the House and the Senate (25 and 30 years, respectively) is higher than the threshold for voting (18 years). In Norway, any citizen can vote in parliamentary elections but eligibility requires residence in the Kingdom for at least ten years.

(2) E is a proper subgroup of V. Deputies represent E. The case of cross-voting belongs here. In theory, there might be other cases, but I have not come across any. One could imagine, perhaps, the following case. Rather than representing different geographical districts, Parliament represents different age groups. Representatives of a given group are chosen by and from the members of that group, with the exception of those who represent the age slice from 16 to 18 years. If it is believed that some members of this group have issue competence but that because of their immaturity many lack even voting competence, members of all age groups might be given a vote in electing their representatives. This procedure is imaginable only because of differential competence among the voting groups. If representation were on a geographical basis, the idea of giving members of A a vote in choosing representatives for B would be hard to imagine unless members of B had a vote in electing representatives of A, that is, cross-voting.[15]

---

[14] Pierre (1893), pp. 130–31.

[15] Age is not the only conceivable criterion for (real or imagined) differential competence. One could imagine a hierarchical system of estates in which the higher estates would have a vote in selecting representatives of the lower estates to a common assembly, but not vice versa.

(3) V is a proper subgroup of E. Deputies represent V. In elections to the Constituante of 1789, the third estate could and did choose members of the other estates to represent them. Thus Mirabeau and Sieyes were elected from the nobility and clergy, respectively, to represent the third estate. Overall, there were 58 nobles and 3 clergymen elected by the third estate.[16] The third estate had originally opposed this option, fearing that habits of deference would allow the privileged estates to impose themselves. Yet in a decision of December 27, 1788, the King explicitly refused to block this possibility.[17]

In contemporary parliaments, this case is illustrated by the occasional lack of residential requirements for the deputies. In France, deputies represent the nation, not their district (Art. 27 of the constitution is widely understood to express this idea). Hence anyone can stand as a candidate anywhere. People without local attachments may be resented as "parachutistes" or carpet-baggers, but they are not legally prevented from presenting themselves. In Norway, such has also been the practice since 1952.

(4) V is a proper subgroup of E. Deputies represent E. This case is the inverse of case (1) and obtains when there are stricter conditions (income, property, tax payment, age, gender, length of residence, etc.) on suffrage than on eligibility. As we saw in Chapter 3, Bentham advocated an asymmetric system of this kind. Although probably less frequent than the converse asymmetry, the examples offered in Chapter 1 show that it is not negligible. Thus in the Danish constitution of 1849, the age requirement for electing deputies to the lower house was 30 years and that for eligibility to that house 25 years. Although I have not studied the debates preceding the decision, one can imagine a rationale. The framers may have thought that voters below the age of 30 would in general not have voting competence. At the same time, they may have thought that some individuals below that age would be sufficiently mature to have not only voting competence but even issue competence. Voters older than 30 would, because of their greater maturity, be able to identify and vote for such individuals. A similar rationale might explain the cases in which women became eligible before they became voters (see Chapter 1), if it was believed that some women had issue competence but that many or most lacked even voting competence.

At the Federal Convention, Gouverneur Morris said, "If qualifications are proper, he wd. prefer them in the electors rather than the elected." Madison "concurred with Mr. Govr. Morris in thinking that qualifications in the Electors would be much more effectual than in the elected. The former would discriminate between real & ostentatious property in the latter."[18] The last sentence refers to Madison's earlier observation that "It had often happened that men who had acquired landed property on credit, got into the Legislatures with a view of promoting an unjust protection agst. their Creditors."[19] The reasoning

[16] Tackett (1996), p.23.
[17] AP 1, p. 494 ff.
[18] Farrand (1966), vol. 2, pp. 121, 124.
[19] Ibid., p. 123.

seems a bit confused. For the electors to discriminate between real and ostentatious property, they would presumably themselves have to own "real" property only; otherwise men who had acquired landed property on credit would vote for similar individuals as deputies. But if it was possible to distinguish between real and ostentatious property in the electors, why couldn't one do the same for the deputies? Be this as it may, in the end the Convention did not impose any conditions on suffrage, but left the matter to the states.

Can anything be said about the comparative merits of systems (1) and (4)? I limit myself to age qualifications. There are (at least) three desiderata in systems of representation. First, the deputy should be chosen "from us." This condition is satisfied in case (4), but not in case (1). Second, he should be chosen "by us." This condition is satisfied in case (1), but not in case (4). Third, he should have issue competence. Tensions arise because some of "us" may lack either issue competence or voting competence. Let us make three (plausible) assumptions. First, at all age levels issue competence is more rare than voting competence. Second, for either kind of competence, the proportion of competent individuals increases with age. Third, for either kind of competence the proportion of competent individuals falls well short of 100 percent at all age levels. In case (1), more eligibles have issue competence, but since the electorate has less voting competence they might still choose deputies with little issue competence. In case (4), the voters have more voting competence, but there are more issue incompetent eligibles. Without more specific assumptions, the net outcome of the comparison along this dimension is indeterminate.

III. CROSS-VOTING AT THE ESTATES-GENERAL

In France, the Estates-General, composed of delegates from the clergy, the nobility, and the third estate, were called at irregular intervals from 1302 to 1789. Their political role, although real, was limited. France never became a *Ständestaat* in the sense of some of the North European countries, although there were occasional attempts to force the King to share power with the three estates (or orders). Yet France remained a *Ständegesellschaft*, in the sense that social relations were dominated by considerations of rank and hierarchy. It does not seem unreasonable to think that France never became a Ständestaat precisely because it was a Ständegesellschaft. In the 16th and 17th centuries, the arrogant contempt with which the upper clergy and the nobility treated the third estate when the Estates met prevented the formation of any common front against the King. Although Tocqueville was probably mistaken when he thought the division due to divide-and-conquer policies by the kings, it certainly worked out to their benefit.[20]

The delegates had a double electoral base, being chosen both by estate and by electoral district. On several occasions, the choice was made by cross-voting, so

[20] Elster (2009b), pp. 155–56.

that within a given electoral district (*balliage* or *sénéchaussée*), members of all orders cast a vote on the choice of the deputies from each order. It might seem illogical that deputies *elected jointly* would meet and *vote separately* by order once they assembled. In 1484, when cross-voting was the rule in most circumscriptions, the Estates were in fact divided into six geographical provinces rather than in estates.[21]

The *Journal* of Jean Masselin, a deputy from the clergy to the Estates of 1484, casts an interesting light on how the deputies perceived the practice of cross-voting. When a deputy from the clergy demanded that their travel expenses be paid out of general taxes rather than at their own expense, a deputy from the third estate replied that

> [It] seems fair that the men sent by the Church to discuss the matters concerning it should be paid out of the wealth that it possesses in abundance. We say the same about the nobles, persuaded as we are that it is already enough for the third estate to pay for its own deputies as far as it is in its power, and that one would commit an injustice towards this estate if it were to pay for the nobility and the clergy, an injustice all the more unworthy of them as it would force the poorest to give alms to the richest.[22]

The indignant response of Philippe de Poitiers, a deputy for the nobility, is worth citing at some length:

> I dare affirm ... that the clergy and the nobility, by their efforts and according to their mandate, have been superior defenders of the cause of the poor people.... Which men, after the people itself, have the most to lose from the sufferings of the people and must have the greatest concern for its interests? I answer with great confidence that these are the ecclesiastics and the nobles, whose ease and fortune depend entirely on those of the people and who love it much more than lawyers and magistrates, who are the last to care about its poverty and who continue to enrich themselves even when it is miserable. The clergy and above all the nobility do not present this scandalous spectacle, because it is impossible for them to be rich if the people is not. But why would the others claim so loudly to be the exclusive defender of the people? Listening to them it would seem that the clergy is here only to occupy itself with matters of the church, the nobles only with matters of war, and that only they are here to care of the affairs of the nation.... But I beg them to read from beginning to end the text of their convocation: it will prove to them that the clergy and the nobility are no less than they the mandatories of the people.... All the deputies are supposed to receive their powers from the united voters of all three estates.... The elected deputies are to treat in common the common interests of the kingdom and to work together for the welfare of the nation.... Will they claim that they have a prior right to be consulted in the people's cause, because they have a particular interest in determining its taxes, which they also have to pay? I reply that ... even though they are in fact deputies of the people and delegates of the third estate, they are usually exempt from paying taxes.... This reasoning shows conclusively that it is not necessary for the deputies for the people to be taken from the people.[23]

---

[21] Picot (1888), vol. 5, pp. 249–52.
[22] Masselin (1835), p. 497, translated from the French translation of the Latin original.
[23] Ibid., pp. 499, 501, 503.

As evidence of cross-estate solidarity, these comments are not compelling. It is true, of course, that the nobility and the clergy had an interest in lower *taxes* on the people, but mainly to facilitate greater feudal exactions. Although it would be false to assert that the welfare of the people in the French countryside was at all times at the lowest sustainable level, the double exploitation of the peasants left them with a relatively small margin above subsistence.[24] Philippe de Poitiers's charge against the third estate is more convincing than his defense of the privileged orders, since its city-dwelling deputies were in fact often exempt from the taxes they voted.

On later occasions, cross-voting was practiced only occasionally. In 1576 and in 1614, the elections in Brittany of delegates to the Estates took the extreme form of having delegates for each estate elected only by votes of members of the other two estates.[25] The intention behind cross-voting seems to have been to promote the spirit of the province at the expense of the spirit of the estate. The deputies came, as it were, as ambassadors from their province. If all districts in the nation had adopted the procedure, the outcome would have been a conflict among the provinces rather than among the estates. There is no reason to think that it would have promoted the national or *general* interest.

In the elections to the French Assemblée Constituante in 1789, the normal pattern was that members of one estate in a given electoral district chose a representative among themselves to represent them. The electoral rules allowed, however, delegates of all three estates to the electoral assemblies to vote jointly on who should represent a given estate.[26] This could only happen if each order, voting separately, agreed to this system. The King could have imposed it, but he did not. A few districts, notably the Dauphiné, took advantage of this possibility.[27] The system could obviously work in peculiar ways. As noted in a memorandum written by dissident clergy and nobles in the Dauphiné some time between the elections there and the opening of the Estates-General, "it might happen that not a single deputy for the nobility received a single vote

[24] According to Milanovic, Lindert, and Williamson (2011), in 1788 the French elites extracted about 75 percent of the feasible maximum, a rate comparable to that of the Roman Empire. By contrast, in 1759 the elites in England and Wales extracted only about 55 percent of the maximum. I conjecture that taxation and feudal dues combined were even harsher in the 15th century.

[25] Picot (1888), vol. 5, pp. 271–72.

[26] AP 1, p. 623.

[27] To my knowledge, there is no systematic study of the subject. For the Dauphiné, see discussion and references later in the chapter. Harris (1986) p. 436, asserts that "about twelve" districts used this method, but does not say which these were. Canon Coster, deputy for the clergy from Verdun, notes in his journal that he had been elected by all three orders (Houtin 1916, p. 134). Verdun sent a total of four deputies, who presumably were chosen in the same manner. According to Moreau (1995), p. 191, the system was also used in the selection of the single deputy (of the third estate) from Arles. Lefebvre (1989), p. 105, says that in addition to the Dauphiné, the procedure had been adopted "in some electoral districts," but does not say which. Lafayette tried, but without success, to get the Dauphiné system adopted in Auvergne (Gottschalk and Maddox, 1969, p. 22). In the electoral district of Nîmes, the three orders in one of three subdistricts expressed a desire for cross-voting (Moreau 1995, pp. 113, 130).

from the nobility."[28] At the same time, Tocqueville thought the system might have had good effects if adopted across the board:

In the Dauphiné, it was the assembly of the estates that chose in common deputies from the three orders. This assembly was made up of the three orders, each having been elected separately and representing only itself. But the deputies to the Estates General were elected by the assembly: in this way each nobleman had some bourgeois among his electors and each bourgeois some nobles; and while remaining distinct the three deputations became in a way homogeneous. If the orders had been represented in this way, they might not have been able to agree [*s'entendre*] but at least to avoid confronting each other too violently.[29]

Prior to the elections, there was in the Dauphiné, as in many other parts of France, a strong movement demanding that when the Estates-General met in Versailles, the three estates should vote in joint sessions and with votes taken individually rather than (as in the traditional system) by estate. In the Dauphiné, that principle was also adopted in choosing deputies to the Estates-General. The idea seems first to have been formulated by the Comte de Virieu in 1787. He proposed that "in this new election *all* be elected by *all*, so that there is no deputy from one Order that does not also have the support (*voeu*) of the other two. Although each deputy is destined to communicate the interest of the body to which he belongs, he is nevertheless not its special mandatory, and thus is not obligated to embrace exclusively its particular passions and views, but becomes through this mode of election the representative of all."[30]

The system was adopted in the fall of 1788 by an assembly of the three estates convened by the King for the purpose of organizing the meeting of the provincial Estates. Mounier – the leading spirit in the reform movement in the Dauphiné – justified it as follows: "This form offers a precious advantage: that of having all the Orders contribute to the choice of their respective deputies. They all become the mandatories of the people as a whole (*le peuple en corps*), and this union of the various classes of electors will be a new motive for representatives to consult only the interests they have in common."[31]

The new system was implemented at the meeting of the provincial Estates in January 1789, when each elector – 45 from the clergy, 89 from the nobility, and 119 from the third estate – established a list of 30 candidates: 5 from the clergy, 10 from the nobility, and 15 from the third estate. Anyone whose name appeared on more than half of the lists (*lorsqu'on réunissait la moitié des votes*) was elected as a deputy to the Estates-General. As some names dropped out, the lists were completed by new names.[32] This brief description does not enable us to understand how the system worked, but presumably it did work.

[28] Ilovaïsky (1974), p. 429; see also p. 359.
[29] Tocqueville (2004b), pp. 497–98 ; see also p. 532, where he says that cross-voting might have "favored agreement."
[30] Cited after Joubert (1990), p. 349.
[31] Egret (1942), p. 76.
[32] Ibid., p. 153.

Members of the privileged orders had considerable misgivings about the system. In November, the Comte de Morges wrote to another noble that "many members of the nobility strongly fear the nomination of deputies to the Estates-General by the three orders. The third estate does not know the nobility, which knows even less about the third estate, which is also strongly suspected of choosing those most favorable to it."[33] After the elections had taken place, a number of dissident clergy and nobles declared that "being attentive to all that may concern the dignity and the interests of the two first orders, we observe with the greatest pain that the choice of our deputies to the Estates-General is absolutely dependent on those whose interests or even passions might induce to choose those subjects who would have the smallest part of the confidence of our orders."[34]

By juxtaposing this criticism of the system with the defense offered by Virieu we observe a striking opposition. The critics cite the tendency of deputies from the third estate to be led by their "interests and passions" when voting for the deputies that shall represent the privileged orders. The defense claims that the system will *reduce* the importance of the "particular passions and views" of each order.

The point of view of the critics is easy to understand. When choosing among candidates for the clergy and nobility, members of the third estate would cast their votes for those who were closest to their own position or to their own views. They might be expected, for instance, to favor the parish priests over the high clergy and the liberal nobility over the entrenched defenders of privilege. Perhaps their passions might even induce them to act out of revenge – for instance, by not casting their vote for a particular noble or bishop who had offended by his insulting or condescending manners. The numbers obviously matter. The third estate would because of its numerical superiority have a strong influence on the selection of its own deputies. The clergy, by contrast, would be pretty much at the mercy of the third estate and the liberal nobility combined. The nobility would be in an intermediate position. The traditional nobility would be supported by the high clergy, which dominated the first estate, but deserted by the liberal nobility. They would have good reasons to fear that their interests would be badly represented.

The point of view of the defense is more opaque. The system might simply affect the *attitude* of the chosen deputies, making them more sensible to the common interest, or it could modify the actual *selection* of deputies. The statements by Virieu and Mounier are sufficiently general to be compatible with either. Focusing on the second and more interesting reading, Mounier's claim that the new electoral system would induce a tendency to consider the common interest can be spelled out as follows. A member of the third estate would not have an interest in voting for a member of the privileged orders who would represent and promote only the interests of those orders. He could not, to be

---

[33] Cited after Egret, ibid., p. 70.
[34] Cited after Egret (1950), p. 40. See also the complaint cited in the text that it might happen that "not a single deputy for the nobility received a single vote from the nobility."

sure, expect to find a member of the privileged orders who would represent and promote only the interests of the third estate, but he might find and vote for some members who were willing to consider the general interest. In France in 1789, this meant mainly equality of taxation and abolition of privilege in the access to civil and military office. Correspondingly, members of the privileged orders might vote for members of the third estate who would recognize the importance of property (including feudal dues) and the social utility of distinctions (including noble titles).

Suppose, for a numerical example, that within each estate two thirds want only to promote the particular interests of that estate and one third want to promote the general interest. Suppose also that rather than the numerical proportions in the Dauphiné we have the more common proportion of 30 clergy, 30 nobles and 60 from the third estate.[35] Let us also suppose (contrary to what was the case in the Dauphiné) that the candidates are to be chosen from within the electoral assembly itself, which has to elect 15, 15, and 30 deputies from the three orders. Suppose finally that the candidates elected are those who receive the largest number of votes. Within the clergy, each of the 10 members who want to promote the general interest will receive 10 votes from the clergy, 30 votes from the nobility, and 60 votes from the third estate, 100 votes altogether. These 10 candidates among them will receive 1,000 votes. The total number of votes to be cast is $15(30+30+60) = 1,800$. The remaining 800 votes could in theory be cast for 7 candidates who would each receive more than 100 votes. At worst, therefore, only 8 of the 15 deputies from the clergy will represent the general interest. In practice, the votes for those who do not represent the general interest will be so diluted that all will receive fewer than 100 votes. In that case, 10 out of 15 deputies from the clergy will represent the general interest. The same reasoning holds for the nobility.

Within the third estate, the 20 members who want to promote the general interest will receive 20 votes from their own estate and 30 votes from each of the other estates, 80 votes altogether. These 20 candidates among them will receive 1,600 votes. The total number of votes to be cast is $30 (30+30+60) = 3,600$. The remaining 2,000 votes could in theory be cast for 24 candidates who would each receive more than 80 votes. On that worst-case assumption, only 6 out of 30 deputies from the third estate would represent the general interest. On the more plausible best-case assumption, the 2,000 remaining votes would be divided more or less equally among the forty remaining candidates. All would receive fewer than 80 votes, and ten would be elected. In that case, 20 out of 30 deputies from the third estate would represent the general interest. This outcome would in fact be realized as long as the candidate ranked eleven among the forty candidates received fewer than 80 votes. It would take considerable coordination to bring the vote of the eleventh-ranked above this threshold.

---

[35] In the assemblies where the third estate had as many deputies as the other orders taken together, the usual pattern was for the clergy and the nobility to have equal numbers of representatives. The Dauphiné was an exception.

The numbers are arbitrary. What the exercise shows is that even when 2/3 in each group are concerned only with the interests of that group, cross-voting can produce an assembly in which 2/3 of the members care only about the general interest. Whether, given the constellation of motives in 1789, this result was actually produced, in the Dauphiné or elsewhere, is another matter. The intensely negative reaction that the provincial Estates elicited in many members of the privileged orders suggests that cross-voting did have some effect in reducing group interest representation.[36]

Virieu's claim that cross-voting is likely to reduce the influence of passion could be supported along similar lines. For specificity, let us make the following assumptions. The upper fraction of the third estate, aspiring to be ennobled, is so envious and resentful of the recently ennobled that it never votes for them ("neighborhood envy").[37] Conversely, the recently ennobled, eager to pull up the ladder behind them, are so contemptuous of the upstarts that they would never vote for them. (I ignore the more conjectural emotional attitudes among or toward the clergy.) Let us also assume that those who are motivated by group interest or by the general interest will never vote for those who are emotionally motivated, perhaps because they believe them to be unreliable. One cannot exclude the possibility that passion might affect the choice of deputies, but cross-voting can under certain circumstances make it less likely that the deputies themselves will be motivated by passion. Suppose, for instance, that a large majority of the noble electors consisted of the recently ennobled. If their deputies were chosen by and from their order, there would be some fraction that were intensely jealous of their newly acquired privileges and extremely unwilling to give them up. With cross-voting, by contrast, some of these would be kept out by the other two orders. In fact, those aspiring to be ennobled would vote against them (that is, abstain from voting for them) out of envy or resentment, so that passion would neutralize passion, and others would vote against them to reduce the influence of passion.

The elections to the Estates-General are special in ways that make it hard to generalize. The numerical superiority of the third estate in the electoral assembly gave it, at least potentially, a preponderant influence on selection of deputies from the other groups. It would have been more fair, perhaps, to adjust either the size of the delegations or the weights of the votes so that each order would have had the same influence on the other two. At the same time, even with a number of electors equal to the sum of electors in the other two orders, the third estate was vastly underrepresented in the electoral assemblies. In a total French population of perhaps 25 million, there were at most 100,000 priests, monks, and nuns and 400,000 nobles. The rest, about 98 percent, constituted the third estate. I assume that proportions in the Dauphiné were roughly similar. In that perspective, there is nothing unjust about the third estate having a preponderant influence in selecting deputies to the Estates-General.

[36] Chagny (1988), pp. 152–57.
[37] Elster (1999), p. 170.

When the Estates-General met in May 1789, the first task was to verify the credentials of their deputies. The question that held up the proceedings for six weeks was whether the verification should be done separately, with each order verifying the credentials of its delegates, or jointly by "cross-verification." This issue was closely related to two others, one already decided and one undecided. It had been decided that the third estate would have twice as many delegates as each of the other orders (the "doublement du tiers"). It was left unresolved whether the Estates-General would vote by order or by "head," that is, individually. It was widely argued that the "doublement du tiers" logically implied voting by head: what other reason could the King and Necker have for imposing it? (See Chapter 4 for the knowledge-aggregation argument they offered.) Yet the King and his minister did not themselves draw that implication, but left it to the assembly to decide how it would vote, subject to the constraint that voting by head would have to be approved by all three orders.

The privileged orders were heavily against cross-verification, for two reasons. First, they argued that this procedure would set a precedent and open the way for voting by head in the assembly.[38] Second, they argued that given the "doublement du tiers," the third estate would have an excessive influence on the composition of the two other orders.[39] The idea underlying this objection was presumably that the third estate might use its numerical superiority to exclude delegates from the privileged orders that it disliked, or at least do so in contested cases rather than judging them on their merit. The argument seems implausible and was in fact much less important than the first. In taking its final stance, however, the nobility did concede that cross-verification was at least appropriate for members of the delegations who had been elected by cross-voting.[40]

One of the 40-odd noble delegates who showed consistent sympathy with the cause of the third estate argued that even – in fact especially – with voting by order, joint verification was essential. Since each order would have veto over the others, each order had an interest in assuring that the delegates of the other orders were truly representative of the nation.[41] If one could plausibly stipulate that verification in common would not lead to voting by head, the argument might have had merit. Under the circumstances, however, that stipulation was implausible. It is nevertheless noteworthy that here, as in the case of cross-voting in the Dauphiné, some deputies argued that cross-verification could be abused

---

[38] For one example among many, "[La Gallissonnière] spoke four or five times to establish the true principles concerning voting by order or by head and showed the dangers of beginning common verification for the three orders, which would have led to voting by head" (Ilovaïsky 1974, p. 213).

[39] Procès-verbal (1789), pp. 24, 50; Ilovaïsky (1974), p. 221.

[40] Lefebvre (1989), p. 105.

[41] In the internal deliberations of the nobility, the Comte de Castellane said that "Especially on the hypothesis where the orders would remain separated all three would have an interest in assuring that their members are truly the representatives of the nation, since each of its members can, by his influence, determine the veto that each order might use against the decisions of the two others" (Ilovaïsky 1974, pp. 210–11).

and others that it might prevent abuses.[42] Many incentive schemes have this feature.

IV. CROSS-VOTING IN THE UNITED STATES, 1787–1789

In this Section I consider three American episodes of cross-voting. The Federal Convention in Philadelphia used cross-voting at some crucial junctures in their proceedings. The procedure proposed for electing the President was also based on the anticipated benefits of cross-voting. Finally, the first federal elections in Georgia and Maryland relied on this system.

In the course of their debates, the 1787 framers appointed six grand committees: the committee on representation that proposed the Great Compromise; another committee on representation that specified the number of representatives of the states in the lower house; the committee on the assumption of state debts; the committee on slave trade and navigation acts; the committee on commercial discrimination; and the committee on remaining matters (including the mode of electing the President). The members were chosen by secret voting: delegates from all states voted to decide who, from a given state delegation, should represent it. In addition, there were five committees with three to five members also selected by secret ballot: the committee on rules, the committee on apportionment, the committee of detail, the committee on interstate comity and bankruptcy, and the committee on style.

The cross-voting used to appoint the Grand Committees was a peculiar system. As it was entirely up to the states how many delegates they wanted to send, the state delegations were of very unequal size, ranging from eight (Pennsylvania) to two (New Hampshire). There was a weak tendency for delegations from larger states to have more members. To the extent that this was the case, the cross-voting system represented an element of proportional voting at the Convention, which otherwise voted by "One state, one vote." To the extent that it was not the case, the system allowed for arbitrary differences in voting power. There was also a weak tendency for states at greater distance from Philadelphia to have smaller delegations.

Judging by the matters that the Federal Convention referred to grand committees and to other committees, we may infer that the former were intended to deal with contentious substantive issues and the latter mainly with procedural and technical issues.[43] There is no direct evidence, however, about why the

---

[42] In Chapter 4 I mentioned a possible instance of cross-voting at the Constituante, when members of the Committee of the Constitution were chosen to represent the three orders, arguably by deputies from all estates voting to determine the representatives of each of them. Since the evidence is inferential I have not included this case here.

[43] The Convention turned down a proposal to have the committee of detail organized as a Grand Committee and adopted instead a proposal to have it consist of five members (Farrand 1966, vol. 2, pp. 95–96). The committee on apportionment is only an apparent exception. It was created to deal with one of the recommendations of the first grand committee on representation, and its most important recommendation was handed over to the second grand committee on representation.

framers chose to have the representatives of the states in the grand committees elected jointly by all delegates rather than selected by the delegations. Several explanations are conceivable. First, it may simply have been a practical necessity. The state delegations were sometimes evenly divided on important issues, and hence would presumably also be divided on the question of who should represent them on those issues. That explanation is not quite satisfactory, however, as the same situation also arose frequently in the Continental Congress without causing a move to individual voting. Second, the framers may have wanted the members of the committees to think of themselves as representing all delegates rather than their own state delegation. If all are chosen by all rather than some by some and others by others, the tendency to parochial thinking may be attenuated. Third, if all are chosen by all, the choice of representatives may itself be different, weeding out extremists and favoring moderates. Even if the second and third accounts do not enter into the *explanation* of the adoption of the system, they may nevertheless point to possible *effects* of the system once it had been adopted on pragmatic grounds.

Calvin Jillson argues that the committee system biased the selection of representatives toward the center. "Whenever they were faced with a conflict that seemed to be insoluble under normal decision procedures, the delegates would deliberately select a compromise committee composed of moderates on the issue."[44] Thus framers whose range of positions on a given issue ranged from 0 to 10 might chose committee members whose positions ranged (say) from 2 to 8 or from 3 to 7. This procedure would allow compromises to be reached that would have been unacceptable to the intransigent extremists.

Jillson's claim is demonstrably not true, however, for the first and most important grand committee, and probably not for the last either. The committee formed on July 2 to propose a mode of representation of the states in the Senate "was composed of adamant small-staters and malleable large-staters,"[45] suggesting something more like a range of positions from 0 to 7. In fact, Jillson himself makes the same observation: "The compromise committee not only failed to include Wilson and Madison, but omitted every one of the strong spokesmen for proportional representation," whereas the smaller states were

---

[44] Jillson (1988), p. 24.

[45] Rossiter (1987), p. 187. See also McLaughlin (1905), p. 234: "One would fain know the political manoeuvring that preceded the election of the committee. The moment that it was chosen, the large-state party was beaten in its effort to have proportional representation in both houses; for not one of the really strong men of the nationalists was chosen. From Massachusetts came not clear-minded King, but Gerry; from Pennsylvania, not vigorous Wilson, but accommodating Franklin; from Virginia, not the broad-minded Madison, but Mason, who was now lukewarm and was to change into an avowed enemy of the Constitution he had helped to frame. On the other hand, the committee contained Ellsworth, Yates, Paterson, the irrepressible Bedford of Delaware, the obstinate Martin of Maryland, Baldwin of Georgia, by whose vote Georgia had for the moment been lost from the ranks of the large-state party, and Davie of North Carolina, who had already given signs of indecision. The eleventh member was Rutledge of South Carolina."

represented "by an effective mix of their most persuasive and intransigent spokesmen."[46]

A compromise between compromising and uncompromising committee members is likely to be a biased one.[47] What the small states gave up (the right of the Senate to originate or amend money bills) was far less than what they got (equal representation in the Senate).[48] Perhaps there was a tacit norm to choose moderates, and the small-staters violated it. It is also possible, however, that whereas few large-staters were willing to walk out of the Convention if they did not get their way, some small-staters were (or were believed to be). In that case, moderate large-staters would not cast their votes for Madison or Wilson, if they were thought to be willing to report back that no agreement could be reached.

The delegates to the Committee on Postponed Matters that proposed the mode of electing the President "were almost entirely separationists [opponents of election by Congress] and their allies," a fact reflected in its report and in the Constitution. It is possible that this lop-sided composition of the committee reflected the votes of the large delegation from Pennsylvania, which had 8 delegates (out of at most 44) at the time the committee was elected, and which had a strong separationist bias.[49] The committee was elected to report on a number of issues, and it is possible that the presidency did not have the same salience for the other states that it had for the Pennsylvanians.

The second case concerns the procedure the Convention proposed for electing the President. Article II.1 of the U.S. Constitution says that in choosing the President "The electors shall meet in their respective States, and vote by ballot for two persons, of whom one at least shall not be an inhabitant of the same State with themselves." As in the central cases of cross-voting, each voter is asked to cast more than one vote. As in the other cases, one vote has to be for a candidate from outside the voter's constituency. In some cross-voting cases, it is also required that one vote *must* be for a candidate in the voter's own constituency, but in voting for the President this is optional rather than mandatory.

---

[46] Jillson (1988), p. 93.

[47] "Once upon a time two boys found a cake. One of them said, 'Splendid! I will eat the cake.' The other one said, 'No, that is not fair! We found the cake together, and we should share and share alike, half for you and half for me.' The first boy said, 'No, I should have the whole cake!' Along came an adult who said, "Gentlemen, you shouldn't fight about this: you should compromise. Give him three quarters of the cake'" (Smullyan 1980, p. 56).

[48] In fact, the Convention later reneged on the money-bill promise. Franklin and Mason, who had been members of the Grand Committee, affirmed that the lack of power of the Senate to initiate or amend money bills was part of the compromise (Farrand 1966, vol. 2, p. 233). Gerry, also a member, later made the same claim (ibid., vol. 3, p. 265). Randolph, who was not on the committee, also asserted that it was part of the compromise (ibid., vol. 2, p. 263). Charles Pinckney, who was not on the committee, denied that it was (ibid., 262).

[49] Riker (1984), pp. 6, 13. The size of the Pennsylvanian delegation did not reflect the size of the state but the fact that the state could afford to send many delegates since the Convention took place in the state capital. For the same reason, the Pennsylvanian delegates were less likely to be absent from the Convention on business or family matters.

When Gouverneur Morris first proposed this procedure at the Convention, Madison "thought something valuable might be made of the suggestion.... The second best man in this case would probably be the first, in fact."[50] Following "second best," Madison had originally written and then crossed out "in the partial Judgment of each citizen towards his immediate fellow citizen." These cryptic statements can be interpreted as saying that the vote cast for the candidate outside the state of the elector would be more likely to reflect an impartial judgment motivated by the general interest. Madison added that

the only objection which occurred was that each Citizen after havg. given his vote for his favorite fellow Citizen, wd. *throw away his second* on some obscure Citizen of another State, in order to ensure the object of his first choice. But it could hardly be supposed that the Citizens of many States would be so sanguine of having their favorite elected, as *not to give their second vote with sincerity* to the next object of their choice.[51]

At this stage of the Convention, details about the electoral college were yet to be settled – for instance, whether it would choose the President by majority or plurality. Toward the end of the Convention, the Grand Committee animated by Gouverneur Morris proposed the solution that later found its way into the Constitution: "The Person having the greatest number of votes shall be the President, if such number be a majority of the whole number of the Electors appointed."[52] When George Mason moved to delete "if such number be a majority of that of the electors," James Wilson apparently "remarked that striking the words out would have the effect of *inducing the large States to throw away the vote* to be given to a person out of the State in order to increase the chances of its own Citizens."[53] Although it is hard to tell whether the inducement would be strong enough to trigger strategic behavior, it would certainly be stronger than under majority voting.

A third case of cross-voting in the United States occurred in the first federal elections in Maryland and Georgia.[54] Below I focus on Maryland, as little is known about Georgia except the bare fact that on January 23, 1789, the House

---

[50] Farrand (1966), vol. 2, p. 114.
[51] Ibid.; my italics. Amar (2005), pp. 167–68, notes that the double-ballot system would lead to the election "of men who might be everyone's second choice – broadly acceptable leaders of wide geographic repute." For Madison, this outcome would be produced because an elector would not be able to count on the election of his in-state candidate. Amar suggests that it would occur because the electors might also desire a competent vice president if their in-state candidate was elected. (He also cites the fact that "the nation's first vice president would *end up* [ex post] tipping the Senate balance on twenty separate occasions" as evidence that the electors "thus *had good reasons* [ex ante] to take their out-of-state votes seriously." There is an obvious tension between the phrases I have italicized.) The idea that the president would be chosen by votes cast with the need for a competent vice president in mind seems implausible and not supported, to my knowledge, by any texts.
[52] Farrand (1966), vol. 2, p. 494. In the absence of a majority, the election would be left to Congress.
[53] Ibid., p. 513; my italics. I say "apparently" because the lines were crossed out in Madison's notes, perhaps because he was not sure who had made the remark.
[54] I am indebted to Jack Rakove for drawing my attention to these elections as an example of cross-voting.

of the legislature decided that each voter should cast three votes, one for electing representatives in each of the three electoral districts of the state.[55]

In an article by "Numa" [*sic*] in the Pennsylvania Gazette of July 16, 1788, addressed to the "Inhabitants of the States That Have Adopted the New Constitution," cross-voting was defended by five arguments:

You will soon be called upon to enact laws for choosing members of the House of Representatives in the new federal legislature. The following mode of electing them is hereby recommended.... Divide the state into as many districts as there are members to be chosen, and direct the electors to fix upon a member from *each* district, and then let the whole state vote for the whole number of members. By these means [1] a knowledge of the local interests of every part of the state will be carried to Congress, but in such a manner, as [2] not to interfere with the *general* interest of the whole state. When members are chosen by the *whole* state, they will [3] consider themselves as servants of the *whole* state, and [4] not suffer themselves to be misled by the local prejudices or interests of a few men who often govern counties and districts.... By these means [5] none but men of real character and abilities will be returned, for such men are generally best known throughout every part of a state.[56]

Cross-voting ensures the representation of the *knowledge* of local interest [1], while excluding the direct *representation* of that interest [4]. (See Chapter 4 for this distinction.) It will ensure the promotion of the general interest [2] through the two channels identified: by affecting the attitude of the representatives [3] and by influencing the choice of representatives [5].

Cross-voting might thus offer a solution to the dilemma identified by Madison in *Federalist* No. 10: "By enlarging too much the number of electors, you render the representative too little acquainted with all their local circumstances and lesser interests; as by reducing it too much, you render him unduly attached to these, and too little fit to comprehend and pursue great and national objects." Madison's own solution – "the great and aggregate interests being referred to the national, the local and particular, to the state legislatures" – is not necessarily superior. This being said, the argument in [5] obviously trades on the Madisonian idea (also in No. 10) that "in the large republic ... it will be more difficult for unworthy candidates to practise with success the vicious arts, by which elections are too often carried."

To my knowledge, Madison did not explicitly comment on the cross-voting procedure. Yet in the mention of a "middle course" in a letter to Jefferson of October 8, 1788, we may perhaps see an indirect reference to that idea:

A law has ... been passed [in Pennsylvania] providing for the election of members for the House of Representatives and electors of the President. The act proposes that every citizen throughout the state shall vote for the whole number of members allotted to the State. This mode of election will confine the choice to characters of general notoriety, and so far

[55] DenBoer (1984), pp. 456–57.
[56] Jensen and Becker (1976), p. 246.

be favorable to merit. It is however liable to some popular objections urged against the tendency of the new system. In Virginia, I am inclined to think the State will be divided into as many districts, as there are to be members. And in others again a middle course be taken. It is perhaps to be desired that various modes should be tried, as by that means only the best mode can be ascertained.[57]

On December 22, 1788, the Maryland legislature enacted legislation requiring "that *every person* coming to vote for representatives for this state in the congress of the United States, shall have *a right to vote for six persons*, one whereof shall be a resident of each of [six] districts, and the candidate in each district having the greatest number of votes of all the candidates residing in that district, shall be declared to be duly elected for that district" (my italics). The editors of *The Documentary History of the First Federal Elections* explain the adoption of the law by the determination of the Federalists "to draft provisions that would shut Antifederalists out of the representation. Thus, with each voter entitled to vote for six Representatives ... the Federalists would be able to neutralize Antifederalist voting strength concentrated in Anne Arrundel, Baltimore, and Harford counties and in the town of Baltimore."[58]

In February 1789 a debate ensued in the *Maryland Journal* over the wisdom and constitutionality of this law. Of particular interest is an article by "A Moral Politician," addressed to a "poor, industrious and well-meaning man, with little leisure to read compacts, and less propensity to sift into their meaning." The author first sets out to rebut the charge that the law is unconstitutional:

New-York, New-Jersey, Pennsylvania, and Maryland, have adopted modes of election, each differing from each other, while each is strictly conformable to the constitution. The reason perhaps why the constitution lays down no rule to direct the states, is to afford room for the discovery of the best mode of election, which would have been precluded had it imposed on the States a fixed and uniform rule.... How much better had it been to have confessed this truth, and then the poor man, instead of being mislead [sic], would have perceived that the Federals having prevailed in our Assembly, constructed the law in such a manner, as to afford the highest probability of obtaining a complete federal representation, and that had the antifederals been superior in number, it would have been formed so as, if possible, to have produced a contrary kind of representation. By such an open proceeding, the poor man would have been enabled at the next, or some future election, to make choice of such men as would repeal the law, if found not to have answered the purpose for which it was framed.[59]

These observations are partly insightful, partly confused and naive. The author begins with a statesmanlike, Madisonian insight about the several states as a reservoir for experimentation – without telling us (any more than Madison does) who is to draw the conclusions from the experiment and implement

---

[57] Cross-voting is not the only "middle course" between at-large elections and district elections. Yet the alternative compromise, which is to have some delegates elected in at-large and others in district elections, emerged only after the Civil War (Zagarri 1987, p. 105 n.).

[58] Denboer (1984), p. 123. The law is cited from ibid., p. 138.

[59] Ibid., p. 219.

them. He goes on in a more realistic mode when noting that the choice of an electoral system depends on group interests rather than on abstract criteria of optimality. In the last sentence he seems to lose sight of this idea, arguing as if it would be easy for "Antifederals" to use an electoral law designed by the "Federals" to topple them from power. In a subsequent part of the article he returns to the high moral ground in a substantive argument for the law: "the making the votes of the different Counties *checks* upon each other, may improve *representation*, as the checks of the different branches have improved *legislation*."[60] The analogy with the usual system of checks and balances is obviously not perfect. The concurrence of electoral districts in the choice of representatives for each of them does not proceed in the same way as the concurrence of lower house, upper house, and executive in law-making, nor is the purpose of the mutual checking the same. Yet at a more abstract level the comparison is suggestive.

An opponent of the law – the one who provoked the "Moral Politician" into writing his article – rested his case on what he saw as its perverse properties: "Is it just and wise to compel the People to vote for Persons they do not know? Is it proper that Washington and Frederick Counties should elect for the People of Baltimore and Hartford Counties, and thereby prevent them from having the Man of their Choice, and impose on them the Man they very generally reject?"[61] The author might have made his point in the very same terms used by the Dauphiné nobility and clergy in their argument against cross-voting: "it might happen that the deputy for a county received not a single vote from that county." In addition, the author made constitutional objections to the requirement that representatives be residents of the district from which they are elected.[62]

As suggested by the "Moral Politician," the elections turned on the conflict between Federalists and Antifederalists. After the victory of the former, George Washington congratulated the Governor of the state on the outcome:

The whole number of representatives being federal and the large majority by which there chosen, is the most decisive proof that could be given of the attachment of your State to the general Government – and must effectually silence any assertion that may be made in future that the sentiment of the People was not in unison with that of the Convention which adopted the Constitution by so large a majority. – It is somewhat singular that among so large a number of votes as you mention [none] to have been found opposed to the federal ticket – it was a circumstance not to be expected in any County.[63]

Whether sincere or disingenuous (recall from Chapter 3 that Washington was not above using subterfuge to win elections), these remarks are inaccurate. As we have seen, Maryland's cross-voting law owed its adoption to the desire of the Federalists to reduce the influence of the Antifederalists. As the latter were

[60] Ibid., p. 220.
[61] Ibid., p. 212.
[62] Ibid., The author returns more forcefully to the residency argument in a later article (ibid., pp. 217–18).
[63] George Washington to John Howard, February 2, 1789, ibid., p. 211.

concentrated in certain electoral districts, cross-voting enabled residents in other districts to exclude them by voting for the federalist candidates. Cross-voting *prevented the expression of local conceptions of the general interest*, rather than letting the expression of local interest converge toward the general interest.

For the next federal elections, Georgia and Maryland gave up the "middle Course" of cross-voting and opted for one of the two pure systems: at-large elections in Georgia and district elections in Maryland.[64] We can only speculate about the reasons. As Maryland adopted the district system that also requires local residency for representatives, that feature of cross-voting cannot have been decisive, although the common objection that this requirement prevents voters from choosing the best candidate may have played a role in Georgia.[65] The non-representative aspect of cross-voting is perhaps more likely to have been decisive.

V. SOME CONTEMPORARY EXAMPLES

For societies divided on ethnic or other grounds, politicians and scholars have proposed forms of electoral centripetalism to attenuate conflict and facilitate the election of moderate candidates. In particular, cross-voting seems an attractive procedure for generating with broad electoral appeal.[66] The system has in fact been adopted or proposed in three formerly British colonies: Rhodesia, Fiji, and Cyprus.

Not only the practice but the very term "cross-voting" was adopted in the 1961 Rhodesian constitution. Prima facie, the system was designed to enable the election of moderate politicians in a racially divided country. By allowing black voters to cast a vote in white electoral units and vice versa, extremists in either camp would be under a disadvantage. A succinct description of the system is as follows:

There were two types of seats (50 constituencies and 115 districts) and two classes of voters (A-roll and B-roll). Essentially the constituencies were European seats elected by A-roll voters and the districts were African seats determined by the B-roll.... A new provision allowed voters on each roll to vote for a candidate in both a district and a constituency. This was called cross-voting, and in theory it intended to give A-roll voters up to 25 percent in district voting and B-roll voters the same influence in constituencies. Where cross-voting exceeded 25 percent of the predominant roll's vote, the result would be devalued proportionately. Because so few Africans ever registered or voted, cross-voting had no effect in the two elections (1962 and 1965) held under the 1961 constitution.[67]

Although seemingly designed to promote impartiality, the system was largely make-believe. "The qualifications for each roll were based on a complex mix of

---

[64] Zagarri (1987), p. 114.

[65] For this objection, see ibid., p. 110.

[66] The "alternative vote" system has also been advocated on the grounds that it tends to produce election of moderate candidates, by cross-ethnic voting rather than by cross-voting. For sharply opposed views on its efficacy, see Fraenkel and Grofman (2006) and Horowitz (2007).

[67] Bowman (1973) p. 34; see also Palley (1966), pp. 414–16.

income, property, and education. Translated into the realities of Rhodesian life, the A-roll was almost entirely white (and provisions were made for regularly raising the qualifications) and the B-roll was limited to a handful of Africans – perhaps 20,000 in an African population of 3.5 million."[68]

In Fiji, the British government introduced cross-voting in 1965 as a compromise between at-large elections and communal rolls in which representatives would be chosen by and from the ethnic groups.[69] In the system as modified after independence in 1970, the ethnic balance of the 52-seat Parliament was predetermined. Among the 27 "communal seats," 12 were reserved for Fijians, 12 reserved for Indo-Fijians, and 3 for "General Electors" (i.e., Europeans, Chinese, and other minorities). Among the 25 "national seats," which required voters from one ethnic community to vote for candidates from a different community, 10 were reserved for Fijians, 10 reserved for Indo-Fijians, and 5 for General Electors. Each elector was to cast no less than *four* votes: one for a communal (co-ethnic) representative, and one for a "national" candidate from each of the three communal groups. An indigenous Fijian voter, for example, would vote for a Fijian candidate in his or her communal electorate, and then cast three additional votes – one for a Fijian, one for an Indo-Fijian, and one for a General Elector – in the national electorates. There is no evidence, however, that the cross-voting component of the system had the intended effect of attenuating ethnic conflicts. The idea of electing moderates within each ethnic group was incompatible with the "plural society syndrome" of Fijian politics that was "initiated and sustained through two mechanisms: the doctrine of the paramountcy of Fijian interests and the concept of Fijian cultural homogeneity."[70]

In Cyprus, the idea of cross-voting between the Greek and Turkish communities goes back to the 1970s.[71] While not adopted, it is a central idea in some proposals currently being negotiated. Although the former de facto President of the Turkish Republic of Cyprus conceded the principle of cross-voting demanded by the Greek community, his nationalist successor Dervis Eroglu has expressed the hope of an independent Turkish Cypriot state. In one form, cross-voting would operate as shown in Figure 5.1. It involves, in fact, both cross-voting at the bottom and cross-designation at the top. The long thin arrows at the bottom of the diagram indicate that each community would have a weighted vote of about 20 percent in the choice of presidential candidate for the other community. As shown at the top, the Federal Council would be chosen by the President and Vice President each appointing two members from their own community and one from the other.

Since the system has not been tried, one cannot tell whether it would work. As with cross-voting generally, the hope is that it would "favor moderate candidates who have appeal beyond their ethnic communities" and offer "space in the

---

[68] Bowman (1973), p. 174 n. 44.
[69] Studies include Aikman (1999) and Fraenkel (2001).
[70] Lawson (1990), p. 795.
[71] Loizides and Keskiner (2004); Lordos, Kaymak, and Tocci (2009).

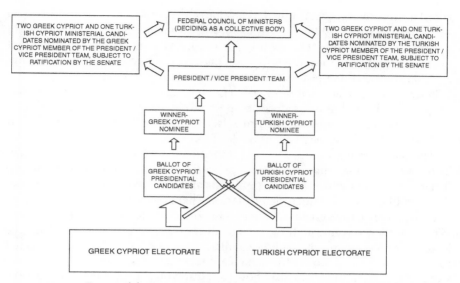

FIGURE 5.1. Proposal for cross-voting in Cyprus. *Source*: Lordos, Kaymak, and Tocci (2009), p. 95.

political system for individuals and movements that aim to represent the whole country rather than ethnically specific interests."[72]

Cross-voting has also been proposed as the solution to the seemingly ungovernable state of affairs in Belgium. Under the heading of the "Multiple Proportional Vote," Laurent de Briey has proposed a scheme that is defined by the following features:

1. The representatives of the different communities included in the society are elected separately by using a List-PR electoral system.
2. Those representatives are elected not only by the voters of their own group, but also by the voters of every other group included in the society.
3. The value of the total of all internal votes (that means votes from a member of a specific community in favor of a candidate or a party from her own community) is higher than the value of the total of all external votes (that means votes from a member of a specific community in favor of a candidate or a party of another community).[73]

The proposed system differs from the French model and the Maryland model in that it excludes the possibility of a deputy being elected without a single vote from her own community. As we saw, that feature of these two systems could be deeply destabilizing. This effect is probably what de Briey refers to when he cites "the obvious necessity of giving to C [the ratio of the value of internal to external

[72] Loizides and Keskiner (2004), p. 162.
[73] De Briey (2005).

votes] a value over 0.5." As noted, the value of that ratio was zero in Brittany in 1576 and 1614, 1/6 in Maryland in 1789, and 1/3 in the Estates-General of 1484 and (in the districts using cross-voting) of 1789. At the same time, the larger that ratio, the smaller the incentive for candidates from one community to adopt positions that might appeal to the other community or communities. Whether a balance could be struck that reconciles legitimacy and moderation seems entirely conjectural. In addition, as de Briey points out, the system is vulnerable to strategic voting by voters from Brussels, who would "define themselves [as Flemish or French] at the moment of election."

The last remark provides a natural transition to a very different and, I think, instructive example, that of electoral primaries. I first consider a hypothetical American case, in which both Republicans and Democrats could vote in *both* the Republican and Democratic primaries. That system would obviously have undesirable incentive effects, similar to the ones pointed out by Madison and Wilson at the Convention. It would encourage (say) Democrats to vote for the Republican candidate who had the smallest chances of eventually being elected to the Presidency. In 2012, for instance, they might vote massively for Newt Gingrich. The system might also, however, lead voters to cast their vote for the candidate of the other party who would, from their point of view, be the best President if elected. In that case, they would vote for a centrist Republican, or for a less extremist one. Which effect would dominate would depend on a myriad of factors that I cannot even begin to enumerate. The realistic possibility that the first effect could dominate is sufficient to exclude the system as a practical option.

Let me now turn to a real American case, which involves *crossover voting* rather than cross-voting stricto sensu. In the 20-odd states that currently have open or semi-open primaries in the United States, both Republicans and Democrats can vote in *either* the Republican or the Democratic primaries. Hence (as in cross-voting) voters have to make two choices: the choice of a primary and the choice of a candidate in that primary. In the spirit of cross-voting generally, one might expect some voters to engage in *hedging*. If, for instance, the outcome in the Democratic primary can be taken for granted whereas that of the Republican primary is more uncertain, Democrats might cast their vote in the Republican primaries for the candidate whom they would prefer as President to the other Republican candidates. They might also use this opportunity if they believe that *any* Democratic candidate will very likely lose.

Open primaries can also, however, create an inducement to *raiding*, if members of one party intentionally vote for a weak candidate from another party to decrease the latter party's chance of winning in the general election. Although raiding seems to be rare,[74] it happens. "On March 3, 2008, Rush Limbaugh advised his 13 million listeners to 'hold their noses,' participate in the March 4th, 2008 Democratic primaries, and vote for Hillary Clinton....

---

[74] Sides, Cohen, and Citrin (2002).

Reading published polls ... conservatives may ... have found Obama a more serious threat to John McCain, the presumptive Republican nominee, than Hillary Clinton."[75] Presumably some of his 13 million listeners followed his advice.[76] When the electorally weaker candidate is also the more extreme, raiding behavior could have the socially undesirable effect of causing the election of an extremist president. In fact, if both parties successfully engage in raiding on these grounds, that outcome is inevitable.

Some American states have taken precautions against strategic voting in primaries.[77] (Practice also varies across parties.) Some states impose closed primaries in which only voters registered with a given party can vote in its primaries. In some states, however, voters can register on election day. Even when a longer lead time is required, strategic registration for the purpose of raiding remains possible. Other states use semi-closed primaries, in which independents can vote but voters registered with a party may vote only in that party's primary. Here, too, raiding remains possible in principle. In Illinois, voters must declare their party affiliation at the polling place to a judge who must then announce it in "a distinct tone of voice, sufficiently loud to be heard by all persons in the polling place." If there is no challenge, the voter is given the ballot for his preferred party.[78]

VI. CONCLUSION: THE FRAGILITY OF INCENTIVE SYSTEMS

In electoral units (be they districts, states, or estates) that fall short of the nation as a whole (in Israel and in the Netherlands, the nation is the only unit), the idea of representation is intrinsically ambiguous. On the one hand, representatives are supposed to represent the interests of their units. Residential requirements,

---

[75] Donovan (2008). Cho and Kang (2008) offer a formal model, assuming hyperrational voters, to determine when hedging, raiding, and other forms of strategic voting will occur. That assumption is, however, unrealistic (Sides, Cohen, and Citrin 2002, pp. 12–13).

[76] In 2012, Democrat activists in Michigan encouraged Democrats to vote in the Republican race against Mitt Romney, to make the less electable Rick Santorum the Republican nominee. Piggybacking on this move, Santorum authorized automated calls to encourage Democrats to participate in the Michigan Republican primary and to vote against Romney. "Santorum did get a boost from Democrats; 13 percent of his votes came from them, according to exit polls, compared with 4 percent for Romney" (*Washington Post*, March 2, 2012). In 1992, Romney did the same when he voted for the Democrat Paul Tsongas: "'In Massachusetts, if you register as an independent, you can vote in either the Republican or Democratic primary,' Romney told ABC News. 'When there was no real contest in the Republican primary, I'd vote in the Democrat primary, vote for the person who I thought would be the weakest opponent for the Republican'" (ibid.).

[77] For information and analysis, see www.fairvote.org/open-and-closed-primaries.

[78] By contrast, the requirement for voting in the primaries of the French Socialist Party in the presidential elections of 2012 was limited to signing a *written* statement affirming adherence to "the values of the left" and payment of at least one euro. Although speculations abounded on the Internet about the possibility of supporters of UMP (the main right-wing party) raiding the Socialist primaries, it is difficult to imagine a *public* call for strategic voting similar to Rush Limbaugh's or a calm acknowledgment of the practice similar to Romney's. The civilizing force of hypocrisy may be greater in France.

where they exist, reflect this concern. On the other hand, they are supposed to represent the interest of the nation. The ban on imperative mandates that one finds in several constitutions and that goes back to famous arguments made by Burke in 1774 and Sieyes in 1789 reflects this consideration. Even earlier, Thomas Hutchinson wrote to a friend in 1766 that the practice of bound mandates "is unconstitutional and contradicts the very idea of a parliament the members whereof are supposed to debate and argue in order to convince and be convinced."[79]

One might argue that this ambiguity or tension is spurious. If all interests are represented, they can engage in logrolling that yields Pareto-improvements and approximates the general interest. Yet as we saw in Chapter 1, vote-trading between two groups can impose costs on third parties that more than offset the gains achieved by the logrollers. When the third party is an indefinite number of future generations, the likelihood of a net loss is particularly high.

Another argument is that "the public interest is served indirectly, as the by-product of competition for scarce resources among competing elites. Norms of justice and ideas of the common good are not politically powerless, therefore; but they can be asserted most effectively *when rival unjust interests are relatively well-balanced.*"[80] An instance may be the way suffrage in classical Athens was extended as the result of political competition among elite groups.[81] Marx cites the English proverb, "When thieves fall out, honest men come into their own," adding that the noisy quarrel between landowners and industrial capitalists "was the midwife of truth."[82] In colonial America, the "expansion of popular politics originated not because the mass of people pressed upward from below with new demands but because competing gentry, for their own parochial and tactical purposes, courted the people."[83] Nobody can deny that such things happen, but do they happen with enough regularity to ensure that the public interest will, by and large, prevail?

---

[79] Cited after Pole (1966), p. 72. Pole (1983), p. 103, traces the idea back to 1721. Burke claimed, however, to be the first newly elected MP to make this argument to his own electors (Langford 1991, p. 189).

[80] Holmes (2003), p. 52; my italics.

[81] Ober (1989), p. 85, notes that "by the time of Cleisthenes, the elites recognized mass ambitions as a new weapon to use against each other. As a result, politically ambitious elites actively sponsored democratizing reforms.... Ironically, as the elites gained victories over their enemies by sponsoring democratic reforms, there were fewer and fewer institutions that they could control directly." Similarly, Ostwald (1986), pp. 179–80, writes that "Ephialtes' reforms had the effect of establishing the sovereignty of the people in political affairs, but that does not mean this was their intent. His primary purpose may well have been to outflank those who had been most effective in supporting Cimon's now-discredited policy of giving a higher priority to the interests of Sparta than to the expansion of his own country." Ober's comment is especially interesting, in that it suggests that the elites were engaged in something like a Prisoner's Dilemma, in which they all lost power by trying to outdo each other in appealing to the people.

[82] Marx (1967), p. 675.

[83] Wood (1991), p. 173; also Tocqueville (1991), p. 100.

An alternative to the idea that the public interest arises out of the clash of group interests or negotiation among group interests is to make group interests more sensitive to the public interest in the first place. This is the idea underlying proposals and practices of cross-voting. The core idea is that *individuals in one group have an interest in other groups having representatives who are not exclusively concerned with the interest of those other groups*. If those in group A, therefore, can have a say in choice of representatives of group B, they will tend to vote for the more impartial-minded, and less group-minded, members of group B. When this happens across groups, as in cross-voting, the representatives may contain a larger proportion of deputies genuinely concerned with the general interest.

As we have seen repeatedly, however, this is at most a possibility theorem. Cross-voting does not necessarily lead members of group A to vote for the most impartial members of group B. It could also lead them to vote for the most inept or extremist members of B. Moreover, if a group does not contain perceived internal differentiation between extremists and moderates, as may have been the case in Fiji, cross-voting has no purchase.

The comments by the "Moral Politician" and by the editors of the *Documentary History of the First Federal Elections* point to another normative problem. In Maryland, there were two groups of voters, Federalists and Antifederalists, referred to hereafter as A and B. The comments are consistent with the following arbitrary assumptions. A had a 70 percent majority in four of the six electoral districts and were in a 30 percent minority in the remaining two. Each district had 10,000 voters. Assuming single candidacies from each bloc, an A-candidate would get 6,000 votes from the two B-majority districts and 28,000 from the four A-majority districts, or 34,000. With only 26,000 votes, the B-candidate would be defeated in all districts. As the editors of the *Documentary History* write, cross-voting "assured a Federalist sweep of the elections."

In itself, this might not seem to be objectionable. Let us stipulate, for the sake of argument, that the Federalists represented the general interest and the Antifederalists local, unprincipled interests.[84] A system that produces a broader representation of the general interest, while also respecting the importance for each district of being represented by someone who knows its situation and needs, would seem to be an ideal one. Yet if we reinterpret A and B in terms of ethnic groups, cross-voting is less defensible. Keeping the same numbers, a total population of 34,000 whites and 26,000 blacks would elect six white representatives, whereas district elections would yield four white and two black representatives. Under these assumptions, cross-voting ensures total political domination by

---

[84] Local interests need not be unprincipled if they recognize the legitimacy and validity of other local interests (Nagel 1991, p. 38 and *passim*). At the national level, it is one thing to be a states-righter (a local and principled attitude) and another to simply favor one's own state (a local and unprincipled attitude). At the Federal Convention, Madison was strongly opposed to the principle of states' rights. Afterward, he became a stalwart defendant of the rights of Virginia (Ketcham 1971, pp. 310–12).

the majority ethnic group even when a (large) minority forms the majority in some electoral districts.

Furthermore, the question arises whether deputies chosen by cross-voting represent those who *by whom* or those *from whom* they are chosen. (As we saw in Section II, this ambiguity arises whenever E ≠ V.) To eliminate the ambiguity one might either follow Maryland and adopt district elections or Georgia and adopt at-large elections. In the elections to the Estates-General, the equivalent alternatives would be to retain the system of election by and from each estate or to abolish the estates systems entirely. The first solution belonged to the past, the second to the future.

Given the pervasive lack of tolerance for ambiguity that characterizes the human mind, this last feature of cross-voting is perhaps the most plausible explanation for its demise or non-adoption. Although representation in multi-district electorates is always intrinsically ambiguous, cross-voting brings out that ambiguity in what may be an intolerably explicit manner. The paradox that has been noted in the Dauphiné and in Maryland, that a representative of a given estate or state might be *elected without a single vote from the group he is to represent*, is especially poignant in this respect. Today, Seattle and some other cities elect candidates in at-large voting and ask each elector to cast *n* votes in determining who shall be elected for each of *n* seats. "[One] variation of at-large voting has numbered seats that correspond to specific neighborhoods of the city, and candidates for those seats may be required to be residents of those areas. This arrangement, however, *creates some ambiguity about whom the winning candidates actually represent*. This is because these officials are not elected solely by voters in these neighborhoods, but by voters citywide. So a candidate preferred by most votes in a neighborhood may be defeated by one preferred by a citywide majority."[85] Even worse, a candidate not receiving a single vote from his neighborhood may be chosen as its representative.

Even if we ignore issues of perverse effects and representativeness, we may ask about the *motives* for adopting a system of cross-voting? Why would electors mainly motivated by group interest adopt a system that would produce deputies mainly motivated by the general interest? (Remember that in the elections of deputies to the Estates-General, each order had to agree to cross-voting for this system to be used.) In principle, one might propose the following answer. In a choice restricted to the diagonal outcomes (from the upper left hand to the bottom right hand) in a Prisoner's Dilemma, even selfish actors would choose universal cooperation over universal non-cooperation. Similarly, the interest of all groups would make them prefer a system in which all groups had some impartial representation over a system in which all groups had representation based only on group interest. This stark statement would obviously require many qualifications, but the basic idea seems right.

[85] Amy (2000), p. 59; my italics.

Prospect theory suggests, however, that this argument could be undermined by *loss aversion*, that is, by the well-documented tendency to count a loss about twice as heavily as an equal-sized gain. The adoption of cross-voting can be seen as an exchange. A group gives up the exclusive right to select its own representative in exchange for a right to contribute to the choice of representatives for other groups. What is lost in this exchange is the option of choosing a representative who would promote its interest vigorously and aggressively. What is gained is the elimination of candidates who would oppose that interest with equal vigor and aggression. Even if an observer judged that the gains outweigh the losses, the actors might think differently. The following argument might apply, *mutatis mutandis*, to the present case as well:

Imagine two countries negotiating the number of missiles that they will keep and aim at each other. Each country derives security from its own missiles and is threatened by those of the other side. Thus, missiles eliminated by the other side are evaluated as gains, and missiles one must give up are evaluated as losses, relative to the status quo. If losses have twice the impact of gains, then each side will require its opponent to eliminate twice as many missiles as it eliminates – not a promising start for the achievement of an agreement.[86]

Loss aversion can be reinforced by *reactive devaluation*, that is, by the tendency to discount a proposal merely because it is made by a party with opposite interests.[87] If the third estate proposed cross-voting in electing deputies to the Estates-General, the other two orders might react with suspicion and assume that the general-interest defense of the proposal was merely "Aesopian language" for some special interest of the third estate.

The point I want to stress is not that there are good arguments both for and against cross-voting, as is true of other systems of representation.[88] Rather, it is that even the arguments in favor of the system are too fragile. The proposal has an obvious intuitive attraction, as shown by the fact that it has appeared independently in many times and places. It has some of the flavor of the paradigm of perfect procedural justice, "I divide, you choose." Yet when we move from that simple case to real politics, we come up against the difficulty of designing good incentive-based electoral systems, and in fact incentive schemes more generally. Benthamite schemes are more robust, since they are based on *removing opportunities* to do mischief rather than on *creating incentives* to behave in socially desirable ways.

To bring the point home, let me consider a very different example, the decision by the Federal Convention – nine states to two – to have senators chosen by the state legislatures rather than by direct elections or by the lower

---

[86] Kahneman and Tversky (1995), p. 56.

[87] Ross (1995), pp. 26–42.

[88] Amy (2000), ch. 2, enumerates 19 criteria for assessing systems of representation. As his book abundantly demonstrates, no system comes close to satisfying most of them.

house of Congress. The framers argued that indirect elections were needed to represent the commercial interest, to promote wisdom, and to protect the States:

[The] people have two great interests, the landed interest, and the commercial, including the stockholders. To draw both branches from the people will leave no security to the latter interest; the people being chiefly composed of the landed interest, and erroneously, supposing that the other interests are adverse to it.[89]

Wisdom was one of the characteristics which it was in contemplation to give the second branch. Would not more of it issue from the Legislatures, than from an immediate election by the people.[90]

It has been agreed on all hands that an efficient Govt. is necessary that to render it such it ought to have the faculty of self-defence, that to render the different branches effectual each of them ought to have the same power of self-defence.... He ... wondered that there should be any disagreement about the necessity of allowing the State Govts. the same self-defence. If they are to be preserved as he conceived to be essential, they certainly ought to have this power, and the only mode left of giving it to them, was by allowing them to appoint the 2d. branch of the Natl. Legislature.[91]

My impression is that the arguments from property and from the defense of the states were the most important. Be this as it may, fifty years later Tocqueville emphasized the argument from wisdom:

The men elected in this way are [always] precisely representative of the ruling majority, but they represent only the lofty thoughts at large in the nation, the generous instincts that animate it, and not the petty passions that often agitate it or the vices that dishonor it. It is easy to foresee a time in the future when the American republics will be forced to multiply two-stage elections in their electoral system or else come to grief on democracy's shoals.[92]

Writing 80 years later, in the last edition of *The American Commonwealth* (1914), James Bryce observed that the opposite of what Tocqueville predicted had come to pass: rather than being generalized, two-stage elections even to the Senate were abolished by the Seventeenth Amendment. As Bryce explains, the system had become completely transformed and perverted:

Choice by a legislature had come to mean choice by a party majority in a legislative caucus, and the determination of that caucus had often been prearranged by a small group of party managers; or if that did not happen secretly, it had been settled in a party convention which directed the members of the party in the legislature how to cast their votes. There was anyhow little room left for free selection by the legislature. The people or rather those wire-pullers who manage the people and act in their name had usually settled the matter beforehand. *So hard is it to make any scheme of indirect election work according to its original design; so hard is it to keep even a written and rigid constitution from bending and warping under the actual forces of politics.*[93]

---

[89] Gerry, in Farrand (1966), vol. 1, p. 152.
[90] Ellsworth, ibid., p. 406.
[91] Mason, ibid., p. 407.
[92] Tocqueville (2004a), p. 230.
[93] Bryce (1995), p. 90.

Bryce also offers a striking example to illustrate the statements I have italicized:

In 1904 Oregon provided, by a law passed by the people under the initiative method of legislation contained in the constitution of that state, that the political parties might in the party primaries nominate persons for election as United States senators, and that the people might at the ensuing election of the state legislature select by their votes one of these nominees as their choice for senator. Along with this it was also enacted that a candidate for the state legislature might on his nomination either: (1) declare that he would, if elected, vote for that person as United States senator who had received the largest popular vote and thus become "the people's choice"; or, (2) declare that he would consider the popular vote as merely "a recommendation." Or he might make no declaration at all. In 1908 a majority of the members elected to the legislature, having made the former declaration, felt bound to carry it out, and the person who had received the highest popular vote was accordingly elected by that majority, although he was a Democrat and they were Republicans. Thus the people got their way and the federal Constitution was not formally transgressed.[94]

This attempt at positive institutional engineering ran into problems similar to those of cross-voting. Political actors will often subvert the design if they can, and their ingenuity often provides them with the means to do so. I agree, then, with the following statements. "It may be impossible to anticipate the many ways in which a particular incentive scheme may be gamed.... There are a virtually infinite number of dimensions along which strategic ... personnel can act to game the current system."[95]

The problem is not limited to politics. Many readers will know the perverse effects of the use of citation counts, the Shanghai ranking, and so on in allocating funds to research institutions. Today, individual scholars and research institutions waste much time gaming these systems. In a letter to *Science*, an astrophysicist recounts that he received a generous offer from the King Abdulaziz University in Saudi Arabia, but turned it down when he discovered that the only reason for their interest was his inclusion in ISIHighlyCited.com, a database that lists the 250 most-cited scientists for each of the 22 major subfields of science. Commenting on his experience, he refers to

the ridiculous system of university rankings, which is exacerbated by the naivety of decision-makers who take these university rankings so seriously. The situation is extremely damaging for academia because the university ranking metrics are often used as the basis for policy-making and funding.

University ranking tables can also be seen in a wider context – namely as part of the constant pressure to be accountable, to produce, and to be "the best in the world." The Saudi action illustrates the danger of fostering such a competitive, target-based approach in all walks of life. The distorting, sometimes counterproductive, effects of such a philosophy are obvious in areas as diverse as the targeted reduction of hospital waiting

[94] Ibid., pp. 90–91.
[95] Jakob and Levitt (2003), pp. 843, 871.

lists, published rankings of schools, pressure on traffic wardens to dole out a specific number of parking tickets, and bonuses for bankers that sell large numbers of irresponsible mortgages.[96]

As another example, consider a comment on one of the many rescue plans for the euro: "By the end of June 2012, banks are expected to establish a core-capital ratio of 9%. In principle, this is laudable. But if banks have months to reach their target, they can avoid raising new equity, which would dilute their shareholders, and instead move to the required ratio by shrinking their balance-sheets. That would be a terrible outcome: by depriving Europe's economy of credit, it would worsen the downturn."[97]

Incentive systems can be fragile for several reasons.

First, they can create multiple incentives, some for desirable and others for undesirable behaviors. A large monetary prize for winning a race will set up an incentive to practice hard *and* an incentive to trip up the competition. When school boards use student test scores to punish or reward schools, the effect may be that teachers cheat on the scores they report rather than making an effort to improve the performance of students.[98] We have seen that cross-voting is vulnerable to a problem of this kind, by creating an incentive to vote for incompetent candidates from another constituency.

Second, systems that rely on agents responding rationally to incentives may fail if agents are subject to one of the numerous forms of irrationality uncovered by behavioral economics. When choosing an insurance or pension scheme, people often prefer the default option even though another option might be superior from the point of view of their rational self-interest. I have suggested that loss aversion might provide one reason why cross-voting has often seemed unattractive.

Third, incentive systems based on monetary rewards can backfire and reduce the performance of the agents.[99] In a famous experiment, it was found that when parents were fined for being late in picking up their child from a child-care center, the frequency of late pick-ups increased.[100] The fine was perceived as a price.

Finally, by a closely related mechanism, negative incentives (punishments and fines) may create resentment against those who impose them. The draconian tax measures recently adopted by several governments in southern Europe might end up generating less revenue rather than more.[101] Those who try to instill *fear* in a population by draconian punishments may find that the *hatred* they trigger

---

[96] Miley (2012), pp. 1041–42. The ranking-induced practice of coercive citations (Wilhite and Fong 2012), provides another illustration.
[97] *The Economist*, October 29, 2011.
[98] Jacob and Levitt (2003).
[99] Fehr and Falk (2002).
[100] Gneezy and Rustichini (2000).
[101] Gneezy and Rustichini (2000), p. 16, make a similar point.

makes the targets more prone to rebel rather than less.[102] The dilemma is nicely captured in a cartoon in the London *Observer* on January 4, 2009, showing a young boy on a heap of rubble in Gaza, watching Israeli bombers and asking himself, "Is this going to make me more or less likely to fire rockets at Israel when I grow up?"

Although the last two mechanisms do not apply specifically to cross-voting, they are highly relevant in the general Benthamite perspective. A designer of incentive schemes that rely on fundamental preferences remaining stable over time might find to his dismay that they are, on the contrary, affected by the schemes.

---

[102] "Kings by clemency gain a security more assured, because repeated punishment, while it crushes the hatred of a few, stirs the hatred of all" (Seneca, *De Clementia*, I, 8). Seneca proposed that (what might one might call) "Benthamite rulers" might choose instead to keep their subjects in a state of pluralistic ignorance: "A proposal was once made in the senate to distinguish slaves from free men by their dress; it then became apparent how great would be the impending danger if our slaves should begin to count our number" (ibid., I, 23).

Conclusion

The negative Benthamite approach to collective decision making has a number of definite implications. Let me cite some representative examples from earlier chapters:

- Screening jurors and voters from bribes and threats
- Screening constitution-makers from soldiers and crowds
- Separating the constituent and legislative powers
- Combining ex ante secrecy and ex post publicity of voting in juries and assemblies
- Publishing the names of abstainers in national elections
- Enforcing a ban on the sale and serving of liquor to jurors and voters
- Enforcing a delay between the last public debates and opinion polls on the one hand and election day on the other
- Putting the assets of public officials into blind trusts
- Adopting a ban on *cumul des mandats* by representatives
- Adopting a cap on aggregate campaign contributions
- Adopting the constructive vote of no confidence
- Seating deputies on benches rather than at desks
- Seating jurors in unadorned rooms
- Selecting jury forepersons by secret ballot
- Offering jurors information in ways that minimize cognitive bias, for example, in terms of natural frequencies rather than probabilities
- Disallowing knowledge of a defendant's previous criminal record
- Delaying jury trials in highly publicized cases

I shall not belabor the virtues of the general Benthamite framework, but take up the issues I mentioned in the Introduction: the costs of decision making, the value of diversity, the need for institutional overrides, the question of whether the negative approach might be indeterminate, and the need for a political will.

I. COSTS

For Bentham, reducing the cost of political decision making was a crucial desideratum. As I noted in Chapter 3, he thought, somewhat incoherently, that the measures that would maximize the aptitude of deputies and officials would also minimize expenses. In reality, there is often a trade-off. We may not be able, however, to determine its shape.

The costs of decision making can be incurred by the legal or political system as a whole, ultimately funded by taxes, or by the decision makers themselves. Although one might think that the latter procedure is the least costly for society at large, we shall see that the opposite is often true. First, however, let me spell out some of the main costs of legal and political decision making.

First, there are *direct costs* of operation. Deputies, judges, and jurors have to be paid; voters, too, have sometimes been paid. Buildings for courts, parliaments, and other institutions have to be raised, and decisions have to be published. In some cases, the costs of these operations could certainly be reduced without loss on other counts. There is no reason to think that Italian deputies would perform worse if they lost some of their privileges and had their salaries cut in half. Nor is there any reason to believe that the extraordinary expenses incurred in the construction of new headquarters of the Bank of Norway were in any way justified by expected performance.

On the other hand, low payment to jurors may offer an example of *misplaced economizing*. Citizens who normally earn more than they receive as jurors are in fact asked to pick up part of the costs themselves. As a result, many potential jurors try, often successfully, to get out of jury duty. As those who remain in the pool are unlikely to form a representative cross-section, the desideratum of diversity may suffer.

When a lawyer or a witness communicates inadmissible information to the jury (see Chapter 2), the judge can either declare a mistrial or instruct the jury to disregard the evidence. Since the first option is costly, it may not be chosen. Instead, judges often assume – in good or bad faith – that the jury will be able to ignore what they heard. Given the considerable body of evidence against that assumption,[1] this practice amounts to sacrificing accuracy in order to reduce costs. Usually, the trade-off is indeterminate.

A frequently cited objection to the jury system as a whole is that it is much more costly to operate than a judge-based system. In 2000, the English Home Secretary claimed that one could save more than £120 million a year by denying those accused of "either-way offenses" the right to opt for trial by jury.[2] The

---

[1] In *United States v. Gruenwald*, 1956, p. 574, Judge Frank referred to the assumption as a "judicial lie." According to one survey, "98% of the lawyers questioned and 43% of the judges believed that jurors would not comply with ... instructions" to allow an item of evidence for the purpose of assessing credibility while disregarding it for the purpose of determining guilt (Kassin and Studebaker 1998, p. 423). See also discussion in Chapter 2.

[2] Lloyd-Bostock and Thomas (2000), p. 63. Somewhat surprisingly, the estimate included savings arising from lighter sentencing by magistrates.

move from jury unanimity to a qualified majority has also been defended by the cost of hung juries and subsequent retrials, which arise more frequently in the first regime. These two reforms involve very different trade-offs. If we accept the commonly made claim that the existence of a single dissenter ipso facto shows that the accused is not guilty "beyond a reasonable doubt,"[3] the move away from unanimity would save costs at the expense of accuracy. One consequence is (somehow) traded off against another. By contrast, the main objection of the reassignment of "either-way" cases to judges has been based on *perceived legitimacy* rather than on *consequences*:

> In the interests of efficiency and the reduction of costs, there have been several attempts in England and Wales to limit the defendants' "right" to opt for jury trial by making various "either-way" offences, primarily petty dishonesty and minor violence, triable only under summary procedure. However, these proposals have been criticized as an attack on citizens' civil liberties and contrary to due process. In Scotland, on the other hand, the accused has never had any such "right," and, perhaps more significantly, there has never been any pressure to grant the accused such an option. Thus, what in England is often perceived to be a fundamental principle of trial by jury is revealed simply to be the product of the way in which the institution happened to develop in that jurisdiction.[4]

When comparing the cost of trials by judge and by jury, one should take account not only of out-of-pocket expenses but also of the costs of false convictions and false acquittals. Generally speaking, jury trials have higher, sometimes much higher, acquittal rates than trials by judges. In itself, this fact tells us little, because the cases that go before juries and judges can differ in systematic ways. When the French Vichy government replaced pure jury trials by mixed courts in 1941 and the acquittal rate fell immediately and dramatically, the causal relationship was not in doubt, however. Other findings point in the same direction. Conjecturally, the difference might be explained by the fact that if asked to assign a numerical value to n in the statement "It is better that n guilty go free than that one innocent be convicted," jurors would in general choose a larger number than judges do.[5] As jurors are selected more or less

[3] Stephen (1883), vol. 1, pp. 304–5; Abramson (2000), p. 186, citing the claim of the defendant in *Johnson v. Louisiana*.
[4] Duff (2000), p. 254; see also pp. 260 and 272. This example provides a good illustration of the relative and historical nature of perceived legitimacy.
[5] Volokh (1997) reports variations in n ranging from 1 to 100. Esmein (1913), p. 473, cites stunningly comical statements from the 1808 French debates on jury reform warning against adoption of the jury system in France on the grounds that the French, compared to the English, were too compassionate. The criminal court of Aveyron pointed to the difference between Shakespeare and Racine as proof of "those feelings of toleration and natural pity in the Frenchman which incline his heart to commiseration." The court of Doubs likewise observed that "the Englishman at the theater cares only for apparitions, madmen, dreadful criminals and murders long drawn out," whereas "the Frenchman ... is delicate in all his tastes; he eagerly flees from any sight which could disagreeably awaken his sensitiveness; could he have any pleasure in wielding the bleeding sword of justice?" The judges writing these opinions clearly thought that French jurors, unlike English ones, would assign much too high values of n.

randomly among the citizens, their preference would presumably reflect that of the population at large. The preference for the jury system might, then, be linked to the belief that it minimizes an appropriately weighted sum of costs from type I and type II errors.

Second, decision making can have *opportunity costs* that justify speedy procedures. In wartime, military courts often adopt simplified procedures and do not allow appeals. The rush of anti-terrorist legislation in the wake of September 11, 2001, also provides a dramatic example of decision making under urgency.[6] Among the many possible reasons for the rapid adoption of laws whose complexity would normally have dictated years of committee discussion before the final vote, the perceived risk of an imminent attack might seem to justify the truncated procedure.[7] In a famous example: if you see a shape on the path that could be either a snake or a branch, it makes sense to run away rather than to inspect it more closely.[8] Assemblies and courts ought to have fast-track procedures that enable them to face emergencies of this kind, while at the same time having built-in protections against decisions based on unjustified panics or exaggerated fears. "It is the task of the Assembly to know how to protect itself against the danger of improvised votes that are not required by anything."[9] Warning against this danger in a legal context, Frank Murphy wrote in a dissenting Supreme Court opinion in the trial of General Yamashita that "in all this *needless* and unseemly haste there was no serious attempt to charge or prove that he committed a recognized violation of the laws of war."[10]

Justice expedited is justice denied; so is justice delayed. In legal proceedings delays should count as a cost even when they do not involve out-of-pocket expenses. In criminal cases, the accused should be able to achieve closure and get on with their lives. (Prisoners on death row constitute an exception.) In civil cases, plaintiffs will want to receive their awards before they die. Although the cost of delay can be offset by incurring the cost of appointing more judges, the trade-off may be hard or impossible to assess. Moreover, the removal of delay by appointing more judges could itself cause more delay (to be remedied by even more judges), since "fewer litigants will waive their right to jury trial."[11]

Third, consider costs associated with *hyperrationality*. If one aims at the decision that would have been best if found instantly and costlessly, the outcome can be far from optimal. The mechanisms leading to suboptimality include neglect of direct costs, neglect of opportunity costs (notably of delays), and

[6] In the United States, the Patriot Act was signed into law on October 26, 2001. For the similarly accelerated processes in England, France, and Germany, see Haubrich (2003).
[7] I say "might seem" because the actions of the United States may have been dictated by the desire for revenge rather than by fear. Whereas fear can justify haste, the desire for revenge usually does not. Revenge does, however, typically *cause* haste.
[8] LeDoux (1996), p. 268.
[9] Pierre (1893), p. 890.
[10] *Yamashita v. Styer*, 327 U.S. 1 (1946); my italics. See also more generally Elster (2009c).
[11] Zeisel, Kalven, and Buchholz (1959), p. 59.

neglect of harms created by the procedure itself. For an example of the last, consider contested custody cases where legal procedures aimed at determining the custody arrangement that would be in the best interest of the child can, because of the pain and suffering they impose on the child, work against that interest.[12] One writer refers to the need for "managing the iatrogenic risks of risk management."[13]

Consider finally costs associated with *participation* in collective decision making. Because these costs may have received less attention than they deserve,[14] I shall offer several examples.

In modern Western democracies, the costs of political assemblies are borne by the state (or by a local authority). Deputies, in particular, are paid by the government and not by their constituents. One might imagine, therefore, that cost factors might enter into the determination of the optimal size of the assembly, together with the other factors that I discuss in Chapters 3 and 4. To my knowledge, however, costs have never been a practical consideration in determining the number of deputies, nor have costs entered into theoretical discussions of the issue.[15] Presumably, assembly designers have assumed, almost certainly correctly, that this factor was a second-order consideration they could safely ignore.

In earlier centuries, things were often organized differently, with the constituencies bearing the burden of paying travel, meals, and lodging for their deputies. Analogous to the misplaced economy in the payment of jurors, this system could lead to severe inefficiencies; it could also cause distributive injustice. The salient fact is that the size of delegations was often smaller when deputies had to travel a long distance to the assembly. I shall discuss three American cases in which this fact had important effects, the first from several state legislatures in the 1780s, the second from the Continental Congress, and the third from the Federal Convention. In the second case, cost considerations led to inefficiency, in the first and third cases to malapportionment.

1. In the American states, elections to the councils or legislatures used either regional or proportional representation. States using the former mode often wrote underrepresentation of the backcountry into their charters or constitutions, the Carolinas and Virginia being especially notorious. In states using the latter mode, geography and costs conspired to produce the same result. The case of Massachusetts was emblematic in this regard. Although several members of the Convention that drafted the 1780 Constitution demanded that the state assume all costs of the delegates,

---

[12] Elster (1989b), ch. 3; Elster (2007a), ch. 13; Elster (2010a), ch. 2. A different and in some ways more intractable case arises in suspected child abuse, when the welfare agency needs to weigh the risks of intervening too early and possibly violating the rights of the parents against intervening too late and possibly exposing the child to more abuse.

[13] Wiener (1998).

[14] Stasavage (2010) is a rare exception.

[15] Estlund (2012), pp. 243–47, does not cite costs among what he calls the "shrinking factors" in the determination of assembly size.

[the] Constitution as drafted and adopted provided that each town should pay the expenses of its own representatives incurred in attending the session.... The point about payment was of very great consequence and of greater practical signification, in all probability, than the question of the precise basis of representation. Interior towns, especially those at more than a day's journey from Boston, very frequently failed to send a member at all. The cost of maintaining a representative in the capital through the legislative session was a heavy burden to which the frugal farmers saw little reason to subject themselves; were it necessary to be represented, in order to put the town's view in some dispute, a single member would be cheaper than two. For the seaboard towns the capital was relatively accessible. Their greater wealth also made it easier for them to maintain representatives. *All the normal circumstances of economic and political life therefore tended to give the advantages to the east coast.*[16]

In Pennsylvania, the 1776 constitution substituted proportional for regional representation and thus did away with the legal underrepresentation of the western counties. These areas were, however, disadvantaged in other respects. "Farmers struggling to get from under a load of unpaid debts and taxes could not afford to leave the plow to spend months in Philadelphia debating laws."[17] To obtain legal title to land on the frontier, poor settlers had to make the expensive trip to Philadelphia.[18] Without the title, they could not vote. Whether de jure or de facto, the underrepresentation of the backcountry in the state legislatures, at the Federal Convention, and in the ratifying conventions was probably a necessary condition for the adoption of the Constitution.[19]

2. Under the Articles of Confederation, a state delegation to the Continental Congress required a quorum of two members to cast a vote. That minimum easily became a maximum, especially for the states that were at some distance from where Congress met and that were reluctant to fund large delegations. When two-state delegations were divided and thus could not cast a vote, their virtual absence was added to the physical absence of states that had not even sent a delegation. In many cases, the result was that the quorum of states in Congress was not reached. After 1783, this fact was one of the several causes of the near-paralysis of the body. Congress was fully aware of the problem, as shown by a remarkable resolution adopted on April 19, 1784:

Resolved that the Legislatures of the several States be informed that whilst they are respectively represented in Congress by two Delegates only, such an unanimity for conducting the most important public concerns is necessary as can rarely be expected: that if each of the thirteen States should be represented by the two Members five out of twenty-six being only a fifth of the whole may negative any measure requiring the voice of nine States. That of eleven States now on the floor of Congress, nine being represented by only two Members from each, it is in the power of three out of twenty-five

---

[16] Pole (1966), p. 204; my italics.
[17] Bouton (2007), p. 129.
[18] Ibid., pp. 121–22.
[19] Elster (2012).

making one eighth of the whole to negative such a measure notwithstanding that by the articles of confederation, the dissent of five out of thirteen, being more than one third of the number, is necessary for such a negative. That in a representation of three Members from each State, not less than ten of thirty-nine could so negative a matter requiring the voice of nine States. That from facts under the observation of Congress they are clearly convinced that a representation of two Members from the several States is extremely injurious by producing delays, and for this reason is likewise much more expensive than a general representation of three Members from each State. That therefore Congress conceive it to be indispensably necessary and earnestly recommend that each State at all times when Congress are sitting, be hereafter represented by three Members at least; as the most injurious consequences may be expected from the want of such representation.

In one of their many failures to overcome collective action problems, the states did not listen to the call from Congress. Each may have thought that its share of the benefits from contributing to the public good of efficient decision making by sending three rather than two delegates were inferior to the costs, even though all states would benefit if all states adopted the proposed policy. An apparently simpler solution would have been to allocate the same (odd) number of delegates to all the states and have them paid by Congress. That solution could only have worked, however, if the states had paid the requisitions imposed on them by Congress for that purpose – another collective action problem!

3. At the Federal Convention, the size of the delegations was unregulated. States sent from two to eight delegates, partly reflecting the size of the states and partly the distance from Philadelphia. Pennsylvania had the largest delegation, no doubt because six of its delegates lived in Philadelphia and one very close to the city, with attendance costs close to zero. On one of the occasions (see Chapter 5) when votes were taken by individuals rather than by states, the Pennsylvanians may have used their numerical clout to bias an important committee in favor of their preferred solution. To prevent this geographical bias, Congress could have required the states to send equal-size (and odd-numbered!) delegations; alternatively, the Convention could have had the members of the Grand Committees elected by the states rather than by the delegates.[20]

The upshot of this discussion is unsurprising: the costs of participating in collective decision making should be borne by the collective and not by the participants. Because of pervasive free-rider problems, however, this principle has not always been respected. Its adoption has itself been an important collective decision.

---

[20] The Convention proposed that representatives be paid out of the national treasury, partly out of concern for the states ("Payment by the States would be unequal as the distant States would have to pay for the same term of attendance and more days in travelling to & from the seat of the Govt," Hamilton in Farrand, vol. 1, p. 373) and partly out of concern for the federal government ("If the States were to pay the members of the Natl. Legislature, a dependence would be created that would vitiate the whole System," Randolph, p. 372).

II. DIVERSITY

The claim that all virtue – at least all virtue that can be reliably enhanced by institutional design – is negative does not necessarily extend to the *virtues of collectives* as such. Condorcet claimed that under certain conditions, *large groups* are more likely to track the truth than smaller ones. For several reasons, including those I discussed in Chapter 3, the relevance of this claim for institutional design is doubtful. A more powerful idea is that a *diverse group* of decision makers, selected by simple or stratified lotteries or by proportional voting in the population at large, may produce better decisions than a group of individually excellent decision makers. As a group may have to be large to generate sufficient diversity, and since large groups may be at a disadvantage in some respects, diversity might have some undesirable effects. In the following, I shall ignore this issue, however.

I shall focus on the value of diversity that stems from the *exchange of information* among the decision makers, each of whom may possess specialized knowledge. The movie *Twelve Angry Men* vividly illustrates how such exchanges could lead to a better decision. Although diversity may arguably have good effects even when there is no pooling of information, such as ensuring that the beliefs and preferences of each actor are independent from those of the others, I shall ignore them. The choice of jurors and *nomothetai* by lot in Athens in the fourth century B.C. certainly generated diversity (attenuated, however, by self-selection of those who presented themselves each morning to form the lottery pool), but its value, if any, did not come from communication, which was discouraged.[21]

In previous chapters I have cited several examples of mandatory or recommended diversity. In the two great 18th-century constituent assemblies that I have constantly cited, diversity of deputies was either sought ex ante for its information-pooling effect or praised ex post for having this effect. Constitutional courts and central bank committees may deliberately seek diversity among their members. Diversity is usually cited as an important rationale for random selection of jurors.

Even disregarding distortions caused by challenges for cause and by peremptory challenges, random selection does not, of course, guarantee diversity in the jury that results from the draw. As an alternative, one might use stratified random selection. In Norway, juries have to contain roughly equal numbers of men and women. Boards of a certain category of Norwegian companies are also constrained by law to contain at least 40 percent women. If a company doesn't comply, it can be shut down. The system can be gamed, since companies can change their legal status to avoid the requirement. Noncompliance with the similar French law entails that all nominations to the board are invalidated, except those of women. Noncompliance with the French law requiring that political parties nominate equal numbers of men and women triggers only

---

[21] For juries, see Chapter 2; for *nomothetai*, see Rhodes (2003).

financial penalties. The parties have by and large been quite willing to pay the fines to avoid diversity in their nominations. I conjecture that they defend themselves by claiming that compliance would entail electoral losses. If that is in fact their argument, it is (at most) valid, for a given party, only if other parties do not comply. Bentham might have imposed the automatic dissolution of any company or party that did not fulfill the requirement.

Generally speaking, however, stratification has two obvious drawbacks: because there are so many potentially relevant dimensions, it would be *impractical* in small-group decisions to stratify along all of them; because they are all relevant, it would be *unfair* or *arbitrary* to choose just one or a few. Mathias Risse (personal communication) suggests the following solution: one might, for a given jury, determine its score on an appropriately constructed *diversity index* and then, among many randomly chosen juries, empanel the one with the highest score.

The *precise mechanism* by which diversity improves decisions remains to be discussed. In Chapter 3 I distinguished between two potential contributions of diversity in assemblies: *identifying problems* (where the shoe pinches) and *identifying solutions* (how to make better shoes). In the case of juries, diversity may enable the emergence of *better narratives*. If jurors are chosen from different backgrounds, the chances are better that one juror, by virtue of her experience, will be able to make sense of seemingly obscure or conflicting evidence than if they all come from a narrow segment of the population. An all-male jury might not have detected the incongruous behavior of the woman who claimed to suffer severe back pain after a car accident and yet did not wince when, wearing high heels, she stepped off the raised witness stand. As a final mechanism, good decisions may be enhanced by creativity, creativity by brainstorming, and brainstorming by diversity.

Scott Page has done much to bring formal rigor to the study of diversity.[22] Although I have tried, I have not been able to link his models to actual processes of collective decision making. As is also the case for Condorcet's jury theorem, it is difficult to verify that the assumptions of the theorems hold in any given case. His illustrative examples in which these assumptions hold are compelling, but also highly stylized. When presenting real-world empirical evidence on the benefits of diversity, he does not relate them to the assumptions. To the extent that diversity works by generating creativity ("thinking outside the box"), as in the example Page gives from the Chicago Transport Authority,[23] the benefits can hardly be predicted from a model.

It is quite possible that future work will bring the models closer to reality. It is also possible that I underestimate their power, and they are in fact already closer to reality than they seem to me. Be this as it may, I want to mention an important

[22] Page (2007, 2010). Some of his arguments (notably in Page 2010) show that diversity may bring benefits even in the absence of interaction. Because of my purposes in the present book, I shall ignore these results.
[23] Page (2007), pp. 86–88.

argument that Page raises concerning the *net effect* of diversity on the quality of decisions.[24] It seems plausible that cognitive diversity will often be correlated with motivational diversity. Although the former can be very valuable, the latter can, as I discussed in Chapter 1, have undesirable effects. Heterogeneous preferences have the potential for generating majority cycles, leaving the collective decision essentially arbitrary. Although we do not know how frequently the potential is realized, we cannot afford to ignore it. Also, an individual might have an incentive to withhold private information if releasing it would benefit her opponents. If these behave in the same way, the collective decision might be Pareto-suboptimal. Of my two main case studies, I believe that juries are relatively immune to these problems. In constituent assemblies, however, they might well arise. Which effect will dominate is an open question.

III. OVERRIDES

I have argued that when we have done all we can to remove distorting factors from the decision-making process, we should simply let the chips fall where they may and accept the outcome, whatever it is. As I said in Chapter 1, we may think of this recommendation as "impure procedural justice" – impure because complete removal of distorting factors will never be possible. The question I shall now address is whether the risk of bad decisions resulting from any remaining distortions could justify some kind of overriding mechanism. I shall argue that constitutional courts should be allowed to override legislative decisions on procedural but not on substantive grounds, and that judges should be allowed to override convictions by juries. The override of elections seems unfeasible.

I shall use John Hart Ely's *Democracy and Distrust* as a point of departure. Although he does not cite Bentham's writings on institutional design, Ely's approach is very close to Bentham's, as suggested by the title of his book. Although its subtitle is *A Theory of Judicial Review* – referring to an institution decried by Bentham – the negative spirit of Ely's work nevertheless places him in the same camp. Let me quote him at some length:

The approach to constitutional adjudication recommended here is akin to what might be called an "antitrust" as opposed to a "regulatory" orientation to economic affairs – rather than to dictate substantive results it intervenes only when the "market," in our case the political market, is systematically malfunctioning.... Our government cannot fairly be said to be "'malfunctioning" simply because it sometimes generates outcomes with which we disagree, however strongly (and claims that it is reaching results with which "the people" really disagree – or would "if they understood" – are likely to be little more than self-deluding projections). In a representative democracy value determinations are to be made by our elected representatives, and if in fact most of us disapprove we can vote them out of office. Malfunction occurs when the process is undeserving of trust, when (1) the ins are choking off the channels of political change to ensure that they will stay in and the outs will stay out, or (2) though no one is actually denied a voice or a vote,

---

[24] Ibid., ch. 11.

representatives beholden to an effective majority are systematically disadvantaging some minority out of simple hostility or a prejudiced refusal to recognize commonalities of interest, and thereby denying that minority the protection afforded other groups by a representative system.[25]

I argued in Chapter 3 that legislatures cannot be left entirely to their own devices, and that they need to be limited by constitutional constraints. Today, judicial review is the privileged instrument for the *enforcement* of those limits. Let me now ask whether one should always let the chips fall where they may as long as the system is not malfunctioning. In the following passage, Ely affirms unambiguously that one should:

[Imagine] a law, passed pursuant to a free and democratic process, that does something frightful to all of us and thus does not single out a powerless minority for victimization. Harry Wellington suggests an example, "a statute making it a crime for any person to remove any other person's gall bladder, except to save that person's life." Surely, he says, *that* has to be unconstitutional. Now Wellington has me (sort of): I don't think that law is unconstitutional. Curtains for my theory? I've led you all this way to confess error at the very end? Well, no, since that law couldn't conceivably pass. . . . It is an entirely legitimate response to the gall bladder law to note that it couldn't pass and refuse to play any further. In fact it can only deform our constitutional jurisprudence to tailor it to laws that couldn't be enacted, since constitutional law appropriately exists for those situations where representative government cannot be trusted, not those where we know it can.[26]

With regard to legislative assemblies, Ely's argument provides a necessary but not sufficient set of precautionary measures. Because of its focus on elections, it does not exhaust the set of procedural remedies one might want to apply before letting the chips fall where they may. Nothing in Ely's argument would exclude, for instance, the *cumul des mandats* or require that deputies put their assets in a blind trust. A Benthamite extension of Ely's argument dictates that measures to promote the active, moral, and intellectual aptitude of deputies should also be put into the constitution and be enforced by judicial review.

I agree with Ely's criticism of *substantive* judicial review based on the legal and political philosophy of the judges. They have no business overriding the decisions of a properly elected and properly organized legislature. The substantive decisions of supreme courts and of constitutional courts are usually based on abstract and general clauses about individual rights, interpreted through a body of previous decisions that have often a very tenuous connection to the text of the constitution. In practice, this creates an unacceptably large scope for arbitrary and ideologically based decisions. This is not the place, however, to defend that highly contentious claim.

Let me now consider juries and more briefly elections in the same perspective.

[25] Ely (1980), pp. 102–3.
[26] Ely (1980), pp. 182–83. Ely's response to the objection amounts to a refusal to consider purely possibilistic reasoning (ch. 1).

In their chapter on "Cross-overs" in *The American Jury*, Harry Kalven and Hans Zeisel argue that in the United States there is (and should be) an asymmetry in the role of judges in acquittals and convictions by juries. The cross-over cases are those in which the judges presiding over the cases said that they would have been more lenient than the jury was. Kalven and Zeisel cite a number of such cases, many of them turning on the indignation of jurors triggered by legally irrelevant factors of the defendant's behavior. Two examples follow:

A young Negro boy is charged with indecent exposure in a theatre. The undisputed facts are that the manager of the theatre, using a flashlight, discovers him masturbating in the dark. The judge acquits on the grounds that the crime of indecent exposure requires exposure to the public. The jury overrides this distinction, because on these facts it is offended by the boy's conduct, whether or not anyone saw it. The judge tells us: "The jury could not get the moral of the case out of their mind. They saw only a colored boy masturbating in the theatre with white women and children in the audience."

[Another case concerns] an auto accident where defendant's auto knocks down a female pedestrian. The jury finds him guilty of reckless driving, the judge only of the lesser crime of leaving the scene.... The unusual feature of this case is that the jury is so incensed at the defendant that it is not satisfied to find him guilty of the very crime that angers them but most go on to find him guilty of reckless driving.[27]

In the first case, one might perhaps have eliminated the racial bias by institutional design, although it is hard to imagine exactly how this result could have been achieved. In the second, by contrast, I believe that no design measure could have prevented the jurors' anger from triggering the excessive verdict.

In such cases, the judge has the power to set aside the conviction or to impose the minimum penalty. There is a sharp asymmetry between acquittal and conviction:

As a matter of law [the judge] has no power over jury verdicts which, in his view, are too favorable to the defendant. In the cross-over case, however, the judge may have legal power to intervene.... In the end *the institutional arrangement is impressive*. It gives the jury autonomy to do equity on behalf of the criminal defendant. Where the jury's freedom leads to "illegally" harsh results, the judge is at hand, ready to erase them.[28]

Kalven and Zeisel report that in 56 percent of the 103 cross-over cases in their sample, the judge let stand a verdict he would not have reached himself. In trials for a serious crime, the percentage falls to 39 percent.[29] The override mechanism, although not perfect, had a considerable effect.

Wrongful convictions by a jury are certain to be less frequent when decisions have to be unanimous than when they can be taken by simple or qualified

[27] Kalven and Zeisel (1966), pp. 298, 299.

[28] Ibid., pp. 411, 413; my italics. Risinger (2004), p. 1315, is less impressed with the role of the judge as "the thirteenth juror." Zalman (2008), p. 85, suggests that "some procedures in the French system of judicially directed inquiry [by a *juge d'instruction*] have the potential to catch potential wrongful convictions early in the process." While this may be so, the recent Outreau case shows that this potential is not always realized.

[29] Kalven and Zeisel (1966), pp. 412, 413.

majorities. In the latter cases, the need for an institutional override becomes especially acute and has in fact been introduced in the law. Under a law of 1795, French juries were allowed to convict by a majority of seven to five. Napoleon's Code of Criminal Procedure introduced two override procedures:

> Article 351 ... stipulated that if the jury convicted the accused of the principal charge by a vote of seven to five, the judges were to be polled on the verdict. If four of the five judges accepted the opinion of the minority of the jury, the accused was then acquitted by a vote of nine to eight. Article 352 stated that even when the jury voted for conviction by a majority greater than seven, if the judges were unanimously convinced that there had been a miscarriage of justice, they could suspend the verdict and send the case to trial in the next court session, to be submitted to a new jury, from which all of those who first tried the case was excluded. Both articles concerned only convictions; acquittals could not be overturned.[30]

In Scotland, where juries can convict by a bare majority of eight to seven, the right to appeal against convictions was introduced in 1926 and further stream-lined in 1980.[31] In Norway, judges can overturn jury acquittals as well as convictions, but the requirements for overrides are more stringent for acquittals. There have notably been several overrides of acquittals for rape. The diversity requirement that half the members of the jury be women is likely to lead to fewer acquittals in rape cases in any case.

Overrides of assemblies by courts and of juries by judges, whether desirable or undesirable, certainly do occur. It is harder, perhaps impossible, to find examples of institutional mechanisms for overriding *the outcome of elections* in cases where the impact of distorting factors has been reduced as much as possible. Overrides happen, to be sure. In Algeria, the Islamic Salvation Front (ISF) won 188 out of 232 seats in the first electoral round in 1991, and was confidently expected to win sufficiently many of the 198 seats to be allocated in the second round to form the 75 percent majority in Parliament required to change the constitution and create an Islamic state. The government canceled the second round, "saving democracy" by violating it.[32] Since the ISF owed its victory in part to massive electoral fraud, the assumption that distorting factors had been minimized does not hold. Moreover, the override was purely ad hoc, not based on an institutional mechanism.

It seems highly unlikely that a procedurally sound democratic election could produce the abolition of democracy as its outcome, especially if we stipulate, as I think we can, that parties with that abolition on their platform should be banned from participating. Hitler's rise to power certainly does not fit that scenario. Yet if that outcome were to be produced, it is hard to imagine an override mechanism that would not lend itself to abuses. Vesting the power to cancel elections in the head of state or in the constitutional court, on the basis of

[30] Donovan (2010), p. 41. In Belgium, a provision similar to Article 351 is still in force.
[31] Duff (2000), pp. 277–79.
[32] Bouandel (2005).

a discretionary judgment that the winner represents a threat to democracy, would almost certainly be a remedy worse than the ill it was supposed to prevent.

IV. INDETERMINACY

An institutional reform that will predictably reduce the impact of one of the distorting factors I have been discussing – interest, passion, prejudice, and bias – may predictably enhance the impact of another. The following cases will illustrate the problem.

> Whereas publicity will drive interest underground, it will provide a fertile breeding ground for passion. Secrecy tends to have the opposite effect. Although I claimed that in the special case of constituent assemblies this dilemma is attenuated if the decision makers focus on issues on which interest has no purchase, this solution is not available to ordinary legislatures.

> Whereas rotation of officials and term limits of deputies may reduce the risk of capture by interest groups, these measures will have a negative impact on their knowledge of the issues.

> Whereas the selection of jurors who are ignorant about a high-profile case they are to decide will eliminate bias caused by pre-trial publicity, jurors who do not read newspapers or watch TV are likely to be lacking in intellectual or active aptitude.

> Whereas banning the presence of other witnesses during witness testimony reduces the risk that a witness might distort the truth because he is subject to conformism or intimidation, their presence would deter him from telling falsehoods in the presence of someone who may know the truth.

> Whereas large electoral (single-deputy) districts reduce the active aptitude of voters, small districts produce large assemblies and reduce the active aptitude of deputies.

> Whereas one can mitigate the "primacy effect" (the tendency to form rigid first impressions) by presenting important information or witnesses at a late stage in legal proceedings, "the recency effect" might then cause them to be given undue importance.

> Whereas imposing a high age threshold on representatives may on average enhance their intellectual aptitude, Bentham claimed that it would reduce their moral aptitude.

> Whereas anonymizing CVs in job applications would reduce the opportunity of employers to engage in negative discrimination, that measure would also reduce their opportunity for positive discrimination.

Often, attempts to evaluate the net effect of such reforms and adopt them only if they do more good than harm prove futile. The idea of fine-tuning electoral reform by choosing the size of electoral districts that minimizes the sum of free-riding effects on voters and on deputies is quite unrealistic. Determining the optimal length of tenure by officials and deputies is also a fragile project, except that a very short tenure and life tenure are definitely undesirable.

When a departure from the status quo can be predicted to have significant positive as well as negative effects, institutional designers have to tread carefully. Often, the combination of *uncertainty* concerning the long-term net effect of reform and the *transaction costs* of reform will provide a compelling argument for retaining the status quo. *The burden of proof is on the reformer*, simply because reform always has short-term costs. When, upon becoming President of France in 1981, François Mitterrand renamed the Ministry of Foreign Affairs (Ministère des affaires étrangères) as the Ministry of External Relations (Ministère des relations extérieures), the decision certainly had substantial costs in terms of new stationery, new inscriptions on buildings, and so on. Did it have any nonconjectural benefits?

This emphasis on indeterminacy confers an undeniably conservative slant to my argument. It does not, however, amount to a "cult of complexity, with its inevitable strong suggestion that any but the most piecemeal and modest tinkering with the social mechanism [is] ill-fated."[33] The conservatism is offset by the radical character of many Benthamite proposals, such as the promotion of active aptitude and the adoption of secret-public voting. If carried out systematically, the program would imply a thoroughgoing purge of many institutions.

V. POLITICAL WILL

Yet this claim brings me to the final question, concerning the political will to carry out the program. This issue can be broken down along three dimensions: the nature of the decision-making body, the nature of the influence from which it should be protected, and the nature of the body whose political will is required. These meta-decisions can be heteronomous or autonomous. The most difficult case is when a body has to reform itself.

In jury reform, it is hard to see why legislators should be opposed to measures that reduce the impact of self-interest, passion, and cognitive bias on jurors. Prejudice is a different matter: racist legislators have often, for example, adopted mechanisms favoring the choice of racist jurors.

It is also hard, although not quite as hard, to see why anyone would be opposed to measures, in any arena, that would reduce the impact of passion and bias. On any given occasion, a group or an individual might wish these influences to operate, but in the long run there is little benefit to be had from irrational decision makers.

The hardest question arises with regard to measures to curb the impact of self-interest in elections and, especially, in assemblies. Why would a parliament adopt legislation to prevent vote-buying if all parties believe that it might one day be in their interest to use this stratagem? Why would framers motivated by

---

[33] Novick (1988), p. 324. I may have been indulging in this cult in earlier writings, notably Elster (1989b), ch. 4.

partisan interests create a central bank that would render monetary policy independent of partisan interests?[34] Why would a parliament abolish the *cumul des mandats* or adopt strict rules to punish members for being absent if all deputies would like to retain these options?

As I remarked in the Introduction, these problems might be overcome at the constitutional stage, but only if the framers follow the example of Solon and leave political life. At the post-constitutional stage, much depends on the nature of the issue and on the motivation of the deciders. Let me illustrate with two reforms to promote active aptitude in the American Congress, past and present. In the 19th century, some representatives may well have understood that public business would be carried out more efficiently if they sat on benches rather than at desks, yet opposed the reform if they cared more about carrying out their private business. In the 21st century, a reform limiting the time representatives spend on financing their reelection would enable them to carry out their public business more efficiently, with no sacrifice of their private interest.

The purpose of this book has been to set out and illustrate important aims that for their realization require political will. I wish I could have said more about the conditions for political will formation. If it is true that nothing great is ever done without passion, and that passions are unpredictable and ungovernable, the failure was perhaps inevitable.

[34] Przeworski and Limongi (1993).

References

Abramovsky, A. (1996), "Cameras in the jury room," *Arizona State Law Journal* 28, 865–92.

Abramovsky, A. and Edelstein, J. (1998–99), "Anonymous juries: In exigent circumstances only," *St. John's Journal of Legal Commentary* 13, 457–90.

Abramson, J. (2000), *We, the Jury*, Cambridge, MA: Harvard University Press.

Abramson, P. et al. (2010), "Comparing strategic voting under FPTP and PR," *Comparative Political Studies* 43, 61–90.

Ackerer, A. (2008), *The Termination of the Stay of Aliens*, Munich: Grin.

Ackerman, B. and Katyal, N. (1995), "Our unconventional founding," *University of Chicago Law Review* 62, 475–573.

Adair, D. (1998), *Fame and the Founding Fathers*, Indianapolis, IN: Liberty Press.

Adams, C. and Bourgeois, M. (2006), "Separating compensatory and punitive damage award decisions by trial bifurcation," *Law and Human Behavior* 30, 11–30.

Adams, G. and Stephen, H. (1914), *Select Documents of English Constitutional History*, London: Macmillan.

Adams, W. P. (2001), *The First American Constitutions*, New York: Rowman and Littlefield.

Adler, S. (1994), *The Jury: Trial and Error in the American Courtroom*, New York: Crown.

Aikman, C. (1999), "Making a multi-racial democracy work in Fiji," *Asia Pacific Viewpoint* 40, 285–94.

Allouche-Pourcel, B. (2010), *Kant et la Schwärmerei*, Paris: Harmattan.

Alschuler, A. 1989, "The Supreme Court and the jury: Voir dire, peremptory challenges, and the review of jury verdicts," *University of Chicago Law Review* 56, 153–233.

Alter, A. et al. (2007), "Overcoming intuition," *Journal of Experimental Psychology: General* 136, 569–76.

AM = *L'Ancien Moniteur*, Paris 1840–45.

Amar, A. (1994–95), "Reinventing juries: Ten suggested reforms," *University of California Davis Law Review* 28, 1169–94.

Amar, A. (2005), *America's Constitution: A Biography*, New York: Random House.

Amy, D. J. (2000), *Behind the Ballot Box*, Westport, CT: Praeger.

Anderson, T. (1993), *Creating the Constitution*, University Park: Pennsylvania State Press.

Antonetti, G. (1994), *Louis-Philippe*, Paris: Fayard.

AP = *Archives Parlementaires*, Serie I: 1787–99, Paris, 1875–88.

Arato, A. (2009), *Constitution-making under Occupation*, New York: Columbia University Press.

Arato, A. (2010), "Democratic constitution making and unfreezing the Turkish process," *Philosophy and Social Criticism* 36, 473–88.

Arato, A. and Miklósi, Z. (2010), "Constitution making in Hungary 1989–1996," in L. Miller and L. Aucoin (eds.), *Framing the State in Times of Transition: A Comparative Study of Constitution Making Processes*, Washington, DC: USIP Press, pp. 350–90.

Arkes, H. and Blumer, C. (1985), "The psychology of sunk cost," *Organizational Behavior and Human Decision Processes* 35, 124–40.

Arrow, K. and Hurwicz, L. (1971), "An optimality criteron for decision-making under uncertainty," in C. F. Carter and J. L. Ford (eds.), *Uncertainty and Expectations in Economics*, Clifton, NJ: Kelley, pp. 1–11.

Asch, G. (1951), "Effects of group pressure upon the modification and the distortion of judgment," in H. Guetzkow (ed.), *Groups, Leadership and Men*, Pittsburgh, PA: Carnegie Press, pp. 177–90.

Aulard, A. (1882), *Les orateurs de la Révolution Française*, Paris: Hachette.

Aulard, A. (1921), *Histoire politique de la Révolution Française*, Paris: Armand Colin.

Axelsson, R. (2011), "Comments on the decision of the Supreme Court to invalidate the election to the Constitutional Assembly," http://stjornarskrarfelagid.is/wp-content/uploads/2011/07/Article_by_Reynir_Axelsson.pdf.

Ayres, I. (2000), "Disclosure versus anonymity in campaign finance," in I. Shapiro and S. Macedo (eds.), *Designing Democratic Institutions*, New York: New York University Press, pp. 19–54.

Ayres, I. and Donahue, J. (2003), "Shooting down the 'more guns, less crime' hypothesis," *Stanford Law Review* 55, 1193–1312.

Babelon, J. P. (1982), *Henri IV*, Paris: Fayard.

Bach, L. (2009), "Faut-il interdire le cumul des mandats?" Working Paper, Ecole d'Economie de Paris, www.jourdan.ens.fr/~lbach/documents/Cumul_Bach.pdf.

Bailly, J.-S. (1804), *Mémoires*, Paris.

Balinski, M. and Laraki, R. (2010), *Majority Judgment*, Cambridge, MA: MIT Press.

Balinski, M. and Laraki, R. (2012), "Judge: Don't Vote!" unpublished manuscript, Ecole Polytechnique, Paris.

Banfield, E. (1958), *The Moral Basis of a Backward Society*, Glencoe, IL: Free Press.

Banner, S. (1988), "Disqualifying elected judges from cases involving campaign contributors," *Stanford Law Review* 40, 449–90.

Baron, D. and Ferejohn, J. (1989), "Bargaining in legislatures," *American Political Science Review* 83, 1181–1206.

Baron, J. (2008), *Thinking and Deciding*, Cambridge: Cambridge University Press.

Barry, R. (1942), *Mr. Rutledge of South Carolina*, Salem, NH: Ayer.

Bassett, G. and Spersky, J. (1999), "Robust voting," *Public Choice* 99, 299–310.

Bastid, P. (1945), *Doctrines et institutions politiques de la Seconde République*, Paris: Hachette.

Bastid, P. (1956), *Le gouvernement d'assemblée*, Paris: Cujas.

Baumeister, R. et al. (2001), "Bad is stronger than good," *Review of General Psychology* 5, 323–70.

Bayliss, F. (1957), "The independent members of the British Wages Councils and Boards," *British Journal of Sociology* 8, 1–25.

Beard, C. (1986), *An Economic Interpretation of the Constitution*, New York: Free Press.

Beardsley, J. (1972), "The Constitutional Council and constitutional liberties in France," *American Journal of Comparative Law* 20, 431–52.

Bell, J. (1994), *French Constitutional Law*, Oxford: Oxford University Press.

Bentham, J. (1776), *A Fragment on Government*, London.

Bentham, J. (1843a), *The Works of Jeremy Bentham*, vol. III (ed. John Bowring), Edinburgh: Tait.

Bentham, J. (1843b), *The Works of Jeremy Bentham*, vol. V (ed. John Bowring), Edinburgh: Tait.

Bentham, J. (1983), *Constitutional Code*, vol. 1, Oxford: Oxford University Press.

Bentham, J. (1989), *First Principles Preparatory to a Constitutional Code*, Oxford: Oxford University Press.

Bentham, J. (1990), *Securities against Misrule and other Constitutional Writings for Tripoli and Greece*, Oxford: Oxford University Press.

Bentham, J. (1999), *Political Tactics*, Oxford: Oxford University Press.

Bentham, J. (2002), *Rights, Representation, and Reform*, Oxford: Oxford University Press.

Berend, D. and Paroush, J. (1998), "When is Condorcet's jury theorem valid?" *Social Choice and Welfare* 15, 481–88.

Bertram, C. (2004), *Rousseau and the Social Contract*, London: Routledge.

Bèze, T. de (1882), *Histoire ecclésiastique des églises réformées*, Toulouse: Société des livres religieux.

Bierce, A. (2002), *The Unabridged Devil's Dictionary*, Atlanta: University of Georgia Press.

Bikhchandani, S., Hirshleifer, D., and Welch, I. (1998), "Learning from the behavior of others: Conformity, fads, and informational cascades," *Journal of Economic Perspectives* 12, 151–70.

Blais, A. (2004), "Y a-t-il un vote stratégique en France?," in B. Cautrès et N. Mayer (eds.), *Le nouveau désordre électoral*, Paris: Presses de Sciences Po.

Blewett, N. (1965), "The franchise in the United Kingdom 1885–1918," *Past and Present* 32, 27–56.

Blinder, A. (2007), "Monetary policy by committee: Why and how?" *European Journal of Political Economy* 23, 106–23.

Blinder, A. and Morgan, J. (2008), "Do monetary policy committees need leaders?" *American Economic Review: Papers and Proceedings* 98, 224–29.

Bodin, J. (1788), "Journal de Bodin," in C. J. Mayer (ed.), *Des états généraux et autres assemblées nationales*, t. XIII, Paris.

Bogdanor, V. (2003), *The British Constitution in the Twentieth Century*, Oxford: Oxford University Press.

Bonime-Blanc, A. (1987), *Spain's Transition to Democracy*, Boulder, CO: Westview Press.

Bonnefon, J.-F. (2007), "How do individuals solve the doctrinal paradox in collective decisions?" *Psychological Science* 18, 753–55.

Bonnefon, J.-F. (2009), "Behavioral evidence for framing effects in the resolution of the doctrinal paradox," *Social Choice and Welfare* 34, 631–41.

Boralevi, L. (1983), "Jeremy Bentham's writings on sexual non-conformity," *Topoi* 2, 123–48.

Borgeaud, C. (1895), *Adoption and Amendments of Constitutions*, New York: Macmillan.

Bornstein, B. H. (1999), "The ecological validity of jury simulations: Is the jury still out?" *Law and Human Behavior* 23, 75–91.

Boster, F., Hunter, J., and Hale, J. (1991), "An information-processing model of jury decision making," *Communication Research* 18, 524–47.

Bouandel, Y. (2005), "Reforming the Algerian electoral system," *Journal of Modern African Studies* 43, 393–415.

Bougrab, J. (2002), *Aux origines de la constitution de la IVᵉ République*, Paris: Dalloz.

Bouton, T. (2007), *Taming Democracy*, Oxford: Oxford University Press.

Bowman, L. (1973), *Politics in Rhodesia*, Cambridge, MA: Harvard University Press.

Brady, D., Ferejohn, J., and Pope, J. (2007), "Congress and civil rights policy: An examination of endogenous preferences," in I. Katznelson and B. Weingast (eds.), *Preferences and Situations*, New York: Russell Sage, pp. 62–86.

Brassart, P. (1998), *Paroles de la Révolution. Les assemblées révolutionnaires 1789–94*, Paris: Minerve.

Breau, D. and Brook, B. (2007), "'Mock' mock juries: A field experiment on the ecological validity of jury simulations," *Law and Psychology Review* 31, 77–92.

Brehm, J. (1966), *A Theory of Psychological Reactance*, New York: Academic Press.

Brette, A. (1902), *Histoire des édifices où ont ont siégé les assemblées parlementaires de la révolution*, Paris: Imprimerie Nationale.

Brewer-Carías, A. (2010), "The 1999 Venezuelan constitution-making process," in L. Miller (ed.), *Framing the State in Times of Transition*, Washington, DC: United States Institute of Peace Press, pp. 505–31.

Brinks, D. (2004), *Legal Tolls and the Rule of Law*, Ph.D. Dissertation, University of Notre Dame.

Brunell, T. L., Dave, C., and Morgan, N. C. (2009), "Factors affecting the length of time a jury deliberates: Case characteristics and jury composition," *Review of Law and Economics* 5, 556–578.

Bruyère, J. de la (2007), *Caractères*, Paris: Garnier.

Bryce, J. (1905), *Constitutions*, Oxford: Oxford University Press.

Bryce, J. (1995), *The American Commonwealth*, Indianapolis, IN: Liberty Fund.

Brynner, R. (1993), *Fire Beneath Our Feet: Shays's Rebellion and Its Constitutional Impact*, Ph. D. Dissertation, Department of History, Columbia University.

Buchstein, H. (2000), *Öffentliche und geheime Stimmabgabe*, Baden-Baden: Nomos.

Buechler, R., Griffin, D., and Ross, M. (2002), "Inside the planning fallacy," in T. Gilovich, D. Griffin, and D. Kahneman (eds.), *Heuristics and Biases*, Cambridge: Cambridge University Press, pp. 250–70.

Burdeau, G., Hamon, F., and Troper, L. (1991), *Droit Constitutionnel*, 22e édition, Paris: Librairie Générale de Droit et de Jurisprudence.

Burnett, E. (1964), *The Continental Congress*, New York: Norton

Burns, J. H. (1966), "Bentham and the French Revolution," *Transactions of the Royal Historical Society* 16, 95–14.

Butler, P. (2006–07), "When judges lie (and when they should)," *Minnesota Law Review* 91, 1785–1828.

Cairncross, A. (2004), "Keynes, John Maynard," in *Dictionary of National Biography*, Oxford: Oxford University Press, vol. 31, pp. 483–98.

Cameron, N., Potter, S., and Young, W. (2000), "The New Zealand jury: Towards reform," in N. Vidmar (ed.), *World Jury Systems*, Oxford: Oxford University Press, pp. 167–210.

Caminker, E. (1999), "Strategic and sincere voting norms on multimember courts," *Michigan Law Review* 97, 2297–380.

Campbell, E. (1985), "Jury secrecy and contempt of court," *Monash Law Review* 11, 169–200.

Caron, P. (1906–07), "La tentative de contre-révolution de Juin-Juillet 1789," *Revue d'histoire moderne et contemporaine* 8, 5–34 and 649–78.

Castaldo, A. (1989), *Les méthodes de travail de la Constituante*, Paris: Presses Universitaires de France.

Chagny, R. (1988), "Printemps 89 ... ou comment les Dauphinois, sans y avoir été invités, ont exprimé leurs doléances," in V. Chomel (ed.), *Les débuts de la Révolution Française en Dauphiné*, Grenoble: Presses Universitaires de Grenoble, pp. 143–72.

Chernow, R. (2004), *Alexander Hamilton*, New York: Penguin.

Chernow, R. (2010), *George Washington*, New York: Penguin.

Chesterman, M. (2000), "Criminal trial juries in Australia," in N. Vidmar (ed.), *World Jury Systems*, Oxford: Oxford University Press, pp. 125–66.

Cho, S. and Kang, I. (2008), "Open primaries and crossover voting," paper presented at the 2008 meeting of the Midwest Political Science Association, Chicago, IL.

Christin, O. (1997), *La paix de religion*, Paris: Seuil.

Christin, O. (2009), "Putting faith to the ballot," Paper presented at a conference on Majority Decisions, Collège de France.

Claussen, C. and Røisland, Ø. (2010a), "A quantitative discursive dilemma," *Social Choice and Welfare* 35, 49–64.

Claussen, C. and Røisland, Ø. (2010b), "The discursive dilemma in monetary policy," Bank of Norway Working Paper no. 5.

Claverie, E. (1984), "De la difficulté de faire un citoyen: Les 'acquittements scandaleux' du jury dans la France provinciale du début du XIXᵉ siècle," *Études Rurales* 95–96, 143–66.

Cochin, A. (1979), *L'esprit du Jacobinisme*, Paris: Presses Universitaires de France.

Cohen, M. (2010), "Sincerity and reason-giving," *DePaul Law Review* 59, 1091–1150.

Coles, E. (1856), *History of the ordinance of 1787*, Philadelphia: Historical Society of Pennsylvania.

Comité National chargé de la publication des travaux préparatoires des institutions de la Vᵉ République (1987), *Documents pour server à l'histoire de l'élaboration de la constitution du 4 octobre 1958*, Paris: La Documentation Française.

Condorcet, Marquis de (1785), "Essai sur l'application de l'analyse à la probabilité des decision rendues à la pluralité des voix," in Condorcet, *Sur les élections*, Paris: Fayard, pp. 7–177.

Condorcet, Marquis de (1788), "Essai sur la constitution et les fonctions des assemblées provinciales," in Condorcet, *Sur les elections*, Paris: Fayard, pp. 273–435.

Condorcet, Marquis de (1789a), "On the need for the citizens to ratify the Constitution," in I. McLean and F. Hewitt (eds.), *Condorcet: Foundations of Social Choice and Political Theory*, Aldershot, England: Edward Elgar, 1994, pp. 271–80.

Condorcet, Marquis de (1789b), "Est-il utile de diviser une assemblée en plusieurs chambres," in Condorcet, *Oeuvres*, vol. IX, Paris, 1847, pp. 333–64.

Condorcet, Marquis de (1792), "Révision des travaux de la première legislature," in Condorcet, *Oeuvres*, vol. X, Paris, 1847, pp. 371–442.

Coniez, H. (2008), *Ecrire la démocratie*, Paris: Harmattan.

Connes, F. (2009), *La sécurité des systèmes de vote*, Thèse de droit, Université de Paris II.

Constant, B. (1815), *Principes de politique*, Paris: Eymery.

Coquille, G. (1789), "Comment on doit considerer les Etats, et quelle est la nature de leur pouvoir," in C. Mayer (ed.), *Des états généraux et autres assemblées nationales*, t. VII, Paris, pp. 285–96.

Courselle, D. (2005–06), "Struggling with jury secrecy, jury independence, and jury reform," *South Carolina Law Review* 57, 203–54.

Coutant, A. (2009), *1848, quand la République combattait la Démocratie*, Paris: Mare et Martin.

Cover, R. (1984), *Justice Accused*, New Haven, CT: Yale University Press.

Cowan, R. (1959), "Reorganization of federal Arkansas, 1862–65," *Arkansas Historical Quarterly* 18, 32–57.

Craig, G. (1981), *Germany 1866–1945*, Oxford: Oxford University Press.

Crawley, C. (1939), "French and English influences in the Cortes of Cadiz," *Cambridge Historical Journal* 6, 176–208.

Cromwell, O. (1845), *Letters and Speeches*, vol. 2, ed. T. Carlyle, New York: Wiley and Putnam.

Daly, G. (2004), "Jury secrecy: R v Mirza; R v Connor and Rollock," *International Journal of Evidence and Proof* 8, 184–90.

Damaska, M. (1997), *Evidence Law Adrift*, New Haven, CT: Yale University Press.

Dana, J., Cain, D., and Dawes, R. (2006), "What you don't know can't hurt me," *Organizational Behavior and Human Decision Processes* 100, 193–201.

Daudet, E. (1834), *Histoire de la Restoration*, Paris: Hachette.

Dawes, R. (1964), "Social selection based on multidimensional criteria," *Journal of Abnormal and Social Psychology* 68, 104–9.

Dawes, R. (1994), "Notes on the sampling of stimulus cases and the measurement of responses in research on juror decision making," in R. Hastie (ed.), *Inside the Juror: The Psychology of Jury Decision Making*, Cambridge: Cambridge University Press, pp. 225–28.

Dawes, R. M., Faust, D., and Meehl, P. E. (1989) "Clinical versus actuarial judgment," *Science* 243, 1668–674.

Debré, M. (1955), "Trois caractéristiques du système parlementaire français," *Revue Française de Science Politique* 5, 21–48.

De Briey, L. (2005), "Centripetalism in consociational democracy: The multiple proportional vote," Working Paper, Université Catholique de Louvain.

De Lolme, J. (1807), *The Constitution of England*, London.

DenBoer, G., ed. (1984), *The Documentary History of the First Federal Elections 1788–1790*, vol. 2, Madison: University of Wisconsin Press.

Descartes, R. (1637), *Discours de la méthode*.

Desposato, S. (2007), "How does vote buying shape the legislative arena?" in F. Schafer (ed.), *Elections for Sale*, Boulder, CO: Lynn Rienner, pp. 101–22.

Devine, D. et al. (2001), "Jury decision-making: 45 years of empirical research on deliberating groups," *Psychology, Public Policy, and Law* 7, 622–727.

Devons, E. (1965), "Serving as a juryman in Britain," *Modern Law Review* 28, 561–70.

Diamond, S., Casper, J., and Ostergren, L. (1989), "Blindfolding the jury," *Law and Contemporary Problems* 52, 247–68.

Dicey, A. V. (1915), *The Law of the Constitution*, 8th ed., reprint: Indianapolis, IN: Liberty Fund Classics, 2001.

Diermeier, D. and Gailmard, S. (2006), "Self-interest, inequality and entitlement in majoritarian decision-making," *Quarterly Journal of Political Science* 1, 327–50.

Dietrich, F. (2008), "The premises of Condorcet's Jury Theorem are not simultaneously satisfied," *Episteme* 5, 56–73.

Dijksterhuis, A. et al. (2006), On making the right choice: The deliberation-without-attention effect," *Science* 311, 1005–07.

Dijksterhuis, A. and Nordgren, L. (2006), "A theory of unconscious thought," *Perspectives on Psychological Science* 1, 95–109.

Dijksterthuis, A. and van Olden, Z. (2006), "On the benefits of thinking unconsciously," *Journal of Experimental Social Psychology* 42, 627–31.

Diller, P. (2008), "When Congress passes an intentionally unconstitutional law: The Military Commissions Act of 2006," *SMU Law Review* 61, 281–335.

Dixon, S. (2011), "From ceremonial to sexualities: A survey of scholarship on Roman marriage," in B. Rawson (ed.), *Families in the Greek and Roman Worlds*, London: Blackwell, pp. 245–61.

Donahue, J. and Wolfers, J. (2005), "Uses and abuses of empirical evidence in the death penalty debate," *Stanford Law Review* 58, 791–46.

Donovan, J. (2010), *Juries and the Transformation of Criminal Justice in France*, Chapel Hill: University of North Carolina Press.

Donovan, T. (2008), "The Limbaugh effect," *The Forum* 6(2), 1–8.

Douai, M. de (1813), *Répertoire universel et raisonné de jurisprudence*, Paris: Garnery.

Dover, K. (1994), *Greek Popular Morality in the Time of Plato and Aristotle*, Indianapolis, IN: Hackett.

Downs, A. (1957), *An Economic Theory of Democracy*, New York: Harper and Row.

Droz, J. (1860), *Histoire du règne de Louis XVI*, Paris: Renouard.

Dryzek, J. and List, C. (2003), "Social choice theory and deliberative democracy: A reconciliation," *British Journal of Political Science* 33, 1–28.

Duff, P. (2000), "The Scottish criminal jury," in N. Vidmar (ed.), *World Jury Systems*, Oxford: Oxford University Press, pp. 249–82.

Dummett, M. (1998), "The Borda count and electoral manipulation," *Social Choice and Welfare* 15, 287–96.

Dumont, E. (1832), *Souvenirs sur Mirabeau*, London: Bull.

Duquesnoy, A. (1894), *Journal sur l'Assemblée Constituante*, vol. I, Paris: Alphonse Picard

Durant, T. and Weintraub, M. (2011), "Winner-take-turns as a robust alternative to winner-take-all," Working Paper, Department of Economics, New York University.

Duverger, M. (1974), "Un gramme de démocratie," *Le Monde*, October 11.

ECHR 2010 = Judgment of the European Court of Human Rights in Taxquet v. Belgium, at www.menschenrechte.ac.at/orig/10_6/Taxquet.

Egret, J. (1942), *Les derniers Etats de Dauphiné*, Grenoble: Arthaud.

Egret, J. (1950), *La révolution des notables*, Paris: Armand Colin.

Egret, J. (1975), *Necker, ministre de Louis XVI*, Paris: Champion.

Eisenberg, T. and Johnson, S. (2004), "Implicit racial bias in death penalty lawyers," *DePaul Law Review* 53, 1539–56.

Elliot, J. (1836), *The Debates in the Several State Conventions, on the Adoption of the Federal Constitution*, Washington, DC: Printed for the Editor.

Ellis, R. and Wildavsky, A. (1989), *Dilemmas of Presidential Leadership*, New Brunswick, NJ: Transaction Books.

Ellsworth, P. (1989), "Are twelve heads better than one?" *Law and Contemporary Problems* 52, 207–24.

Elster, J. (1983), *Sour Grapes*, Cambridge: Cambridge University Press.

Elster, J. (1984), *Ulysses and the Sirens*, rev. ed., Cambridge: Cambridge University Press.

Elster, J. (1985), *Making Sense of Marx*, Cambridge: Cambridge University Press.

Elster, J. (1986), "The market and the forum," in J. Elster and A. Hylland (eds.), *Foundations of Social Choice Theory*, Cambridge: Cambridge University Press, pp. 103–32.

Elster, J. (1989a), *The Cement of Society*, Cambridge: Cambridge University Press.

Elster, J. (1989b), *Solomonic Judgments*, Cambridge: Cambridge University Press.

Elster, J. (1993), "Constitutional bootstrapping in Philadelphia and Paris," *Cardozo Law Review* 14, 549–76.

Elster, J. (1995), "Transition, constitution-making and separation in Czechoslovakia," *Archives Européennes de Sociologie* 36, 105–34.

Elster, J. (1999), *Alchemies of the Mind*, Cambridge: Cambridge University Press.

Elster, J. (1999–2000), "Arguing and bargaining in two constituent assemblies," *University of Pennsylvania Journal of Constitutional Law* 2, 345–421.

Elster, J. (2000), *Strong Feelings*, Cambridge, MA: MIT Press.

Elster, J. (2001), *Ulysses Unbound*, Cambridge: Cambridge University Press.

Elster, J. (2003). "Don't burn your bridges before you come to them," *Texas Law Review* 81, 1751–87.

Elster, J. (2004a), "Mimicking impartiality," in K. Dowding, R. Goodin, and C. Pateman (eds.), *Justice and Democracy*, Cambridge: Cambridge University Press, pp. 112–26.

Elster, J. (2004b), *Closing the Books*, Cambridge: Cambridge University Press.

Elster, J. (2006a), "Drawing a veil over equality," in C. Sypnowich (ed.), *The Egalitarian Conscience*, Oxford: Oxford University Press, pp. 36–55.

Elster, J. (2006b), "Altruistic behavior and altruistic motivations," in S.-C. Kolm and J. M. Ythier (eds.), *Handbook of the Economics of Giving, Altruism and Reciprocity*, vol. 1, Amsterdam: Elsevier, pp. 183–206.

Elster, J. (2006c), *Raison et Raisons*, Paris: Fayard.

Elster, J. (2007a), *Explaining Social Behavior*, Cambridge: Cambridge University Press.

Elster, J. (2007b), "The night of August 4 1789: A study in collective decision making," *Revue Européenne des sciences sociales* 45, 71–94.

Elster, J. (2009a), *Le désintéressement*, Paris: Seuil.

Elster, J. (2009b), *Alexis de Tocqueville: The First Social Scientist*, Cambridge: Cambridge University Press.

Elster, J. (2009c), "Urgency," *Inquiry* 52, 399–411.

Elster, J. (2009d), "Excessive ambitions," *Capitalism and Society* 4, 1–30.

Elster, J. (2010a), *L'irrationalité*, Paris: Seuil.

Elster, J. (2010b), "L"aveuglement volontaire chez Proust," *Cahiers de Littérature Française* IX–X, 55–68.

Elster, J. (2010c), "Emotional choice and rational choice," in P. Goldie (ed.), *Oxford Handbook of Philosophy of Emotion*, Oxford: Oxford University Press, pp. 263–81.

Elster, J. (2011), "The two great fears of 1789," *Social Science Information* 50, 317–29.

Elster, J. (2012), "Constitution-making and violence," *Journal of Legal Analysis* 4, 7–39.

Elster, J. and Roemer, J., eds. (1991), *Interpersonal Comparisons of Utility*, Cambridge: Cambridge University Press.

Ely, J. (1980), *Democracy and Distrust*, Cambridge, MA: Harvard University Press.

Emerson, T. (1955), "The doctrine of prior restraint," *Law and Contemporary Problems* 20, 648–71.

Eskridge, W. and Ferejohn, J. (2001), "Structuring lawmaking to reduce cognitive bias: A critical view," *Cornell Law Review* 87, 616–47.

Esmein, A. (1913), *A History of Continental Criminal Procedure*, Boston: Little, Brown.

Estlund, D. (2012), "Democracy counts," in H. Landemore and J. Elster (eds.), *Collective Wisdom*, Cambridge: Cambridge University Press, pp. 230–50.

Eule, J. (1987), "Temporal limits on the legislative mandate: Entrenchment and retroactivity," *American Bar Foundation Research Journal* 12, 380–460.

Eyck, F. (1968), *The Frankfurt Parliament 1848–49*, London: Macmillan.

Farrand, M. (1966), *Records of the Federal Convention*, New Haven, CT: Yale University Press.

Favoreu, L. (1984), "Le conseil constitutionnel et l'alternance," *Revue française de science politique* 34, 1002–29.

Fearon, J. (1998), "Deliberation as discussion," in J. Elster (ed.), *Deliberative Democracy*, Cambridge: Cambridge University Press, pp. 44–68.

Feer, R. (1966), "Shays's rebellion and the Constitution," *New England Quarterly* 42, 388–410.

Fehr, E. and Falk, A. (2002), "The psychological foundations of incentives," *European Economic Review* 46, 687–724.

Feldkamp, M. (1998), *Der Parlamentarische Rat 1948–1949*, Göttingen: Vandenhoek and Ruprecht.

Ferejohn, J. (2012), "Legislation, planning, deliberation," in H. Landemore and J. Elster (eds.), *Collective Wisdom*, Cambridge: Cambridge University Press, pp. 97–117.

Ferguson, E. (1961), *The Power of the Purse*, Chapel Hill: University of North Carolina Press.

Ferreres, V. (2004), "The consequences of centralizing constitutional review in a special court," *Texas Law Review* 82, 1705–36.

Ferrières, Marquis de (1932), *Correspondance Inédite*, Paris: Armand Colin.

Festinger, L. and Carlsmith, J. (1959), "Cognitive consequences of forced compliance," *Journal of Abnormal and Social Psychology* 58, 203–10.

Finkelman, P. 1996, "Slavery and the Constitutional Convention," in R. Beeman, S. Botein and E. Carter (eds.), *Beyond Confederation*, Chapel Hill: University of North Carolina Press, pp. 188–225.

Finley, M. (1983), *Politics in the Ancient World*, Cambridge: Cambridge University Press.

Finocchiaro, C. and Jenkins, J. (2008). "In search of killer amendments in the modern U.S. House," *Legislative Studies Quarterly* 33, 263–94.

Firth, C. H. (1891). *The Putney Debates*, London: The Historical Society.

Fischhoff, B. (1982), "Debiasing," in D. Kahneman., P. Slovic, and A. Tversky (eds.), *Judgment under Uncertainty*, Cambridge: Cambridge University Press, pp. 422–44.

Fishkin, J. et al. (2008), "Returning deliberative democracy to Athens: Deliberative polling for candidate selection," paper presented at the 2008 meeting of the American Political Science Association, Boston, MA.

Fishkin, J. et al. (2010), "Deliberative democracy in an unlikely place: Deliberative polling in China," *British Journal of Political Science* 40, 435–48.

Fitzsimmons, M. (1994), *The Remaking of France*, Cambridge: Cambridge University Press.

Flaig, E. (1993), "Die spartanische Abstimmung nach der Lautstärke," *Historia* 42, 139–60.

Fletcher, A. (1981), *The Outbreak of the English Revolution*, New York: New York University Press.

Fogarty J. (1997), "Reactance theory and patient noncompliance," *Social Science and Medicine* 45, 1277–88.

Føllesdal, D. (1979), "Some ethical aspects of recombinant DNA research," *Social Science Information* 18, 401–19.

Foner, E. (2010), *The Fiery Trial*, New York: Norton.

Fontaine, G. and Kiger, R. (1978), "The effects of defendant dress and supervision on judgment of simulated jurors," *Law and Human Behavior* 2, 63–71.

Forsyth, W. (1873), *History of Trial by Jury*, Jersey City: Lynn.

Fox, D., Gallón-Girado, G., and Stetson, A. (2010), "Lessons of the Colombian constitutional reform of 1991," in L. Miller (ed.), *Framing the State in Times of Transition*, Washington, DC: United States Institute of Peace Press, pp. 467–82.

Fox, J. and Stephenson, M. (2011), "The distributional effects of minority-protective judicial review," Working Paper, Harvard Law School.

Fraenkel, J. (2001), "The alternative vote system in Fiji," *Commonwealth and Comparative Politics* 39, 1–31.

Fraenkel, J. and Grofman, B. (2006), "Does the alternative vote foster moderation in ethnically divided societies?" *Comparative Political Studies* 39, 623–51.

Freedman, D. (2005), *Statistical Models*, Cambridge: Cambridge University Press.

FRUS = *Foreign Relations of the United States*, 1948: II and 1949: III, Washington, DC: Department of State.

Gabba, E. (1984), "The Collegia of Numa," *Journal of Roman History* 74, 81–86.

Garde, P. (2001), "The Danish jury," *International Review of Penal Law* 72, 87–120.

Garrett, B. (2011), *Convicting the Innocent*, Cambridge, MA: Harvard University Press.

Gauthier, P. (1994), "Les rois héllenistiques et les juges étrangers" *Journal des Savants* 2, 165–95.

Gerhardt, M. J. (2000), *The Federal Appointments Process*, Durham, NC: Duke University Press.

Gialdroni, S. (2009), "They are incorporated," paper presented at the Summer School of Università degli Studi di Roma Tre.

Giannetti, D. (2010), "Secret voting in the Italian parliament," paper presented at the conference "Scrutin secret et vote public, huis clos et débat ouvert," Collège de France.

Gibbon, E. (1995), *The History of the Decline and Fall of the Roman Empire*, London: Penguin.

Gigerenzer, G. and Goldstein, D. (1996), "Reasoning the fast and frugal way," *Psychological Review* 103, 65–69.

Gilbert, M., ed. (1986), *The Oxford Book of Legal Anecdotes*, Oxford: Oxford University Press.

Ginsburg, T. (2002), "Economic analysis and the design of constitutional courts," *Theoretical Inquiries in Law* 3, Article 3.

Ginsburg, T., Elkin, Z., and Blount, J. (2009), "Does the process of constitution-making matter?" *Annual Review of Law and Society* 5, 201–23.

Gneezy, U. and Rustichini, A. (2000), "Pay enough or don't pay at all," *Quarterly Journal of Economics* 115, 791–810.

Gobert, J. (1997), *Justice, Democracy and the Jury*, Brookfield, VT: Ashgate.

Goguel, F. (1963), "Le référendum du 28 octobre et les élections des 18–25 novembre 1962," *Revue Française de Science Politique* 13, 289–314.

Golay, J. (1958), *The Founding of the Federal Republic of Germany*, Chicago: University of Chicago Press.

Goldie, P., ed. (2010), *The Oxford Handbook of the Philosophy of Emotion*, Oxford: Oxford University Press.

Goldin, C. and Rouse, C. (2000), "Orchestrating impartiality," *American Economic Review* 90, 715–41.

Golding, J. and Long, D. (1998), "Forgetting: An integrative review," in J. Golding and C. MacLeod (eds.), *Intentional Forgetting*, Mahwah, NJ: Lawrence Erlbaum, pp. 59–102.

Goldstein, D. and Gigerenzer, G. (2002) "Models of ecological rationality: The recognition heuristic," *Psychological Review* 109, 75–90.

Goodsell, C. (1988), "The architecture of parliaments," *British Journal of Political Science* 18, 287–302.

Gordon, R. (1987), *The Structure of Emotions*, Cambridge: Cambridge University Press.

Gottschalk, L. and Maddox, M. (1969), *Lafayette in the French Revolution through the October Days*, Chicago: University of Chicago Press.

Government of Canada (1991), "The process for amending the constitution of Canada," *A Report of the Special Joint Committee of the Senate and the House of Commons*.

Grabbe, H. (1978), "Die deutsch-alliierte Kontroverse um den Grundgesetzentwurf im Frühjahr 1949," *Vierteljahrshefte fur Zeitgeschichte* 26, 393–418.

Grant, R. (2011), *Strings Attached: Untangling the Ethics of Incentives*, Princeton, NJ: Princeton University Press.

Green, T. (1985), *Verdict According to Conscience*, Chicago: University of Chicago Press.

Green, T. (1986), *Lectures on the Principles of Political Obligation*, Cambridge: Cambridge University Press.

Greenwald, A. and Krieger, L. (2006), "Implicit bias: Scientific foundations," *California Law Review* 94, 945–67.

Greenwald, A., McGhee, D., and Schwartz, J. (1998), "Measuring individual differences in implicit cognition: The Implicit Association Test," *Journal of Personality and Social Psychology* 74, 1464–80.

Griffin, M. (2000), *Nero*, New York: Routledge.

Grofman, B. and Feld, S. (1988), "Rousseau's general will," *American Political Science Review* 82, 567–76.

Grofman, B. and Feld, S. (1989), in D. Estlund et al., "Democratic theory and the public interest: Condorcet and Rousseau revisited," *American Political Science Review* 83, 1328–40.

Gross, S. and O'Brien, B. (2008), "Frequency and predictors of false conviction," *Journal of Empirical Legal Studies* 5, 927–62.

Grossman, S. and Stiglitz, J. (1980), "On the impossibility of informationally efficient markets," *American Economic Review* 70, 393–408.

Grunfeld, C. (1964), "Statutes," *Modern Law Review* 27, 682–704.

Guennifey, P. (1993), *Le nombre et la raison*, Paris: Editions de l'EHESS.

Guidi, M. (2010), "Jeremy Bentham, the French Revolution, and the political economy of representation (1788 to 1789)," *European Journal of the History of Political Thought*, 17, 579–605.

Guillaume, S. (2004), "Le 'cartel des non,'" *Parlement[s], Revue d'Histoire Politique*, Nº Hors Série 1, 45–64.

Gylfason, T. (2012), "From collapse to constitution," Working Paper, Department of Economics, University of Iceland.

Habermas, J. (1992), *Faktizität und Geltung*, Frankfurt a.m.: Suhrkamp.

Hahn, E. (1995), "The occupying powers and the constitutional reconstruction of Germany, 1945–1949," in E. Hahn et al., *Cornerstone of Democracy: The West German Grundgesetz 1949–1989*, Washington, DC: German Historical Institute, pp. 7–36.

Ham, J. and van den Bos, K. (2010), "On unconscious morality: The effects of unconscious thinking on moral decision making," *Social Cognition* 28, 74–83.

Ham, J., van den Bos, K., and van Doorn, E. (2009), "Lady justice thinks unconsciously: Unconscious thought can lead to more accurate justice judgments," *Social Cognition* 27, 509–21.

Hamilton, A. (1780), Letter of September 3 to James Duane, in P. Kurland and J. Lerner (eds.), *The Founders' Constitution*, Chicago: University of Chicago Press, vol. 1, ch. 5, document 2.

Hannan, J., Auchterlonie, M., and Holden, K., eds. (2000), *International Encyclopedia of Women's Suffrage*, Santa Barbara, CA: ABC-CLIO.

Hansen, M. (1991), *The Athenian Democracy in the Age of Demosthenes*, Oxford: Blackwell.

Harrington, J. (1977), "Oceana," in J. A. Pocock (ed.), *The Political Works of James Harrington*, Cambridge: Cambridge University Press.

Harris, R. (1986), *Necker and the French Revolution*, Lanham, MD: University Press of America.

Harris, W. (1997), *With Charity for All*, Lexington: University of Kentucky Press.

Hart, H. (1982), *Essays on Bentham*, Oxford: Oxford University Press.

Haslam, S. et al. (1998), "Inspecting the emperor's clothes: Evidence that random selection of leaders can enhance group performance," *Group Dynamics* 2, 168–84.

Hastie, R. (2008), "Conscious and nonconscious cognitive processes in jurors' decisions," in C. Engel and W. Singer (eds.), *Better than Conscious?* Cambridge, MA: MIT Press, pp. 371–90.

Hastie, R., Penrod, S., and Pennington, N. (1983), *Inside the Jury*, Cambridge, MA: Harvard University Press.

Haubrich, D. (2003), "September 11, anti-terror laws, and civil liberties," *Government and Opposition* 38, 3–28.

Hausman, D. (2011), *Preference, Value, Choice, and Welfare*, Cambridge: Cambridge University Press.

Henningsen, D. et al. (2004), "It's good to be leader: The influence of randomly and systematically selected leaders on decision-making groups," *Group Dynamics* 8, 62–76.

Hermann, B., Thöni, C., and Gächter, S. (2008), "Antisocial punishment across societies," *Science* 319, 1362–67.

Hoar, R. S. (1917), *Constitutional Conventions*, Boston: Little, Brown.

Hodge, C. (1986–87), "Three ways to lose a republic: The electoral politics of the Weimar SPD," *European History* 17, 165–93.

Hoeffel, J. (2005), "Risking the Eighth Amendment: Arbitrariness, juries, and discretion in capital cases," *Boston College Law Review* 46, 705–70.

Hoffrage, U. et al. (2000), "Representation facilitates reasoning," *Cognition* 84, 343–52.

Holland, R. (2006), "Improving criminal jury verdicts: Learning from the court-martial," *Journal of Criminal Law and Criminology* 97, 101–46.

Holmes, S. (2003), "Lineages of the rule of law," in J. Maravall and A. Przeworski (eds.), *Democracy and the Rule of Law*, Cambridge: Cambridge University Press, pp. 19–61.

Holton, W. (2004), "'From the labours of others': The war bonds controversy and the origins of the constitution in New England," *William and Mary Quarterly* 61, 271–316.

Holton, W. (2007), *Unruly Americans*, New York: Hill and Wang.

Horowitz, D. (2007), "Where have all the parties gone?" *Public Choice* 133, 13–23.

Horowitz, D. (2007–08), "Conciliatory institutions and constitutional processes in post-conflict states," *William and Mary Law Quarterly* 49, 1213–48.

Horowitz, I. (2007–08), "Jury nullification: An empirical perspective," *Northern Illinois University Law Review* 28, 425–51.

Horwitz, A. (2004–05), "Mixed signals and subtle cues: Jury independence and judicial appointment of the jury foreperson," *Catholic University Law Review* 54, 829–78.

Houtin, A., ed. (1916), *Les séances du clergé aux Etats Généraux de 1789*, Paris: Société de l'Histoire de la Révolution Française.

Hovland. C. et al. (1957), *The Order of Presentation in Persuasion*, New Haven, CT: Yale University Press.

Howard, B. (1904), "Trial by jury in Germany" *Political Science Quarterly* 19, 650–72.

Huber, E.R. (1978), *Deutsche Verfassungsgeschichte seit 1789*, vol. 5, Stuttgart: Kohlhammer.

Hume, D. (1742), "On the independency of Parliament," in Hume, *Essays: Moral, Political, and Literary*.

Hurst, H. (1990–91), "Judicial rotation in juvenile and family courts," *Juvenile and Family Court Journal* 42, 13–23.

Hyman, R. and Brough, I. (1975), *Social Values and Industrial Relations*, Oxford: Blackwell.

Ilovaïsky, O., ed. (1974), *Recueil de documents relatifs aux séances des Etats Généraux*, T.II.i, Paris: CNRS

Inoue, K. (1991), *MacArthur's Japanese Constitution*, Chicago: University of Chicago Press.

Isenberg, D. (1986), "Group polarization," *Journal of Personality and Social Psychology* 50, 1141–51.

Jackson, J. and Kovalev, N. (2006) "Lay Adjudication and Human Rights in Europe," *Columbia Journal of European Law* 13, 83–123.

Jackson, J., Quinn, K., and O'Malley, T. (1999). "The jury system in contemporary Ireland," *Law and Contemporary Problems* 62, 203–31.

Jacob, B. and Levitt, S. (2003), "Rotten apples," *Quarterly Journal of Economics* 118, 843–77.

Jaurès, J. (1968), *Histoire socialiste de la Révolution Française*, vol. 1, Paris: Editions Sociales.

Jedrzejewicz, W. (1982), *Pilsudski*, New York: Hippocrene Books.

Jensen, M. (1959), *The Articles of Confederation*, Madison: University of Wisconsin Press.

Jensen, M. and Becker, R., eds. (1976), *The Documentary History of the First Federal Elections, 1788–1790*, Madison: University of Wisconsin Press, vol. 1.

Jillson, C. (1988), *Constitution making: Conflict and consensus in the Federal Convention of 1787*, New York: Algora.

Jillson, C. and Wilson, R. (1994), *Congressional Dynamics: Structure, Coordination and Choice in the First American Congress 1774–1790*, Stanford, CA: Stanford University Press.

Johansen, L. (1977), "The theory of public goods: Misplaced emphasis?" *Journal of Public Economics* 7, 147–52.

Johansen, L. (1979), "The bargaining society and the inefficiency of bargaining," *Kyklos* 32, 497–522.

Jonakait, R. (2003), *The American Jury System*, New Haven, CT: Yale University Press.

Jones, G.W. (1985), "The Prime Minister's power," in A. King (ed.), *The British Prime Minister*, London: Macmillan, pp. 195–220.

Jones, R.V. (1978), *Most Secret War*, London: Penguin.

Jouanna, A. (1998), "Les temps des guerres de religion en France (1550–1598)," in A. Jouanna et al. (eds.), *Histoire et Dictionnaire des Guerres de Religion*, Paris: Laffont, pp. 3–445.

Joubert, J.-P. (1990), "1788 en Dauphiné," in R. Chagny (ed.), *Aux origines provinciales de la Révolution*, Grenoble: Presses Universitaires de Grenoble, pp. 344–59.

Jourdan, A. (2006), *La Révolution, une exception française?* Paris: Flammarion.

Kahneman, D. (2011), *Thinking, Fast and Slow*, New York: Farrar, Straus and Giroux.

Kahneman, D. and Tversky, A. (1982), "The simulation heuristics," in D. Kahneman, P. Slovic, and A. Tversky (eds.), *Judgment under Uncertainty*, Cambridge: Cambridge University Press, pp. 201–09.

Kahneman, D. and Tversky, A. (1995), "Conflict resolution: A cognitive perspective," in K. Arrow et al. (eds.), *Barriers to Conflict Resolution*, New York: Norton, pp. 44–60.

Kalven, H. (1958), "The jury, the law, and the personal injury damage award," *Ohio State Law Journal* 19, 158–78.

Kalven, H. and Zeisel, H. (1966), *The American Jury*, Chicago: University of Chicago Press.

Kalyvas, S. (1996), *The Rise of Christian Democracy*, Ithaca, NY: Cornell University Press.

Kant. I. (1764), "Versuch über die Krankheiten des Kopfes," in Kant, *Gesammelten Werken* (Akademie-Ausgabe) II, pp. 257–71.

Kant, I. (1790), *Critique of Judgment*, Cambridge: Cambridge University Press, 2000.

Kant, I. (1797), "The metaphysics of morals," in Kant, *Practical Philosophy*, Cambridge: Cambridge University Press, 1996.

Kant, I. (1798), "Conflict of faculties," in Kant, *Religion and Rational Theology*, Cambridge: Cambridge University Press, 1996.

Karotkin, D. and Paroush, J. (2003), "Optimal committee size," *Social Choice and Welfare* 20, 429–41.

Kassin, S. and Studebaker, C. (1998), "Instructions to disregard the jury," in J. Golding and C. MacLeod (eds.), *Intentional Forgetting*, Mahwah, NJ: Lawrence Erlbaum, pp. 413–34.

Kassin, S. and Wrightsman, L. (1988), *The American Jury on Trial*, Bristol, PA: Taylor and Francis.

Katz, D. and Allport F. (1931), *Student Attitudes*, Syracuse, NY: Craftsman.

Kemp, B. (1965), *King and Commons 1650–1832*, London: Macmillan.

Kerr, N. and Bray, R. (2005), "Simulation, realism, and the study of the jury," in N. Brewer and K. Williams (eds.), *Psychology and Law*, New York: Guilford Press, pp. 322–64.

Kerr, N. and MacCoun, R. (1985), "The effects of jury size and polling method on the process and product of jury deliberation," *Journal of Personality and Social Psychology* 48, 349–63.

Kerr, N., Nerenz, D., and Herrick, D. (1979), "Role playing and the study of jury behavior," *Sociological Methods and Research* 7, 337–55.

Kershaw, I. (1998), *Hitler 1889–1936*, New York: Norton.

Kerwin, J. and Shaffer, D. (1994), "Mock jurors versus mock juries," *Personality and Social Psychology Bulletin* 20, 153–62.

Kessel, P. (1969), *La nuit du 4 août 1789*, Paris: Arthaud.

Ketcham, R. (1971), *James Madison*, Newtown, CT: American Political Biogaphy Press.

Keyssar, A. (2000), *The Right to Vote*, New York: Basic Books.

King, N. (1996a), "Silencing jury nullification inside the jury room and outside the courtroom," *University of Chicago Law Review* 65, 433–500.

King, N. (1996b), "Nameless justice," *Vanderbilt Law Review* 49, 123–60.

Kline, M.-J. (1978), *Gouverneur Morris and the New Nation, 1775–1788*, New York: Arno Press.

Kolarova, R. and Dimitrov, D. (1996), "The roundtable talks in Bulgaria," in J. Elster (ed.), *The Roundtable Talks and the Breakdown of Communism*, Chicago: University of Chicago Press, pp. 178–212.

Konopczyński, L. (1930), *Le liberum veto: Etude sur le développement du principe majoritaire*, Paris: Champion.

Kornhauser, L. and Sager, L. (1986), "Unpacking the Court," *Yale Law Journal* 96, 82–117

Kornhauser, L. and Sager, L. (1993), "The one and the many," *California Law Review* 81, 1–59.

Kruger, J. and Dunning, D. (1999), "Unskilled and unaware of it," *Journal of Personality and Social Psychology* 77, 1121–34.

Kruman, M. (1997), *Between Authority and Liberty: State Constitution Making in Revolutionary America*, Chapel Hill: University of North Carolina Press.

Kugler, M. and Rosenthal, H. (2005), "Checks and balances: An assessment of the institutional separation of political powers," in A. Alesina (ed.), *Institutional Reforms: The Case of Colombia*, Cambridge, MA: MIT Press, pp. 75–102.

Lally-Tolendal, T.-G. (1790), *Deuxième lettre à ses commettans*, Paris: Desenne.

Landemore, H. and Elster, J., eds. (2012), *Collective Wisdom*, Cambridge: Cambridge University Press.

Lang, A. (2007), "But is it for real? The British Columbia's citizen assembly as a model of state-sponsored citizen empowerment," *Politics and Society* 35, 35–69.

Langbein, J. (1977–78), "The criminal trial before the lawyers," *University of Chicago Law Review* 45, 263–316.

Langbein, J. (1981), "Mixed court and jury court," *American Bar Foundation Research Journal* 6, 195–220.

Langbein, J. (2003), *The Origins of Adversary Criminal Trial*, Oxford: Oxford University Press.

Lange, A. et al. (2010), "On the self-interested use of equity in international climate negotiations," *European Economic Review* 54, 359–75.

Langford, P. (1991), *Public Life and the Propertied Englishman, 1698–1798*, Oxford: Oxford University Press.

Lanni, A. and Vermeule, A. (2012), "Constitutional design in the ancient world," *Stanford Law Review* 64, 907–50.

Larson, E. (2011), *In the Garden of Beasts*, New York: Crown.

Lawson, S. (1990), "The myth of cultural homogeneity and its implications for chiefly power and politics in Fiji," *Comparative Studies in Society and History* 32, 795–821.

Lebègue, E. (1910), *Thouret*, Paris: Alcan.

LeDoux, J. (1996), *The Emotional Brain*, New York: Simon and Schuster.

Lee, R. (1989), "Equal protection and a deaf person's right to serve as a juror," *Review of Law and Social Change* 17, 81–114.

Leeman, L. and Mares, I. (2011), "From 'open secrets' to the secret ballot," Working Paper, Department of Political Science, Columbia University.

Lefebvre, G. (1963), *Etudes sur la Révolution Française*, Paris: Presses Universitaires de France.

Lefebvre, G. (1988), *La grande peur de 1789*, Paris: Armand Colin.

Lefebvre, G. (1989), *La Révolution Française*, Paris: Presses Universitaires de France.

Lehmberg, S. (1970), *The Reformation Parliament*, Cambridge: Cambridge University Press.

Leib, E. (2008), "A comparison of criminal jury decision rules in democratic countries," *Ohio State Journal of Criminal Law* 5, 629–44.

Lempert, R. and Salzburg, S. (1977), *A Modern Approach to Evidence*, St. Paul, MN: West Publishing.

Lendon, J. (2001), "Voting by shouting in Sparta," in E. Tylawski and C. Weiss (eds.), *Essays in Honor of Gordon Williams*, New Haven, CT: Henry Schwab, pp. 169–75.

Lenowitz, J. (2007), "Rejected by the people: Failed U.S. state constitutional conventions in the 1960s and 70s," Department of Political Science, Columbia University.

Le Pillouer, A. (2003), *Le pouvoir non-constituant des assemblées constituantes*, Paris: Dalloz-Sirey.

Levinson, S. (1993), Review of Perry (1991), *Virginia Law Review* 79, 717–39.

Levy, D. and Peart, S. (2002), "Galton's two papers on voting as robust estimation," *Public Choice* 113, 357–65.

Levy, E. (2003), *Sparte*, Paris: Seuil.

Lewis, M., Haviland-Jones, J., and Barrett, L., eds. (2007), *Handbook of Emotions*, 3rd ed., New York: Guilford Press.

Lieberman, J. and Sales, B. (1997), "What social science teaches us about the jury instruction process," *Psychology, Public Policy, and Law* 3, 589–644.

Lintott, A. (1999), *The Constitution of the Roman Republic*, Oxford: Oxford University Press.

List, C. et al. (2007), "Deliberation, single-peakedness and the possibility of deliberative democracy," Working Paper, London School of Economics.

List, C. and Pettit, P. (2011), *Group Agency*, Oxford: Oxford University Press.

Little, E. (2000), "Envy and jealousy: A study of separation of powers and judicial review," *Hastings Law Journal* 52, 47–121.

Lloyd-Bostock, S. and Thomas, C. (2000), "The continuing decline of the English jury," in N. Vidmar (ed.), *World Jury Systems*, Oxford: Oxford University Press, pp. 52–91.

Lock, F. (1998), *Edmund Burke 1730–1784*, Oxford: Oxford University Press.

Locke, J. (1979), *An Essay Concerning Human Understanding*, Oxford: Oxford University Press.

Loewenstein, G. and Schkade, D. (1999), "Wouldn't it be nice? Predicting future feelings," in D. Kahneman, E. Diener, and N. Schwartz (eds.), *Well-Being*, New York: Russell Sage, pp. 85–105.

Loizides, N. and Keskiner, E. (2004), "The aftermath of the Annan plan referendums: Cross-voting moderation for Cyprus?" *Southeast European Politics* 5, 158–71.

Lopes, L. (1993), "Two conceptions of the juror," in R. Hastie (ed.), *Inside the Juror: The Psychology of Jury Decision Making*, Cambridge: Cambridge University Press, pp. 255–62.

López-Guerra, C. (2011a), "The enfranchisement lottery," *Politics, Philosophy and Economics* 10, 211–33.

López-Guerra, C. (2011b), "Enfranchisement and constitution-making," unpublished manuscript.

Lordos, A., Kaymak, E., and Tocci. N. (2009), *A People's Peace in Cyprus*, Brussels: Centre for European Policy Studies.

Lovejoy, A. (1961), *Reflections on Human Nature*, Baltimore, MD: Johns Hopkins University Press.

Loyrette, J. and Gaillot, L. (1982–83), "The French nationalizations," *George Washington Journal of International Law and Economics* 17, 17–62.

Luchaire, F. (1974), "Le Conseil Constitutionnel et la protection des droits et libertés des citoyens," in *Mélanges Waline*, Paris: LGDJ, vol. 2, pp. 563–74.

Luchins, A. (1957), "Experimental attempts to minimize the impact of first impressions," in C. Hovland et al., *The Order of Presentation in Persuasion*, New Haven, CT: Yale University Press, pp. 62–75.

Lynd, S. (2009), *Class Conflict, Slavery, and the United States Constitution*, Cambridge: Cambridge University Press.

MacCunn, J. (1913), *The Political Philosophy of Burke*, New York: Longmans.

MacDowell, D. (1978), *The Law in Classical Athens*, Ithaca, NY: Cornell University Press.

Mackie, G. (2003), *Democracy Defended*, Cambridge: Cambridge University Press.

Magnette, P. (2004), "La convention européenne," *Revue Française de Science Politique* 54, 5–42.

Magnette, P. and Nicolaïdis, K. (2004), "The European Convention," *West European Politics* 27, 381–404.

Maier, Pauline (2010), *Ratification: Americans Debate the Constitution*, New York: Simon and Schuster.

Maier, Philippe (2010), "How Central Banks take decisions," in P. L. Siklos, M. T. Bohl, and M. E. Wohar (eds.), *Challenges in Central Banking*, Cambridge: Cambridge University Press, Cambridge, pp. 320–56.

Majone, G. (1989), *Evidence, Argument and Persuasion in the Policy Process*, New Haven, CT: Yale University Press.

Manin, B. (1997), *The Principles of Representative Government*, Cambridge: Cambridge University Press.

Marion, M. (1923), *Dictionnaire des institutions de la France aux XVIIe et XVIIIe siècles*, Paris: Picard

Markovitz, A. (2000–01), "Jury secrecy during deliberations," *Yale Law Journal* 110, 1493–1530.

Marsh, D. (1992), *The Bundesbank*, London: Mandarin.

Marshall, G. (1986), *Constitutional Conventions*, Oxford: Oxford University Press.

Marx, K. (1967), *Capital*, vol. 1, New York: International Publishers.

Masselin, J. (1835), *Journal des Etats Généraux de Tours*, Paris: Imprimerie Royale.

Mathiez, A. (1898), "Etude critique sur les journées des 5 & 6 octobre 1789," *Revue Historique* 67, 241–84.

Matthews, D. (1973), *US Senators and Their World*, New York: Norton.

McAdams, A. (1996), "The Honecker trial: The East German past and the German future," *Review of Politics* 58, 53–80.

McDonald, F. (1982), *We the People: The Economic Origins of the Constitution*, New Brunswick, NJ: Transaction Books.

McGuire, R. (2003), *To Form a More Perfect Union*, Oxford: Oxford University Press.

McLaughlin, A. (1905), *The Confederation and the Constitution*, New York: Collier.

McLean, I. and Hewitt, F. (1994), "Introduction" to *Condorcet: Foundations of Social Choice and Political Theory*, Northampton, MA: Edward Elgar.

Meade, E. and Stasavage, D. (2008), "Publicity of debate and the incentive to dissent," *Economic Journal* 118, 695–717.

Melilli, K. (1995–96), "*Batson* in practice," *Notre Dame Law Review* 71, 447–504.

Merkl, P. (1963), *Origin of the West German Republic*, Oxford: Oxford University Press.

Merleau-Ponty, M. (1945), *Phénoménologie de la perception*, Paris: Gallimard.

Michelet, J. (1998), *Histoire de la Révolution Française*, Paris: Robert Laffont.

Michels, A. (1967), *The Calendar of the Roman Republic*, Princeton, NJ: Princeton University Press.

Milanovic, B., Lindert, P., and Williamson, J. (2011), "Pre-industrial inequality," *Economic Journal* 121, 255–72.

Miley, G. (2012), "Saudi university policy: Overvalued rankings," *Science* 335, 1041–42.

Miller, D. (1999), "The norm of self-interest," *American Psychologist* 54, 1053–60.

Miller, D. and McFarlane, C. (1987), "Pluralistic ignorance," *Journal of Personality and Social Psychology* 53, 298–305.

Miller, L. (2010), "Designing constitution-making processes," in L. Miller (ed.), *Framing the State in Times of Transition*, Washington, DC: United States Institute of Peace Press, pp. 601–65.

Miller, V. (2002), "The Laeken Declaration and the Convention on the Future of Europe," London: House of Commons Research Paper 02/14.

Miller, W. (1996), *Arguing about Slavery*, New York: Knopf.

Mirabeau, Comte de (1851), "Note pour la Cour du 23 décembre 1790," in A. de Bacourt (ed.), *Correspondance entre le comte de Mirabau et le comte de la Marck*, Brussels: Pagny.

Monselet, C. (1853), *Histoire anecdotique du tribunal révolutionnaire*, Paris: Giraud et Dagneau.

Montaigne, M. de (1991), *Essays*, London: Allen Lane.

Moore, R. and Robinson, D. (2002), *Partners for Democracy*, Oxford: Oxford University Press.

Moreau, B. (1995), *Voter en 1789*, Paris: Publisud.

Morris, J. (2003), "The anonymous accused: Protecting defendants' rights in high-profile criminal cases," *Boston College Law Review* 44, 901–46.

Moses, R. (2009) "Scratch the juror's itch – the defender's role in creating a fair deliberative process," at http://juryargument.homestead.com/Sample4.html.

Mousnier, R. (2005), *Les institutions de la monarchie absolue*, Paris: Presses Universitaires de France.

Mueller, D. (2003), *Public Choice III*, Cambridge: Cambridge University Press.

Mukhopadhaya, K. (2003), "Jury size and the free rider problem," *Journal of Law, Economics and Organization* 19, 24–44.

Müller, I. (1991), *Hitler's Justice*, Cambridge, MA: Harvard University Press.

Muthoo, A. (2000), "A non-technical introduction to bargaining theory," *World Economics* 1, 145–65.

Nagel, T. (1991), *Equality and Partiality*, Oxford: Oxford University Press.

Nash, J. (2003), "A context sensitive voting protocol paradigm for multimember courts," *Stanford Law Review* 56, 75–159.

Necheles, R. (1974), "The curés in the Estates General of 1789," *Journal of Modern History* 46, 425–44.

Necker, J. (1791), Sur l'Administration de M. Necker par lui-même, in Necker, *Oeuvres Complètes*, Paris 1821, vol. 6.

Needham, J. (1956), *Science and Civilization in China*, vol. II, Cambridge: Cambridge University Press.

Nemeth, C. et al. (2004), "The liberating role of conflict in group creativity," *European Journal of Social Psychology* 34, 365–74.

Nisbett, R. and Ross, L. (1980), *Human Inference*, Upper Saddle River, NJ: Prentice Hall.

Nooteboom, B. 1999 "The triangle: Roles of the go-between," in S. M. Gabbay and R. Leenders (eds.), *Corporate Social Capital*, Dordrecht: Kluwer, pp. 341–55.

Note (1983), "Public disclosures of jury deliberations," *Harvard Law Review* 96, 886–906.

Note (2005), "Trumping the race card: Permitting criminal defendants to remain anonymous and absent from trials to eliminate racial jury bias," *Georgetown Journal of Legal Ethics* 18 (2005), 1150–60.

Novak, S. (2011), *La prise de décision au Conseil de l'union européenne*, Paris: Dalloz.

Novick, P. (1988), *That Noble Dream: The 'Objectivity' Question and the American Historical Profession*, Cambridge: Cambridge University Press.

Nugent, D. (1974), *Ecumenism in the Age of the Reformation: The Colloque of Poissy*, Cambridge, MA: Harvard University Press.

Ober, J. (1989), *Mass and Elite in Democratic Athens*, Princeton, NJ: Princeton University Press.

Ogloff, J. and Rose, V. (2005), "The comprehension of judicial instructions," in N. Brewer and K. Williams (eds.), *Psychology and Law*, New York: Guilford Publications, 407–44.

Ohanian, H. (2008), *Einstein's Mistakes*, New York: Norton.

OIV (1994) = Organisation internationale de la vigne et du vin, *Standard for International Wine competitions*.

Oldham, J. (1983), "The origins of the special jury," *University of Chicago Law Review* 50, 137–221.

Olivetti, M. (2004), "Foreign influences on the Italian constitutional system," paper presented at the 6th World Congress of the International Association of Constitutional Law, Santiago, Chile.

Olivier-Martin, F. (2010), *Histoire du droit français*, Paris: CNRS Editions.

Ostwald. M. (1986), *From Popular Sovereignty to the Sovereignty of Law*, Berkeley: University of California Press.

Page, S. (2007), *The Difference*, Princeton, NJ: Princeton University Press

Page, S. (2010), *Diversity and Complexity*, Princeton, NJ: Princeton University Press

Paine, T. (1791), *The Rights of Man*.

Palley, C. (1966), *The Constitutional History of Southern Rhodesia*, Oxford: Oxford University Press.

Parfit, D. (2011), *On What Matters*, vol. 1, Oxford: Oxford University Press.

Patterson, S. (1972), "Party opposition in the legislature," *Polity* 4, 344–66.

Pehe, J. (1993), "The waning popularity of the Czech Parliament," *Radio Free Europe*, November 12.

Perelman, C. and Olbrechts-Tyteca (1969), *The New Rhetoric*, Notre Dame, IN: University of Notre Dame Press.

Perry, H. (1991), *Deciding to Decide: Agenda Setting in the United States Supreme Court*, Cambridge, MA: Harvard University Press.

Pettit, P. (2001), "Deliberative democracy and the discursive dilemma," *Philosophical Issues* (supplement to *Nous* 11), 268–99.

Peyrefitte, A. (1994), *C'était de Gaulle*, vol. I, Paris: Fayard.

Picot, G. (1888), *Histoire des Etats Généraux*, Paris.

Pierre, E. (1893), *Traité de droit politique électoral et parlementaire*, Paris: Librairies-Imprimeries Réunies.

Pitkin, H. (1967), *The Concept of Representation*, Berkeley: University of California Press.

Poggi, I. (2007), "Enthusiasm and its contagion: Nature and function," in A. Paiva, R. Prada, and R. W. Picard (eds.), *Affective Computing and Intelligent Interaction*, Berlin: Springer, pp. 410–21.

Poisson, S.-D. (1837), *Recherches sur la probabilité des jugements en matière criminelle et en matière civile*, Paris: Bachelier.

Pole, J. R. (1966), *Political Representation in England and the Origins of the American Republic*, Berkeley: University of California Press.

Pole, J. R. (1983), *The Gift of Government*, Atlanta: University of Georgia Press.

Posey, A. and Wrightsman, L. (2005), *Trial Consulting*, Oxford: Oxford University Press.

Posner, R. (1988), "The Constitution as an economic document," *George Washington Law Review* 56, 4–49.

Posner, R. (2005), *Catastrophe, Risk, and Response*, Oxford: Oxford University Press.

Powe, L. (2010), "The obscenity bargain," *Journal of Supreme Court History* 35, 166–76.

Procès-verbal (1789) = *Procès-verbal des conférences sur la vérification des pouvoirs*, Paris.

Proust, M. (1988a), A l'ombre des jeunes filles en fleurs, in *A la recherche du temps perdu*, vol. II, Paris: Gallimard.

Proust, M. (1988b), Sodome et Gomorrhe, in *A la recherche du temps perdu*, vol. III, Paris: Gallimard.

Przeworski, A. (1991), *Democracy and Markets*, Cambridge: Cambridge University Press.

Przeworski, A. (2009), "Conquered or granted? A history of suffrage extensions," *British Journal of Political Science* 39, 291–321.

Przeworski, A. (2010), *Democracy and the Limits of Self-Government*, Cambridge: Cambridge University Press.

Przeworski, A. and Limongi, F. (1993), "Political regimes and economic growth," *Journal of Economic Perspectives* 7, 51–69.

Rachlinski, J. et al. (2008), "Does unconscious racial bias affect trial judges?" *Notre Dame Law Review* 84, 1195–245.

Rakove, J. (1979), *The Beginning of National Politics*, New York: Knopf.

Randall, L. (2011), *Knocking on Heaven's Door*, New York: Ecco.

Rapaczynski, A. (1991), "Constitutional politics in Poland," *University of Chicago Law Review* 58, 595–632.

Rapine, F. (1651), *Recueil très exact et curieux de tout ce qui s'est passé de singulier & memorable en l'Assemblée générale des Etats tenus à Paris en l'année 1614 & particulierement en chacune séance du tiers ordre*, Paris.

Rastgoufard, B. (2003), "Pay attention to that green curtain: Anonymity and the courts, *Case Western Reserve Law Review* 53, 1009–40.

Rawls, J. (1971), *A Theory of Justice*, Cambridge, MA: Harvard University Press.

Raz, J. (1979), *The Authority of Law*, Oxford: Oxford University Press.

Reilly, B. (2001), *Democracy in Divided Societies*, Cambridge: Cambridge University Press.

Reilly, B. (2011), "Centripetalism," in S. Wolff and C. Yakinthou (eds.), *Conflict Management in Divided Societies*, London: Routledge, pp. 57–65.

Report of the City Commissioners of the City of Boston (1895), vol. 26, Boston: Rockwell and Churchill.

Rhodes, P. J. (2003), "Sessions of *nomothetai* in fourth-century Athens," *Classical Quarterly* 53, 124–29.

Richards, C. (1994), *The Founders and the Classics*, Cambridge, MA: Harvard University Press.

Richards, L. (2002), *Shays's Rebellion*, Philadelphia: University of Pennsylvania Press.

Ricoeur, P. (1969), *Le conflit des interprétations*, Paris: Seuil.

Riker, W. (1962), *The Theory of Political Coalitions*, New Haven, CT: Yale University Press.

Riker, W. (1982), *Liberalism against Populism*, San Francisco: Freeman.

Riker, W. (1984), "The heresthetics of constitution-making: The Presidency in 1787," *American Political Science Review* 78, 1–16.

Riker, W. (1987), "The lessons of 1787," *Public Choice* 55, 5–34.

Riker, W. and Brams, S. (1973), "The paradox of vote trading," *American Political Science Review* 67, 1235–47.

Risinger, D. (2004), "Unsafe verdicts," *Houston Law Review* 41, 1281–1336.

Risinger, D. (2007), "Innocents convicted," *Journal of Criminal Law and Criminology* 97, 761–806.

Ritov, I. and Baron, J. (1990), "Reluctance to vaccinate: Omission bias and ambiguity," *Journal of Behavioral Decision Making* 3, 263–77.

Robertson, G. (1993), *Freedom, the Indivdual, and the Law*, London: Penguin.

Roll, C. (1969), "We, some of the people: Apportionment in the thirteen state conventions ratifying the Constitution," *Journal of American History* 56, 21–40.

Rosanvallon, P. (1992), *Le sacre du citoyen*, Paris: Gallimard.

Rosen, F. (1982), *Jeremy Bentham and Representative Democracy*, Oxford: Oxford University Press.

Ross, L. (1995), "Reactive devaluation in negotiation and conflict resolution," in K. Arrow et al. (eds.), *Barriers to Conflict Resolution*, New York: Norton 1995, pp. 27–42.

Rossiter, C. (1987), *The Grand Convention*, New York: Norton.

Roth, A. Murnighan, J and Schoumaker, F. (1998), "The deadline effect in bargaining: Some experimental evidence," *American Economic Review* 78, 806–23.

Roussel, E. (2002), *Charles de Gaulle*, Paris: Gallimard.

Rubenfeld, J. (2001), *Freedom and Time*, New Haven, CT: Yale University Press.

Ruprecht, C. (1997), "Are verdicts, too, like sausages?" *University of Pennsylvania Law Review* 146, 217–67.

Russell. P. (1993), *Constitutional Odyssey*, 2nd ed., Toronto: University of Toronto Press.

Saari, D. (1995), *The Basic Geometry of Voting*, Berlin: Springer.

Saint-Priest, Comte de (1929), *Mémoires*, vol. 1, Paris: Calman-Lévy.

Sajó, A. (2011), *Constitutional Sentiments*, New Haven, CT: Yale University Press.

Saks, M. J. (1997), "What do experiments tell us about how juries (should) make decisions," *Southern California Interdisciplinary Law Journal* 6, 1–54.

Saleilles, R. (1895), "The development of the present constitution of France," *Annals of the American Academy of Political and Social Science* 6, 1–78.

Sander, D. and Scherer, K., eds. (2009), *Oxford Companion to Emotion and the Affective Sciences*, Oxford University Press.

Sanders, A., Young, R., and Burton, M. (2010), *Criminal Justice*, Oxford: Oxford University Press.

Satterthwaite, M. (1973), *The Existence of a Strategy Proof Voting Procedure*, Ph.D. Dissertation, University of Wisconsin.

Scanlon, T. (1975), "Preference and urgency," *Journal of Philosophy* 72, 655–669.

Schauer, F. (2010), "When and how (if at all) does law constrain official action?" *Georgia Law Review* 44, 769–801.

Scheflin, A. and van Dyke, J. (1979–80), "Jury nullification," *Law and Contemporary Problems* 43, 51–115.

Schmitt, C. (2008), *Constitutional Theory*, Durham, NC: Duke University Press.

Schofield, P. (2006), *Utility and Democracy: The Political Thought of Jeremy Bentham*, Oxford: Oxford University Press.

Schwartz, E. (2006), "Secret ballot or a show of hands?" *Lawyers Weekly USA*, February 27.

Schwartz, H. (2000), *Constitutional Justice in Central and Eastern Europe*, Chicago: University of Chicago Press.

Seidman, A. (1945), "Church and State in the early years of the Massachusetts Bay Colony," *New England Historical Review* 18, 211–33.

310

References

Selth, J. (1997), *Firm Heart and Capacious Mind*, Lanham, MD: University Press of America.

Shoemaker, P. (1982), "The expected utility model," *Journal of Economic Literature* 20, 529–63.

Shmooa, S. (1990), "Minority status in an ethnic democracy," *Ethnic and Racial Studies* 13, 389–413.

Sides, J., Cohen, J., and Citrin, J. (2002), "The causes and consequences of crossover voting in the 1998 California elections," in B. Cain and E. Gerber (eds.), *Voting at the Fault Line: California's Experiment with the Blanket Primary*, Berkeley: University of California Press, pp. 77–106.

Siegismund, E. (2000), "The function of honorary judges in criminal proceedings in Germany," Presentation to the 120th International Senior Seminar, Berlin, pp. 114–25.

Sieyes, Abbé de (1789), "Vues sur les moyens d'exécution dont les Représentans de la France pourront disposer en 1789," in *Oeuvres de Sieyes*, t. I, Paris: Edhis 1989.

Simmel, G. (1908), *Soziologie*, Berlin: Duncker and Humblot.

Simon, D. (2004), "A third view of the black box," *University of Chicago Law Review* 71, 511–86.

Sinnott-Armstrong, W., Young, L., and Cushman, F. (2010), "Moral intuitions," in J. Doris et al. (eds.), *The Moral Psychology Handbook*, Oxford: Oxford University Press, pp. 246–72.

Skidelsky, R. (2000), *John Maynard Keynes: Fighting for Britain 1937–1946*, London: Macmillan.

Skinner, G. W. (1975), "Cities and the hierarchy of local systems," in G. W. Skinner (ed.), *The City in Late Imperial China*, Stanford, CA: Stanford University Press, pp. 275–364.

Smith, J. (2992), *Lucius Clay*, New York: Henry Holt.

Smullyan, R. (1980), *This Book Needs No Title*, Englewood Cliffs, NJ: Prentice-Hall.

Spevack, E. (2002), *Allied Control and German Freedom*, New Brunswick, NJ: Transaction.

Spranca, M., Minsk, E., and Baron, J. (1989), "Omission and commission in judgment and choice," *Journal of Experimental Social Psychology* 27, 76–105.

Staël, Mme de (2000), *Considérations sur la Révolution Française*, Paris: Tallandier.

Stasavage, D. (2010), "When distance mattered," *American Political Science Review* 104, 625–43.

Staveley, E. (1972), *Greek and Roman Voting and Elections*, Ithaca, NY: Cornell University Press.

Steen, S. (1951), *1814*, Oslo: Cappelen.

Stephen, J. (1883), *A History of the Criminal Law of England*, London: Macmillan.

Stokke, T. (2011), "The Scandinavian system of labor mediation and arbitration," paper prepared for a conference on the Neutral Third Party in Conflict Resolution, Collège de France.

Stone, A. (1992), *The Birth of Judicial Politics in France*, Oxford: Oxford University Press.

Storing, H. (1981), *The Complete Anti-Federalist*, Chicago: University of Chicago Press.

Stratmann, T. (1997), "Logrolling," in D. Mueller (ed.), *Perspectives on Public Choice*, Cambridge: Cambridge University Press 1997, pp. 322–41.

Sunstein, C. (1992), "Neutrality in constitutional law," *Columbia Law Review* 92, 1–52.

Sunstein, C. (1995), "Incompletely theorized agreements," *Harvard Law Review* 108, 1733–72.

Sunstein, C. et al., eds. (2002), *Punitive Damages*, Chicago: University of Chicago Press.

Surowiecki, J. (2005), *The Wisdom of Crowds*, New York: Anchor Books.

Sydnor, C. (1952), *Gentlemen Freeholders*, Chapel Hill: University of North Carolina Press.

Tackett, T. (1996), *Becoming a Revolutionary*, Princeton, NJ: Princeton University Press.

Tanchoux, P. (2004), *Les procédures et pratiques électorales en France*, Paris: Comité des travaux historiques et scientifiques.

Taubman, W. (2003), *Khrushchev*, New York: Norton.

Taylor, D, (1982), "Pluralistic ignorance and the spiral of science," *Public Opinion Quarterly* 46, 311–35.

Taylor, T. (1992), *The Anatomy of the Nuremberg Trials*, New York: Knopf.

Thagard, P. (1989), "Explanatory coherence," *Behavioral and Brain Sciences* 12, 435–67.

Thaman, S. (1998), "Spain returns to trial by jury," *Hastings International and Comparative Law Review* 21, 241–538.

Thaman, S. (2000), "Europe's new jury systems," in N. Vidmar (ed.), *World Jury Systems*, Oxford: Oxford University Press, pp. 319–52.

Thayer, J. (1898), *A Preliminary Treatment on Evidence at Common Law*, Boston: Little, Brown.

Thayer, J, (1900), *A Selection of Cases on Evidence at the Common Law*, Cambridge, MA: Sever.

Theakston, K. (2003), "Review of Richard Crossman: *The Diaries of a Cabinet Minister*," *Public Policy and Administration* 18, 20–40.

Thompson, J. (1971), "A defense of abortion," *Philosophy and Public Affairs* 1, 47–66.

Thompson, W. and Fuqua, J. (1998), "'The jury will disregard ... '" in J. Golding and C. MacLeod (eds.), *Intentional Forgetting*, Mahwah, NJ: Lawrence Erlbaum, pp. 435–52.

Tideman, N. (2006), *Collective Decisions and Voting*, Farnham, Surrey: Ashgate.

Tocqueville, A. de (1968), *Journeys to England and Ireland*, New Brunswick, NJ: Transaction Books.

Tocqueville, A. de (1985), "Notes pour un discours," in Tocqueville, *Œuvres Complètes*, Vol. VII.2, Paris: Gallimard.

Tocqueville, A. de (1987), *Recollections*, New Brunswick, NJ: Transaction Books.

Tocqueville, A. de (1991), Voyage en Amérique, in *Oeuvres*, vol. I (Pléiade), Paris: Gallimard.

Tocqueville, A. de (2004a), *Democracy in America*, New York: Library of America.

Tocqueville, A. de (2004b), "Considérations sur la Révolution," in *Oeuvres*, vol. III (Pléiade), Paris: Gallimard.

Tocqueville, A. de (2011), *The Ancien Régime and the French Revolution*, Cambridge: Cambridge University Press.

Todd, S. (1993), *The Shape of Athenian Law*, Oxford: Oxford University Press.

Tréanton, P. (1909–10), "La loi du 31 mai 1850," *Revue d'Histoire Moderne et Contemporaine* 13, 277–304, and 14, 44–79, 297–331.

Troper, M. (2006), *Terminer la Révolution: La Constitution de 1795*, Paris: Fayard.

Turner, R. R. (1913), "The Peerage Bill of 1719," *English Historical Review* 28, 243–59.

Urfalino, P. (2007), "La décision par consensus apparent," *Revue Européenne des Sciences Sociales* 45, 47–70.

Urfalino, P. and Costa, P. (2010), "Public and oral voting in FDA's advisory committee," paper presented at the Conference "Private and Public Debate and Voting," Collège de France.

U.S. Senate (1956), "Recording of jury deliberations," Washington, DC: Government Printing Office.

Vacca, R. (1921), "Opinioni individuali e deliberazione collettive," *Rivista Internazionale di Filosofia del Diritto* 52, 52–59.

Van Dyke, J. (1977), *Jury Selection Procedures*, Cambridge, MA: Ballinger.

Van Effenterre, H. and Van Effenterre, M. (1988), "L'acte de fraternisation de Namone," *Mélanges de l'Ecole Française de Rome. Antiquités* 100, 687–700.

Van Hees, M. and Dowding, K. (2007), "In praise of manipulation," *British Journal of Political Science* 38, 1–15.

Vermeule, A. (2004), "Constitutional law of Congressional procedure," *University of Chicago Law Review* 71, 361–437.

Vermeule, A. (2005), "Submajority rules," *Journal of Political Philosophy* 13, 74–98.

Vermeule, A. (2007), *Mechanisms of Democracy*, Oxford: Oxford University Press.

Vermeule, A. (2009), "The force of majority rule," Paper presented at a Conference on Majority Decisions, Collège de France.

Vermeule, A. (2010), "Intermittent institutions," Harvard Public Law Working Paper 10–13.

Vernier, D. (2007), *Jury et démocratie*, Thèse de Doctorat, Ecole Normale Supérieure de Cachan.

Veyne, P. (1976), *Le pain et le Cirque*, Paris: Seuil.

Veyne, P. (2005), *L'empire greco-romain*, Paris: Seuil.

Vidmar, N. (2000a), "A historical and comparative perspective on the common law jury," in N. Vidmar (ed.), *World Jury Systems*, Oxford: Oxford University Press, pp. 1–52.

Vidmar, N. (2000b), "The Canadian criminal jury," in N. Vidmar (ed.), *World Jury Systems*, Oxford: Oxford University Press, pp. 211–48.

Vidmar, N. and Hans, V. (2007), *American Juries: The Verdict*, Amherst, NY: Prometheus Books.

Vile, J. (2005), *The Constitutional Convention of 1787*, Santa Barbara, CA: ABC-CLIO.

Voas, R. et al. (2009), "Implied consent laws," *Journal of Safety Research* 40, 77–83.

Volokh, A. (1997), "n guilty men," *University of Pennsylvania Law Review* 146, 173–218.

Waldron, J. (1999), *Law and Disagreement*, Oxford: Oxford University Press.

Wang, J. (2007), "The evolution of China's internal trade policy," in Y. Lee (ed.), *Economic Development through World Trade*, Alphens an den Riin (the Netherlands): Kluwer, pp. 191–213.

Weber, M. (1988), Contributions to the debates over the draft of a German constitution, in W. Mommsen and W. Schwentker (eds.), *Max Weber zur Neuordnung Deutschlands*, Tübingen: Mohr.

Webster, P. (1785), "A plea for the poor soldiers," in *Political Essays* (1791), pp. 269–305.

Wegner, D. M. (1989), *White Bears and other Unwanted Thoughts*, New York: Viking.

White, M. (1987), *Philosophy, The Federalist, and the Constitution*, Cambridge, MA: Harvard University Press.

Wiener, J. (1998), "Managing the iatrogenic risks of risk management," *Risk: Health, Safety and Environment* 9, 39–82.

Wilhite, A. and Fong, E. (2012), "Coercive citation in academic publishing," *Science* 335, 542–43.

Wilkerson, J. (1999), "'Killer amendments' in Congress," *American Political Science Review* 93, 535–52.

Wilms, H. (1999), *Ausländische Einwirkungen auf die Entstehung des Grundgesetzes*, Stuttgart: Kohlhammer.

Wilson, T. and Schooler, J. (1991), "Thinking too much," *Journal of Personality and Social Psychology* 60, 181–92.

Wood, G. (1987), "Interest and disinterestedness in the making of the constitution," in R. Beeman, S. Botein, and E. Carter (eds.), *Beyond Confederation*, Chapel Hill: University of North Carolina Press, pp. 69–109.

Wood, G. (1991), *The Radicalism of the American Revolution*, New York: Vintage.

Wood, G. (2009), *Empire of Liberty*, Oxford: Oxford University Press.

Woolrych, A. (1987), *Soldiers and Statesmen*, Oxford: Oxford University Press.

Woolrych, A. (2002), *Britain in Revolution 1625–1660*, Oxford: Oxford University Press.

Yaari, M. and Bar-Hillel, M. (1984), "On dividing justly," *Social Choice and Welfare* 1, 1–24.

Young, A. (1794), *Travels during the Years 1787, 1788, and 1789*, 2nd ed., London: Richardson.

Young, J. (1986), *The Washington Community 1800–1828*, New York: Columbia University Press.

Zagarri, R. (1987), *The Politics of Size*, Ithaca, NY: Cornell University Press.

Zajac, E. (1995), *The Political Economy of Fairness*, Cambridge, MA: MIT Press.

Zalman, M. (2008), "The adversary system and wrongful conviction," in C. Huff and M. Killias (eds.), *Wrongful Conviction*, Philadelphia, PA: Temple University Press, pp. 71–91.

Zeisel, H., Kalven, H. and. Buchholz, B. (1959), *Delay in the Court*, Boston: Little, Brown.

Zhao, C. (2008), "Deliberation or bargaining?" *Asia Europe Journal* 6, 427–40.

Zitzewitz, E. (2006), "Nationalism in winter sports judging and its lessons for organizational decision making," *Journal of Economics and Management Strategy* 15, 67–99.

Index

abortion, 51–52, 58
Acheson, Dean, 200
active aptitude, 75, 106, 119, 120, 202, 217
  of citizens, 149
  of deputies, 151–60
  Plutarch on, 157
Adams, Sam, 23
Adenauer, Konrad, 197, 199
aggregation, 31, 60–66
  of beliefs, 62–66
  of beliefs and policy preferences jointly,
    65–66, 75–76
  of conclusions, 63–65
  mixed with arguing, 33–34
  mixed with bargaining, 34
  of policy preferences, 60–62
  of premises, 63–65
  pure, 32–33
  strategic forms of, 72–84
alcohol, 2–3
Alexander I, 142
Amar, Akhil, 139 n. 187, 255 n. 51
American Academy of Arts and Sciences, 33 n. 65
amoral familism, 91
analogies, 51–55, 70 n. 192
  between alcohol consumption and virus
    infection, 52
  between ban on abortion and forced organ
    donation, 52
  between church members and liverymen, 240
  between juries and assemblies, 133
  between jurors and voters, 53, 110, 133,
    139 n. 187
  between manhood suffrage and abolition of
    private property, 53
  between the right to vote and the right to drive
    a car, 53

anonymity, 8, 89, 109, 111, 113, 123
antidosis, 19
Antiphon, 48
apella (Sparta), 19
Areopagites, 85, 111
arguing, 30, 31–32, 33–36, 42–60
  vs. bargaining, 230
  mixed with aggregation, 33
  mixed with bargaining, 34
  pure, 31–32
argument, 31
  ad hominem, 49
  conditional, 49–58
  consistency constraint on, 69, 91–92
  from first principles, 57, 58–60
  imperfection constraint on, 69, 92
  strategic uses of, 69–72
  from *tu quoque*, 55–58
  uncoerced force of the better, 2, 49 n. 119, 216
Aristotle, 12, 43, 91, 120, 149, 150
Arrow paradox, 67
Articles of Confederation, 165 n. 129, 172, 208,
  277
Assemblée des Notables (1788), 147, 168,
  231 n. 170
assemblies
  admission of public to, 173
  admission of women to, 174
  benches vs. desks in, 156, 163, 287
  order of speaking in, 158–59
  seating arrangements in, 159–60
Athens (classical), 90, 98, 120–21, 132, 264, 279
August 4, 1789, 3, 161, 180, 204
Avery v. Georgia, 106

backcountry (American), 80, 225, 277
Bailly, Jean Sylvain, 205

Index

Rubenfeld, Jed, 90
R v Connor and Rollock, 127
R v Mirza, 127

Salle, Jean-Baptiste, 182
Santorum, Rick, 263
Satterthwaite, Mark, 74–75
Savage, Sir Arnold, 9
Schmid, Carlo, 192
Schmitt, Carl, 8–9
Schumacher, Kurt, 197, 198
Scott, John, 207
secrecy, 6, 7–9
    and anonymity, 111
    of debates, 9, 130 n. 154
    and privacy, 8
    of voting, 7–9; in assemblies, 9, 10, 96 n. 285, 135, 169–70; in elections, 7–8; ex ante with publicity ex post, 128; ex ante without publicity ex post, 131; ex post, 89; in juries, 7, 27, 128–36
self-denying ordinance (1791), 213
self-selection, 279
    of assembly members, 206 n. 65, 227
    of jurors, 122, 279
    of *nomothetai*, 227, 279
    reduces diversity, 279
Seneca, 129, 271 n. 102
Senate, American, *see* Congress (U.S.): Senate
separation of powers, 217–19
Septennial Act (1715), 167
Sexby, Edward, 54–55
Shanghai ranking, 269
Shays's rebellion, 203, 225 n. 136, 229
Sieyes, abbé de, 12, 155, 192, 217, 231, 243, 264
signaling, 72, 73, 83
Simmel, Georg, 89
slavery (American), 55, 57, 79–80, 240
social-choice theory, 33, 38–40, 60–62; *see also* independence of irrelevant alternatives; non-dictatorship; Pareto-optimality; strategy-proofness; universal domain
Solon, 287
Sparta, 33, 112 n. 67
Staël, Mme de, 5, 156
Stalin, 168 n. 154, 198
Steyn, Lord Johan, 127
strategic behavior, 68–84, 262
strategy-proofness, 73–74
suffrage, 26, 36, 238–44
    age requirements for, 26, 49, 53, 242

endogenous vs. exogenous determinants of, 240–41
    function vs. right, 224
    literacy requirements for, 147–48
    property requirements for, 26, 29, 146
    tax payment requirements for, 26, 146–47, 242
sunk-cost fallacy, 86
Sunstein, Cass, 51–52
Supreme Court (Iceland), 8
Supreme Court (U.S.), 24 n. 28, 33, 52, 64, 124, 183, 190
Swain v. Alabama, 124

Taxquet v. Belgium, 125
Talleyrand, Charles-Maurice de, 70
Tanner v. United States, 3, 52
Taubira, Christiane, 77, 84
Terror, the (in the French Revolution), 133, 134, 161
Thompson, Judith Jarvis, 51, 56
Thucydides, 112, 132
Tocqueville, Alexis de, 4, 91, 144–45, 146, 161, 169, 184, 214, 217, 225, 244, 247, 268–69
Trade Union (Amalgamation) Act (1964), 227 n. 148
transubstantiation, 58–59
Twelve Angry Men, 279

unconscious thought, theory of, 123
unicameralism, 65–66, 76, 177, 180, 181
Unfunded Mandates Reform Act (1995), 25 n. 35, 153
United States v. Dougherty, 114
United States v. Gruenwald, 23 n. 1
universal domain, condition of, 61
Urfalino, Philippe, 35
urgency, 44, 45, 181, 205
utilitarianism, 38
utility, 16, 32
    interpersonal comparisons of, 37, 62

Vacca, Roberto, 63
vanity, 89
veil of ignorance, *see* ignorance
Vergniaud, Pierre-Victurnien, 134
Veyne, Paul, 69
Villèle, Jean-Baptiste de, 78
Virieu, François Henri, comte de, 247–48
voir dire, 107
vote trading, *see* logrolling